THE ENTAIL

JOHN GALT was born in Irvine, Ayrshire, in 1779 and was trained for business. At the age of twenty-four he moved to London. He was by turns continental traveller (for a time the companion of Byron), businessman in a variety of ventures, parliamentary lobbyist, colonial administrator in Canada (where his family ultimately settled), and, at all times, an indefatigable writer. He was the author of over forty books but his literary reputation was established and remains based on a series of Tales of the West, novels drawing on his memories of the Glasgow and Ayrshire region in which he grew up. His *Annals of the Parish* (1821), *The Provost* (1822), and *The Entail* (1822) are deeply felt studies of small-town life in eighteenth-century Scotland. He moved, with no great success, to historical fiction and in 1832 produced *The Member*, the first political novel in English. Though an invalid in his later years, he continued to write, and published a series of novellas. He died in 1839.

IAN A. GORDON is Emeritus Professor of English in the University of Wellington, New Zealand. He has edited several of Galt's novels and written a biography. Among his other books are *John Skelton*, *Katherine Mansfield*, *Shenstone's Miscellany*, *A Word in Your Ear*, and *The Movement of English Prose*.

THE WORLD'S CLASSICS

JOHN GALT

The Entail
or
The Lairds of Grippy

Edited with an Introduction by
IAN A. GORDON

Oxford   New York
OXFORD UNIVERSITY PRESS
1984

Oxford University Press, Walton Street, Oxford OX2 6DP

London Glasgow New York Toronto
Delhi Bombay Calcutta Madras Karachi
Kuala Lumpur Singapore Hong Kong Tokyo
Nairobi Dar es Salaam Cape Town
Melbourne Auckland

and associated companies in
Beirut Berlin Ibadan Mexico City Nicosia

Oxford is a trade mark of Oxford University Press

Introduction, Notes, Bibliography, and Chronology
© Oxford University Press 1970, 1984

First published 1970 by Oxford University Press
First issued as a World's Classics paperback 1984

British Library Cataloguing in Publication Data
Galt, John
The entail.——(The World's classics)
I. Title II. Gordon, Ian A. (Ian Alistair)
823'.7[F] PR4708.G2
ISBN 0-19-281694-2

Library of Congress Cataloging in Publication Data
Galt, John, 1779–1839.
The entail, or, The Lairds of Grippy.
(The World's classics)
Bibliography: p.
I. Gordon, Ian Alistair, 1908– . II. Title.
III. Title: Lairds of Grippy.
[PR4708.G2E5 1984] 823'.7 84-958
ISBN 0-19-281694-2 (pbk.)

Printed in Great Britain by
Hazell Watson & Viney Ltd
Aylesbury, Bucks

CONTENTS

[1] The Galt–Blackwood letters cited in this edition are excerpted from the Blackwood papers in the National Library of Scotland and from the early Letter Books (cited as L.B. 1–4) of William Blackwood and Sons, Edinburgh, by courtesy of the National Library of Scotland and of the present head of the firm, G. D. Blackwood, Esq.

INTRODUCTION

JOHN GALT was over forty before he began the set of Scottish regional stories on which his literary reputation firmly stands. Before that point he had published copiously travel, biography, drama, verse, political and social commentary, schoolbooks—anything, almost, that editors and publishers would accept, to supplement the income of a London-based Scot who had tried both law and the world of business without so far making a notable success of anything. It is likely that this blend of affairs and casual journalism would have continued unchanged had not the appearance in 1817 of *Blackwood's Edinburgh Magazine* suggested a further outlet. After having a few of his general articles accepted, Galt submitted the plan of what was to become *The Ayrshire Legatees*; this episodic tale of a Scottish family's journey to London pleased both the founder William Blackwood and 'Christopher North' his helper; publication began in *Blackwood* in June 1820 and ran till February 1821. In Christopher North's words, it 'increased our sale prodigiously'.[1]

Galt was established within the space of a few months as a successful and popular writer, a role he had not previously enjoyed, and the material—even the shape—of his succeeding books was thereby determined. Sir Walter Scott's mixture of realism and romance was evidently not the only formula for an acceptable Scottish tale. There was clearly an audience—and hence a willing publisher—for Galt's accurately observed studies of small-town characters. Galt's first reaction to his success was almost disastrous —it was to offer Blackwood *The Earthquake*, a 'European' novel he had written some years before and was now having printed in London.[2] Blackwood took over the sheets, published the work late in 1820, and even (though with some natural diffidence) arranged for it to be reviewed in his own magazine.[3] But *The Earthquake*

[1] *Blackwood*, June 1822, p. 744.
[2] Galt to Blackwood, 29 May 1820, Nat. Lib. Scot. MS. 4005, f. 85.
[3] Blackwood to Galt, 23 Jan. 1821, L.B. 1, f. 208.

pleased no one—a London reviewer even doubted if it could be by the author of *The Ayrshire Legatees*. The diverse reception of these two works combined to persuade both Galt and Blackwood where his real talents lay.

Before he had corrected the last proof of *The Earthquake*, and while *The Ayrshire Legatees* was still running in *Blackwood*, Galt had resurrected the draft of another old project, 'The Pastor of the Parish', a chronicle of Scottish village life that had been turned down some years before by Constable. Blackwood liked it, though it would (he thought) 'require a gentle pruning', and invited Galt in addition to begin a 'new Series of any kind'.[1] Galt's response was immediate, the first instalment of *The Steamboat*, a loose bundle of stories told on a steamboat journey between Scotland and London, the whole scheme held together by the character of Mr. Duffle, cloth merchant of Glasgow. It must have given Blackwood quiet satisfaction with the productivity of his new author to see in print in one issue of his magazine the last instalment of *The Ayrshire Legatees* and the first of *The Steamboat*. Galt in the same letter to Blackwood in which he offered *The Steamboat* indicated further that given 'sufficient encouragement' he would make a beginning on a 'novel on the progress of a Scotch man in London'.[2] Blackwood's encouragement (which included satisfying and prompt payment) was certainly producing results.

The year 1821 saw these promises become solid achievement. *The Steamboat* began in *Blackwood* in February and ran till December. 'The Pastor'—Blackwood's 'gentle pruning' had extended to altering the title to *Annals of the Parish*—was published in one volume in May and achieved an immediate success. In the same month Galt wrote to Blackwood that a further work, *The Provost*, was 'in a thriving way'.[3] *The Ayrshire Legatees*, reprinted from the magazine in a one-volume format, appeared in June. By July, Galt was able to report to Blackwood that the novel on the progress of the Scotchman in London (who had now become Sir Andrew Wylie) was two-thirds finished and he tempted Blackwood's appetite by letting him know that John Murray had made an offer of 500 guineas for it.[4] Blackwood duly made the no–doubt-

[1] Blackwood to Galt, 23 Jan. 1821, L.B. 1, f. 208.
[2] Galt to Blackwood, 30 Jan. 1821, Nat. Lib. Scot. MS. 4006, ff. 219–20.
[3] Galt to Blackwood, 28 May 1821, Nat. Lib. Scot. MS. 4006, f. 235.
[4] Galt to Blackwood, 30 July 1821, Nat. Lib. Scot. MS. 4006, f. 240.

expected counter-offer and, from the October issue onwards of
Blackwood, *Sir Andrew Wylie of that Ilk* was announced as being
'in the Press'. There were in addition articles printed in *Blackwood*,
and Galt's receipts from the firm for the last six months of 1821
amounted to £480.[1] It had been for Galt a busy and a fruitful year.

The pressure and the mounting success continued throughout
1822. In January, *Sir Andrew Wylie* was published in three volumes.
The edition of 1,500 copies sold steadily. In March, Blackwood
published the second edition of *Annals of the Parish*. May saw the
publication, in one volume, of *The Provost*, which further extended
Galt's studies of small-town characters. Once again Galt had
caught the market. An edition of 2,000 sold in a fortnight. A second
edition the following month was reported in *Blackwood* as melting
away 'like snaw aff a dyke'.[2] In July, *The Steamboat* series was
reprinted from the magazine as a single volume. A second edition
of *Sir Andrew Wylie* came out in the same month, and in September
Blackwood carried a long comic sketch, *The Gathering of the West*,
in which the now familiar gallery of small-town West of Scotland
characters assembled in Edinburgh for the visit of George IV.

It was in the midst of all this activity and with the exciting sense
of having at last in his early forties succeeded, that Galt set to work
on the novel which was to be his masterpiece. I use the term 'novel'
of *The Entail* with intent. But Galt was never happy with 'novel'
as the proper designation of his works of this period. During a few
busy years (virtually between 1820 and 1822) within which he
evolved his studies of Scottish society, he was quite consciously
working towards his own kind of art-form:

> They would be more properly characterised, in several instances, as
> theoretical histories, than either as novels or romances. A consistent fable
> is as essential to a novel as a plot is to a drama, and yet those, which are
> deemed my best productions, are deficient in this essential ingredient.[3]

Galt, indeed, took some pride in the originality of his genre:

> I do not think I have had numerous precursors, in what I would call my
> theoretical histories of society, limited, though they were required by the
> subject, necessarily to the events of a circumscribed locality.[4]

---

[1] The receipted returns are in Nat. Lib. Scot. MS. 4006, f. 245.
[2] *Blackwood*, June 1822, p. 744.
[3] *Autobiography* (1833), ii. 219.
[4] Ibid., 220.

The sequence of 'theoretical histories' that began with *The Ayrshire Legatees* and continued through *Annals of the Parish*, *Sir Andrew Wylie*, *The Provost*, and *The Entail*, was conceived by Galt as a series of plotless studies of middle-class Scottish life, each an independent work, but each linked to the others by common characters and thematic cross-references. Galt wanted the essential unity of the series stressed by having the whole group entitled 'Tales of the West'. But Blackwood would have none of it: such a 'general title' would be a 'disadvantage to those books'[1] and Galt—who had indeed anticipated by about a century the *roman-fleuve*—had no option but to withdraw.

Blackwood's influence had further effects on the series. While he appreciated the lifelike verisimilitude of Galt's studies, he hankered for more in the way of a *story*. In spite of the obvious acceptance by the public of Galt's episodic genre, whether presented serially or in book form, he urged on Galt, then engaged on *Sir Andrew Wylie*: 'A great matter is to construct a good and striking story with which to interweave your graphic sketches of actual life and manners.'[2]

Galt evidently felt he had no option but to give way. With considerable reluctance he reshaped the book he was working on to conform closer to the conventional plotted novel of the period. Some ten years later, in his *Autobiography*, he recounted with regret that he had been induced to provide *Sir Andrew Wylie* with a 'beginning, middle, and end . . . like an ordinary novel'. He had planned, he wrote, a novel 'with no particular story'.[3]

When Galt, in the first half of 1822, came to plan *The Entail*, he was operating under several pressures. There was, on the one hand, the sheer pressure of creation, the urge to push ahead with what was clearly intended as the culminating 'theoretical history' in his series of studies of the society of the west of Scotland. On the other hand, there was his publisher (and not ungenerous paymaster) demanding—against Galt's whole instinct—a 'good and striking story' or (in Galt's more formal language) 'a consistent fable'. A further pressure which shaped the novel was its projected size. Galt had so far (apart from the artificially filled-out *Sir Andrew Wylie*) worked in terms of a single volume. *The Entail* was planned

[1] Blackwood to Galt, 20 May 1821, L.B. 2, f. 32.
[2] Blackwood to Galt, 25 Apr. 1821, L.B. 2, f. 7.
[3] *Autobiography* (1833), ii. 239.

from the beginning as Galt's major work. He had hopes—and they were to be fulfilled—that he would receive permission to dedicate it to the King. It was to be a solid work, in three volumes, and Galt was aware that the current three-volume format imposed its own pattern on the final structure of a work.

The Entail is a horrifying study of greed and mercantile lust for possessions and 'gear'; Claud Walkinshaw rises from poverty to a thriving business, then to the ownership of the farm of Grippy and piece by piece of the whole family estate of Kittlestonheugh. He entails it through a succession of male heirs to ensure, not the happiness of his family, but the preservation of the estate. All of Galt's earlier preoccupations are here—the life of a Scottish town in the eighteenth century, the 'truth of the metaphysical anatomy of the characters',[1] the complexity of relationships in family life, the gallery of 'humorous' characters, the delicately accurate rendering of Scottish speech at different social levels. What was new was the sense of tragedy, the suffocating atmosphere of meanness that overpowers one victim of the entail after another. What elevates the novel to the status of a major work is the skilful setting-off of all this lust, greed, and meanness against the forces of life: Claud Walkinshaw's obsessions are in the end frustrated; Watty the daftie is a better human being than his shrewd and sane business-man brother George; Girzy Hypel, who begins her married life as little more than a chattel, another bit of Claud's 'gear', survives him, to emerge in full vernacular rhetoric and warm humanity as the Leddy, recognized by Scott and Byron and many later readers as one of the great creations of fiction. *The Entail* is the study of an inhuman obsession; the values it enshrines are richly human.

Once he had settled on the theme of *The Entail*, Galt—as the extant, though still unpublished, correspondence shows—gave the book all his abundant energies. He wrote to Blackwood in June 1822 that 'during the summer I intend to devote myself exclusively to "The Entail" which I foresee will extend to three volumes', and since he needed maintenance during the period hoped that Blackwood would 'do as much for me this year as last'.[2] Blackwood read the 'outline' of the novel (a document that unfortunately has not survived) and urged Galt to 'manage it so as that the hero tells the

[1] Galt to Blackwood, 12 Apr. 1826, Nat. Lib. Scot. MS. 4017, f. 22.
[2] Galt to Blackwood, 8 June 1822, Nat. Lib. Scot. MS. 4008, f. 179.

story' because Galt can 'identify the individual, and the Author himself never appears' and 'this is greatly lost when given in the third person'.[1] Galt quietly ignored the advice, but told Blackwood to announce the novel forthwith—'the very fecundity becomes an advertising topic'.[2] Blackwood had doubts—'folks are apt to say you are in too great hurry'—but he did advertise the novel and repeated his advice about a story 'in the third person'.[3]

Galt in his next letter makes it clear that he has thought his way through the new project. The recent good reception in the south of *Sir Andrew Wylie* and *The Provost* has

> . . . given me renewed heart and confidence, in so much that I have con-structed the whole fable of my Entail, determined the characters and most of the incidents—I may be mistaken in my anticipation, but I think it will be out of all comparison the most vigorous and lively work I have yet attempted. . . . It has taken full possession of my fancy and I always know that when I am myself interested I do not fail in the effort.

In this revealing statement he goes on to say that the new work will contain a great deal of matter 'similar in compass' to the *Annals* and *The Provost*, but he will need three months in Scot-land 'to add to my vernacular vocabulary'. If Blackwood can advance him a bill the book will be ready 'before Christmas for the public'.[4]

Blackwood as ever was prompt and business-like. He offered Galt £525 for the copyright, payable in a series of bills.[5] Galt left for Scotland and settled down in Greenock to complete the novel in the countryside in which it is set. His letters to Blackwood during the remainder of the year give an admirable picture of him at work, his energy, his 'fecundity', and his careful attention to details, including proof correction. Proofs shuttle between Greenock and the printing-house in Edinburgh. He asks for a tally of the pages already set up 'as it is time to think of completing the first volume'.[6] Sending in further manuscript, he asks for proofs 'as far as the

[1] Blackwood to Galt, 11 June 1822, L.B. 2, f. 340.
[2] Galt to Blackwood, 15 June 1822, Nat. Lib. Scot. MS. 4008, f. 181.
[3] Blackwood to Galt, 22 June 1822, L.B. 3, ff. 4-5.
[4] Galt to Blackwood, 23 June 1822, Nat. Lib. Scot. MS. 4008, ff. 182-3. See Appendix for full text of this important letter.
[5] Galt's letter of acceptance of 31 Aug. 1822 of these terms is in Nat. Lib. Scot. MS. 4008, f. 184.
[6] Galt to Blackwood, 3 Sept. 1822, Nat. Lib. Scot. MS. 4008, f. 186.

matter goes'—like Jane Austen, he consciously planned the dramatic structure of his story in terms of the volume division: 'I wish the second volume to begin with the commencement of a new act in the story—and may have occasion to write a chapter or two to extend the first.'[1] Half-way through October he sent in the conclusion of volume I and had completed 'a considerable portion of vol. II'.[2] No letters to Blackwood seem to have survived from the remainder of Galt's period in Greenock. But he must have pushed ahead at high speed with the third volume—the dedication to the King was dated 3 December and the three volumes were on sale in London by 11 December, when Galt (just back from Scotland) saw the first copies arrive in Richardson's shop.[3]

There is clear evidence in the correspondence between the two men that the publisher conceived himself as more than a mere passive partner of the novelist. Though Galt was pleased with Blackwood's support, he had to pay the price of listening and on occasion yielding to Blackwood, his insistent demand for a 'story' and his repeated instructions on how to present it. Galt had planned the structure of The Entail as a 'theoretical history' set in a 'circumscribed locality', 'similar in compass' to the Annals and The Provost: 'the chief business lies in Glasgow'.[4] But he was not able finally to resist Blackwood's pressures. The result is that the original plan of the book—a relentless cumulation of incidents from the family history of 'the lairds of Grippy' (which is in fact the subtitle of the book), the story set in Glasgow and the rural west of Scotland—this Galt was able to sustain superbly through the first two volumes.

In the third volume, however, where the closeness of the dates of composition and of publication makes it clear that Galt was working at speed, there are alien elements of melodramatic 'story' and shift of scene which it is not difficult to ascribe to Blackwood's pressure. The series of contrived journeys by the main characters away from the 'circumscribed locality' of Glasgow and the Grippy, the supernatural 'astrologising' of Mrs. Eadie, the 'borrowed' storm scene, and the shipwreck with its implausible coincidences disrupt the planned linear structure of the novel. The demand for

---

[1] Galt to Blackwood, 8 Oct. 1822, Nat. Lib. Scot. MS. 4008, f. 189.
[2] Galt to Blackwood, 11 Oct. 1822, Nat. Lib. Scot. MS. 4008, f. 191.
[3] Galt to Blackwood, 11 Dec. 1822, Nat. Lib. Scot. MS. 4008, f. 193.
[4] Galt to Blackwood, 8 June 1822, Nat. Lib. Scot. MS. 4008, f. 179.

a 'lively story' thus satisfied, Galt permitted himself an ironic comment on the intrusion (in chapter xxvi) as he shifted the story back to Glasgow and the original theme.[1]

Galt clearly resented the pressure, though (unlike Scott, who had a similar experience with Blackwood) he appears to have said nothing at the time. But the interference rankled, and his novels during the following two years were published by Oliver and Boyd. When he returned to Blackwood in 1825-6 with *The Last of the Lairds*, the publisher's demands for reshaping became now so insistent that Galt was forced into an angry protest, which provides further evidence for Blackwood's intrusions in the earlier (and more important) novels:

> In one word my good friend I should have thought by this time you must have known—that nobody can help an author with a conception of a character nor in the evolution of a story—detached passages and special parts may be improved by friendly suggestions, but criticism touching the vitals of what is character and plot rarely if ever improves either the one or the other. The defects of the Annals of the Parish are not mine—though some of the omissions I acknowledge were judicious—Sir Andrew Wylie—the most original of all I have ever done was spoilt by your interference, and the main fault of the Entail was also owing to my being over-persuaded. . . . I do not know how it is, but I cannot proceed if I am interfered with. I know it is very silly to be so chary but I cannot help it. It does *not* come of arrogance but of having confidence in myself.[2]

Galt's 'confidence in himself' was justified by the reception of *The Entail*. It did not have the immediate wide popularity of his more 'comic' Scottish novels. But it drew a quick response from discerning readers: Scott and Byron both read it no fewer than three times; the partisan but none the less discriminating 'Christopher North' reviewed it in *Blackwood* in January 1823 as 'out of all sight the best thing he has done'. The discerning but non-partisan Jeffrey described it in the October *Edinburgh Review* of that year as 'of a far higher order' than his earlier Scottish novels and 'a work undoubtedly of no ordinary merit'. Galt—ever sensitive to commercial success—found the early sales in London 'very satisfactory and flattering'.[3] Blackwood assured him from Edinburgh some two months later that 'every body continues to speak

---

[1] See notes to volume III.
[2] Galt to Blackwood, 23 Aug. 1826, Nat. Lib. Scot. MS. 4017, ff. 37-8.
[3] Galt to Blackwood, 8 Jan. 1823, Nat. Lib. Scot. MS. 4010, f. 146.

highly of the Entail' and reported the sales though 'not now very great' were 'still continuing'.[1]

A high critical estimate and a relatively modest commercial success was, in fact, to be the early history of *The Entail*. It has come properly to be regarded as Galt's masterpiece. Yet of his better-known Scottish novels, it alone did not achieve a second edition in his lifetime. For this slower rise to a popular success, two reasons may be put forward. Initially, the tragic tone, the very seriousness and scale of the work must have put off many readers who had grown to expect, on the basis of the previous two years, merely a further instalment of Scots comedy and pawky humour.

A second difficulty was almost certainly the language. Throughout his series of 'theoretical histories' Galt with each succeeding book had silently increased the Scots element. In the earliest, *The Ayrshire Legatees*, the dialect content is minimal—yet Galt had insisted on its being accurate—'Tell our friend Mr. North', he had written to Blackwood, 'not to touch one of the Scotticisms'.[2] He even, as Professor Kinsley has pointed out, increased the dialect element between successive editions of the same book, 'weighting it a little' in his 1822 revision of the 1821 *Annals of the Parish*.[3] This progressive weighting of his Scots from book to book had not affected his reputation either north or south of the Border. His popularity with the buying public had increased, and by the end of 1822 all of his first four Scottish novels were in reprints. Galt, in deciding to write what was to be his major 'theoretical history', decided also that in language he could afford to be uncompromisingly Scottish. His special visit to Scotland for 'vernacular vocabulary' was directed to that end. For the first time, he would employ, with his customary sensitivity but with heightened accuracy, the full resources of his 'vernacular' of west-country Scots.

The result in *The Entail* is a linguistic triumph. The characters are differentiated with great subtlety by their speech: the 'gentle' Bell Fatherlans and the 'educated' George speak current English; Robina, the 'young lady' heroine of the romantic latter section, declaims the over-emphatic English of the sentimental novel; clergymen and lawyers speak what is generally transcribed as

---

[1] Blackwood to Galt, 24 Feb. 1823, L.B. 4.
[2] Galt to Blackwood, 1 May 1820, Nat. Lib. Scot. MS. 4005, f. 83.
[3] *Annals of the Parish*, ed. James Kinsley (1967), p. xix.

English (which the careful reader knows must be read with a Scots accent); the full west-country dialect—accurately transcribed in virtually phonetic spelling—is mainly reserved for Claud, Watty, and the Leddy (all, as it happens, his most memorable characters). It is not claiming too much to say that *The Entail* is effective as a novel almost precisely to the degree to which Galt exploits the dialect for which he had such a remarkable ear. The consequences are obvious enough. The best of Galt is generally on those very pages that require most effort from the reader—the bereavement of Watty with his 'wee Betty Bodle', the masterly balance between pathos and comedy in the Glasgow court scene, the devastating portrayals of Claud's snarling avarice, the resilience and resourcefulness of the Leddy. The difficulties must be accepted. Galt—like James Joyce or Mark Twain—must finally be met on his own linguistic terms.

NOTE ON THE TEXT

THE text is printed from the British Museum copy of the only edition published in Galt's lifetime. It was printed in Edinburgh in three volumes 12mo by George Ramsay and Co. and published in Edinburgh by Blackwood and, for him, by Cadell in London. The printer, in the colophon to volume III, dated the book 1822. The date on the title-page was 1823, but the work was selling well in London and in Edinburgh in early December 1822 (Galt having fulfilled his promise to Blackwood to have it 'before Christmas for the public').

No subsequent edition has any textual authority. With one exception, all later editions are reprinted from the posthumous second which appeared in 1842 in Blackwood's Standard Novels. For this edition a decision was made in Blackwood's offices that Galt's language must be made easier; accordingly someone—probably D. M. Moir, who was Galt's editor for this series—worked over the entire text. Dialect spellings were modified to bring them closer to English; Galt's west-country Scots was frequently 'translated' into the south-east Lothian/Border variety which Sir Walter Scott had made acceptable, and in which Moir himself wrote; the punctuation was considerably lightened. Hundreds of alterations were made; some samples are given in Appendix I. The great majority of readers of *The Entail*, both in this century and the last, have read it in a version anonymously modified in Blackwood's Edinburgh office in the 1840s.

The unique authority of the 1822/3 text is confirmed in the unpublished correspondence between Galt and Blackwood, which shows Galt regularly receiving 'proofs', 'slips', and 'sheets' of his work from Blackwood, and correcting them with care. There are specific references to his overseeing the proofs of volumes I and II of *The Entail*. The internal evidence of the text demonstrates that he paid particular attention to dialect spellings. Except for regularizing, as recorded in the Textual Notes, certain inconsistencies that appear to have escaped both Galt and the original Blackwood reader, the present edition restores the text of 1822/3. A few obvious misprints, like misplaced quotation marks, have been silently corrected.

SELECT BIBLIOGRAPHY

The Entail was reprinted, with many slight textual alterations, in Black-wood's Standard Novels, 1842 (reissued 1850, 1869) and, in the 1842 text with a new title-page, by Maclaren and Co., n.d. [early 1900s]. An edition was printed and published, n.d. [1880s] by Charles Murchland, Irvine. The World's Classics edition, 1913, was edited by John Ayscough from the 1822/3 text with an introductory essay and vocabulary.

COLLECTED EDITIONS (MAIN NOVELS ONLY). *The Works of John Galt*, ed. D. S. Meldrum, introductions by S. R. Crockett, illustr., 8 vols. (Blackwood, 1895); *The Works of John Galt*, ed. D. S. Meldrum and W. Roughead, introductions by S. R. Crockett, illustr., 10 vols. (John Grant, 1936).

BIBLIOGRAPHY. Harry Lumsden, *The Bibliography of John Galt*, Records of the Glasgow Bibliographical Society (ix), 1931; B. A. Booth in the *Bulletin of Bibliography* (xvi), 1936. See also the books by R. K. Gordon, J. W. Aberdein, Ian Jack and Ian Gordon noted below; and Lucien Leclaire, *A General Analytical Bibliography of the Regional Novelists of the British Isles 1800–1950* (Paris, 1954), pp. 31–5.

BIOGRAPHY AND CRITICISM. The primary sources are Galt's *Auto-biography*, 2 vols. (1833), and his *Literary Life, and Miscellanies*, 3 vols. (1834). The earliest memoir is by 'Δ' (D. M. Moir) in the 1841 edition of the *Annals*. Modern biographies by Jennie W. Aberdein (1936) and Ian A. Gordon (1972). For early criticism see *Blackwood's Magazine*, June 1822 (on his Scottish works prior to *The Entail*), January 1823 (on *The Entail*); *Edinburgh Review*, October 1923 ('Secondary Scottish Novels'). Modern studies: J. H. Millar, *Literary History of Scotland* (1903); John Ayscough, 'The Entail: an appreciation' in *The Dublin Review*, cli, July 1912, pp. 25–52 (reprinted and expanded in his *Levia Pondera*, 1913); John Ays-cough, Introduction to World's Classics edition (1913); R. K. Gordon, *John Galt* (1920, University of Toronto Studies); W. Roughead, 'The Centenary of "The Entail"' in *Juridical Review*, Edinburgh, March 1923, pp. 1–38; G. Kitchin in *Edinburgh Essays on Scots Literature*, ed. H. J. C. Grierson (1933); F. H. Lyell, *A Study of the Novels of John Galt* (1942;

Princeton Studies in English, no. 28); Lucien Leclaire, *Le Roman région-aliste dans les Iles Britanniques 1800-1950* (Paris, 1954); Erik Frykman, *John Galt's Scottish Stories 1820-1823* (Uppsala, 1959); David Craig, *Scottish Literature and the Scottish People 1680-1830* (1961); Ian Jack, *English Literature 1815-1832* (1963), chap. viii; W. M. Parker, *Susan Ferrier and John Galt* (1965); Marion Lockhead, 'John Galt', *Maga* (1968); L. B. Hall, 'Peripety in John Galt's *The Entail*', *Studies in Scottish Literature* (1968); Ian A. Gordon, *John Galt. The Life of a Writer* (1972); K. M. Costain, 'Mind Forg'd Manacles; *The Entail* as Romantic Tragicomedy', in *John Galt 1779–1979* (1979).

A CHRONOLOGY OF JOHN GALT

TO THE KING

THE ENTAIL

CHAPTER I

CLAUD WALKINSHAW was the sole surviving male heir of the Walkinshaws of Kittlestonheugh. His grandfather, the last Laird of the line, deluded by the golden visions that allured so many of the Scottish gentry to embark their fortunes in the Darien Expedition,[1] sent his only son, the father of Claud, in one of the ships fitted out at Cartsdyke, and with him an adventure in which he had staked more than the whole value of his estate. But, as it is not our intention to fatigue the reader with any very circumstantial account of the state of the Laird's family, we shall pass over, with all expedient brevity, the domestic history of Claud's childhood. He was scarcely a year old when his father sailed, and his mother died of a broken heart, on hearing that her husband, with many of his companions, had perished of disease and famine among the swamps of the Mosquito shore. The Kittlestonheugh estate was soon after sold, and the Laird, with Claud, retired into Glasgow, where he rented the upper part of a back house, in Aird's Close, in the Drygate. The only servant whom, in this altered state, he could afford to retain, or rather the only one that he could not get rid of, owing to her age and infirmities, was Maudge Dobbie, who, in her youth, was bairnswoman[2] to his son. She had been upwards of forty years in the servitude of his house; and the situation she had filled to the father of Claud did not tend to diminish the kindliness with which she regarded the child, especially when, by the ruin of her master, there was none but herself to attend him.

The charms of Maudge had, even in her vernal years, been confined to her warm and affectionate feelings; and, at this period, she was twisted east and west, and hither and yont, and Time, in the shape of old age, hung so embracingly round her neck, that his weight had bent her into a hoop. Yet, thus deformed and aged, she was not without qualities that might have endeared her to a more generous boy. Her father had been schoolmaster in the village of

Kittleston; and under his tuition, before she was sent, as the phrase then was, to seek her bread in the world, she had acquired a few of the elements of learning beyond those which, in that period, fell to the common lot of female domestics: and she was thus enabled, not only to teach the orphan reading and writing, but even to supply him with some knowledge of arithmetic, particularly addition and the multiplication table. She also possessed a rich stock of goblin lore and romantic stories, the recital of which had given the father of Claud the taste for adventure that induced him to embark in the ill-fated expedition. These, however, were not so congenial to the less sanguine temperament of the son, who early preferred the history of Whittington and his Cat to the achievements of Sir William Wallace; and 'Tak your auld cloak about you,' ever seemed to him a thousand times more sensible than Chevy Chace. As for that doleful ditty, the Flowers of the Forest, it was worse than the Babes in the Wood; and Gil Morrice more wearisome than Death and the Lady.[1]

The solitary old Laird had not been long settled in his sequestered and humble town-retreat, when a change became visible both in his appearance and manners. He had been formerly bustling, vigorous, hearty, and social; but from the first account of the death of his son, and the ruin of his fortune, he grew thoughtful and sedentary, and shunned the approach of strangers, and retired from the visits of his friends. Sometimes he sat for whole days, without speaking, and without even noticing the kitten-like gambols of his grandson; at others he would fondle over the child, and caress him with more than a grandfather's affection; again, he would peevishly brush the boy away as he clasped his knees, and hurry out of the house with short and agitated steps. His respectable portliness disappeared; his clothes began to hang loosely upon him; his colour fled; his face withered; and his legs wasted into meagre shanks. Before the end of the first twelve months, he was either unwilling or unable to move unassisted from the old arm chair, in which he sat from morning to night, with his grey head drooping over his breast; and one evening, when Maudge went to assist him to undress, she found he had been for some time dead.

After the funeral, Maudge removed with the pennyless orphan to a garret-room in the Saltmarket, where she endeavoured to earn for him and herself the humble aliment of meal and salt, by working stockings; her infirmities and figure having disqualified her from the more profitable industry of the spinning-wheel. In this condition she remained for some time, pinched with poverty, but still patient with her lot, and preserving, nevertheless, a neat and decent exterior.

It was only in the calm of the summer Sabbath evenings that she indulged in the luxury of a view of the country; and her usual walk on those occasions, with Claud in her hand, was along the brow of Whitehill,[1] which she perhaps preferred, because it afforded her a distant view of the scenes of her happier days; and while she pointed out to Claud the hills and lands of his forefathers, she exhorted him to make it his constant endeavour to redeem them, if possible, from their new possessors, regularly concluding her admonition with some sketch or portrait of the hereditary grandeur of his ancestors.

One afternoon, while she was thus engaged, Provost Gorbals[2] and his wife made their appearance.

The Provost was a man in flourishing circumstances, and he was then walking with his lady to choose a scite[3] for a country-house which they had long talked of building. They were a stately corpulent couple, well befitting the magisterial consequence of the husband.

Mrs Gorbals was arrayed in a stiff and costly yellow brocade, magnificently embroidered with flowers, the least of which was peony; but the exuberance of her ruffle cuffs and flounces, the richness of her lace apron, with the vast head-dress of catgut and millinery, together with her blue satin mantle, trimmed with ermine, are items in the gorgeous paraphernalia of the Glasgow ladies of that time, to which the pencil of some abler limner can alone do justice.

The appearance of the Provost himself became his dignity, and corresponded with the affluent garniture of his lady: it was indeed such, that, even had he not worn the golden chains of his dignity, there would have been no difficulty in determining him to be some personage dressed with at least a little brief authority. Over the magisterial vestments of black velvet, he wore a new scarlet cloak, although the day had been one of the sultriest in July; and, with a lofty consequential air, and an ample display of the corporeal acquisition which he had made at his own and other well furnished tables, he moved along, swinging at every step his tall golden headed cane with the solemnity of a mandarine.

Claud was filled with wonder and awe at the sight of such splendid examples of Glasgow pomp and prosperity, but Maudge speedily rebuked his juvenile admiration.

'They're no worth the looking at,' said she; 'had ye but seen the last Leddy Kittlestonheugh, your ain muckle respekit grandmother, and her twa sisters, in their hench-hoops,[1] with their fans in their han's—the three in a row would hae soopit[2] the whole breadth o' the Trongate—ye would hae seen something. They were nane o' your new-made leddies, but come o' a pedigree. Foul would hae been the gait, and drooking[3] the shower, that would hae gart them jook their heads intil the door o' ony sic thing as a Glasgow bailie—Na; Claudie, my lamb, thou maun lift thy een aboon the trash o' the town, and ay keep mind that the hills are standing yet that might hae been thy ain; and so may they yet be, an thou can but master the pride o' back and belly, and seek for something mair solid than the bravery o' sic a Solomon in all his glory as yon Provost Gorbals. —Heh, sirs, what a kyteful o' pride's yon'er! and yet I would be nane surprised the morn to hear that the Nechabudnezzar was a' gane to pigs and whistles, and driven out wi' the divors bill to the barren pastures of bankruptcy.'

CHAPTER II

AFTER taking a stroll round the brow of the hill, Provost Gorbals and his lady approached the spot where Maudge and Claud were sitting. As they drew near, the old woman rose, for she recognised in Mrs Gorbals one of the former visitors at Kittlestonheugh. The figure of Maudge herself was so remarkable, that, seen once, it was seldom forgotten, and the worthy lady, almost at the same instant, said to the Provost,—

'Eh! Megsty, gudeman, if I dinna think yon's auld Kittleston-heugh's crookit bairnswoman. I won'er what's come o' the Laird, poor bodie,[7] sin' he was rookit[8] by the Darien. Eh! what an altera-tion it was to Mrs Walkinshaw, his gudedochter.[9] She was a bonny bodie; but frae the time o' the sore news, she croynt awa,[10] and her life gied out like the snuff o' a can'le. Hey, Magdalene Dobbie, come hither to me, I'm wanting to speak to thee.'

Maudge, at this shrill obstreperous summons, leading Claud

by the hand, went forward to the lady, who immediately said,—

'Ist 'tou aye[1] in Kittlestonheugh's service, and what's come o' him, sin' his lan' was roupit?'[2]

Maudge replied respectfully, and with the tear in her eye, that the Laird was dead.

'Dead!' exclaimed Mrs Gorbals, 'that's very extraordinare. I doubt[3] he was ill off at his latter end. Whar did he die, poor man?'

'We were obligated,' said Maudge, somewhat comforted by the compassionate accent of the lady, 'to come intil Glasgow, where he fell into a decay o' nature.' And she added, with a sigh that was almost a sob, ''Deed, it's vera true, he died in a sare straitened circumstance, and left this helpless laddie upon my hands.'

The Provost, who had in the meantime been still looking about in quest of a site for his intended mansion, on hearing this, turned round, and putting his hand in his pocket, said,—

'An' is this Kittlestonheugh's oe?[4] I'm sure it's a vera pityful thing o' you, lucky,[5] to tak compassion on the orphan; hae, my laddie, there's a saxpence.'

'Saxpence, gudeman!' exclaimed the Provost's lady, 'ye'll ne'er even your han' wi' a saxpence to the like of Kittlestonheugh, for sae we're bound in nature to call him, landless though his laird-ship now be; poor bairn, I'm wae for't.[6] Ye ken his mother was sib[7] to mine by the father's side, and blood's thicker than water ony day.'

Generosity is in some degree one of the necessary qualifications of a Glasgow magistrate, and Provost Gorbals being as well endowed with it as any of his successors have been since, was not displeased with the benevolent warmth of his wife, especially when he understood that Claud was of their own kin. On the contrary, he said affectionately,—

'Really it was vera thoughtless o' me, Liezy, my dear; but ye ken I have na an instinct to make me acquaint wi' the particulars of folk, before hearing about them. I'm sure no living soul can have a greater compassion than mysel' for gentle blood come to need-cessity.'

Mrs Gorbals, however, instead of replying to this remark—indeed, what could she say, for experience had taught her that it was perfectly just—addressed herself again to Maudge.

'And whar dost t'ou[1] live? and what hast t'ou to live upon?'

'I hae but the mercy of Providence,' was the humble answer of honest Maudge, 'and a garret-room in John Sinclair's lan'.[2] I ettle[3] as weel as I can for a morsel, by working stockings; but Claud's a rumbling laddie,[4] and needs mair than I hae to gi'e him:[5] a young appetite's a growing evil in the poor's aught.'[6]

The Provost and his wife looked kindly at each other, and the latter added,—

'Gudeman, ye maun do something for them. It'll no fare the waur[7] wi' our basket and our store.'

And Maudge was in consequence requested to bring Claud with her that evening to the Provost's house in the Bridgegate. 'I think,' added Mrs Gorbals, 'that our Hughoc's auld claes will just do for him; and Maudge, keep a good heart, we'll no let thee want. I won'er 'tou did na think of making an application to us afore.'

'No,' replied the old woman, 'I could ne'er do that—I would hae been in an unco[8] strait before I would hae begget on my own account; and how could I think o' disgracing the family? Any help that the Lord may dispose your hearts to gi'e, I'll accept wi' great thankfulness, but an almous is what I hope he'll ne'er put it upon me to seek; and though Claud be for the present a weight and burden, yet, an he's sparet, he'll be able belyve[9] to do something for himsel.'

Both the Provost and Mrs Gorbals commended her spirit; and, from this interview, the situation of Maudge was considerably improved by their constant kindness. Doubtless, had Mr Gorbals lived, he would have assisted Claud into business, but, dying suddenly, his circumstances were discovered to be less flourishing than the world had imagined, and his widow found herself constrained to abridge her wonted liberality.

Maudge, however, wrestled with poverty as well as she could, till Claud had attained his eleventh year, when she thought he was of a sufficient capacity to do something for himself. Accordingly, she intimated to Mrs Gorbals that she hoped it would be in her power to help her with the loan of a guinea to set him out in the world with a pack.[10] This the lady readily promised, but advised her to make application first to his relation Miss Christiana Heritage.

'She's in a bein[11] circumstance,' said Mrs Gorbals, 'for her father, auld Windywa's, left her weel on to five hundred pounds, and her cousin, Lord Killycrankie, ane of the fifteen[1] that ay staid in our house when he rode the Circuit, being heir of entail to her father, alloos her the use of the house, so that she's in a way to do muckle[2] for the laddie, if her heart were so inclined.'

Maudge, agreeably to this suggestion, went next day to Windywalls; but we must reserve our account of the mansion and its mistress to enrich our next chapter, for Miss Christiana was, even in our day and generation, a personage of no small consequence in her own eyes: indeed, for that matter, she was no less in ours, if we may judge by the niche which she occupies in the gallery of our recollection, after the lapse of more than fifty years.

CHAPTER III

IN the course of the same summer in which we commenced those grammar-school acquirements, that, in after life, have been so deservedly celebrated, our revered relative, the late old Lady Havers, carried us in her infirm dowagerian chariot to pay her annual visit to Miss Christiana Heritage. In the admiration with which we contemplated the venerable mansion and its ancient mistress, an indistinct vision rises in our fancy of a large irregular white-washed house, with a tall turnpike stair-case;[3] over the low and dwarfish arched door of which a huge cable was carved in stone, and dropped in a knotted festoon at each side. The traditions of the neighbourhood ascribed this carving to the Pictish sculptors, who executed the principal ornaments of the High Kirk of Glasgow.[4]

On entering under this feudal arch we ascended a spiral stair, and were shown into a large and lofty room, on three sides of which, each far in a deep recess, was a narrow window glazed with lozens[5] of yellow glass, that seemed scarcely more transparent than horn. The walls were hung with tapestry, from which tremendous forms, in warlike attitudes and with grim aspects, frowned in apparitional obscurity.

But of all the circumstances of a visit, which we must ever consider as a glimpse into the presence-chamber of the olden time, none made so deep and so vivid an impression upon our young remembrance as the appearance and deportment of Miss Christiana herself. She had been apprised of Lady Havers coming, and was seated in state to receive her, on a large settee adorned with ancestral needle work. She rose as our venerable relation entered the room. Alas! we have lived to know that we shall never again behold the ceremonial of a reception half so solemnly performed.

Miss Christiana was dressed in a courtly suit of purple Genoese velvet; her petticoat, spread by her hoop, extended almost to arms-length at each side. The ruffle cuffs which hung at her elbows loaded with lead, were coëval with the Union, having been worn by her mother when she attended her husband to that assembly of the States of Scotland, which put an end to the independence and poverty of the kingdom.[1] But who, at this distance of time, shall presume to estimate the altitude of the Babylonian tower of toupees and lappets which adorned Miss Christiana's brow?

It is probable, that the reception which she gave to poor Maudge and Claud was not quite so ceremonious as ours; for the substantial benison of the visit was but half-a-crown. Mrs Gorbals, on hearing this, exclaimed with a just indignation against the near-be-gawn[2] Miss Christiana, and setting herself actively to work, soon collected, among her acquaintance, a small sum sufficient to enable Maudge to buy and furnish a pack for Claud. James Bridle the saddlemaker, who had worked for his father, gave him a present of a strap to sling it over his shoulder; and thus, with a judicious selection of godly and humorous tracts, curtain rings, sleeve buttons, together with a compendious assortment of needles and pins, thimbles, stay-laces and garters, with a bunch of ballads and excellent new songs, Claud Walkinshaw espoused his fortune.

His excursions at first were confined to the neighbouring villages, and as he was sly and gabby, he soon contrived to get in about the good-will of the farmers' wives, and in process of time, few pedlars in all the west country were better liked, though every one complained that he was the dearest and the gairest.[3]

His success equalled the most sanguine expectations of Maudge, but Mrs Gorbals thought he might have recollected, somewhat better than he did, the kindness and care with which the affectionate old creature had struggled to support him in his helplessness. As often, however, as that warm-hearted lady inquired if he gave her any of his winnings, Maudge was obliged to say, 'I hope, poor lad, he has more sense than to think o' the like o' me. Is na he striving to make a conquest of the lands of his forefathers?

Ye ken he's come o' gentle blood, and I am nae better than his servan'.'

But although Maudge spoke thus generously, still sometimes, when she had afterwards become bedrid, and was left to languish and linger out the remnant of age in her solitary garret, comforted only by the occasional visits and charitable attentions of Mrs Gorbals, the wish would now and then rise, that Claud, when he was prospering in the traffic of the Borders, would whiles[1] think of her forlorn condition. But it was the lambent play of affection, in which anxiety to see him again before she died was stronger than any other feeling, and as often as she felt it moving her to repine at his inattention, she would turn herself to the wall, and implore the Father of Mercies to prosper his honest endeavours, and that he might ne'er be troubled in his industry with any thought about such a burden as it had pleased Heaven to make her to the world.

After having been bedrid for about the space of two years, Maudge died. Claud, in the mean time, was thriving as well as the prigging[2] wives and higgling[3] girls in his beat between the Nith and the Tyne would permit. Nor was there any pedlar better known at the fairs of the Border towns, or who displayed on those occasions such a rich assortment of goods. It was thought by some, that, in choosing that remote country for the scene of his itinerant trade, he was actuated by some sentiment of reverence for the former consequence of his family. But, as faithful historians, we are compelled to remind the reader, that he was too worldly wise to indulge himself with any thing so romantic; the absolute fact being, that, after trying many other parts of the country, he found the Borders the most profitable, and that the inhabitants were also the most hospitable customers,—no small item in the arithmetical philosophy of a pedlar.

CHAPTER IV

ABOUT twenty years after the death of Maudge, Claud returned to Glasgow with five hundred pounds above the world, and settled himself as a cloth-merchant, in a shop under the piazza[4] of a house which occupied part of the ground where the Exchange now stands.[5] The resolution which he had early formed to redeem the inheritance of his ancestors, and which his old affectionate bene-factress had perhaps inspired, as well as cherished, was grown into a habit. His carefulness, his assiduity, his parsimony, his very honesty, had no other object nor motive; it was the actuating principle of his life. Some years after he had settled in Glasgow, his savings and gathering enabled him to purchase the farm of Grippy, a part of the patrimony of his family.

The feelings of the mariner returning home, when he again beholds the rising hills of his native land, and the joys and fears of the father's bosom, when, after a long absence, he approaches the abode of his children, are tame and calm, compared to the deep and greedy satisfaction with which the persevering pedlar received the earth and stone that gave him infeftment[1] of that cold and sterile portion of his forefathers' estate. In the same moment he formed a resolution worthy of the sentiment he then felt,—a senti-ment which, in a less sordid breast, might have almost partaken of the pride of virtue. He resolved to marry, and beget children, and entail the property, that none of his descendants might ever have it in their power to commit the imprudence which had brought his grandfather to a morsel, and thrown himself on the world. And the same night, after maturely considering the prospects of all the heiresses within the probable scope of his ambition, he resolved that his affections should be directed towards Miss Girzy Hypel, the only daughter of Malachi Hypel, the Laird of Plealands.

They were in some degree related, and he had been led to think of her from an incident which occurred on the day he made the purchase. Her father was, at the time, in Glasgow, attending the Circuit; for, as often as the judges visited the city, he had some dispute with a neighbour or a tenant that required their inter-position. Having heard of what had taken place, he called on Claud to congratulate him on the recovery of so much of his family inheritance.

'I hear,' said the Laird, on entering the shop, and proffering his hand across the counter, 'that ye hae gotten a sappy[2] bargain o' the Grippy. It's true some o' the lands are but cauld;[3] howsever, cousin, ne'er fash your thumb,[4] Glasgow's on the thrive, and ye hae as many een[5] in your head, for an advantage, as ony body I ken. But now that ye hae gotten a house, wha's to be the leddy?[6] I'm sure ye might do waur than cast a sheep's e'e in at oure door; my dochter Girzy's o' your ain flesh and blood; I dinna see ony moral impossibility in her becoming, as the Psalmist says, "bone of thy bone."'

Claud replied in his wonted couthy[1] manner:

'Nane o' your jokes, Laird,—me even mysel to your dochter? Na, na, Plealands,[2] that canna be thought o' now a days. But, no to make a ridicule of sic a solemn concern, it's vera true that, had na my grandfather, when he was grown doited,[3] sent out a' the Kittlestonheugh in a cargo o' playocks[4] to the Darien, I might hae been in a state and condition to look at Miss Girzy; but, ye ken, I hae a lang clue to wind[5] before I maun think o' playing the ba' wi' Fortune, in ettling[6] so far aboun my reach.'

'Snuffs o' tobacco,' exclaimed the Laird,—'are nae ye sib to oursels? and, if ye dinna fail by your ain blateness,[7] our Girzy's no surely past speaking to. Just lay your leg, my man, o'er a side o' horse flesh, and come your ways, some Saturday, to spier[8] her price.'

It was upon this delicate hint that Grippy was induced to think of Miss Girzy Hypel; but finding that he was deemed a fit match for her, and might get her when he would, he deferred the visit until he had cast about among the other neighbouring lairds' families for a better, that is to say, a richer match. In this, whether he met with repulsive receptions, or found no satisfactory answers to his inquiries, is not quite certain; but, as we have said, in the same night on which he took legal possession of his purchase, he resolved to visit Plealands; and in order that the family might not be taken unawares, he sent a letter next day by the Ayr carrier[9] to apprise the Laird of his intention, provided it was convenient to receive him for a night. To this letter, by the return of Johnny Drizen, the carrier, on the week following, he received such a cordial reply, that he was induced to send for Cornelius Luke, the tailor, a douce[10] and respectable man, and one of the elders of the Tron Kirk.

'Come your ways, Cornie,' said the intending lover; 'I want to speak to you anent what's doing about the new kirk on the Green Know.'[11]

'Doing, Mr Walkinshaw!—it's a doing that our bairns' bairns will ne'er hear the end o'—a rank and carnal innovation on the spirit o' the Kirk o' Scotland,' replied the elder—'It's to be after the fashion o' some prelatic Babel in Lon'on, and they hae christened it already by the papistical name o' St Andrew—a sore thing that,

Mr Walkinshaw; but the Lord has set his face against it, and the builders thereof are smitten as wi' a confusion o' tongues, in the lack o' siller to fulfil their idolatrous intents—Blessed be His name for evermore! But was na Mr Kilfuddy, wha preached for Mr Anderson last Sabbath, most sweet and delectable on the vanities of this life, in his forenoon lecture? and did na ye think, when he spoke o' that seventh wonder o' the world, the temple of Diana, and enlarged wi' sic pith and marrow on the idolaters in Ephesus, that he was looking o'er his shouther[1] at Lowrie Dinwiddie and Provost Aiton, who are no wrang't in being wytid wi' the sin o' this inordinate superstructure?—Mr Walkinshaw, am nae pro-phet,[2] as ye will ken, but I can see that the day's no far aff, when ministers of the gospel in Glasgow will be seen chambering[3] and wantoning to the sound o' the kist fu' o' whistles,[4] wi' the seven-headed beast routing its choruses at every o'ercome o' the spring.'

Which prediction was in our own day[5] and generation to a great degree fulfilled; at the time, however, it only served to move the pawkie cloth-merchant to say,

'Nae doubt, Cornie, the world's like the tod's whelp, aye the aulder the waur;[6] but I trust we'll hear news in the land before the like o' that comes to pass. Howsever, in the words of truth and holiness, "sufficient for the day is the evil thereof;" and let us hope, that a regenerating spirit may go forth to the ends o' the earth, and that all the sons of men will not be utterly cut up, root and branch.'

'No: be thankit,' said Cornelius, the tailor—'even of those that shall live in the latter days, a remnant will be saved.'

'That's a great comfort, Mr Luke, to us a',' replied Claud;— 'but, talking o' remnants, I hae a bit blue o' superfine; it has been lang on hand, and the moths are beginning to meddle wi't—I won'er if ye could mak me a coat o't?'

The remnant was then produced on the counter, and Cornelius, after inspecting it carefully, declared, that, 'with the help of a steek or twa[7] of darning, that would na be percep, it would do very well.' The cloth was accordingly delivered to him, with strict injunctions to have it ready by Friday, and with all the requisite et ceteras to complete a coat, he left the shop greatly edified, as he told his wife, by the godly salutations of Mr Walkinshaw's spirit; 'wherein,' as he said, 'there was a kithing[8] of fruit meet for repentance; a foretaste o' things that pertain not to this life; a receiving o' the erls[9] of righteousness

and peace, which passeth all understanding, and endureth for
evermore.'

'I'm blithe to hear't,' was the worthy woman's answer, 'for he's
an even down Nabal[1]—a perfect penure pig,[2] that I ne'er could
abide since he wauld na lend poor old Mrs Gorbals, the provost's
widow, that, they say, set him up in the world, the sma' soom o'
five pounds, to help her wi' the outfit o' her oe,[3] when he was gaun
to Virginia, a clerk to Bailie Cross.'

CHAPTER V

WHEN Claud was duly equipped by Cornelius Luke, in the best
fashion of that period, for a bien[4] cloth-merchant of the discreet
age of forty-seven,[5] a message was sent by his shop lad, Jock Gleg,
to Rob Wallace, the horse-couper in the Gallowgate, to have his
beast in readiness next morning by seven o'clock, the intending
lover having, several days before, bespoke it for the occasion.

Accordingly, at seven o'clock on Saturday morning, Rob was
with the horse himself, at the entry to Cochran's Land,[6] in the
Candleriggs, where Claud then lodged, and the wooer, in the
sprucest cut of his tailor, with a long silver-headed whip in his
hand, borrowed from his friend and customer, Bailie Murdoch,
attended by Jock Gleg, carrying a stool, came to the close mouth.[7]

'I'm thinking, Mr Walkinshaw,' said Rob, the horse-couper,
'that ye would na be the waur of a spur, an it were only on the
ae heel.'

'We maun do our best without that commodity, Rob,' replied
Claud, trying to crack his whip in a gallant style, but unfortunately
cutting his own leg through the dark blue rig-and-fur gamashins;[8]
for he judiciously considered, that, for so short a journey, and that,
too, on speculation, it was not worth his while to get a pair of
boots.

Rob drew up the horse, and Jock having placed the stool, Claud
put his right foot in the stirrup, at which Rob and some of the
students of the college, who happened to be attracted to the spot,
with diverse others then and there present, set up a loud shout of
laughter, much to his molestation. But surely no man is expected
to know by instinct the proper way of mounting a horse; and this

was the first time that Claud had ever ascended the back of any quadruped.

When he had clambered into the saddle, Rob led the horse into the middle of the street, and the beast, of its own accord, walked soberly across the Trongate towards the Stockwell. The conduct of the horse, for some time, was indeed most considerate, and, in consequence, although Claud hung heavily over his neck, and held him as fast as possible with his knees, he passed the bridge, and cleared the buildings beyond, without attracting, in any particular degree, the admiration of the public towards his rider. But, in an unguarded moment, the infatuated Claud rashly thought it necessary to employ the Bailie's whip, and the horse, so admonished, quickened his pace to a trot. 'Heavens, ca' they this riding?' exclaimed Claud, and almost bit his tongue through in the utterance. However, by the time they reached Cathcart,[1] it was quite surprising to see how well he worked in the saddle; and, notwithstanding the continued jolting, how nobly he preserved his balance. But, on entering that village, all the dogs, in the most terrifying manner, came rushing out from the cottage doors, and pursued the trotting horse with such bark and bay, that the poor animal saw no other for't, but to trot from them faster and faster. The noise of the dogs, and of a passenger on horseback, drew forth the inhabitants, and at every door might be seen beldams with flannel caps, and mothers with babies in their arms, and clusters of children around them. It was the general opinion among all the spectators, on seeing the spruce new clothes of Claud, and his vaulting horsemanship, that he could be no less a personage than the Lord Provost of Glasgow.

Among them were a few country lads, who, perceiving how little the rider's seat of honour was accustomed to a saddle, had the wickedness to encourage and egg on the dogs to attack the horse still more furiously; but, notwithstanding their malice, Claud still kept his seat, until all the dogs but one devil of a terrier had retired from the pursuit: nothing could equal the spirit and pertinacity with which that implacable cur hung upon the rear, and snapped at the heels of the horse. Claud, who durst not venture to look behind, lest he should lose his balance, several times damned the dog with great sincerity, and tried to lash him away with Bailie Murdoch's silver-headed whip, but the terrier would not desist.

How long the attack might have continued, there is certainly no

telling, as it was quickly determined by one of those lucky hits of
fortune which are so desirable in life. The long lash of the Bailie's
whip, in one of Claud's blind attempts, happily knotted itself
round the neck of the dog. The horse, at the same moment, started
forward into that pleasant speed at which the pilgrims of yore were
wont to pass from London to the shrine of St Thomas a Becket at
Canterbury, (which, for brevity, is in vulgar parlance called, in
consequence, a canter;) and Claud dragged the terrier at his whip-
string end, like an angler who has hooked a salmon that he cannot
raise out of the water, until he met with Johnny Drizen, the Ayr
carrier, coming on his weekly journey to Glasgow.

'Lordsake, Mr Walkinshaw!' exclaimed the carrier, as he drew
his horse aside—'in the name of the Lord, whare are ye gaun,[1] and
what's that ye're hauling ahint[2] you?'

'For the love of Heaven, Johnny,' replied the distressed cloth-
merchant, pale with apprehension, and perspiring at every pore,—
'for the love of Heaven, stop this desperate beast!'

The tone of terror and accent of anguish in which this invoca-
tion was uttered, had such an effect on the humanity and feelings
of the Ayr carrier, that he ran towards Claud with the ardour of a
philanthropist, and seized the horse by the bridle rings. Claud, in
the same moment, threw down the whip, with the strangled dog at
the lash; and, making an endeavour to vault out of the saddle, fell
into the mire, and materially damaged the lustre and beauty of his
new coat. However, he soon regained his legs, but they so shook
and trembled, that he could scarcely stand, as he bent forward with
his feet widely asunder, being utterly unable for some time to
endure in any other position the pain of that experience of St
Sebastian's martyrdom which he had locally suffered.

His first words to the carrier were, 'Man, Johnny, this is the
roughest brute that ever was created. Twa dyers wi' their beetles[3]
could na hae done me mair detriment. I dinna think I'll e'er be
able to sit down again.'

This colloquy was, however, speedily put an end to, by the
appearance of a covered cart, in which three ministers were returning from the synod[4] to their respective parishes in Ayrshire; for at
that time neither post-chaise nor stage-coach was numbered
among the luxuries of Glasgow. One of them happened to be
the identical Mr Kilfuddy of Braehill, who had lectured so
learnedly about the Temple of Diana on the preceding Sunday in

the Tron Church; and he being acquainted with Claud, said, as he looked out and bade the driver to stop,—

'Dear me, Mr Walkinshaw, but ye hae gotten an unco cowp.[1] I hope nae banes are broken?'

'No,' replied Claud a little pawkily,[2] 'no; thanks be and praise—the banes, I believe, are a' to the fore;[3] but it's no to be expressed what I hae suffer't in the flesh.'

Some further conversation then ensued, and the result was most satisfactory, for Claud was invited to take a seat in the cart with the ministers, and induced to send his horse back to Rob Wallace by Johnny Drizen the carrier. Thus, without any material augmentation of his calamity, was he conveyed to the gate which led to Plealands. The Laird, who had all the morning been anxiously looking out for him, on seeing the cart approaching, left the house, and was standing ready at the yett[4] to give him welcome.

CHAPTER VI

PLEALANDS house stood on the bleak brow of a hill. It was not of great antiquity, having been raised by the father of Malachi; but it occupied the site of an ancient fortalice, the materials of which were employed in its construction; and as no great skill of the sculptor had been exerted to change the original form of the lintels and their ornaments, it had an air of antiquity much greater than properly belonged to its years.

About as much as the habitation had been altered from its primitive character, the master too had been modernized. But, in whatever degree he may have been supposed to have declined from the heroic bearing of his ancestors, he still inherited, in unabated vigour, the animosity of their spirit; and if the coercive influence of national improvement prevented him from being distinguished in the feud and foray, the books of sederunt, both of the Glasgow Circuit and of the Court of Session,[5] bore ample testimony to his constancy before them in asserting supposed rights, and in vindicating supposed wrongs.

In his personal appearance, Malachi Hypel had but few pretensions to the gallant air and grace of the gentlemen of that time. He was a coarse hard-favoured fresh-coloured carl,[6] with a few white hairs thinly scattered over a round bald head. His eyes were small and grey, quick in the glance, and sharp in the expression. He spoke thickly and hurriedly, and although his words were all very cogently strung together, there was still an unaccountable obscurity in the precise meaning of what he said. In his usual style of dress he was rude and careless, and he commonly wore a large flat brimmed blue bonnet; but on the occasion when he came to the gate to receive Claud, he had on his Sunday suit and hat.

After the first salutations were over, he said to Claud, on seeing him walking lamely and uneasily, 'What's the matter, Grippy,[1] that ye seem sae stiff and sair?'

'I met wi' a bit accident,' was Claud's reply: 'Rob Wallace, the horse-couper, gied me sic a deevil to ride as, I believe, never man before mounted. I would na wish my sworn enemy a greater ill than a day's journey on that beast's back, especially an he was as little used to riding as me.'

The latter clause of the sentence was muttered inwardly, for the Laird did not hear it; otherwise he would probably have indulged his humour a little at the expence of his guest, as he had a sort of taste for caustic jocularity, which the hirpling[2] manner of Claud was, at the moment, well calculated to provoke.

On reaching the brow of the rising ground where the house stood, the leddy,[3] as Mrs Hypel was emphatically called by the neighbouring cottars, with Miss Girzy, came out to be introduced to their relative.

Whether the leddy, a pale, pensive, delicate woman, had been informed by the Laird of the object of Claud's visit, we do not thoroughly know, but she received him with a polite and friendly respectfulness. Miss Girzy certainly was in total ignorance of the whole business, and was, therefore, not embarrassed with any virgin palpitations, nor blushing anxieties; on the contrary, she met him with the ease and freedom of an old acquaintance.

It might here be naturally expected that we should describe the charms of Miss Girzy's person, and the graces of her mind; but, in whatever degree she possessed either, she had been allowed to reach the discreet years of a Dumbarton youth[4] in unsolicited maidenhood; indeed, with the aid of all the prospective interest of the inheritance around her, she did not make quite so tender an impression on the heart of her resolved lover

as he himself could have wished. But why should we expatiate
on such particulars? Let the manners and virtues of the family
speak for themselves, while we proceed to relate what ensued.

CHAPTER VII

'GIRZY,' said the Laird to his daughter, as they entered the
dining-room, 'gae to thy bed and bring a cod[1] for Mr Walkinshaw,
for he'll no can thole[2] to sit down on our hard chairs.'

Miss Girzy laughed as she retired to execute the order, while
her mother continued, as she had done from the first introduction,
to inspect Claud from head to foot, with a curious and something
of a suspicious eye; there was even an occasional flush that gleamed
through the habitual paleness of her thoughtful countenance,
redder and warmer than the hectic glow of mere corporeal indisposition. Her attention, however, was soon drawn to the
spacious round table, in the middle of the room, by one of the
maids entering with a large pewter tureen, John Drappie, the man
servant, having been that morning sent on some caption and horning business of the Laird's to Gabriel Beagle, the Kilmarnock
lawyer. But, as the critics hold it indelicate to describe the details
of any refectionary supply, however elegant, we must not presume to enumerate the series and succession of Scottish fare,
which soon crowned the board, all served on pewter as bright as
plate. Our readers must endeavour, by the aid of their own fancies,
to form some idea of the various forms in which the head and
harigals[3] of the sheep, that had been put to death for the occasion,
were served up, not forgetting the sonsy,[4] savoury, sappy haggis,
together with the gude fat hen, the float whey,[5] which, in a large
china punch-bowl, graced the centre of the table, and supplied the
place of jellies, tarts, tartlets, and puddings.

By the time the table was burdened, Miss Girzy had returned
with the pillow, which she herself placed in one of the armchairs,
shaking and patting it into plumpness, as she said,—

'Come round here, Mr Walkinshaw,—I trow ye'll fin' this a saft
easy seat,—well do I ken what it is to be saddle-sick mysel'. Lordsake,
when I gaed in ahint my father to see the robber hang'd at Ayr, I was
for mair than three days just as if I had sat doun on a heckle.'[6]

When the cloth was removed, and the ladies had retired, the Laird opened his mind by stretching his arm across the table towards his guest, and, shaking him again heartily by the hand,—

'Weel, Grippy,' said he, 'but am blithe to see you here; and, if am no mistaen, Girzy will no be ill to woo.—Is na she a coothy[1] and kind creature?—She'll make you a capital wife.—There's no another in the parish that kens better how to manage a house.—Man, it would do your heart gude to hear how she rants among the servan' lasses, lazy sluts, that would like nothing better than to live at heck and manger,[2] and bring their master to a morsel; but I trow Girzy gars them keep a trig house and a birring wheel.'[3]

'No doubt, Laird,' replied Claud, 'but it's a comfort to hae a frugal woman for a helpmate; but ye ken now-a-days it's no the fashion for bare legs to come thegither—The wife maun hae something to put in the pot as well as the man.—And, although Miss Girzy may na be a'thegither objectionable, yet it would still be a pleasant thing baith to hersel' and the man that gets her, an ye would just gi'e a bit inkling o' what she'll hae.'

'Is na she my only dochter? That's a proof and test that she'll get a',—naebody needs to be teld[4] mair.'

'Vera true, Laird,' rejoined the suitor, 'but the leddy's life's in her lip,[5] and if ony thing were happening to her, ye're a hale man, and wha kens what would be the upshot o' a second marriage?'

'That's looking far ben,'[6] replied the Laird, and he presently added, more briskly, 'My wife, to be sure, is a frail woman, but she's no the gear that 'ill traike.'[7]

In this delicate and considerate way, the overture to a purpose of marriage was opened; and, not to dwell on particulars, it is sufficient to say, that, in the course of little more than a month thereafter, Miss Girzy was translated into the Leddy of Grippy;[8] and in due season presented her husband with a son and heir, who was baptized by the name of Charles.

When the birth was communicated to the Laird, he rode expressly to Grippy[9] to congratulate his son-in-law on the occasion; and, when they were sitting together, in the afternoon, according to the fashion of the age, enjoying the contents of the gardevin[10] entire, Claud warily began to sound him on a subject that lay very near his heart.

'Laird,' said he, 'ye ken the Walkinshaws of Kittlestonheugh are o' a vera ancient blood, and but for the doited[11] prank o' my grandfather, in sending my father on that gouk's errand[1] to the Darien, the hills are green and the land broad that should this day hae been mine; and, therefore, to put it out o' the power of posterity to play at any sic wastrie[2] again, I mean to entail the property of the Grippy.'

'That's a very good conceit,' replied the Laird, 'and I hae my-sel' had a notion of entailing the Plealands likewise.'

'So I hae heard you say,' rejoined Claud, 'and now that the bairn's born, and a laddie too, we may make ae work o't.'

'Wi' a' my heart,' replied the Laird, 'nothing can be more agree-able to me; but as I wish to preserve the name of my family, than whilk[3] there's no a more respectit in Scotland, I'll only covenant that when Charlie succeeds me, that he'll take the name o' Hypel.'

'Ye surely, Laird, would ne'er be so unreasonable,' replied Grippy, a little somewhat hastily; 'ye can ne'er be sae unreasonable as to expect that the lad would gie up his father's name, the name o' Walkinshaw, and take only that of Hypel.'

''Deed would I,' said the Laird, 'for no haeing a son o' my own to come after me, it's surely very natural that I would like the Hypels to kittle again in my oe[4] through my only dochter.'

'The Walkinshaws, I doubt,' replied Claud emphatically, 'will ne'er consent to sic an eclipse as that.'

'The lands of Plealands,' retorted the Laird, 'are worth some-thing.'

'So it was thought, or I doubt the heir o't would nae hae been a Walkinshaw,' replied Claud, still more pertinaciously.

'Weel, weel,' said the Laird, 'dinna let us argol bargol about it; entail your own property as ye will, mine shall be on the second son; ye can ne'er object to that.'

'Second son, and the first scarce sax days auld! I tell you what it is, an ye'll no make the entail on the first, that is, on Charlie Walkinshaw, to be Walkinshaw, mind that, I'll no say what may happen in the way o' second sons.'

'The Plealands' my ain, and though I canna weel will it awa', and ne'er will sell't, yet get it wha will, he maun tak the name o' Hypel. The thing's sae settled, Grippy, and it's no for you and me to cast out about it.'

Claud made several attempts to revive the subject, and to per-suade the Laird to change his mind, but he was inflexible. Still, however, being resolved, as far as in him lay, to anticipate the indiscretion of his heirs, he executed a deed of entail on Charles; and for a considerable time after the Laird was not a little confirmed in his determination not to execute any deed in favour of Charles, but to reserve his lands for the second son, by the very reason that might have led another sort of person to act differently, namely, that he understood there was no prospect of any such appearing.

Towards the end, however, of the third year after the birth of Charles, Claud communicated to the Laird, that, by some unaccountable dispensation, Mrs Walkinshaw was again in the way to be a mother, adding, 'Noo, Laird, ye'll hae your ain way o't;' and, accordingly, as soon as Walter, the second son, was born, and baptized, the lands of Plealands were entailed on him, on condition, as his grandfather intended, that he should assume the name of Hypel.

CHAPTER VIII

FOR several years after the birth of Walter, no event of any consequence happened in the affairs of Claud. He continued to persevere in the parsimonious system which had so far advanced his fortune. His wife was no less industrious on her part, for, in the meantime, she presented him with a daughter and another son, and had reared calves and grumphies innumerable, the profit of which, as she often said, was as good as the meal and malt o' the family. By their united care and endeavours, Grippy thus became one of the wealthiest men of that age in Glasgow; but although different desirable opportunities presented themselves for investing his money in other and more valuable land, he kept it ever ready to redeem any portion of his ancestral estate that might be offered for sale.

The satisfaction which he enjoyed from his accumulative prospects was not, however, without a mixture of that anxiety with which the cup of human prosperity, whether really full, or only foaming, is always embittered. The Laird, his father-in-law, in the deed of entail which he executed of the Plealands, had reserved to himself a power of revocation, in the event of his wife dying before him, in the first instance, and of Walter and George, the two younger sons of Grippy, either dying under age, or refusing to take the name of Hypel, in the second. This power, both under the circumstances, and in itself, was perfectly reasonable; and perhaps it was the more vexatious to the meditations of Claud, that it happened to be so. For he often said to his wife, as they sat of an evening by the fire-side in the dark, for the Leddy was no seam-stress, and he had as little taste for literature, of course, they burned no candles when by themselves, and that was almost every night,—'I marvel, Girzy, what could gar[1] your father put that most unsafe claw[2] in his entail. I would na be surprised if out o' it were to come a mean of taking the property entirely frae us. For ye see, if your mither was dead, and, poor woman, she has lang been in a feckless way, there's no doubt but your father would marry again,—and married again, there can be as little doubt that he would hae childer,—so what then would become o' ours—'

To this the worthy Leddy of Grippy would as feelingly reply,

'I'm thinking, gudeman, that ye need na tak the anxieties sae muckle to heart; for, although my mither has been, past the memory o' man, in a complaining condition, I ken nae odds o' her this many a year; her ail's like[3] water to leather; it makes her life the tougher; and I would put mair confidence in the durability of her complaint than in my father's health; so we need na fash[4] our-selves wi' controverting anent what may come o' the death o' either the t'ane or the t'ither.'

'But then,' replied Claud, 'ye forget the other claw about Watty and Geordie. Supposing, noo, that they were baith dead and gone, which, when we think o' the frush green kail-custock-like nature of bairns,[5] is no an impossibility in the hands of their Maker. Will it no be the most hardest thing that ever was seen in the world for Charlie no to inherit the breadth o' the blade of a cabaudge o' a' his father's matrimonial conquest? But even should it please the Lord to spare Watty, is't no an afflicting thing, to see sic a braw[6] property as the Plealands destined to a creature that I am sure his brother Geordie, if he lives to come to years o' discretion, will no fail to tak the law o' him for a haverel?'[7]

'I won'er to hear you, gudeman,' exclaimed the Leddy, 'ay mislikening Watty at that gait.[8] I'm sure he's as muckle your ain as ony o' the ither bairns; and he's a weel-tempered laddie, lilting like a linty at the door-cheek[9] frae morning to night, when Charlie's rampaging about the farm, riving his claes[10] on bush and brier a' the summer, tormenting the birds and mawkins[1] out o' their vera life.'

'Singing, Girzy, I'm really distressed to hear you,' replied the father; 'to ca' yon singing; it's nothing but lal, lal, lal, lal, wi' a bow and a bend, backwards and forwards, as if the creature had na the gumpshion o' the cuckoo, the whilk has a note mair in its sang, although it has but twa.'

'It's an innocent sang for a' that; and I wish his brothers may ne'er do waur than sing the like o't. But ye just hae a spite at the bairn, gudeman, 'cause my father has made him the heir to the Plealands. That's the gospel truth o' your being so fain to gar folk trow[2] that my Watty's daft.'

'Ye're daft, gudewife—are na we speaking here in a rational manner anent the concerns o' our family? It would be a sair heart to me to think that Watty, or any o' my bairns, were na like the lave o' the warld;[3] but ye ken there are degrees o' capacity, Girzy, and Watty's, poor callan, we maun alloo, between oursels, has been meted by a sma' measure.'

'Weel, if ever I heard the like o' that—if the Lord has dealt the brains o' our family in mutchkins and chapins,[4] it's my opinion, that Watty got his in the biggest stoup;[5] for he's farther on in every sort of education than Charlie, and can say his questions[6] without missing a word, as far as "What is forbidden in the tenth commandment?" And I ne'er hae been able to get his brother beyond "What is effectual calling?" Though, I'll no deny, he's better at the Mother's Carritches;[7] but that a' comes o' the questions and answers being so vera short.'

'That's the vera thing, Girzy, that disturbs me,' replied the father, 'for the callan[8] can get ony thing by heart, but, after all, he's just like a book, for every thing he learns is dead within him, and he's ne'er a prin's worth[9] the wiser o't. But it's some satisfaction to me, that, since your father would be so unreasonably obstinate as to make away the Plealands past Charlie, he'll be punished in the gouk he's chosen for heir.'

'Gude[10] guide us; is na that gouk your ain bairn?' exclaimed the indignant mother. 'Surely the man's fey[11] about his entails and his properties, to speak o' the illess laddie, as if it were no better than a stirk or a stot.[12]—Ye'll no hae the power to wrang my wean,[13] while the breath o' life's in my bodie; so, I redde ye, tak tent to[14] what ye try.'

'Girzy, t'ou has a head, and so has a nail.'

'Gudeman, ye hae a tongue, and so has a bell.'

'Weel, weel, but what I was saying a' concerns the benefit and advantage o' our family,' said Claud, 'and ye ken as it is our duty to live for one another, and to draw a' thegither, it behoves us twa, as parents, to see that ilk is properly yocket,[1] sin' it would surely be a great misfortune, if, after a' our frugality and gathering, the cart were cowpit[2] in the dirt at last by ony neglek on our part.'

'That's ay what ye say,' replied the Leddy,—'a's for the family, and nothing for the dividual bairns—noo that's what I can never understand, for is na our family, Charlie, Watty, Geordie, and Meg?'—

'My family,' said Claud emphatically, 'was the Walkinshaws of Kittlestonheugh, and let me tell you, Girzy Hypel, if it had na been on their account, there would ne'er hae been a Charlie nor a Watty either between you and me to plea about.'

'I'm no denying your parentage—I ne'er said a light word about it, but I canna comprehend how it is, that ye would mak step-bairns o' your ain blithesome childer on account o' a wheen auld dead patriarchs[3] that hae been rotten, for ought I ken to the contrary, since before Abraham begat Isaac.'

'Haud thy tongue, woman, haud thy tongue. It's a thrashing o' the water, and a raising o' bells,[4] to speak to ane o' thy capacity on things so far aboon thy understanding. Gae but the house,[5] and see gin the supper's ready.'

In this manner, the conversations between Grippy and his Leddy were usually conducted to their natural issue, a quarrel, which ended in a rupture that was only healed by a peremptory command, which sent her on some household mission, during the performance of which the bickering was forgotten.

CHAPTER IX

In the meantime, as much friendliness and intercourse was maintained between the families of Grippy and Plealands as could reasonably be expected from the characters and dispositions of the respective inmates. Shortly, however, after the conversation related in the preceding Chapter had taken place, it happened that, as Malachi was returning on horseback from Glasgow, where he had lost a law-suit, long prosecuted with the most relentless pertinacity against one of his tenants, he was overtaken on the Mairns Moor[1] by one of those sudden squalls and showers, which the genius of the place so often raises, no doubt purposely, to conceal from the weary traveller the dreariness of the view around, and being wetted into the skin, the cold which he caught in consequence, and the irritation of his mind, brought on a fever, that terminated fatally on the fifth day.

His funeral was conducted according to the fashion of the age; but the day appointed was raw, windy, and sleety; not, however, so much so as to prevent the friends of the deceased from flocking in from every quarter. The assemblage that arrived far transcended all that can be imagined, in these economical days, of the attendance requisite on any such occasion. The gentry were shown into the dining-room, and into every room that could be fitted up with planks and deals for their reception. The barn received the tenantry, and a vast multitude—the whole clanjamphry[2] from all the neighbouring parishes—assembled on the green in front of the house.

The Laird in his lifetime maintained a rough and free hospitality; and, as his kindred and acquaintance expected, there was neither scant nor want at his burial. The profusion of the services of seed-cake and wine to the in-door guests was in the liberalest spirit of the time; and tobacco-pipes, shortbread, and brandy, unadulterated by any immersion of the guager's rod,[3] were distributed, with unmeasured abundance, to those in the barn and on the green.

Mr Kilfuddy, the parish minister, said grace to the gentry in the dining-room; and the elders, in like manner, performed a similar part in the other rooms. We are not sure if we may venture to assert, that grace was said to the company out of doors. Mr Taws, the dominie of Bodleton, has indeed repeatedly declared, that he did himself ask a blessing; but he has never produced any other evidence that was satisfactory to us. Indeed, what with the drinking, the blast, and the sleet, it was not reasonable to expect much attention would be paid to any prayer; and therefore we shall not insist very particularly on this point.

The Braehill church-yard was at a considerable distance from Plealands-house, and hearses not being then in fashion in that part of the country, one of the Laird's own carts was drawn out, and the coffin placed on it for conveyance, while the services[1] were going round the company. How it happened, whether owing to the neglect of Thomas Cabinet, the wright, who acted the part of undertaker, and who had, with all his men, more to attend to than he could well manage, in supplying the multitude with refreshments; or whether John Drappie, the old servant that was to drive the cart, had, like many others, got a service overmuch, we need not pause to inquire:—it, however, so happened, that, by some unaccountable and never explained circumstance, the whole body of the assembled guests arranged themselves in funereal array as well and as steadily as the generality of them could, and proceeded towards the church-yard—those in the van believing that the cart with the coffin was behind, and their followers in the rear committing a similar mistake, by supposing that it was before them in front. Thus both parties, in ignorance of the simple fact, that the coffin and cart were still standing at the house door, proceeded, with as much gravity and decorum as possible, to the church-yard gate, where they halted. As the gentlemen in front fell back to the right and left, to open an avenue for the body to be brought up, the omission was discovered, and also that there was no other way of performing the interment but by returning, as expeditiously as possible, to the house for the body.

By this time the weather, which had been all the morning cold and blustering, was become quite tempestuous. The wind raved in the trees and hedges—the sleet was almost thickened into a blinding snow, insomuch, that, when the company reached the house, the greater number of them were so chilled that they stood in need of another service, and another was of course handed round on the green; of which the greater number liberally and freely partaking, were soon rendered as little able to wrestle against

the wind as when they originally set out. However, when the procession was formed a second time, Thomas Cabinet taking care to
send the cart with the coffin on before, the whole moved again
towards the church-yard, it is said, with a degree of less decorum
than in their former procession. Nay, there is no disguising the
fact, that more than two or three of the company, finding themselves, perhaps, unable to struggle against the blast, either lay
down of their own voluntary accord on the road, or were blown
over by the wind.

When the procession had a second time reached the church-
yard, and Thomas Cabinet, perspiring at every pore, was wiping
his bald head with his coat sleeve, his men got the coffin removed
from the cart, and placed on the spokes, and the relatives, according to their respective degrees of propinquity, arranged themselves
to carry it. The bearers, however, either by means of the head-
stones and the graves over which their path lay, or by some other
cause, walked so unevenly, that those on the one side pushed against
their corresponding kindred on the other, in such a manner, that
the coffin was borne rollingly along for some time, but without any
accident, till the relations on the right side gave a tremendous
lurch, in which they drew the spokes out of the hands of the
mourners on the left, and the whole pageant fell with a dreadful
surge to the ground.

This accident, however, was soon rectified; the neighbours,
who were not bearers, assisted the fallen to rise, and Thomas
Cabinet, with his men, carried the coffin to its place of rest, and
having laid it on the two planks which were stretched across the
grave, assembled the nearest kin around, and gave the cords into
their hands, that they might lower the Laird into his last bed. The
betherel[1] and his assistant then drew out the planks, and the sudden
jirk of the coffin, when they were removed, gave such a tug to those
who had hold of the cords, that it pulled them down, head foremost,
into the grave after it. Fortunately, however, none were buried but
the body; for, by dint of the best assistance available on the spot,
the living were raised, and thereby enabled to return to their
respective homes, all as jocose and as happy as possible.

CHAPTER X

ON examining the Laird's papers after the funeral, Mr Keelevin, the father of the celebrated town-clerk of Gudetoun,[1] the lawyer present on the occasion, discovered, in reading over the deed which had been executed by the deceased, in favour of Walter, the second son of Claud, that it was, in some essential points, imperfect as a deed of entail, though in other respects valid as a testamentary conveyance. The opinion of counsel, as in all similar cases, was in consequence forthwith taken; and the suspicions of Mr Keelevin being confirmed, Walter was admitted as heir to the estate, but found under no legal obligation to assume his grandfather's name, —the very obligation which the old gentleman had been most solicitous to impose upon him.

How it happened that the clause respecting so important a point should have been so inaccurately framed, remains for those gentlemen of the law, who commit such inadvertencies, to explain. The discovery had the effect of inducing Claud to apply to our old master, the late Gilbert Omit, writer,[2] to examine the entail of the Grippy, which he had himself drawn up; and it too was found defective, and easily to be set aside. Really, when one considers how much some lawyers profit by their own mistakes, one might almost be tempted to do them the injustice to suspect that they now and then have an eye to futurity, and carve out work for themselves. There have, however, been discoveries of legal errors, which have occasioned more distress than this one; for, instead of giving the old man any uneasiness, he expressed the most perfect satisfaction on being informed, in answer to a plain question on the subject, that it was still in his power to disinherit his first-born. Well do we recollect the scene; being seated at the time on the opposite side of Mr Omit's desk, copying a codicil which Miss Christiana Heritage, then in her ninety-second year, was adding to her will, for the purpose of devising, as heir-looms, the bedstead and blankets in which Prince Charles Edward slept, when he passed the night in her house, after having levied that contribution on the loyal and godly city of Glasgow, for which the magistrates and council were afterwards so laudibly indemnified by Parliament.[3] We were not then quite so well versed in the secrets of human nature as experience has since so mournfully taught us, and the words of Claud at the time sounded strangely and harshly in our ear, especially when he inquired, with a sharp, and as it were a greedy voice, whether it was practicable to get Walter to conjoin with him in a deed that would unite his inheritance of Plealands to the Grippy, and thereby make a property as broad and good as the ancestral estate of Kittlestonheugh?

'Ye ken, Mr Omit,' said he, 'how I was defrauded, as a bodie[1] may say, of my patrimony, by my grandfather; and now, since it has pleased Providence to put it in my power, by joining the heritage of Plealands and Grippy, to renew my ancestry, I would fain mak a settlement with Watty to that effek.'

Mr Omit, with all that calm and methodical manner which a long experience of those devices of the heart, to which lawyers in good practice, if at all men of observation, generally attain, replied,—

'Nothing can be done in that way while Walter is under age. But certainly, when the lad comes to majority, if he be then so inclined, there is no legal impediment in the way of such an arrangement; the matter, however, would require to be well considered, for it would be an unco like[2] thing to hear of a man cutting off his first-born for no fault, but only because he could constitute a larger inheritance by giving a preference to his second.'

Whatever impression this admonitory remark made on the mind of Claud at the moment, nothing further took place at that time; but he thoughtfully gathered his papers together, and, tying them up with a string, walked away from the office, and returned to Grippy, where he was not a little surprised to see Mr Allan Dreghorn's wooden coach at the door; the first four-wheeled gentleman's carriage started in Glasgow, and which, according to the praise-worthy history of Bailie Cleland,[3] was made by Mr Dreghorn's own workmen, he being a timber merchant, carpenter, and joiner. It was borrowed for the day by Mr and Mrs Kilfuddy, who were then in Glasgow, and who, in consequence of their parochial connection with the Plealands family, had deemed it right and proper to pay the Leddy of Grippy a visit of sympathy and condolence, on account of the loss she had sustained in her father.

CHAPTER XI

THE Reverend Mr Kilfuddy was a little, short, erect, sharp-looking, brisk tempered personage, with a red nose, a white powdered wig, and a large cocked hat. His lady was an ample, demure, and solemn matron, who, in all her gestures, showed the most perfect consciousness of enjoying the supreme dignity of a minister's wife in a country parish.

According to the Scottish etiquette of that period, she was dressed for the occasion in mourning; but the day being bleak and cold, she had assumed her winter mantle of green satin, lined with grey rabbit skin, and her hands ceremoniously protruded through the loop holes, formed for that purpose, reposed in full conse-quentiality within the embraces of each other, in a large black satin muff of her own making, adorned with a bunch of flowers in needlework, which she had embroidered some thirty years before, as the last and most perfect specimen of all her accomplishments. But, although they were not so like the blooming progeny of Flora, as a Linwood[1] might, perhaps, have worked, they possessed a very competent degree of resemblance to the flowers they were intended to represent, insomuch that there was really no great risk of mistaking the roses for lilies. And here we cannot refrain from ingeniously suspecting that the limner who designed those cele-brated emblematic pictures of the months which adorned the drawing-room of the Craiglands, and on which the far-famed Miss Mysie Cuningham[2] set so great a value, must have had the image of Mrs Kilfuddy in his mind's eye, when he delineated the matronly representative of November.

The minister, after inquiring with a proper degree of sympathetic pathos into the state of the mourner's health, piously observed, 'That nothing is so uncertain as the things of time. This dis-pensation,' said he, 'which has been vouchsafed, Mrs Walkinshaw, to you and yours, is an earnest of what we have all to look for in this world. But we should not be overly cast down by the like o't, but lippen[3] to eternity; for the sorrows of perishable human nature are erls[4] given to us of joys hereafter. I trust, therefore, and hope, that you will soon recover this sore shock, and in the cares of your young family, find a pleasant pastime for the loss of your worthy father, whom, I am blithe to hear, has died in better circumstances than could be expected, considering the trouble he has had wi' his lawing; leaving, as they say, the estate clear of debt, and a heavy soom of lying siller.'[1]

'My father, Mr Kilfuddy,' replied the lady, 'was, as you well know, a most worthy character, and I'll no say has na left a nest egg—the Lord be thankit, and we maun compose oursels to thole wi'[2] what He has been pleased, in his gracious ordinances, to send upon us for the advantage of our poor sinful souls. But the burial has cost the gudeman[3] a power o' moncy; for my father being the head o' a family, we hae been obligated to put a' the servants, baith here, at the Grippy, and at the Plealands, in full deep mourning; and to hing the front o' the laft in the kirk,[4] as ye'll see next Sabbath, wi' very handsome black cloth, the whilk cost twenty-pence the ell, first cost[5] out o' the gudeman's ain shop; but, considering wha my father was, we could do no less in a' decency.'

'And I see,' interfered the minister's wife, 'that ye hae gotten a bombazeen o' the first quality; nae doubt ye had it likewise frae Mr Walkinshaw's own shop, which is a great thing, Mrs Walkinshaw, for you to get.'

'Na, Mem,' replied the mourner, 'ye dinna know what a misfortune I hae met wi'. I was, as ye ken, at the Plealands when my father took his departal to a better world, and sent for my mournings frae Glasgow, and frae the gudeman, as ye would naturally expck, and I had Mally Trimmings in the house ready to mak them when the box would come. But it happened to be a day o' deluge, so that my whole commodity, on Baldy Slowgaun's cart, was drookit through and through, and baith the crape and bombazeen were rendered as soople as pudding skins. It was, indeed, a sight past expression, and obligated me to send an express to Kilmarnock[6] for the things I hae on, the outlay of whilk was a clean total loss, besides being at the dear rate.[7] But, Mr Kilfuddy, every thing in this howling wilderness is ordered for the best; and, if the gudeman has been needcessited[8] to pay for twa sets o' mournings, yet, when he gets what he'll get frae my father's gear,[9] he ought to be very well content that it's nae waur.'

'What ye say, Mrs Walkinshaw,' replied the minister, 'is very judicious; for it was spoken at the funeral, that your father, Plealands, could nae hae left muckle less than three thousand pounds of lying money.'

'No, Mr Kilfuddy, it's no just so muckle; but I'll no say it's ony waur than twa thousand.'

'A braw soom, a braw soom,' said the spiritual comforter:— but what farther of the customary spirituality of this occasion might have ensued is matter of speculative opinion; for, at this juncture, Watty, the heir to the deceased, came rumbling into the room, crying,

'Mither, mither, Meg Draiks winna gie me a bit of auld daddy's burial bread, though ye brought o'er three farls[2] wi' the sweeties on't, and twa whangs as big as peats[3] o' the fine sugar seed-cake.'

The composity of the minister and his wife were greatly tried, as Mrs Kilfuddy herself often afterwards said, by this 'out-strapolous intrusion;' but quiet was soon restored by Mrs Walkin-shaw ordering in the bread and wine, of which Walter was allowed to partake. The visitors then looked significantly at each other; and Mrs Kilfuddy, replacing her hands in her satin muff, which, during the refectionary treat from the funeral relics, had been laid on her knees, rose and said,—

'Noo, I hope, Mrs Walkinshaw, when ye come to see the leddy, your mither, at the Plealands, that ye'll no neglek to gie us a ca' at the Manse, and ye'll be sure to bring the young Laird wi' you, for he's a fine spirity bairn—every bodie maun alloo[4] that.'

'He's as he came frae the hand o' his Maker,' replied Mrs Walkinshaw, looking piously towards the minister; 'and it's a great consolation to me to think he's so weel provided for by my father.'

'Then it's true,' said Mr Kilfuddy, 'that he gets a' the Plealands property?'

''Deed is't, sir, and a braw patrimony I trow it will be by the time he arrives at the years o' discretion.'

'That's a lang look,' rejoined the minister a little slyly, for Walter's defect of capacity was more obvious than his mother imagined; but she did not perceive the point of Mr Kilfuddy's sarcasm, her attention at the moment being drawn to the entrance of her husband, evidently troubled in thought, and still holding the papers in his hand as he took them away from Mr Omit's desk.

CHAPTER XII

EXPERIENCE had taught Mrs Walkinshaw, as it does most married ladies, that when a husband is in one of his moody fits, the best way of reconciling him to the cause of his vexation is to let him alone, or, as the phrase is, to let him come again to himself. Accordingly, instead of teasing him at the moment with any inquiries about the source of his molestation, she drew Mrs Kilfuddy aside, and retired into another room, leaving him in the hands of the worthy divine, who, sidling up to him, said,—

'I'm weel content to observe the resigned spirit of Mrs Walkinshaw under this heavy dispensation,—and it would be a great thing to us a' if we would lay the chastisement rightly to heart. For wi' a' his faults, and no mere man is faultless, Plealands was na without a seasoning o' good qualities, though, poor man, he had his ain tribulation in a set of thrawn-natured[1] tenants. But he has won away, as we a' hope, to that pleasant place where the wicked cease from troubling, and the weary rest in peace. Nae doubt, Mr Walkinshaw, it maun hae been some sma' disappointment to you, to find that your second son is made the heir, but it's no an affliction past remedy, so ye should na let it fash you oure muckle.'[2]

'No, be thankit,' replied Claud, 'it's no past remede, as Gibby Omit tells me; but I'm a thought troubled anent the means, for my auld son Charlie's a fine callan,[3] and I would grudge to shove him out o' the line o' inheritance. It's an unco pity, Mr Kilfuddy, that it had na pleased the Lord to mak Watty like him.'

The minister, who did not very clearly understand this, said, 'A' thing considered, Mr Walkinshaw, ye'll just hae to let the law tak its course, and though ye canna hae the lairdship in ae lump, as ye aiblins expekit,[4] it's nevertheless in your ain family.'

'I'm no contesting that,' rejoined Claud, 'but I would fain hae the twa mailings in ae aught,[5] for if that could be brought about, I would na doubt of making an excambio[6] o' the Plealands for the Divethill and Kittleston, the twa farms that wi' the Grippy made up the heritage o' my forefathers; for Mr Auchincloss, the present propreeator, is frae the shire o' Ayr, and I hae had an inklin that he would na be ill pleased to mak a swap, if there was ony possibility in law to alloo't.'

'I canna say,' replied the Reverend Mr Kilfuddy, 'that I hae ony great knowledge o' the laws o' man; I should, however, think it's no impossible; but still, Mr Walkinshaw, ye would hae to mak a reservation for behoof of your son Walter, as heir to his grandfather. It would be putting adders in the creel[1] wi' the eggs if ye did na.'

'That's the very fasherie[2] o' the business, Mr Kilfuddy, for it would be na satisfaction to me to leave a divided inheritance; and the warst o't is, that Watty, haverel[3] though it's like to be, is no sae ill as to be cognos't;[4] and what maks the case the mair kittle,[5] even though he were sae, his younger brother Geordie, by course o' law and nature, would still come in for the Plealands afore Charlie. In short, I see nothing for't, Mr Kilfuddy, but to join the Grippy in ae settlement wi' the Plealands, and I would do sae outright, only I dinna like on poor Charlie's account.—Do ye think there is ony sin in a man setting aside his first-born? Ye ken Jacob was alloot to get the blessing and the birthright o' his elder brother Esau.'[6]

Mr Kilfuddy, notwithstanding a spice of worldly-mindedness in his constitution, was, nevertheless, an honest and pious Presbyterian pastor; and the quickness of his temper at the moment stirred him to rebuke the cold-hearted speculations of this sordid father.

'Mr Walkinshaw,' said he severely, 'I can see no point o' comparison between the case o' your twa sons and that o' Jacob and Esau; and what's mair, the very jealousing[7] that there may be sin in what ye wish to do, is a clear demonstration that it is vera sinful; for, O man! it's a bad intent indeed that we canna excuse to oursels. But to set you right in ae point, and that ye may hae nae apology drawn from scriptural acts, for the unnatural inclination to disinherit your first-born, out o' the prideful phantasy of leaving a large estate, I should tell you that there was a mystery of our holy religion hidden in Jacob's mess o' porridge,[8] and it's a profane thing to meddle with that which appertaineth to the Lord, for what He does, and what He permits, is past the understanding o' man, and woe awaits on all those that would bring ought to pass contrary to the manifest course of his ordained method. For example, he taketh the breath of life away at his pleasure, but has he not commanded that no man shall commit murder?—Mr Walkinshaw, Mr Walkinshaw, ye maun strive against this sin of the flesh, ye maun warsle[1] wi' the devil, and hit him weel on the hip till ye gar him loosen the grip that he has ta'en to draw you on to sic an awful sin. Heh, man! an ye're deluded on to do this thing! What a bonny sight it will be to see your latter end, when Belzebub, wi' his horns, will be sitting upon your bosom, boring through the very joints and marrow o' your poor soul wi' the red-het gimblets o' a guilty conscience.'

Claud shuddered at the picture, and taking the reproving minister by the hand, said, 'We canna help the wicked thoughts that sometimes rise, we dinna ken whar frae[2] within us.'

'Ye dinna ken whar frae?—I'll tell you whar frae—frae hell; sic thoughts are the cormorants that sit on the apple trees in the devil's kail-yard, and the souls o' the damned are the carcases they mak their meat o'.'

'For Heaven's sake, Mr Kilfuddy,' exclaimed Claud, trembling in every limb; 'be patient, and no speak that gait,[3] ye gar my hair stand on end.'

'Hair! O man, it would be weel for you, if your precious soul would stand on end, and no only on end, but humlet[4] to the dust, and that ye would retire into a corner, and scrape the leprosy of sic festering sins wi' a potsherd o' the gospel, till ye had cleansed your-self for a repentance unto life.'

These ghostly animadversions may, perhaps, sound harsh to the polite ears of latter days, but denunciation was, at that time, an instrument of reasoning much more effectual than persuasion, and the spiritual guides of the people, in warning them of the danger of evil courses, made no scruple, on any occasion, to strengthen their admonitions with the liveliest imagery that reli-gion and enthusiasm supplied. Yet, with all the powerful aid of such eloquence, their efforts were often unavailing, and the energy of Mr Kilfuddy, in this instance, had, perhaps, no other effect than to make Claud for a time hesitate, although, before they parted, he expressed great contrition for having, as he said, yielded to the temptation of thinking that he was at liberty to settle his estate on whom he pleased.

CHAPTER XIII

AT the death of the Laird of Plealands, the Grippy family, as we have already stated, consisted of three sons and a daughter. Charles, the eldest, was, as his father intimated to Mr Kilfuddy, a fine, generous, open-hearted, blithe-faced boy. Towards him Claud cherished as much affection as the sterile sensibilities of his own bosom could entertain for any object; but Mrs Walkinshaw, from some of those unaccountable antipathies with which nature occasionally perplexes philosophy, almost hated her first-born, and poured the full flow of her uncouth kindness on Walter, who, from the earliest dawnings of observation, gave the most indubitable and conclusive indications of being endowed with as little delicacy and sense as herself. The third son, George, was, at this period, too young to evince any peculiar character; but, in after life, under the appearance of a dull and inapt spirit, his indefatigable, calculating, and persevering disposition demonstrated how much he had inherited of the heart and mind of his father. The daughter was baptized Margaret, which her mother elegantly abbreviated into Meg; and, as the course of our narrative requires that we should lose sight of her for some time, we may here give a brief epitome of her character. To beauty she had no particular pretensions, nor were her accomplishments of the most refined degree; indeed, her chief merit consisted in an innate predilection for thrift and household management; and what few elements of education which she had acquired were chiefly derived from Jenny Hirple, a lameter[1] woman, who went round among the houses of the heritors of the parish with a stilt, the sound of which, and of her feet on the floors, plainly pronounced the words one pound ten. Jenny gave lessons in reading, knitting, and needlework, and something that resembled writing; and under her tuition, Miss Meg continued till she had reached the blooming period of sixteen, when her father's heart was so far opened, that, in consideration of the fortune he found he could then bestow with her hand, he was induced to send her for three months to Edinburgh; there, and in that time, to learn manners, 'and be perfited,' as her mother said, 'wi' a boarding-school education.'

But, to return to Charles, the first-born, to whose history it is requisite our attention should at present be directed, nothing could seem more auspicious than the spring of his youth, notwithstanding the lurking inclination of his father to set him aside in the order of succession. This was principally owing to his grandmother, who had, during the life of the Laird, her husband, languished, almost from her wedding-day, in a state of uninterested resignation of spirit, so quiet, and yet so melancholy, that it partook far more of the nature of dejection than contentment. Immediately after his death, her health and her spirits began to acquire new energy; and before he was six months in the earth, she strangely appeared as a cheerful old lady, who delighted in society, and could herself administer to its pleasures.

In the summer following she removed into Glasgow, and Charles, being then about ten years old, was sent to reside with her for the advantages of attending the schools. Considering the illiterate education of his father, and the rough-spun humours and character of his mother, this was singularly fortunate; for the old lady had, in her youth, been deemed destined for a more refined sphere than the householdry of the Laird of Plealands.

Her father was by profession an advocate in Edinburgh, and had sat in the last assembly of the States of Scotland.[1] Having, however, to the last, opposed the Union with all the vehemence in his power, he was rejected by the Government party of the day; and in consequence, although his talents and acquirements were considered of a superior order, he was allowed to hang on about the Parliament-house, with the empty celebrity of abilities, that, with more prudence, might have secured both riches and honours.

The leisure which he was thus obliged to possess was devoted to the cultivation of his daughter's mind, and the affection of no father was ever more tender, till about the period when she attained her twentieth year. Her charms were then in full blossom, and she was seen only to be followed and admired. But, in proportion as every manly heart was delighted with the graces and intelligence of the unfortunate girl, the solicitude of her father to see her married grew more and more earnest, till it actually became his exclusive and predominant passion, and worked upon him to such a degree, that it could no longer be regarded but as tinctured with some insane malady; insomuch, that his continual questions respecting the addresses of the gentlemen, and who or whether any of them sincerely spoke of love, embittered her life, and deprived her of all the innocent delight which the feminine heart, in the gaiety and triumph of youth, naturally enjoys from the homage of the men.

At this juncture Malachi Hypel was in Edinburgh, drinking the rounds of an advocate's studies; for he had no intention to practise, and with students of that kind the bottle then supplied the place of reviews and magazines. He was a sturdy, rough, hard-riding and free-living fellow, entitled by his fortune and connections almost to the best society; but qualified by his manners and inclinations to relish the lowest more joyously. Unluckily he was among the loudest and the warmest admirers of the ill-fated girl, and one night after supper, flushed with claret and brandy, he openly, before her father, made her a tender of his hand. The old man grasped it with an avaricious satisfaction, and though the heart of the poor girl was ready to burst at the idea of becoming the wife of one so coarse and rugged, she was nevertheless induced, in the space of little more than a month after, to submit to her fate.

The conduct of her father was at that time quite inexplicable, but when he soon afterwards died, unable to witness the misery to which he had consigned his beloved child, the secret came out. His circumstances were in the most ruinous condition; his little patrimony was entirely consumed, and he acknowledged on his death-bed, while he implored with anguish the pardon of his daughter, that the thought of leaving her in poverty had so overset his reason, that he could think of nothing but of securing her against the horrors of want. A disclosure so painful should have softened the harsh nature of her husband towards her, but it had quite a contrary effect. He considered himself as having been in some degree overreached, and although he had certainly not married her with any view to fortune, he yet reviled her as a party to her father's sordid machination. This confirmed the sadness with which she had yielded to become his bride, and darkened the whole course of her wedded life with one continued and unvaried shade of melancholy.

The death of her husband was in consequence felt as a deliverance from thraldom. The event happened late in the day, but still in time enough to allow the original brightness of her mind to shine out in the evening with a serene and pleasing lustre, sufficient to show what, in happier circumstances, she might have been. The beams fell on Charles with the cherishing influence of the summer

twilight on the young plant, and if the tears of memory were sometimes mingled with her instructions, they were like the gracious
dews that improve the delicacy of the flower, and add freshness to
its fragrance. Beneath her care, his natural sensibility was exalted
and refined, and if it could not be said that he was endowed with
genius, he soon appeared to feel, with all the tenderness and intelligence of a poet. In this respect his ingenuous affections served to
recall the long vanished happiness of her juvenile hopes, and yielding to the sentiments which such reflections were calculated to
inspire, she devoted, perhaps, too many of her exhortations in
teaching him to value Love as the first of earthly blessings and of
human enjoyments. 'Love,' she often said to the wondering boy,
who scarcely understood the term, 'is like its emblem fire; it comes
down from Heaven, and when once kindled in two faithful bosoms,
grows brighter and stronger as it mingles its flames, ever rising and
pointing towards the holy fountain-head from whence it came.'—
These romantic lessons were ill calculated to fit him to perform that
wary part in the world which could alone have enabled him to
master the malice of his fortune, and to overcome the consequences
of that disinheritance which his father had never for a moment
ceased to meditate, but only waited for an appropriate opportunity
to carry into effect.

CHAPTER XIV

CHARLES, in due time, was sent to College,[1] and while attending
the classes, formed an intimate friendship with a youth of his own
age, of the name of Colin Fatherlans, the only son of Fatherlans of
that Ilk. He was at this time about eighteen, and being invited by
his companion to spend a few weeks at Fatherlans-house in Ayrshire, he had soon occasion to feel the influence of his grandmother's lectures on affection and fidelity.

Colin had an only sister, and Charles, from the first moment
that he saw her, felt the fascinations of her extraordinary beauty,
and the charms of a mind, still more lovely in its intelligence than
the bloom and graces of her form. Isabella Fatherlans was tall and
elegant, but withal so gentle, that she seemed, as it were, ever in
need of protection; and the feeling which this diffidence of nature

universally inspired, converted the homage of her admirers into
a sentiment of tenderness, which, in the impassioned bosom of
Charles Walkinshaw, was speedily warmed into love.

For several successive years, he had the gratification of spending some weeks in the company of Isabella; and the free intercourse
permitted between them soon led to the disclosure of a mutual
passion. No doubt at that time clouded the sunshine that shone
along the hopes and promises in the vista of their future years.
Every thing, on the contrary, was propitious. His lineage and
prospects rendered him acceptable to her parents, and she was
viewed by his father as a match almost beyond expectation desirable. Time alone seemed to be the only adversary to their affection;
but with him Fortune was in league, and the course of true love
never long runs smooth.

The father of Isabella was one of those unfortunate lairds who
embarked in the Mississippian project of the Ayr Bank,[1] the
inevitable fate of which, at the very moment when the hopes of the
lovers were as gay as the apple boughs with blossoms in the first
fine mornings of spring, came like a nipping frost, and blighted
their happiness for ever. Fatherlans was ruined, and his ruin was
a sufficient reason, with the inflexible Claud, to command Charles
to renounce all thoughts of that fond connection which he had himself considered as the most enviable which his son could hope to
obtain. But the altered fortunes of Isabella only served to endear
her more and more to her lover; and the interdict of his father was
felt as a profane interference with that hallowed enthusiasm of
mingled love and sorrow with which his breast was at the moment
filled.

'It is impossible,' said he; 'and even were it in my power to
submit to the sacrifice you require, honour, and every sentiment
that makes life worthy, would forbid me. No, sir; I feel that
Isabella and I are one; Heaven has made us so, and no human
interposition can separate minds which God and Nature have so
truly united. The very reason that you urge against the continuance of my attachment, is the strongest argument to make me
cherish it with greater devotion than ever. You tell me she is poor,
and must be pennyless. Is not that, sir, telling me that she has
claims upon my compassion as well as on my love? You say her
father must be driven to the door. Gracious Heaven! and in such
a time shall I shun Isabella? A common stranger, one that I had

never before known, would, in such adversity and distress, be
entitled to any asylum I could offer; but Isabella—in the storm
that has unroofed her father's house—shall she not claim that
shelter which, by so many vows, I have sworn to extend over her
through life?'

'Weel, weel, Charlie,'[1] replied the old man, 'rant awa, and tak
thy tocherless[2] bargain to thee, and see what thou'll mak o't. But
mind my words—when Poverty comes in at the door, Love jumps
out at the window.'

'It is true,' said the lover, a little more calmly, 'that we cannot
hope to live in such circumstances as I had so often reason to
expect; but still, you will not refuse to take me into partnership,
which, in the better days of her father, you so often promised?'

'We'll hae twa words about that,' replied the father; 'it's ae
thing to take in a partner young, clever, and sharp, and another to
take a needful man with the prospect o' a family. But, Charlie, I'll
no draw back in my word to you, if ye'll just put off for a year or
twa this calf love connection. May be by and by ye'll think better
o' my counsel; at ony rate, something for a sair foot may be
gathered in the mean time; and neither you nor Bell Fatherlans
are sae auld but ye can afford to bide a while.'

This was said in the old man's most reflective and sedate manner,
and after some farther conversation, Charles did consent to post-
pone for that time his marriage, on condition of being immediately
admitted into partnership, with an understanding, that he should
be free to marry at the end of twelve months, if he still continued
so inclined. Both parties in this arrangement calculated without
their host. The father thought that the necessary change in the
exterior circumstances of Isabella would, in the course of the year,
have a tendency to abate the ardour of her lover, and the son gave
too much credit to his own self-denial, supposing, that, although
the ruin of Fatherlans was declared, yet, as in similar cases, twelve
months would probably elapse before the sequestration and sale
of his estate would finally reduce the condition of his family. From
the moment, however, that the affairs of the banking company
were found irretrievable, Mr Fatherlans zealously bestirred himself to place his daughter above the hazards of want, even while he
entertained the hope that it might not be necessary. He carried her
with him to Glasgow, and, before calling at Claud's shop, secured
for her an asylum in the house of Miss Mally Trimmings, a

celebrated mantua-maker[1] of that time. When he afterwards waited on the inexorable pedlar, and communicated the circumstance, the latter, with unfeigned pleasure, commended the prudence of the measure, for he anticipated that the pride of his son would recoil at the idea of connecting himself with Isabella in her altered state. What the lover himself felt on hearing the news, we shall not attempt to describe, nor shall we so far intrude beyond the veil which should ever be drawn over the anxieties and the sorrows of young affection, under darkened prospects, as to relate what passed between the lovers when they next met. The resolution, however, with which they both separated, was worthy of the purity of their mutual affections, and they agreed to pass the probationary year in a cheerful submission to their lot.

CHAPTER XV

WHEN Charles parted from Isabella, he returned thoughtfully towards Grippy, which was situated on the south side of the Clyde, at the foot of the Cathkin hills.[2] His road, after passing the bridge, lay across the fields as far as Rutherglen, where it diverged towards the higher ground, commanding at every winding a rich and variegated prospect.

The year was waning into autumn, and the sun setting in all that effulgence of glory, with which, in a serene evening, he commonly at that season terminates his daily course behind the distant mountains of Dumbartonshire and Argyle. A thin mist, partaking more of the lacy character of a haze than the texture of a vapour, spreading from the river, softened the nearer features of the view, while the distant were glowing in the golden blaze of the western skies, and the outlines of the city on the left appeared gilded with a brighter light, every window sparkling as if illuminated from within. The colour of the trees and hedges was beginning to change, and here and there a tuft of yellow leaves, and occasionally the berries of the mountain ash, like clusters of fiery embers, with sheaves of corn, and reapers in a few of the neighbouring fields, showed that the summer was entirely past, and the harvest time begun.

The calm diffused over the face of the landscape—the numerous

images of maturity and repose every where around—were calculated to sooth the spirit, to inspire gentle thoughts, and to
awaken pleasing recollections; and there was something in the
feelings with which the lovers had separated, if not altogether in
unison with the graciousness of the hour, still so much in harmony
with the general benignity of nature, that Charles felt his resolution and self-denial elevated with a sentiment of devotion, mingled
with the fond enthusiasm of his passion. 'It is but a short time—
a few months—and we shall be happy,' he exclaimed to himself;
'and our happiness will be the dearer that we shall have earned it
by this sacrifice to prudence and to duty.'

But Charles and Isabella had estimated their fortitude too
highly. They were both inexperienced in what the world really is;
and her tender and sensitive spirit was soon found incapable of
withstanding the trials and the humiliation to which she found
herself subjected.

It was part of her business to carry home the dresses made up
for Miss Mally's customers; and although the Glasgow ladies of
that time were perhaps not more difficult to please with the style
or fashion of their gowns and millinery than those of our own day,
yet some of them were less actuated by a compassionate consideration for the altered fortunes of Isabella than all our fair contemporaries would undoubtedly have been. The unfortunate girl
was, in consequence, often obliged to suffer taunts and animadversions, which, though levelled against the taste or inattention
of her mistress, entered not the less painfully into her young and
delicate bosom. Still, however, she struggled against the harsh
circumstances to which she was exposed; but her sensibilities were
stronger than her courage, and her beauty betrayed what she felt,
and soon began to fade.

Charles was in the practice of accompanying her in the evenings
when she commonly performed her disagreeable errands, and
relieved her of the burden of her band-box, joyfully counting how
much of the probationary year was already past, and cheering her
with the assurance that her misfortunes had only endeared her to
him the more. It happened, however, that, one Saturday, being
late of reaching the place of rendezvous—the foot of the staircase
which led to Miss Mally's dwelling—Isabella had gone away
before he arrived, with a new dress to Mrs Jarvie, the wife of the
far-famed Bailie Nicol, the same Matty who lighted the worthy

magistrate to the Tolbooth, on that memorable night when he, the son of the deacon, found his kinsman Rob Roy there.[1]

Matty at this time was a full-blown lady; the simple, modest, bare-footed lassie, having developed into a crimson, gorgeous, high-heeled madam,—well aware of the augmented width and weight of the bailie's purse, and jealous a little too much of her own consequence, perhaps, by recollecting the condition from which she had been exalted. The dress made up for her was a costly *negligée*; it not only contained several yards of the richest brocade more than any other Miss Mally Trimmings had ever made, but was adorned with cuffs and flounces in a style of such affluent magnificence, that we question if any grander has since been seen in Glasgow. Nor was it ordered for any common occasion, but to grace a formal dinner party, which Provost Anderson and his lady intended to give the magistrates and their wives at the conclusion of his eighth provostry.[2] It was therefore not extraordinary that Mrs Jarvie should take particular interest in this dress; but the moment she began to try it on, poor Isabella discovered that it would not fit, and stood trembling from head to heel, while the bailie's wife, in great glee and good humour with the splendour of the dress, was loud in her praises of the cut of the ruffle-cuffs and the folds of the flounces. Having contemplated the flow of the *negligée* on both sides, and taken two or three stately steps across the room, to see how it would sweep behind, Mrs Jarvie took the wings of the body in her hands, and, drawing them together, found they would not nearly meet.

Isabella, with a beating heart and a diffident hand, approached to smooth the silk, that it might expand; but all would not do. Mrs Jarvie stood a monument of consternation, as silent as Lot's wife, when she looked back, and thought of the charming dresses she had left behind.

'O Chrystal!'[3] were the first words to which the cidevant Matty could give utterance. 'O Chrystal! My God, is nae this moving? Your mistress, doited[4] devil, as I maun ca' her, ought to be skelpit[5] wi' nettles for this calamity. The goun's ruin't—my gude silk to be clippit in this nearbegaun[6] way—past a' redemption. Gang out o' the gait, ye cutty,[7] and no finger and meddle wi' me. This usage is enough to provoke the elect;[8] as 'am[9] a living soul, and that's a muckle word for me to say, I'll hae the old craighling scoot afore the Lords.[10] The first cost was mair than five and twenty guineas.

If there's law and justice atween God and man, she shall pay for't, or I'll hae my satisfaction on her flesh. Hither, maiden, and help me off wi' it. Sicna beauty[1] as it was. Tak it wi' you; tak it to you; out o' the house and my presence. How durst ye dare to bring sic a disgrace to me? But, let me look at it. Is't no possible to put in a gushet[2] or a gore, and to make an eke?'[3]

'I'll take it home and try,' said Isabella, timidly folding up the gown, which she had removed from Mrs Jarvie.

'Try,' said the bailie's wife, relapsing; 'a pretty like story, that sic a gown should stand in the jeopardy o' a try; but how could Miss Mally presume to send a silly thing like t'ee[4] on this occasion? Lay down the gown this precious moment, and gae hame, and order her to come to me direkilty: it's no to seek what I hae to say.'

The trembling and terrified girl let the unfortunate *negligée* fall, and hastily, in tears, quitted the room, and, flying from the house, met, in the street, her lover, who, having learnt where she was, had followed her to the house. A rapid and agitated disclosure of her feelings and situation followed. Charles, on the spot, resolved, at all hazards, rather to make her his wife at once, and to face the worst that might in consequence happen from his father's displeasure, than allow her to remain exposed to such contumelious treatment. Accordingly, it was agreed that they should be married, and on the Monday following, the ceremony was performed, when he conducted her to a lodging which he had provided in the interval.

CHAPTER XVI

ON the morning after his marriage, Charles was anxious, doubtful, and diffident. His original intention was to go at once to his father, to state what he had done, and to persuade him, if possible, to overlook a step, that, from its suddenness, might be deemed rash, but, from the source and motives from which it proceeded, could, he thought, be regarded only as praiseworthy. Still, though this was his own opinion, he, nevertheless, had some idea that the old gentleman would not view it exactly in the same light; and the feeling which this doubt awakened made him hesitate at first, and finally to seek a mediator.

He had long remarked, that 'the lady,'[1] his grandmother, sustained a part of great dignity towards his father; and he concluded, from the effect it appeared to produce, that her superiority was fully acknowledged. Under this delusion, after some consideration of the bearings and peculiarities of his case, he determined to try her interference, and, for that purpose, instead of going to Grippy, as he had originally intended, when he left Isabella, he proceeded to the house of the old lady, where he found her at home and alone.

The moment he entered her sitting-room, she perceived that his mind was laden with something which pressed heavily on his feelings; and she said,

'What has vext you, Charlie? has your father been severe upon you for ony misdemeanour, or hae ye done any thing that ye're afeared to tell?'

In the expression of these sentiments, she had touched the sensitive cord, that, at the moment, was fastened to his heart.

'I'm sure,' was his reply, 'that I hae[2] done no ill, and dinna ken why I should be frightened in thinking on what every bodie that can feel and reflect will approve.'

'What is't?' said the lady, thoughtfully: 'What is't? If it's ought good, let me partake the solace wi' you; and if it's bad, speak it out, that a remedy may be, as soon as possible, applied.'

'Bell Fatherlans,' was his answer; but he could only articulate her name.

'Poor lassie,' said the venerable gentlewoman, 'her lot's hard, and I'm wae both for your sake and hers, Charlie, that your father's so dure[3] as to stand against your marriage in the way he does. But he was aye a bargainer; alack! the world is made up o' bargainers; and a heart wi' a right affection is no an article o' meikle repute in the common market o' man and woman. Poor genty[4] Bell! I wish it had been in my power to hae sweetened her lot; for I doubt and fear she's oure thin-skinned to thole long the needles and prins[5] o' Miss Mally Trimmings' short temper; and, what's far waur, the tawpy[6] taunts of her pridefu' customers.'

'She could suffer them no longer, nor would I let her,' replied the bridegroom, encouraged by these expressions to disclose the whole extent of his imprudence.

Mrs Hypel did not immediately return any answer, but sat for a few moments thoughtful, we might, indeed, say sorrowful—she then said,

'Ye should na, Charlie, speak to me. I canna help you, my dear, though I hae the will. Gang to your father and tell him a', and if he winna do what ye wish, then my poor bairn bravely trust to Providence, that gars[1] the heart beat as it should beat, in spite o' a' the devices o' man.'

'I fear,' replied Charles, with simplicity, 'that I hae done that already, for Bell and me were married yesterday. I could na suffer to see her snooled[2] and cast down any longer by every fat-pursed wife that would triumph and glory in a new gown.'

'Married, Charlie!' said the old lady with an accent of surprise, mingled with sorrow; 'Married! weel, that's a step that canna be untrodden, and your tribulation is proof enough to me that you are awakened to the consequence. But what's to be done?'

'Nothing, Mem, but only to speak a kind word for us to my father,' was the still simple answer of the simple young husband.

'I'll speak for you, Charlie, I can do that, and I'll be happy and proud to gie you a' the countenance in my power; but your father, Charlie—the gude forgie me[3] because he is your father—I'm darkened and dubious when I think o' him.'

'I hae a notion,' replied Charles, 'that we need be no cess[4] on him: we're content to live in a sma' way; only I would like my wife to be countenanced as becomes her ain family, and mair especially because she is mine, so that, if my father will be pleased to tak her, and regard her as his gude-dochter,[5] I'll ask nothing for the present, but do my part, as an honest and honourable man, to the very uttermost o' my ability.'

The kind and venerable old woman was profoundly moved by the earnest and frank spirit in which this was said; and she assured him, that so wise and so discreet a resolution could not fail to make his father look with a compassionate eye on his generous imprudence. 'So gae your ways home to Bell,' said she, 'and counsel and comfort her; the day's raw, but I'll even now away to the Grippy to intercede for you, and by the gloaming be you here wi' your bonny bride, and I trust, as I wish, to hae glad tidings for you baith.'

Charles, with great ardour and energy, expressed the sense which he felt of the old lady's kindness and partiality, but still he doubted the successful result of the mission she had undertaken. Nevertheless, her words inspired hope, and hope was the charm that spread over the prospects of Isabella and of himself, the light, the verdure, and the colours which enriched and filled the distant and future scenes of their expectations with fairer and brighter promises than they were ever destined to enjoy.

CHAPTER XVII

CLAUD was sitting at the window when he discovered his mother-in-law coming slowly towards the house, and he said to his wife,—

'In the name o' gude,[1] Girzy, what can hae brought your mother frae the town on sic a day as this?'

'I hope,' replied the Leddy of Grippy, 'that nothing's the matter wi' Charlie, for he promised to be out on Sabbath to his dinner, and never came.'

In saying these words, she went hastily to the door to meet her mother, the appearance of whose countenance at the moment was not calculated to allay her maternal fears. Indeed, the old lady scarcely spoke to her daughter, but walking straight into the dining-room where Grippy himself was sitting, took a seat on a chair, and then threw off her cloak on the back of it, before she uttered a word.

'What's wrang, grannie?' said Claud, rising from his seat at the window, and coming towards her.—'What's wrang, ye seem fashed?'[2]

'In truth, Mr Walkinshaw, I hae cause,' was the reply—'poor Charlie!'—

'What's happen'd to him?' exclaimed his mother.

'Has he met wi' ony misfortunate accident?' inquired the father.

'I hope it's no a misfortune,' said the old lady, somewhat recovering her self-possession. 'At the same time, it's what I jealouse,[3] Grippy, ye'll no be vera content to hear.'

'What is't?' cried the father sharply, a little tantalized.

'Has he broken his leg?' said the mother.

'Haud that clavering tongue o' thine, Girzy,' exclaimed the Laird peevishly; 'wilt t'ou ne'er devaul' wi' sca'ding thy lips[4] in other folks' kail?'

'He had amaist met wi' far waur than a broken leg,' interposed the grandmother. 'His heart was amaist broken.'

'It maun be unco brittle,' said Claud, with a hem. 'But what's the need o' this summering and wintering anent it?—Tell us what has happened?'

'Ye're a parent, Mr Walkinshaw,' replied the old lady seriously, 'and I think ye hae a fatherly regard for Charlie; but I'll be plain wi' you. I doubt ye hae na a right consideration for the gentle nature of the poor lad; and it's that which gars me doubt and fear that what I hae to say will no be agreeable.'

Claud said nothing in answer to this, but sat down in a chair on the right side of his mother-in-law, his wife having in the meantime taken a seat on the other side.—The old lady continued,—

'At the same time, Mr Walkinshaw, ye're a reasonable man, and what I'm come about is a matter that maun just be endured. In short, it's nothing less than to say, that, considering Fatherlans' misfortunes, ye ought to hae alloo't[1] Charlie and Isabella to hae been married, for it's a sad situation she was placed in—a meek and gentle creature like her was na fit to bide the flyte[2] and flights o' the Glasgow leddies.'

She paused, in the expectation that Claud would make some answer, but he still remained silent.—Mrs Walkinshaw, however, spoke,—

''Deed mither, that's just what I said—for ye ken it's an awfu' thing to thwart a true affection. Troth is't, gudeman; and ye should think what would hae been your ain tender feelings had my father stoppit our wedding after a' was settled.'

'There was some difference between the twa cases,' said the Dowager of Plealands dryly to her daughter;—'neither you nor Mr Walkinshaw were so young as Charlie and Miss Fatherlans— that was something—and may be there was a difference, too, in the character of the parties. Hows'ever, Mr Walkinshaw, marriages are made in heaven; and it's no in the power and faculty of man to controvert the coming to pass o' what is ordained to be. Charlie Walkinshaw and Bell Fatherlans were a couple marrowed by their Maker, and it's no right to stand in the way of their happiness.'

'I'm sure,' said Claud, now breaking silence, 'it can ne'er be said that I'm ony bar till't.[3] I would only fain try a year's probation in case it's but calf love.'

Mrs Hypel shook her head as she said,—'It's vera prudent o' you, but ye canna put auld heads on young shouthers.[4] In a word, Mr Walkinshaw, it's no reasonable to expek that young folk, so encouraged in their mutual affection as they were, can thole¹ so lang as ye would wish. The days o' sic courtships as Jacob's and Rachel's are lang past.'

'I but bade them bide a year,' replied Claud.—'A year's an unco time² to love; but to make a lang tale short, what might hae been foreseen has come to pass, the fond young things hae gotten themselves married.'

'No possible!' exclaimed Claud, starting from his chair, which he instantly resumed.—

'Weel,' said Mrs Walkinshaw,—'if e'er I heard the like o' that! —Our Charlie a married man! the head o' a family!'—

The old lady took no notice of these and other interjections of the same meaning, which her daughter continued to vent, but looking askance and steadily at Claud, who seemed for a minute deeply and moodily agitated, she said,—

'Ye say nothing, Mr Walkinshaw.'

'What can I say?' was his answer.—'I had a better hope for Charlie,—I thought the year would hae cooled him,—and am sure Miss Betty Bodle would hae been a better bargain.'

'Miss Betty Bodle!' exclaimed the grandmother, 'she's a perfect tawpy.'³

'Weel, weel,' said Grippy, 'it mak's no odds noo what she is,— Charlie has ravelled the skein o' his own fortune, and maun wind it as he can.'

'That will no be ill to do, Mr Walkinshaw, wi' your helping hand.—He's your first born, and a better-hearted lad never lived.'

'Nae doubt I maun help him,—there can be nae doubt o' that; but he canna expek, and the world can ne'er expek, that I'll do for him what I might hae done had he no been so rash and disobedient.'

'Very true, Mr Walkinshaw,' said the gratified old lady, happy to find that the reconciliation was so easily effected; and proud to be the messenger of such glad tidings to the young couple, she soon after returned to Glasgow. But scarcely had she left the house, when Claud appeared strangely disturbed,—at one moment he ran hastily towards his scrutoire, and opened it, and greedily seized the title-deeds of his property,—the next he closed it thoughtfully, and retreating to his seat, sat down in silence.

'What's the matter wi' you, gudeman?⁴ ye were na sae fashed⁵ when my mother was here,' said his wife.

'I'll do nothing rashly—I'll do nothing rashly,' was the mysterious reply.

'Eh, mither, mither,' cried Walter, bolting into the room,—'what would you think, our Charlie's grown a wife's gudeman like my father.'

'Out o' my sight, ye ranting cuif,'¹ exclaimed Claud, in a rapture of rage, which so intimidated Walter that he fled in terror.

'It's dreadfu' to be sae tempted,—and a' the gude to gang to sic a haverel,'² added Claud, in a low troubled accent, as he turned away and walked towards the window.

'Nae doubt,' said his wife, 'it's an awfu' thing to hear o' sic disobedience as Charlie in his rashness has been guilty o'.'

'It is, it is,' replied her husband, 'and many a ane for far less hae disinherited their sons,—cut them off wi' a shilling.'

'That's true,' rejoined the Leddy of Grippy. 'Did na Kilmarkeckle gie his only daughter but the legacy o' his curse, for running away wi' the Englisher captain, and leave a' to his niece Betty Bodle?'

'And a' she hae³ might hae been in our family but for this misfortune.—When I think o' the loss, and how pleased her father was when I proposed Charlie for her—It's enough to gar⁴ me tak' some desperate step to punish the contumacious reprobate.—He'll break my heart.'

'Dear keep me, gudeman, but ye're mair fashed than I could hae thought it was in the power o' nature for you to be,'—said Mrs Walkinshaw, surprised at his agitation.

'The scoundrel! the scoundrel!' said Claud, walking quickly across the room—'To cause sic a loss!—To tak' nae advice!—to run sic a ram race!⁵—I ought, I will gar him fin' the weight o' my displeasure. Betty Bodle's tocher⁶ would hae been better than the Grippy—But he shall suffer for't—I see na why a father may na tak' his own course as weel as a son—I'll no be set at nought in this gait.⁷ I'll gang in to Mr Keelevin the morn.'⁸

'Dinna be oure headstrong, my dear, but compose yoursel','—said the lady, perplexed, and in some degree alarmed at the mention of the lawyer's name.—

'Compose thysel, Girzy, and no meddle wi' me,' was the answer, in a less confident tone than the declaration he had just made, adding,

'I never thought he would hae used me in this way. I'm sure I was ay indulgent to him.'

'Overly sae,' interrupted Mrs Walkinshaw, 'and often I told you that he would gie you a het[1] heart for't, and noo ye see my words hae come to pass.'

Claud scowled at her with a look of the fiercest aversion, for at that moment the better feelings of his nature yearned towards Charles, and almost overcame the sordid avidity with which he had resolved to cut him off from his birthright, and to entail the estate of Grippy with the Plealands on Walter,—an intention which, as we have before mentioned, he early formed, and had never abandoned, being merely deterred from carrying it into effect by a sense of shame, mingled with affection, and a slight reverence for natural justice; all which, however, were loosened from their hold in his conscience, by the warrantry which the imprudence of the marriage seemed to give him in the eyes of the world, for doing what he had so long desired to do. Instead, however, of making her any reply, he walked out into the open air, and continued for about half an hour to traverse the green in front of the house, sometimes with quick short steps, at others with a slow and heavy pace. Gradually, however, his motion became more regular, and ultimately ended in a sedate and firm tread, which indicated that his mind was made up on the question, which he had been debating with himself.

CHAPTER XVIII

THAT abysm of legal dubieties, the office of Mr Keelevin, the writer, consisted of two obscure apartments on the ground floor of M'Gregor's Land, in M'Whinnie's Close,[2] in the Gallowgate. The outer room was appropriated to the clerks, and the inner for the darker mysteries of consultation. To this place Claud repaired on the day following the interesting communication, of which we have recorded the first impressions in the foregoing chapter. He had ordered breakfast to be ready an hour earlier than usual; and as soon as he had finished it, he went to his scrutoire, and taking out his title-deeds, put them in his pocket, and without saying any thing to his wife of what he intended to do, lifted his hat and stick from their accustomed place of repose, in the corner of the dining-room, and proceeded, as we have said, to consult Mr Keelevin.

It is not the universal opinion of mankind, that the profession of the law is favourable to the preservation of simplicity of character or of benevolence of disposition; but this, no doubt, arises from the malice of disappointed clients, who, to shield themselves from the consequences of their own unfair courses, pretend that the wrongs and injustice of which they are either found guilty, or are frustrated in the attempt to effect, is owing to the faults and roguery of their own or their adversaries' lawyers. But why need we advocate any revision of the sentence pronounced upon the limbs of the law? for, grasping, as they do, the whole concerns and interests of the rest of the community, we think they are sufficiently armed with claws and talons to defend themselves. All, in fact, that we meant by this apologetic insinuation, was to prepare the reader for the introduction of Mr Keelevin, on whom the corrosive sublimate of a long and thorough professional insight of all kinds of equivocation and chicanery had, in no degree, deteriorated from the purity of his own unsuspicious and benevolent nature. Indeed, at the very time that Claud called, he was rebuking his young men on account of the cruelty of a contrivance they had made to catch a thief that was in the nocturnal practice of opening the window of their office, to take away what small change they were so negligent as to leave on or in their desks; and they were not only defending themselves, but remonstrating with him for having rendered their contrivance abortive. For, after they had ingeniously constructed a trap within the window, namely, a footless table, over which the thief must necessarily pass to reach their desks, he had secretly placed a pillow under it, in order that, when it fell down, the robber might not hurt himself in the fall.

'Gude morning, gude morning, Mr Keelevin; how're ye the day?' said Claud, as he entered.

'Gaily, gaily, Grippy; how're ye yoursel, and how's a' at hame? Come awa ben[1] to my room,' was the writer's answer, turning round and opening the door; for experience had taught him, that visits from acquaintances at that hour were not out of mere civility.

Claud stepped in, and seated himself in an old armed chair which stood on the inner side of the table where Mr Keelevin himself usually wrote; and the lawyer followed him, after saying to the clerks, 'I redde ye, lads, tak tent[2] to what I hae been telling you, and no encourage yourselves to the practice of evil that good may come o't. To devise snares and stratagems is most abominable—all that ye should or ought to do, is to take such precautions that the thief may not enter; but to wile him into the trap, by leaving the window unfastened, was nothing less than to be the cause of his sin. So I admonish you no to do the like o't again.'

In saying this he came in, and, shutting the door, took his own seat at the opposite side of the table, addressing himself to Claud, 'And so ye hae gotten your auld son married? I hope it's to your satisfaction.'

'An he has brewed good yill,[1] Mr Keelevin, he'll drink the better,' was the reply; 'but I hae come to consult you anent a bit alteration that I would fain make in my testament.'

'That's no a matter of great difficulty, Laird; for, sin' we found out that the deed of entail that was made after your old son was born can never stand, a' ye have is free to be destined as ye will, both heritable and moveable.'

'And a lucky discovery that was;—many a troubled thought I hae had in my own breast about it; and now I'm come to confer wi' you, Mr Keelevin, for I would na trust the hair o' a dog to the judgment o' that tavert bodie,[2] Gibby Omit, that gart me pay nine pounds seven shillings and saxpence too for the parchment; for it ne'er could be called an instrument, as it had na the pith o' a windlestrae[3] to bind the property; and over and aboon that, the bodie has lang had his back to the wa', wi' the 'poplexy; so that I maun put my trust in this affair into your hands, in the hope and confidence that ye're able to mak something mair sicker.'[4]

'We'll do our endeavour, Mr Walkinshaw; hae ye made ony sort o'scantling[5] o' what you would wish done?'

'No, but I hae brought the teetles[6] o' the property in my pouch, and ye'll just conform to them. As for the bit saving of lying money, we'll no fash wi' it[7] for the present; I'm only looking to get a solid and right entail o' the heritable.'

'Nothing can be easier. Come as ye're o' an ancient family, no doubt your intent is to settle the Grippy on the male line; and, failing your sons and their heirs, then on the heirs of the body of your daughter.'

'Just sae, just sae. I'll make no change on my original disposition; only, as I would fain hae what cam by the gudewife[8] made part and portion o' the family heritage, and as her father's settlement on Watty canna be broken without a great risk, I would like to begin the entail o' the Grippy wi' him.'

'I see nothing to prevent that; ye could gie Charlie, the auld son, his liferent in't, and as Watty, no to speak disrespectful of his capacity, may ne'er marry, it might be so managed.'

'Oh, but that's no what I mean, and what for may na Watty marry? Is na he o' capacity to execute a deed, and surely that should qualify him to take a wife?'

'But heavens preserve me, Mr Walkinshaw, are ye sensible of the ill ye would do to that fine lad, his auld brother, that's now a married man, and in the way to get heirs? Sic a settlement as ye speak o' would be cutting him off a' thegither. it would be most iniquitous!'

'An it should be sae, the property is my own conquesting, Mr Keelevin, and surely I may mak a kirk and a mill o't an I like.'

'Nobody, it's true, Mr Walkinshaw, has ony right to meddle wi' how ye dispone[1] of your own, but I was thinking ye may be did na reflect that sic[2] an entail as ye speak o' would be rank injustice to poor Charlie, that I hae ay thought a most excellent lad.'

'Excellent here, or excellent there, it was na my fault that he drew up wi' a tocherless tawpy,[3] when he might hae had Miss Betty Bodle.'

'I am very sorry to hear he has displeased you; but the Fatherlans family, into whilk[4] he has married, has ay been in great repute and estimation.'

'Aye, afore the Ayr Bank; but the silly bodie the father was clean broken by that venture.'

'That should be the greater reason, Mr Walkinshaw, wi' you to let your estate go in the natural way to Charlie.'

'A' that may be very true, Mr Keelevin; I did na come here, however, to confer with you anent the like of that, but only of the law. I want you to draw the settlement, as I was saying; first, ye'll entail it on Walter and his heirs-male, syne[5] on Geordie and his heirs-male, and failing them, ye may gang back, to please yoursel, to the heirs-male o' Charlie, and failing them, to Meg's heirs-general.'

'Mr Walkinshaw,' said the honest writer, after a pause of about a minute, 'there's no Christianity in this.'

'But there may be law, I hope.'

'I think, Mr Walkinshaw, my good and worthy friend, that you should reflect well on this matter, for it is a thing by ordinare to do.'

'But ye ken, Mr Keelevin, when Watty dies, the Grippy and the Plealands will be a' ae heritage,[1] and will na that be a braw[2] thing for my family?'

'But what for would ye cut off poor Charlie from his rightful inheritance?'

'Me cut him off frae his inheritance! When my grandfather brake on account o' the Darien,[3] then it was that he lost his inheritance. He'll get frae me a' that I inherited frae our forbears, and may be mair; only, I'll no alloo he has ony heritable right on me, but what stands with my pleasure to gie him as an almous.'[4]

'But consider, he's your own firstborn?'—

'Weel, then, what o' that?'

'And it stands with nature surely, Mr Walkinshaw, that he should hae a bairn's part o' your gear.'[5]

'Stands wi' nature, Mr Keelevin? A coat o' feathers or a pair o' hairy breeks[6] is a' the bairn's part o' gear that I ever heard o' in nature, as the fowls o' the air and the beasts o' the field can very plainly testify.—No, no, Mr Keelevin, we're no now in a state o' nature but a state o' law, and it would be an unco thing[7] if we did na make the best o't. In short, ye'll just get the settlements drawn up as soon as a possibility will alloo, for it does na do to lose time wi' sic things, as ye ken, and I'll come in wi' Watty neest[8] market day and get them implemented.'

'Watty's no requisite,' said Mr Keelevin, somewhat thoughtfully; 'it can be done without him. I really wish ye would think better o't before we spoil any paper.'

'I'm no fear't about the paper, in your hands, Mr Keelevin,— ye'll do every thing right wi' sincerity,—and mind, an it should be afterwards found out that there are ony flaws in the new deed, as there were in the auld, which the doited[9] creature Gibby Omit made out, I'll gar you pay for't yoursel; so tak tent,[10] for your own sake, and see that baith Watty's deed and mine are right and proper in every point of law.'

'Watty's! what do you mean by Watty's?'

'Have na I been telling you that it's my wis[11] that the Plealands and the Grippy should be made one heritage, and is na Watty concos mancos[12] enough to be conjunct[13] wi' me in the like o' that? Ye ken the flaw in his grandfather's settlement, and that, though the land has come clear and clean to him, yet it's no sae tethered but he may wise it awa[1] as it likes him to do, for he's noo past one-and-twenty. Therefore, what I want is, that ye will mak a paper for him, by the whilk he's to 'gree that the Plealands gang the same gait,[2] by entail, as the Grippy.'

'As in duty bound, Mr Walkinshaw, I maun do your will in this business,' said Mr Keelevin; 'but really I ken na when I hae been more troubled about the specialities of any settlement. It's no right o' you to exercise your authority oure Watty; the lad's truly no in a state to be called on to implement ony such agreement as what ye propose. He should na be meddled wi', but just left to wear out his time in the world, as little observed as possible.'

'I canna say, Mr Keelevin, that I like to hear you misliken[3] the lad sae, for did na ye yourself, with an ettling of pains[4] that no other body could hae gane through but yoursel, prove, to the satis-faction of the fifteen at Edinburgh,[5] that he was a young man of a very creditable intellect, when Plealands' will was contested by his cousin?'

'Waes me,[6] Mr Walkinshaw, that ye should cast up to me the sincerity with which I did but my duty to a client. However, as ye're bent on this business, I'll say na mair in objection, but do my best to make a clear and tight entail, according to your instruc-tions   trusting that I shall be accounted hereafter as having been but the innocent agent; and yet I beg you again, before it's oure late, to reflect on the consequence to that fine lad Charlie, who is now the head of a house, and in the way of having a family—It's an awfu' thing ye're doing to him.'

'Weel, weel, Mr Keelevin, as I was saying, dinna ye fash your thumb,[7] but mak out the papers in a sicker[8] manner,—and may be though ye think sae ill o' me, it winna be the waur[9] for Charlie after a's come and gane.'

'It's in the Lord's power certainly,' replied the worthy lawyer piously, 'to make it all up to him.'

'And maybe it's in my power too, for when this is done, I'll hae to take another cast o' your slight o' hand in the way of a bit will for the moveables and lying siller,[10] but I would just like this to be weel done first.'

'Man, Laird, I'm blythe to hear that,—but ye ken that ye told me last year when you were clearing the wadset[11] that was left on the Grippy, that ye had na meikle mair[12] left—But I'm blythe to hear ye're in a condition to act the part of a true father to a' your bairns, though I maun say that I canna approve, as a man and a frien', of this crotchet of entailing your estate on a haverel,[1] to the prejudice of a braw and gallant lad like Charlie. Hows'ever, sin' it is sae, we'll say nae mair about it. The papers will be ready for you by Wednesday come eight days,[2] and I'll tak care to see they are to your wish.'[3]

'Na, an ye dinna[4] do that, the cost shall be on your own risk, for the deil a plack or bawbee[5] will I pay for them, till I hae a satisfaction that they are as they ought to be. Howsever, gude day, Mr Keelevin, and we'll be wi' you on Wednesday by ten o'clock.'

In saying this, Claud, who had in the mean time risen from his seat, left the office without turning his head towards the desk, where the clerks, as he walked through the outer room, were sitting, winking at one another, as he plodded past them, carrying his staff in his left hand behind him, a habit which he had acquired with his ellwand[6] when he travelled the Borders as a pedlar.

CHAPTER XIX

ON the Saturday evening after the instructions had been given to prepare the new deed of entail, Grippy was thoughtful and silent, and his wife observing how much he was troubled in mind, said,

'I'm thinking, gudeman, though ye hae no reason to be pleased with this match Charlie has made for himsel, ye ken, as it canna be helpit noo, we maun just put up wi't.'

To this observation, which was about one of the most sensible that ever the Leddy o' Grippy made in her life, Claud replied, with an ill articulated grumph, that partook more of the sound and nature of a groan than a growl, and she continued,—

'But, poor laddie, bare legs need happing; I would fain hope ye'll no be oure dure;—ye'll hae to try an there be any moully pennies in the neuk o' your coffer that can be spar'd and no miss't.'

'I hae thought o' that, Girzy, my dawty,' said he somewhat more cordially than he was in the practice of doing to his wife; 'and we'll gang o'er the morn and speer for Charlie. I wis[7] he had na been so headstrong; but it's a' his ain fault: howsever, it would na be canny to gang toom-handed,[1] and I hae got a bit bill[2] for five score pounds that I'm mindit to gie him.'

'Five score pounds, gudeman! that's the whole tot[3] o' a hundred. Na, gudeman, I would hae thought the half o't an unco almous frae you.[4] I hope it's no a fedam[5] afore death. Gude preserve us! ye're really ta'en wi' a fit o' the liberalities; but Charlie, or am[6] mista'en, will hae need o't a', for yon Flanders baby[7] is no for a poor man's wife. But for a'that, I'm blithe to think ye're gaun to be sae kind, though I need na wonder at it, for Charlie was ay your darling chevalier,[8] I'm sure nobody can tell what for, and ye ay lookit down on poor good-natured Watty.'

'Haud that senseless tongue o' thine, Girzy; Watty's just like the mither o't, a haverel; and if it were na more for ae thing than anither,[9] the deil a penny would the silly gouk[10] get frae me, aboon an aliment to keep him frae beggary. But what's ordain't will come to pass, and it's no my fault that the sumph[11] Watty was na Charlie. But it's o' nae use to contest about the matter; ye'll be ready betimes the morn's morning[12] to gang in wi' me to the town to see the young folks.'

Nothing more then passed, but Claud, somewhat to the surprise of his lady, proposed to make family worship that evening. 'It's time now, gudewife,' said he, 'when we're in a way to be made ancestors, that we should be thinking o' what's to come o' our sinful souls hereafter. Cry ben[13] the servants, and I'll read a chapter to them and you, by way o' a change, for I kenna what's about me, but this rash action o' that thoughtless laddie fashes[14] me, and yet it would na be right o' me to do any other way than what I'm doing.'

The big ha' Bible[15] was accordingly removed by Mrs Walkinshaw from the shelf where it commonly lay undisturbed from the one sacramental occasion to the other, and the dust being blown off, as on the Saturday night prior to the action sermon,[16] she carried it to the kitchen to be more thoroughly wiped, and soon after returned with it followed by the servants. Claud, in the meantime, having drawn his elbow-chair close to the table, and placed his spectacles on his nose, was sitting when the mistress laid the volume before him ready to begin. As some little stir was produced by the servants taking their places, he accidentally turned up the cover, and looked at the page in which he had inserted the dates of his own marriage and the births of his children. Mrs Walkinshaw observing him looking at the record, said,

'Atweel,[1] Charlie need na been in sic a haste, he's no auld enough yet to be the head o' a family. How auld were ye, gudeman, when we were marriet? But he's no blest wi' the forethought o' you.'

'Will that tongue o' thine, Girzy, ne'er be quiet? In the presence o' thy Maker, wheest,[2] and pay attention, while I read a chapter of His holy word.'

The accent in which this was uttered imposed at once silence and awe, and when he added, 'Let us worship God, by reading a portion of the Scriptures of truth,' the servants often afterwards said, 'he spoke like a dreadfu' divine.'

Not being, as we have intimated, much in the practice of domestic worship, Claud had avoided singing a Psalm, nor was he so well acquainted with the Bible, as to be able to fix on any particular chapter or appropriate passage from recollection. In this respect he was, indeed, much inferior to the generality of the Glasgow merchants of that age, for, although they were considerably changed from the austerity by which their fathers had incurred the vengeance of Charles the Second's government,[3] they were still regular in the performance of their religious domestic duties. Some excuse, however, might be made for Claud, on account of his having spent so many years on the English Borders, a region in no age or period greatly renowned for piety, though plentifully endowed, from a very ancient date, with ecclesiastical mansions for the benefit of the outlaws of the two nations. Not, however, to insist on this topic, instead of reverently waling[4] a portion with judicious care, he opened the book with a degree of superstitious trepidation, and the first passage which caught his eye was the thirty-second verse of the twenty-seventh chapter of Genesis.[5] He paused for a moment; and the servants and the family having also opened their Bibles, looked towards him in expectation that he would name the chapter he intended to read. But he closed the volume over upon his hand, which he had inadvertently placed on the text, and lay back on his chair, unconscious of what he had done, leaving his hand still within the book.

'We're a' ready,' said Mrs Walkinshaw; 'whare's the place?'

Roused by her observation from the reverie into which he had momentarily sunk, without reflecting on what he did, he hastily opened the Bible, by raising his hand, which threw open the leaves, and again he saw and read,—

'And Isaac his father said unto him, Who art thou? and he said, I am thy son,—thy first-born, Esau;
'And Isaac trembled very exceedingly.'

'What's the matter wi' you, gudeman?' said the Leddy; 'are ye no weel?'[1] as he again threw himself back in his chair, leaving the book open before him. He, however, made no reply, but only drew his hand over his face, and slightly rubbed his forehead.

'I'm thinking, gudeman,' added the Leddy, 'as ye're no used wi' making exercise,[2] it may be as weel for us at the beginning to read a chapter intil oursels.'[3]

'I'll chapse[4] that place,' said Walter, who was sitting opposite to his father, putting, at the same time, unobserved into the book a bit of stick which he happened to be sillily gnawing.

Claud heard what his wife suggested, but for about a minute made no answer: shutting the Bible, without noticing the mark which Walter had placed in it, he said,—

'I'm thinking ye're no far wrang, gudewife. Sirs, ye may gae but the house,[5] and ilk[6] read a chapter wi' sobriety, and we'll begin the worship the morn's night,[7] whilk is the Lord's.'

The servants accordingly retired; and Walter reached across the table to lay hold of the big Bible, in order to read his chapter where he had inserted the stick; but his father angrily struck him sharply over the fingers, saying,—

'Hast t'ou neither grace nor gumshion, that t'ou daurs[8] to tak awa the word o' God frae before my very face? Look to thy ain book, and mind what it tells thee, an t'ou has the capacity of an understanding to understand it.'

Walter, rebuked by the chastisement, withdrew from the table; and, taking a seat sulkily by the fireside, began to turn over the leaves of his pocket Bible, and from time to time he read mutteringly a verse here and there by the light of the grate. Mrs Walkinshaw, with Miss Meg, having but one book between them, drew their chairs close to the table; and the mother, laying her hand on her daughter's shoulders, overlooked the chapter which the latter had selected.

Although Claud had by this time recovered from the agitation into which he had been thrown, by the admonition he had as it were received from the divine oracle, he yet felt a profound emotion of awe as he again stretched his hand towards the sacred volume, which, when he had again opened, and again beheld the self-same words, he trembled very exceedingly, in so much that he made the table shake violently.

'In the name of God, what's that!' cried his wife, terrified by the unusual motion, and raising her eyes from the book, with a strong expression of the fear which she then felt.

Claud was so startled, that he looked wildly behind him for a moment, with a ghastly and superstitious glare. Naturally possessing, however, a firm and steady mind, his alarm scarcely lasted a moment; but the pious business of the evening was so much disturbed, and had been to himself so particularly striking, that he suddenly quitted the table, and left the room.

CHAPTER XX

THE Sabbath morning was calm and clear, and the whole face of Nature fresh and bright. Every thing was animated with glee; and the very flowers, as they looked up in the sunshine, shone like glad faces. Even the Leddy o' Grippy partook of the gladdening spirit which glittered and frolicked around her; and as she walked a few paces in front of her husband down the footpath from the house to the highway leading to Glasgow, she remarked, as their dog ran gamboling before them, that

'Auld Colley, wi' his daffing,[1] looks as he had a notion o' the braw wissing[2] o' joy Charlie is to get. The brute, gudeman, ay took up wi' him, which was a wonderfu' thing to me; for he did nothing but weary its life wi' garring it loup[3] for an everlasting after sticks and chucky stanes.[4] Hows'ever, I fancy dogs are like men— leavened, as Mr Kilfuddy says, wi' the leaven of an ungrateful heart—for Colley is as doddy and crabbit[5] to Watty as if he was its adversary, although, as ye ken, he gathers and keeps a' the banes for't.'

'Wilt t'ou ne'er devaul'[6] wi' thy havering tongue? I'm sure the dumb brute, in favouring Charlic, showed mair sense than his mother, poor fellow.'

'Aye, aye, gudeman, so ye say; but every body knows your most unnatural partiality.'

'Thy tongue, woman,' exclaimed her husband, 'gangs like the clatter-bane o' a goose's——'[1]

'Eh, Megsty me!' cried the Leddy; 'wha's yon at the yett tirling at the pin?'[2]

Claud, roused by her interjection, looked forward, and beheld, with some experience of astonishment, that it was Mr Keelevin, the writer.[3]

'We'll hae to turn and gang back with him,' said Mrs Walkinshaw, when she observed who it was.

'I'll be damn'd if I do ony sic thing,' growled the old man, with a fierceness of emphasis that betrayed apprehension and alarm, while it at the same time denoted a rivetted determination to persevere in the resolution he had taken; and, mending his pace briskly, he reached the gate before the worthy lawyer had given himself admittance.

'Gude day, Mr Keelevin!—What's brought you so soon afield this morning?'

'I hae just ta'en a bit canter oure[4] to see you, and to speak anent yon thing.'

'Hae ye got the papers made out?'

'Surely—it can never be your serious intent—I would fain hope—nay, really Mr Walkinshaw, ye maunna[5] think o't.'

'Hoot, toot, toot; I thought ye had mair sense, Mr Keelevin. But I'm sorry we canna gae back wi' you, for we're just sae far in the road to see Charlie and his lady landless.'

''Deed are we,' added Mrs Walkinshaw; 'and ye'll no guess what the gudeman has in his pouch to gie them for hansel[6] to their matrimony: the whole tot of a hundred pound, Mr Keelevin—what think you o' that?'

The lawyer looked first at the Leddy, and then at the Laird, and said, 'Mr Walkinshaw, I hae done you wrong in my thought.'

'Say nae mair about it, but hae the papers ready by Wednesday, as I directed,' replied Claud.

'I hope and trust, Mr Keelevin,' said Mrs Walkinshaw, 'that he's no about his will and testament: I redde ye, an he be,[7] see that I'm no neglekit; and dinna let him do an injustice to the lave[8] for the behoof of Charlie, wha is, as I say, his darling chevalier.'

Mr Keelevin was as much perplexed as ever any member of the profession was in his life; but he answered cheerfully,

'Ye need na be fear't, Mrs Walkinshaw, I'll no wrang either you or any one of the family;' and he added, looking towards her husband, 'if I can help it.'

'Na, thanks be an' praise, as I understand the law, that's no in your power; for I'm secured wi' a jointure on the Grippy by my marriage articles; and my father, in his testament, ordained me to hae a hundred a year out of the barming o' his lying money;[1] the whilk, as I have myself counted, brings in to the gudeman, frae the wadset[2] that he has on the Kilmarkeckle estate, full mair than a hundred and twenty-seven pounds; so I would wis[3] both you and him to ken, that I'm no in your reverence;[4] and likewise, too, Mr Keelevin, that I'll no faik[5] a farthing o' my right.'

Mr Keelevin was still more perplexed at the information contained in this speech; for he knew nothing of the mortgage, or, as the Leddy called it, the wadset which Claud had on his neighbour Kilmarkeckle's property, Mr Omit having been employed by him in that business. Indeed, it was a regular part of Grippy's pawkie[6] policy, not to let his affairs be too well known, even to his most confidential legal adviser; but, in common transactions, to employ any one who could be safely trusted in matters of ordinary professional routine. Thus the fallacious impression which Claud had in some degree made on the day in which he instructed the honest lawyer respecting the entail was, in a great measure, confirmed; so that Mr Keelevin, instead of pressing the remonstrance which he had come on purpose from Glasgow that morning to urge, marvelled exceedingly within himself at the untold wealth of his client.

In the meantime, Grippy and his Leddy continued walking towards the city, but the lawyer remounted his horse, pondering on what he had heard, and almost persuaded that Claud, whom he knew to be so close and wary in worldly matters, was acting a very prudent part. He conceived that he must surely be much richer than the world supposed; and that, seeing the natural defects of his second son, Walter, how little he was superior to an idiot, and judging he could make no good use of ready money, but might, on the contrary, become the prey of knavery, he had, perhaps, determined, very wisely, to secure to him his future fortune by the entail proposed, meaning to indemnify Charles from his lying money. The only doubt that he could not clear off entirely to his satisfaction, was the circumstance of George, the youngest son, being preferred in the limitations of the entail to his eldest brother. But even this admitted of something like a reasonable explanation; for, by the will of the grandfather, in the event of Walter dying without male issue, George was entitled to succeed to the Plealands, as heir of entail; the effect of all which, in the benevolent mind of honest Mr Keelevin, contributed not a little to rebuild the good opinion of his client, which had suffered such a shock from the harshness of his instructions, as to induce him to pay the visit which led to the rencounter described; and in consequence he walked his horse beside the Laird and Leddy, as they continued to pick their steps along the shady side of the road.—Mrs Walkinshaw, with her petticoats lifted half leg high, still kept the van, and her husband followed stooping forward in his gait, with his staff in his left hand behind him—the characteristic and usual position in which, as we have already mentioned, he was wont to carry his ellwand when a pedlar.

CHAPTER XXI

THE young couple were a good deal surprised at the unexpected visit of their father and mother; for although they had been led to hope, from the success of the old lady's mission, that their pardon would be conceded, they had still, by hearing nothing farther on the subject, passed the interval in so much anxiety, that it had materially impaired their happiness. Charles, who was well aware of the natural obduracy of his father's disposition, had almost entirely given up all expectation of ever being restored to his favour; and the despondency of the apprehensions connected with this feeling underwent but little alleviation when he observed the clouded aspect, the averted eye, and the momentary glances, with which his wife was regarded, and the troubled looks from time to time thrown towards himself. Nevertheless, the visit, which was at first so embarrassing to all parties, began to assume a more cordial character; and the generosity of Charles' nature, which led him to give a benevolent interpretation to the actions and motives of every man, soon mastered his anxieties; and he found himself, after the ice was broken, enabled to take a part in the raillery of his mother, who, in high glee and good humour, joked with her blooming and blushing daughter-in-law, with all the dexterity and delicacy of which she was so admirable a mistress.

'Eh!' said she, 'but this was a galloping wedding o' yours, Charlie. It was an unco like[1] thing, Bell—na, ye need na look down, for ye maunna expek me to ca' you by your lang-nebbit[2] baptismal name, now that ye're my gude-dochter[3]—for ceremony's a cauldrife[4] commodity amang near frien's.[5] But surely, Bell, it would hae been mair wiselike[6] had ye been cried in the kirk three distink Sabbaths,[7] as me and your gude-father[8] was, instead o' gallanting awa under the scog[9] and cloud o' night, as if ye had been fain and fey.[10] Howsever, it's done noo; and the gudeman means to be vastly genteel. I'm sure the post should get a hag[11] when we hear o' him coming wi' hundreds o' pounds in his pouch, to gi'e awa for deil-be-licket[12] but a gratus gift o' gude will, in hansel to your matrimonial. But Charlie, your gudeman, Bell, was ay his pett, and so am nane[13] surprised at his unnatural partiality, only I ken they'll hae clear e'en and bent brows that 'ill see him gi'eing ony sic almous[14] to Watty.'

When the parental visitors had sat about an hour, during the great part of which the Leddy o' Grippy continued in this strain of clishmaclaver,[15] the Laird said to her it was time to take the road homeward. Charles pressed them to stay dinner. This, however, was decidedly refused by his father, but not in quite so gruff a manner as he commonly gave his refusals, for he added, giving Charles the bank-bill, as he moved across the room, towards the door,—

'Hae, there's something to help to keep the banes[16] green, but be careful, Charlie, for I doubt ye'll hae need, noo that ye're the head o' a family, to look at baith sides o' the bawbee[17] before ye part wi't.'

'It's for a whole hundred pound,' exclaimed Lady Grippy in an exulting whisper to her daughter-in-law—while the old man, after parting with the paper, turned briskly round to his son, as if to interrupt his thankfulness, and said,—

'Charlie, ye maun come wi' Watty and me on Wednesday; I hae a bit alteration to make in my papers; and, as we need na cry sic things at the Cross,[18] I'm mindit to hae you and him for the witnesses.'

Charles readily promised attendance; and the old people then made their congées and departed.

In the walk homeward Claud was still more taciturn than in the morning; he was even sullen, and occasionally peevish; but his wife was in full pipe and glee; and, as soon as they were beyond hearing, she said,—

'Every body maun alloo that she's a well far't[1] lassie yon; and, if she's as good as she's bonny, Charlie's no to mean[2] wi' his match. But, dear me, gudeman, ye were unco scrimpit[3] in your talk to her —I think ye might hae been a thought mair complaisant and jocose, considering it was a marriage occasion; and I wonder what came o'er mysel that I forgot to bid them come to the Grippy and tak their dinner the morn,[4] for ye ken we hae a side o' mutton in the house; for, since ye hae made a conciliation free gratus wi' them, we need na be standing on stapping-stanes; no that I think the less o' the het[5] heart that Charlie has gi'en to us baith; but it was his forton,[6] and we maun put up wi't. Howsever, gudeman, ye'll alloo me to make an observe to you anent the hundred pound. I think it would hae been more prudent to hae gi'en them but the half o't, or ony smaller sum, for Charlie's no a very gude guide;— siller wi' him gangs like snaw aff a dyke;[7] and as for his lily-white handit madam, a' the jingling o' her spinnit will ne'er make up for the winsome tinkle o' Betty Bodle's tocher[8] purse. But I hae been thinking, gudeman, noo that Charlie's by hand and awa, as the ballad o' Woo't and Married and a'[9] sings, could na ye persuade our Watty to mak up to Betty, and sae get her gear[10] saved to us yet?'

This suggestion was the only wise thing, in the opinion of Claud, that ever he had heard his wife utter; it was, indeed, in harmonious accordance with the tenor of his own reflections, not only at the moment, but from the hour in which he was first informed of the marriage. For he knew, from the character of Miss Betty Bodle's father, that the entail of the Grippy, in favour of Walter, would be deemed by him a satisfactory equivalent for any intellectual defect. The disinheritance of Charles was thus, in some degree, palliated to his conscience as an act of family policy rather than of resentment; in truth, resentment had perhaps very little to say in the feeling by which it was dictated;—for, as all he did and thought of in life was with a view to the restoration of the Walkinshaws of Kittlestonheugh, we might be justified, for the honour of human nature, to believe, that he actually contemplated the sacrifice

which he was making of his first-born to the Moloch of ancestral
pride, with reluctance, nay, even with sorrow.

In the meantime, as he returned towards Grippy with his wife,
thus discoursing on the subject of Miss Betty Bodle and Walter,
Charles and Isabella were mutually felicitating themselves on the
earnest which they had so unexpectedly received of what they
deemed a thorough reconciliation. There had, however, been
something so heartless in the behaviour of the old man during the
visit, that, notwithstanding the hopes which his gift encouraged,
it left a chill and comfortless sensation in the bosom of the young
lady, and her spirit felt it as the foretaste of misfortune. Averse,
however, to occasion any diminution of the joy which the visit of
his parents had afforded to her husband, she endeavoured to suppress the bodement, and to partake of the gladdening anticipations
in which he indulged. The effort to please others never fails to
reward ourselves. In the afternoon, when the old dowager[1] called,
she was delighted to find them both satisfied with the prospect,
which had so suddenly opened, and so far too beyond her most
sanguine expectations, that she also shared in their pleasure, and
with her grandson inferred, from the liberal earnest he had
received, that, in the papers and deeds he was invited to witness,
his father intended to make some provision to enable him to support the rank in society to which Isabella had been born, and in
which his own taste prompted him to move. The evening, in
consequence, was spent by them with all the happiness which the
children of men so often enjoy with the freest confidence, while the
snares of adversity are planted around them, and the demons of
sorrow and evil are hovering unseen, awaiting the signal from
destiny to descend on their blind and unsuspicious victims.

CHAPTER XXII

GRIPPY passed the interval between the visit and the day appointed for the execution of the deeds of entail with as much comfort of mind as Heaven commonly bestows on a man conscious of
an unjust intention, and unable to excuse it to himself. Charles,
who, in the meantime, naturally felt some anxiety to learn the
precise nature of the intended settlement, was early afoot on the

morning of Wednesday, and walked from the lodgings where he resided with his wife in Glasgow to meet his father and brother, on their way to the town. Being rather before the time appointed, he went forward to the house, on the green plot in front of which the old man was standing, with his hands behind, and his head thoughtfully bent downwards.

The approach of his son roused Claud from his reverie; and he went briskly forward to meet him, shaking him heartily by the hand, and inquiring, with more kindness than the occasion required, for the health of his young wife. Such unusual cordiality tended to confirm the delusion which the gift of the bank bill on Sunday had inspired; but the paroxysm of affection produced by the effort to disguise the sense which the old man suffered of the irreparable wrong he was so doggedly resolved to commit, soon went off; and, in the midst of his congratulations, conscience smote him with such confusion, that he was obliged to turn away, to conceal the embarrassment which betrayed the insincerity of the warmth he had so well assumed. Poor Charles, however, was prevented from observing the change in his manner and countenance, by Walter appearing at the door in his Sunday clothes, followed by his mother, with his best hat in her hand, which she was smoothing at the same time with the tail of her apron.

'I redde[1] ye, my bairn,' said she to Walter, as she gave him the hat, 'to take care o' thysel, for ye ken they're an unco crew[2] ay in the Trongate on Wednesday; and mind what I hae been telling you, no to put your hand to pen and ink unless Mr Keelevin tells you it's to be for your advantage; for Charlie's your father's ain chevalier, and nae farther gane than the last Lord's day, he gied him, as I telt you, a whole hundred pound for hansel to his tocherless matrimony.'[3]

Charles, at this speech, reddened and walked back from the house, without speaking to his mother; but he had not advanced many steps towards the gate, when she cried,—

'Hey, Charlie! are ye sae muckle ta'en up wi' your bonny bride, that your mother's already forgotten?'

He felt the reproof, and immediately turned and went back to make some apology, but she prevented him by saying,—

'See that this is no a Jacob and Esau[4] business, Charlie, and that ye dinna wrang poor Watty; for he's an easy good-natured lad, and will just do what either you or his father bids him.'

Charles laughed, and replied,—

'I think, mother, your exhortation should rather be to Watty than me; for ye ken Jacob was the youngest, and beguiled his auld brother of the birth-right.'

The old man heard the remark, and felt it rush through his very soul with the anguish of a barbed and feathered arrow; and he exclaimed, with an accent of remorse as sharp and bitter as the voice of anger,—

'Hae done wi' your clavers,[1] and come awa. Do ye think Mr Keelevin has nothing mair to do than to wait for us, while ye're talking profanity, and taigling at this gait?[2] Come awa, Watty, ye gumshionless cuif,[3] as ever father was plagued wi'; and Charlie, my lad, let us gang thegither, the haverel will follow; for if it has na the colley-dog's sense, it has something like its instinct.'

And so saying, he stepped on hastily towards the gate, swinging his staff in his right hand, and walking faster and more erectly than he was wont.

The two sons, seeing the pace at which their father was going forward, parted from their mother and followed him, Charles laughing and jeering at the beau which Walter had made of himself.

During the journey the old man kept aloof from them, turning occasionally round to rebuke their mirth, for there was something in the freedom and gaiety of Charles's laugh that reproached his spirit, and the folly of Walter was never so disagreeable to him before.

When they reached the office of Mr Keelevin, they found him with the parchments ready on the desk; but before reading them over, he requested the Laird to step in with him into his inner-chamber.

'Noo, Mr Walkinshaw,' said he, when he had shut the door, 'I hope ye have well reflected on this step, for when it is done, there's nae power in the law o' Scotland to undo it. I would, therefore, fain hope ye're no doing this out of any motive or feeling of resentment for the thoughtless marriage, it may be, of your auld son.'

Claud assured him, that he was not in the slightest degree influenced by any such sentiment; adding, 'But, Mr Keelevin, though I employ you to do my business, I dinna think ye ought to catechise me. Ye're, as I would say, but the pen in this matter, and the right or the wrong o't's a' my ain.[4] I would, therefore, counsel you, noo that the papers are ready, that they should be implemented, and for that purpose, I hae brought my twa sons to be the witnesses themselves to the act and deed.'

Mr Keelevin held up his hands, and, starting back, gave a deep sigh as he said,—'It's no possible that Charlie can be consenting to his own disinheritance, or he's as daft as his brother.'

'Consenting here, or consenting there, Mr Keelevin,' replied the father, 'ye'll just bring in the papers and read them o'er to me; ye need na fash to ca' ben¹ the lads, for that might breed strife atween them.'

'Na! as sure's death, Mr Walkinshaw,' exclaimed the honest writer,² with a warmth and simplicity rather obsolete among his professional brethren now-a-days, however much they may have been distinguished for those qualities in the innocent golden age; 'Na! as sure's death, Mr Walkinshaw, this is mair than I hae the conscience to do; the lads are parties to the transaction, by their reversionary interest, and it is but right and proper they should know what they are about.'

'Mr Keelevin,' cried the Laird, peevishly, 'ye're surely growing doited.³ It would be an unco like thing⁴ if witnesses to our wills and testaments had a right to ken what we bequeathe. Please God, neither Charlie nor Watty sall⁵ be ony the wiser o' this day's purpose, as lang as the breath's in my body.'

'Weel, Mr Walkinshaw,' replied the lawyer, 'ye'll tak your own way o't, I see that; but, as ye led me to believe, I hope an' trust it's in your power to make up to Charles the consequences of this very extraordinary entail; and I hope ye'll lose no time till ye hae done sae.'

'Mr Keelevin, ye'll read the papers,' was the brief and abrupt answer which Claud made to this admonition; and the papers were accordingly brought in and read.

During the reading, Claud was frequently afflicted by the discordant cheerfulness of Charles's voice in the outer room, joking with the clerks, at the expence of his fortunate brother; but the task of aforesaids and hereafters being finished, he called them in, with a sharp and peevish accent, and signed the deeds in their presence. Charles took the pen from his father, and also at once signed as witness, while Mr Keelevin looked the living image of amazement; but, when the pen was presented to Watty, he refused to take it.

'What am I to get by this?' said the natural, mindful of his

mother's advice. 'I would like to ken that. Nobody writes papers
without payment.'

'T'ou's a born idiot,' said the father; 'wilt t'ou no do as t'ou's
bidden?'[1]

'I'll do ony other thing ye like, but I'll no sign that drum-head[2]
paper, without an advantage: ye would na get Mr Keelevin to do
the like o't without payment; and what for should ye get me?
Have na I come in a' the gait[3] frae the Grippy to do this; and am I
no to get a black bawbee for my pains?'

The Laird masked the vexation with which this idiot speech of
his destined heir troubled his self-possession, while Charles sat
down in one of the chairs, convulsed with laughter. Claud was not,
however, to be deterred from his purpose by the absurdity of his
son: on the contrary, he was afraid to make the extent of the fool's
folly too evident, lest it might afterwards be rendered instru-
mental to set aside the entail. He called in one of the clerks from
the outer-chamber, and requested him to attest his signature.
Walter loudly complained of being so treated; and said, that he
expected a guinea, at the very least, for the trouble he had been
put to; for so he interpreted the advantage to which his mother
had alluded.

'Weel, weel,' said his father, 'ha'd thy tongue, and t'ou sall[4] get
a guinea; but first sign this other paper,' presenting to him the
second deed; by which, as possessor of the Plealands' estate, he
entailed it in the same manner, and to the same line of succession,
as he had himself destined the Grippy. The assurance of the guinea
was effectual; Walter signed the deed, which was witnessed by
Charles and the clerk; and the disinheritance was thus made
complete.

CHAPTER XXIII

On leaving the office of Mr Keelevin, Charles invited his father
and brother to go home with him; but the old man abruptly turned
away. Walter, however, appeared inclined to accept the invitation,
and was moving off with Charles, when their father looked back,
and chidingly commanded him to come along.

At any other time, this little incident would have been unnoticed by Charles, who, believing the old man had made some liberal provision for him or for his wife, was struck with the harsh contrast of such behaviour to the paternal affection by which he thought him actuated; and he paused, in consequence, thoughtfully looking after him as he walked towards the Cross,[1] followed by Walter.

Grippy had not proceeded above twenty or thirty paces when he stopped, and turning round, called to his son, who immediately obeyed the summons.

'Charlie,' said he, 'I hope t'ou'll let nae daffing nor ploys[2] about this marriage o' thine tak up thy attention frae the shop; for business maun be minded; and I'm thinking t'ou had as weel be making up a bit balance-sheet, that I may see how the counts stand between us.'

This touched an irksome recollection, and recalled to mind the observation which his father had made on the occasion of Fatherlans' ruin, with respect to the hazards of taking into partnership a man with the prospect of a family.

'I hope,' was his reply, 'that it is not your intention, sir, to close accounts with me?'

'No, Charlie, no,' was his answer.—I'll may be mak things better for thee—t'ou'll no be out o' the need o't.[3] But atween hands[4] mak up the balance-sheet, and come doun on Saturday wi' thy wife to Grippy, and we'll hae some discourse anent it.'

With these words, the old man and Walter again went on towards the Cross, leaving Charles standing perplexed, and unable to divine the source and motives of his father's behaviour. It seemed altogether so unaccountable, that for a moment he thought of going back to Mr Keelevin to ask him concerning the settlements; but a sense of propriety restrained him, and he thought it alike indelicate and dishonourable, to pry into an affair which was so evidently concealed from him. But this restraint, and these considerations, did not in any degree tend to allay the anxiety which the mysteriousness of his father's conduct had so keenly excited, so that, when he returned home to Isabella, he appeared absent and thoughtful, which she attributed to some disappointment in his expectations,—an idea the more natural to her, as she had, from the visit on Sunday, been haunted with an apprehension that there was something unsound in the reconciliation.

Upon being questioned as to the cause of his altered spirits, Charles could give no feasible reason for the change. He described what had passed, he mentioned what his father had said, and he communicated the invitation, in all which there was nothing that the mind could lay hold of, nor ought to justify his strange and indescribable apprehension, if that feeling might be called an apprehension, to which his imagination could attach no danger, nor conjure up any thing to be feared. On the contrary, so far from having reason to suspect that evil was meditated against him, he had received a positive assurance that his circumstances would probably receive an immediate improvement; but for all that, there had been, in the reserve of the old man's manner, and in the vagueness of his promises, a something which sounded hollowly to his hope, and deprived him of confidence in the anticipations he had cherished.

While Isabella and he were sitting together conversing on the subject, the old Lady Plealands came in, anxious to hear what had been done, having previously been informed of the intended settlements, but not of their nature and objects. In her character, as we have already intimated, there was a considerable vein, if not of romantic sentiment, unquestionably of morbid sensibility. She disliked her son-in-law from the first moment in which she saw him; and this dislike had made her so averse to his company, that, although their connection was now nearly of four-and-twenty years standing, she had still but a very imperfect notion of his character. She regarded him as one of the most sordid of men, without being aware that avarice with him was but an agent in the pursuit of that ancestral phantom which he worshipped as the chief, almost the only good in life; and, therefore, could neither imagine any possible ground for supposing, that, after being reconciled, he could intend his first-born any injury, nor sympathize with the anxieties which her young friends freely confessed both felt, while she could not but deplore the unsatisfactory state of their immediate situation.

In the meantime, Walter and his father were walking homeward. The old man held no communion with his son; but now and then he rebuked him for hallooing at birds in the hedges, or chasing butterflies, a sport so unbecoming his years.

In their way they had occasion to pass the end of the path which led to Kilmarkeckle, where Miss Bodle, the heiress, resided with her father.

'Watty,' said Grippy to his son, 'gae thy ways hame by thysel, and tell thy mither that am gaun[1] up to the Kilmarkeckle to hae some discourse wi' Mr Bodle, so that she need na weary if I dinna come hame to my dinner.'

'Ye had better come hame,' said Watty, 'for there's a sheep's head in the pat,[2] wi' a cuff o' the neck like ony Glasgow bailie's.[3]— Ye'll no get the like o't at Kilmarkeckle, where the kail's sae thin that every pile o' barley[4] runs roun' the dish, bobbing and bidding gude day to its neighbour.'

Claud had turned into the footpath from the main road, but there was something in this speech which did more than provoke his displeasure; and he said aloud, and with an accent of profound dread,—'I hope the Lord can forgi'e me for what I hae done to this fool!'

Walter was not so void of sense as to be incapable of comprehending the substance of this contrite exclamation; and instantly recollecting his mother's admonition, and having some idea, imperfect as it was, of the peril of parchments with seals on them, he began, with obstreperous sobs and wails, to weep and cry, because, as he said, 'My father and our Charlie had fastened on me the black bargain o' a law plea to wrang me o' auld daddy's mailing.'[5]

Grippy was petrified; it seemed to him that his son was that day smitten in anger to him by the hand of Heaven, with a more disgusting idiocy than he had ever before exhibited, and, instigated by the aversion of the moment, he rushed towards him, and struck him so furiously with his stick, that he sent him yelling homeward as fast as he could run. The injustice and the rashness of the action were felt at once, and, overpowered for a few seconds by shame, remorse, and grief, the old man sat down on a low dry-stone wall that bounded the road on one side, and clasping his hands fervently together, confessed with bitter tears that he doubted he had committed a great sin. It was, however, but a transitory contrition, for, hearing some one approaching, he rose abruptly, and lifting his stick, which he had dropped in his agitation, walked up the footpath towards Kilmarkeckle; but he had not advanced many paces when a hand was laid on his shoulder. He looked round, and it was Walter, with his hat folded together in his hand.

'Father,' said the fool, 'I hae catched a muckle bum-bee; will ye help to haud[6] it till I take out the honey blob?'

'I'll go hame, Watty—I'll go hame,' was the only answer he

made, in an accent of extreme sorrow, 'I'll go hame; I daur do nae mair[1] this day,' and he returned back with Walter to the main road, where, having again recovered his self-possession, he said, 'I'm dafter than thee to gang on in this fool gait; go, as I bade thee, hame and tell thy mother no to look for me to dinner, for I'll aiblins bide wi' Kilmarkeckle.'[2] In saying which, he turned briskly round, and, without ever looking behind, walked with an alert step, swinging his staff courageously, and never halted till he reached Kilmarkeckle-house, where he was met at the door by Mr Bodle himself, who, seeing him approaching up the avenue, came out to meet him.

CHAPTER XXIV

BODLE of Kilmarkeckle, like all the lairds of that time, was come of an ancient family, in some degree related to the universal stock of Adam, but how much more ancient, no historian has yet undertaken to show. Like his contemporaries of the same station, he was, of course, proud of his lineage; but he valued himself more on his own accomplishments than even on the superior purity of his blood. We are, however, in doubt, whether he ought to be described as an artist or a philosopher, for he had equal claims to the honour of being both, and certainly without question, in the art of delineating hieroglyphical resemblances of birds and beasts on the walls of his parlour with snuff, he had evinced, if not talent or genius, at least considerable industry. In the course of more than twenty years, he had not only covered the walls with many a curious and grotesque form, but invented,—and therein lay the principle of his philosophy—a particular classification, as original and descriptive as that of Linnæus.[3]

At an early age he had acquired the habit of taking snuff, and in process of time became, as all regular snuff-takers are, acute in discriminating the shades and inflections of flavour in the kind to which he was addicted. This was at once the cause and the principle of his science. For the nature of each of the birds and beasts which he modelled resembled, as he averred, some peculiarity in the tobacco of which the snuff that they severally represented had been made; and really, to do him justice, it was quite wonderful to hear with what ingenuity he could explain the discriminative qualities in which the resemblance of attributes and character consisted. But it must be confessed, that he sometimes fell into that bad custom remarkable among philosophers, of talking a great deal too much to every body, and on every occasion, of his favourite study. Saving this, however, the Laird of Kilmarkeckle was in other respects a harmless easy-tempered man, of a nature so kind and indulgent, that he allowed all about him to grow to rankness. The number of cats of every size and age which frisked in his parlour, or basked at the sunny side of the house, exceeded all reasonable credibility, and yet it was a common saying among the neighbours, that Kilmarkeckle's mice kittled[1] twice as often as his cats.

In nothing was his easy and indulgent nature more shown than in his daughter, Miss Betty, who having, at an early age, lost her mother, he had permitted to run unbridled among the servants, till the habits which she had acquired in consequence rendered every subsequent attempt to reduce her into the requisite subjection of the sex totally unavailing.

She had turned her twentieth year, and was not without beauty, but of such a sturdy and athletic kind, that, with her open ruddy countenance, laughing eyes, white well-set teeth, and free and joyous step and air, justly entitled her to the nickname of Fun, bestowed by Charles Walkinshaw. She was fond of dogs and horses, and was a better shot than the Duke of Douglas's[2] game-keeper. Bold, boisterous, and frank, she made no scruple of employing her whip when rudely treated, either by master or man; for she frequently laid herself open to freedoms from both, and she neither felt nor pretended to any of her sex's gentleness nor delicacy. Still she was not without a conciliatory portion of feminine virtues, and perhaps, had she been fated to become the wife of a sportsman or a soldier, she might possibly have appeared on the turf or in the tent to considerable advantage.

Such a woman, it may be supposed, could not but look with the most thorough contempt on Walter Walkinshaw; and yet, from the accidental circumstance of being often his playmate in childhood, and making him, in the frolic of their juvenile amusements, her butt and toy, she had contracted something like an habitual affection for the creature; in so much, that, when her father, after Claud's visit, proposed Walter for her husband, she made no

serious objection to the match; on the contrary, she laughed, and
amused herself with the idea of making him fetch and carry as
whimsically as of old, and do her hests and biddings as implicitly
as when they were children. Every thing thus seemed auspicious
to a speedy and happy union of the properties of Kilmarkeckle and
Grippy,—indeed, so far beyond the most sanguine expectations
of Claud, that, when he saw the philosophical Laird coming next
morning, with a canister of snuff in his hand, to tell him the result
of the communication to Miss Betty, his mind was prepared to
hear a most decided, and even a menacing refusal, for having
ventured to make the proposal.

'Come away, Kilmarkeckle,' said he, meeting him at the door;
'come in by—what's the best o' your news this morning? I hope
nothing's wrang at hame, to gar you look sae as ye were fasht?'[1]

'Troth,' replied Kilmarkeckle, 'I hae got a thing this morning
that's very vexatious. Last year, at Beltane,[2] ye should ken, I coft[3]
frae Donald M'Sneeshen, the tobacconist aboon the Cross of
Glasgow, a canister of a kind that I ca'd the Linty.[4] It was sae
brisk in the smeddum,[5] so pleasant to the smell, garring ye trow[6]
in the sniffling that ye were sitting on a bonny green knowe[7] in hay
time, by the side of a blooming whin-bush, hearkening to the blythe
wee birdies singing sangs, as it were, to pleasure the summer's sun;
and what would ye think, Mr Walkinshaw, here is another canister
of a sort that I'll defy ony ordinary nose to tell the difference, and
yet, for the life o' me, I canna gie't[8] in conscience anither name
than the Hippopotamus.'

'But hae ye spoken to your dochter?' said Grippy, interrupting
him, and apprehensive of a dissertation.

'O aye, atweel[9] I hae done that.'

'And what did Miss Betty say?'

'Na, an ye had but seen and heard her, ye would just hae dee't,[10]
Mr Walkinshaw. I'm sure I wonder wha the lassie taks her light-
hearted merriment frae, for her mother was a sober and sedate
sensible woman; I never heard her jocose but ance, in a' the time
we were thegither, and that was when I expounded to her how
Maccaba[11] is like a nightingale, the whilk, as I hae seen and read
in print, is a feathert fowl that has a great notion o' roses.'

'I was fear't for that,' rejoined Claud, suspecting that Miss Betty
had ridiculed the proposal.

'But to gae back to the Linty and the Hippopotamus,' resumed

Kilmarkeckle. 'The snuff that I hae here in this canister—tak a pree o't,[1] Mr Walkinshaw—it was sent me in a present frae Mr Glassford, made out of the primest hogget in his last cargo[2]— what think ye o't? Noo, I would just speer gin[3] ye could tell wherein it may be likened to a hippopotamus, the which is a creature living in the rivers of Afrikaw, and has twa ivory teeth, bigger, as I am creditably informed, than the blade o' a scythe.'

Claud, believing that his proposal had been rejected, and not desirous of reverting to the subject, encouraged the philosopher to talk, by saying, that he could not possibly imagine how snuff could be said to resemble any such creature.

'That's a' that ye ken?' said Kilmarkeckle, chuckling with pleasure, and inhaling a pinch with the most cordial satisfaction. 'This snuff is just as like a hippopotamus as the other sort that was sae like it, was like a linty; and nothing could be plainer; for, even now when I hae't in my nostril, I think I see the creature wallowing and wantoning in some wide river in a lown[4] sunny day, wi' its muckle glad e'en,[5] wamling[6] wi' delight in its black head, as it lies lapping in the clear callour[7] water, wi' its red tongue, twirling and twining round its ivory teeth, and every now and then giving another lick.'

'But I dinna see any likeness in that to snuff, Mr Bodle,' said Claud.

'That's most extraordinary, Mr Walkinshaw; for surely there is a likeness somewhere in every thing that brings another thing to mind; and although as yet I'll no point out to you the vera particularity in a hippopotamus by which this snuff gars me think o' the beast, ye must, nevertheless, allow past a' dispute, that there is a particularity.'

Claud replied with ironical gravity, that he thought the snuff much more like a meadow, for it had the smell and flavour of new hay.

'Ye're no far frae the mark, Grippy; and now I'll tell you wherein the likeness lies. The hay, ye ken, is cut down by scythes in meadows; meadows lie by water sides: the teeth of the hippopotamus is as big as scythes; and he slumbers and sleeps in the rivers of Afrikaw; so the snuff, smelling like hay, brings a' thae things to mind; and therefore it is like a hippopotamus.'

After enjoying a hearty laugh at this triumph of his reasoning, the philosopher alighted from his hobby,[8] and proceeded to tell

Claud that he had spoken to his daughter, and that she had made no objection to the match.

'Heavens preserve us, Mr Bodle!' exclaimed Grippy; 'what were ye havering sae[1] about a brute beast, and had sic blithsome news to tell me?'

They then conversed somewhat circumstantially regarding the requisite settlements, Kilmarkeckle agreeing entirely with every thing that the sordid and cunning bargainer proposed, until the whole business was arranged, except the small particular of ascertaining how the appointed bridegroom stood affected. This, however, his father undertook to manage, and also that Walter should go in the evening to Kilmarkeckle, and in person make a tender of his heart and hand to the blooming, boisterous, and bouncing Miss Betty.

CHAPTER XXV

'WATTY,' said the Laird o' Grippy to his hopeful heir, calling him into the room, after Kilmarkeckle had retired,—

'Watty, come ben[2] and sit down; I want to hae some solid converse wi' thee. Dist t'ou[3] hearken to what I'm saying?—Kilmarkeckle has just been wi' me—Hear'st t'ou me?—deevil an I saw the like o' thee—what's t'ou looking at? As I was saying, Kilmarkeckle has been here, and he was thinking that you and his dochter'—

'Weel,' interrupted Watty, 'if ever I saw the like o' that. There was a Jenny Langlegs[4] bumming at the corner o' the window, when down came a spider wabster as big as a puddock, and claught it[5] in his arms; and he's off and awa wi' her intil[6] his nest;—I ne'er saw the like o't.'

'It's most extraordinar, Watty Walkinshaw,' exclaimed his father peevishly, 'that I canna get a mouthful o' common sense out o' thee, although I was just telling thee o' the greatest advantage that t'ou's ever likely to meet wi' in this world. How would ye like Miss Betty Bodle for a wife?'

'O father!'

'I'm saying, would na she make a capital Leddy o' the Plealands?'

Walter made no reply, but laughed, and chuckingly rubbed his hands, and then delightedly patted the sides of his thighs with them.

'I'm sure ye canna fin' ony fau't wi' her; there's no a brawer nor a better tocher'd[1] lass in the three shires.[2]—What think'st t'ou?'

Walter suddenly suspended his ecstasy; and grasping his knees firmly, he bent forward, and, looking his father seriously in the face, said,—

'But will she no thump me? Ye mind how she made my back baith black and blue.—I'm frightit.'

'Haud thy tongue wi' sic nonsense; that happened when ye were but bairns. I'm sure there's no a blither, bonnier quean[3] in a' the kintra side.'

'I'll no deny that she has red cheeks, and e'en like blobs o' honey dew in a kail-blade; but father—Lord, father! she has a neive like a beer mell.'[4]

'But for a' that, a sightly lad like you might put up wi' her, Watty. I'm sure ye'll gang far, baith east and west, before ye'll meet wi' her marrow; and ye should reflek on her tocher, the whilk is a wull-ease that's no to be found at ilka dykeside.'[5]

'Aye, so they say; her uncle 'frauded his ain only dochter, and left her a stocking fu' o' guineas for a legacy.—But will she let me go halffer?'[6]

'Ye need na misdoubt that; na, an ye fleech her weel,[7] I would na be surprised if she would gi'e you the whole tot; and I'm sure ye ne'er hae seen ony woman that ye can like better.'

'Aye, but I hae though,'[8] replied Watty confidently.

'Wha is't?' exclaimed his father, surprised and terrified.

'My mother.'

The old man, sordid as he was, and driving thus earnestly his greedy purpose, was forced to laugh at the solemn simplicity of this answer; but he added, resuming his perseverance,—

'True! I did na think o' thy mother, Watty—but an t'ou was ance marriet[9] to Betty Bodle, t'ou would soon like her far better than thy mother.'

'The fifth command says, "Honour thy father and thy mother, that thy days may be long in the land;" and there's no ae word[10] about liking a wife in a' the rest.'

'Weel, weel, but what I hae to say is, that me and Kilmarkeckle hae made a paction for thee to marry his dochter, and t'ou maun just gang o'er the night[11] and court Miss Betty.'

'But I dinna ken the way o't, father; I ne'er did sic a thing a' my days; odd, I'm unco blate[1] to try't.'

'Gude forgi'e me,' said Claud to himself, 'but the creature grows sillier and sillier every day—I tell thee, Watty Walkinshaw, to pluck up the spirit o' manhood, and gang o'er this night to Kilmarkeckle, and speak to Miss Betty by yoursel about the wedding.'

'Atweel, I can do that, and help her to buy her parapharnauls,[2]— We will hae a prime apple-pye that night, wi' raisins in't.'

The old man was petrified.—It seemed to him that it was utterly impossible the marriage could ever take place, and he sat for some time stricken, as it were, with a palsy of the mind. But these intervals of feeling and emotion were not of long duration; his inflexible character, and the ardour with which his whole spirit was devoted to the attainment of one object, soon settled and silenced all doubt, contrition, and hesitation; and considering, so far as Walter was concerned, the business decided, he summoned his wife to communicate to her the news.—

'Girzy Hypel,' said he as she entered the room, holding by the neck a chicken, which she was assisting the maids in the kitchen to pluck for dinner, and the feathers of which were sticking thickly on the blue worsted apron which she had put on to protect her old red quilted silk petticoat.

'Girzy Hypel, be nane surprised to hear of a purpose of marriage soon between Watty and Betty Bodle.'

'No possible!' exclaimed the Leddy, sitting down, with vehemence in her astonishment, and flinging, at the same time, the chicken across her lap, with a certain degree of instinctive or habitual dexterity.

'What for is't no possible?' said the Laird, angrily through his teeth, apprehensive that she was going to raise some foolish objection.

'Na, gudeman, an that's to be a come-to-pass—let nobody talk o' miracles to me. For although it's a thing just to the nines[3] o' my wishes, I hae ay jealoused[4] that Betty Bodle would na tak him, for she's o' a rampant nature, and he's a sober weel-disposed lad. My word, Watty, t'ou has thy ain luck—first thy grandfather's property o' the Plealands, and syne'—She was going to add, 'sic a bonny braw-tochered lass as Betty Bodle'—but her observation struck jarringly on the most discordant string in her husband's bosom, and he interrupted her, sharply, saying,—

'Every thing that's ordained will come to pass; and a' that I
hae for the present to observe to you, Girzy, is to tak tent that
the lad gangs over wiselike,[1] at the gloaming, to Kilmarkeckle,
in order to see Miss Betty anent the wedding.'

'I'm sure,' retorted the Leddy, 'I hae no need to green for[2]
weddings in my family, for, instead o' any pleasance to me, the
deil-be-licket's my part and portion o' the pastime but girns
and gowls.[3] Gudeman, ye should learn to keep your temper,
and be of a composed spirit, and talk wi' me in a sedate manner,
when our bairns are changing their life. Watty, my lad, mind
what your mother says—"Marriage is a creel,[4] where ye maun
catch," as the auld byword runs, "an adder or an eel." But,
as I was rehearsing, I could na hae thought that Betty Bodle
would hae fa'en just at ance[5] into your grip; for I had a notion
that she was oure souple in the tail to be easily catched. But
it's the Lord's will, Watty; and I hope ye'll enjoy a' manner
o' happiness wi' her, and be a confort to ane anither, like your
father and me,—bringing up your bairns in the fear o' God,
as we hae done you, setting them, in your walk and conversation, a patren[6] of sobriety and honesty, till they come to years
of discretion, when, if it's ordained for them, nae doubt they'll
look, as ye hae done, for a settlement in the world, and ye maun
part wi' them, as we are obligated, by course of nature, to part
with you.'

At the conclusion of which pathetic address, the old lady lifted
her apron to wipe the gathered drops from her eyes, when Watty
exclaimed,—

'Eh! mother, ane o' the hen's feathers is playing at whirley wi'
the breath o' your nostril!'

Thus ended the annunciation of the conjugal felicity of which
Grippy was the architect.

After dinner, Walter, dressed and set off to the best advantage
by the assistance of his mother, walked, accompanied by his
father, to Kilmarkeckle; and we should do him injustice if we
did not state, that, whatever might be his intellectual defici-
encies, undoubtedly in personal appearance, saving, perhaps,
some little lack of mental light in his countenance, he was cast
in a mould to find favour in any lady's eye. Perhaps he did not
carry himself quite as firmly as if he had been broke in
by a serjeant of dragoons, and in his air and gait we shall not

undertake to affirm that there was nothing lax nor slovenly, but still, upon the whole, he was, as his mother said, looking after him as he left the house, 'a braw bargain of manhood, get him wha would.'

CHAPTER XXVI

AFTER Kilmarkeckle had welcomed Grippy and Walter, he began to talk of the hippopotamus, by showing them the outlines of a figure which he intended to fill up with the snuff on the wall. Claud, however, cut him short, by proposing, in a whisper, that Miss Betty should be called in, and that she and Walter should be left together, while they took a walk to discuss the merits of the hippopotamus. This was done quickly, and, accordingly, the young lady made her appearance, entering the room with a blushing giggle, perusing her Titan of a suitor from head to heel with the beam of her eye.

'We'll leave you to yoursels,' said her father jocularly, 'and, Watty, be brisk wi' her, lad; she can thole a touzle,[1] I'se warrant.'

This exhortation had, however, no immediate effect, for Walter, from the moment she made her appearance, looked awkward and shamefaced, swinging his hat between his legs, with his eyes fixed on the brazen head of the tongs, which were placed upright astradle in front of the grate; but every now and then he peeped at her from the corner of his eye with a queer and luscious glance, which, while it amused, deterred her for some time from addressing him. Diffidence, however, had nothing to do with the character of Miss Betty Bodle, and a feeling of conscious superiority soon overcame the slight embarrassment which arose from the novelty of her situation.

Observing the perplexity of her lover, she suddenly started from her seat, and advancing briskly towards him, touched him on the shoulder, saying,—

'Watty,—I say, Watty, what's your will wi' me?'

'Nothing,' was the reply, while he looked up knowingly in her face.

'What are ye fear't for? I ken what ye're come about,' said she, 'my father has telt me.'

At these encouraging words, he leaped from his chair with an alacrity unusual to his character, and attempted to take her in his arms; but she nimbly escaped from his clasp, giving him, at the same time, a smart slap on the cheek.

'That's no fair, Betty Bodle,' cried the lover, rubbing his cheek, and looking somewhat offended and afraid.

'Then what gart you meddle wi' me?' replied the bouncing girl, with a laughing bravery that soon reinvigorated his love.

'I'm sure I was na gaun to do you ony harm,' was the reply;—'no, as sure's death, Betty, I would rather cut my finger than do you ony scaith,[1] for I like you so weel—I canna tell you how weel; but, if ye'll tak me, I'll mak you the Leddy o' the Plealands in a jiffy, and my mother says that my father will gie me a hundred pound to buy you parapharnauls and new plenishing.'[2]

The young lady was probably conciliated by the manner in which this was said; for she approached towards him, and while still affecting to laugh, it was manifest even to Walter himself that she was not displeased by the alacrity with which he had come to the point. Emboldened by her freedom, he took her by the hand, looking, however, away from her, as if he was not aware of what he had done; and in this situation they stood for the space of two or three minutes without speaking. Miss Betty was the first to break silence:—

'Weel, Watty,' said she, 'what are ye going to say to me?'

'Na,' replied he, becoming almost gallant; 'it's your turn to speak noo. I hae spoken my mind, Betty Bodle—Eh! this is a bonny hand; and what a sonsy[3] arm ye hae—I could amaist[4] bite your cheek, Betty Bodle—I could.'

'Gude preserve me, Watty! ye're like a wud[5] dog.'

'An I were sae, I would worry you,' was his animated answer, while he turned round, and devoured her with kisses; a liberty which she instantaneously resented, by vigorously pushing him from her, and driving him down into her father's easy chair; his arm in the fall rubbing off half a score of the old gentleman's snuffy representatives.

But, notwithstanding this masculine effort of maiden modesty, Miss Betty really rejoiced in the ardent intrepidity of her lover, and said, merrily,

'I redde you, Watty, keep your distance; man and wife's man and wife; but I'm only Betty Bodle, and ye're but Watty Walkinshaw.'

'Od, Betty,' replied Watty, not more than half-pleased, as he rubbed his right elbow, which was hurt in the fall, 'ye're desperate strong, woman; and what were ye the waur o' a bit slaik o' a kiss?[1] Howsever, my bonny dawty,[2] we'll no cast out for a' that; for if ye'll just marry me, and I'm sure ye'll no get any body that can like you half so weel, I'll do any thing ye bid me, as sure's death I will—there's my hand, Betty Bodle, I will; and I'll buy you the bravest satin gown in a' Glasgow, wi' far bigger flowers on't than on any ane in a' Mrs Bailie Nicol Jarvie's aught.[3] And we'll live in the Plealands-house, and do nothing frae dawn to dark but shoo ane another[4] on a swing between the twa trees on the green; and I'll be as kind to you, Betty Bodle, as I can be, and buy you like-wise a side-saddle, and a poney to ride on; and when the winter comes, sowing the land wi' hailstones to grow frost and snaw, we'll sit cosily at the chumley-lug,[5] and I'll read you a chapter o' the Bible, or aiblins Patie and Roger,[6]—as sure's death I will, Betty Bodle.'

It would seem, indeed, that there is something exalting and inspiring in the tender passion; for the earnest and emphatic manner in which this was said gave a degree of energy to the countenance of Watty, that made him appear in the eyes of his sweetheart, to whom moral vigour was not an object of primary admiration, really a clever and effectual fellow.

'I'll be free wi' you, Watty,' was her answer; 'I dinna objek to tak you, but,' and she hesitated.—

'But what?' said Watty, still exalted above his wont.

'Ye maunna hurry the wedding oure soon.'

'Ye'll get your ain time, Betty Bodle, I'll promise you that,' was his soft answer; 'but when a bargain's struck, the sooner pay-ment's made the better; for, as the copy-line at the school says, "Delays are dangerous."'—So, if ye like, Betty, we can be bookit on Saturday, and cried, for the first time, on Sabbath, and syne, a second time next Lord's day, and the third time on the Sunday after, and marriet on the Tuesday following.'[7]

'I dinna think, Watty,' said she, laying her hand on his shoulder, 'that we need sic a fasherie o' crying.'[8]

'Then, if ye dinna like it, Betty Bodle, I'm sure neither do I, so we can be cried a' out on ae day,[9] and married on Monday, like my brother and Bell Fatherlans.'

What more might have passed, as the lovers had now come to a

perfect understanding with each other, it is needless to con-
jecture, as the return of the old gentlemen interrupted their conversation; so that, not to consume the precious time of our readers
with any unnecessary disquisition, we shall only say, that some
objection being stated by Grippy to the first Monday as a day too
early for the requisite settlements to be prepared, it was agreed
that the booking should take place, as Walter had proposed, on the
approaching Saturday, and that the banns should be published,
once, on the first Sunday, and twice on the next, and that the
wedding should be held on the Tuesday following.

CHAPTER XXVII

WHEN Charles and Isabella were informed that his brother and
Betty Bodle were to be bookit on Saturday, that is, their names
recorded, for the publication of the banns, in the books of the kirk-
session,—something like a gleam of light seemed to be thrown on
the obscurity which invested the motives of the old man's conduct.
They were perfectly aware of Walter's true character, and concluded, as all the world did at the time, that the match was entirely
of his father's contrivance; and they expected, when Walter's
marriage settlement came to be divulged, that they would then
learn what provision had been made for themselves. In the meantime, Charles made out the balance-sheet, as he had been desired,
and carried it in his pocket when he went on Saturday with his wife
to dine at Grippy.

The weather that day was mild for the season, but a thin grey
vapour filled the whole air, and saddened every feature of the landscape. The birds sat mute and ourie,[1] and the Clyde, increased by
recent upland rains, grumbled with the hoarseness of his wintry
voice. The solemnity of external nature awakened a sympathetic
melancholy in the minds of the young couple, as they walked
towards their father's, and Charles once or twice said that he felt
a degree of depression which he had never experienced before.

'I wish,' Isabella,' said he, 'that this business of ours were well
settled, for I begin, on your account, to grow anxious. I am not
superstitious; but I kenna what's in't—every now and then a
thought comes over me that I am no to be a long liver—I feel, as

it were, that I have na a firm grip of the world—a sma' shock, I doubt, would easily shake me off.'

'I must own,' replied his wife with softness, 'that we have both some reason to regret our rashness. I ought not to have been so weak as to feel the little hardships of my condition so acutely; but, since it is done, we must do our best to bear up against the anxiety that I really think you indulge too much. My advice is, that we should give up speaking about your father's intents, and strive, as well as we can, to make your income, whatever it is, serve us.'

'That's kindly said, my dear Bell, but you know that my father's no a man that can be persuaded to feel as we feel, and I would not be surprised were he to break up his partnership with me, and what should we then do?'

In this sort of anxious and domestic conversation, they approached towards Grippy-house, where they were met on the green in front by Margaret and George, who had not seen them since their marriage. Miss Meg, as she was commonly called, being at the time on a visit in Argyleshire with a family to whom their mother was related, the Campbells of Glengrowlmaghallochan,[1] and George was also absent on a shooting excursion with some of his acquaintance at the Plealands, the mansion-house of which happened to be then untenanted. Their reception by their brother and sister, especially by Miss Meg, was kind and sisterly, for although in many points she resembled her mother, she yet possessed much more warmth of heart.

The gratulations and welcomings being over, she gave a description of the preparations which had already commenced for Walter's wedding.

'Na, what would ye think,' said she, laughing, 'my father gied him ten pounds to gang intil Glasgow the day to buy a present for the bride, and ye'll hardly guess what he has sent her,—a cradle,— a mahogany cradle, shod wi' roynes,[2] that it may na waken the baby when its rocking.'

'But that would na tak all the ten pounds?' said Charles, diverted by the circumstance; 'what has he done wi' the rest?'

'He could na see any other thing to please him, so he tied it in the corner of his napkin, but as he was coming home flourishing it round his head, it happened to strike the crookit tree at the water side, and the whole tot o' the siller, eight guineas, three half-crowns, and eighteenpence, played whir[3] to the very middle o' the Clyde. He has na got the grief o' the loss greetten out yet.'[1]

Before there was time for any observation to be made on this misfortune, the bridegroom came out to the door, seemingly in high glee, crying, 'See what I hae gotten,' showing another note for ten pounds, which his father had given to pacify him, before Kilmarkeckle and the bride arrived; they being also expected to dinner.

It happened that Isabella, dressed in her gayest apparel for this occasion, had brought in her hand, wrapt in paper, a pair of red Morocco shoes, which, at that period, were much worn among lairds' daughters; for the roads, being deep and sloughy, she had, according to the fashion of the age, walked in others of a coarser kind; and Walter's eye accidentally lighting on the shoes, he went up, without preface, to his sister-in-law, and, taking the parcel gently out of her hand, opened it, and contemplating the shoes, holding one in each hand at arm's length, said, 'Bell Fatherlans, what will ye tak to sell thir bonny red cheeket shoon?[2] — I would fain buy them for Betty Bodle.'

Several minutes elapsed before it was possible to return any answer; but when composure was in some degree regained, Mrs Charles Walkinshaw said, —

'Ye surely would never buy old shoes for your bride? I have worn them often. It would be an ill omen to give her a second-hand present, Mr Walter; besides, I don't think they would fit.'

This little incident had the effect of tuning the spirits of Charles and his wife into some degree of unison with the main business of the day; and the whole party entered the house bantering and laughing with Walter. But scarcely had they been seated, when their father said, —

'Charlie, has t'ou brought the balance-sheet, as I bade thee?'

This at once silenced both his mirth and Isabella's, and the old man expressed his satisfaction on receiving it, and also that the profits were not less than he expected.

Having read it over carefully, he then folded it slowly up, and put it into his pocket, and, rising from his seat, walked three or four times across the room, followed by the eyes of his beating-hearted son and daughter-in-law — at last he halted.

'Weel, Charlie,' said he, 'I'll no be waur[3] than my word to thee — t'ou sall hae a'[4] the profit made between us since we came thegither in the shop; that will help to get some bits o' plenishing for a house—and I'll mak, for time coming, an eke[1] to thy share. But, Charlie and Bell, ca' canny;[2] bairns will rise among you, and ye maun bear in mind that I hae baith Geordie and Meg to provide for yet.'

This was said in a fatherly manner, and the intelligence was in so many respects agreeable, that it afforded the anxious young couple great pleasure. Walter was not, however, satisfied at hearing no allusion to him, and he said,—

'And are ye no gaun to do any thing for me, father?'

These words, like the cut of a scourge, tingled to the very soul of the old man, and he looked with a fierce and devouring eye at the idiot;—but said nothing. Walter was not, however, to be daunted; setting up a cry, something between a wail and a howl, he brought his mother flying from the kitchen, where she was busy assisting the maids in preparing dinner—to inquire what had befallen the bridegroom.

'My father's making a step-bairn[3] o' me, mother, and has gi'en Charlie a' the outcome frae the till, and says he's gaun to hain but for[4] Geordie and Meg.'

'Surely, gudeman,' said the Leddy o' Grippy, addressing her husband, who for a moment stood confounded at this obstreperous accusation—'Surely ye'll hae mair naturality than no to gi'e Watty a bairn's part o' gear?[5] Has na he a right to share and share alike wi' the rest, over and aboon what he got by my father? If there's law, justice, or gospel in the land, ye'll be obligated to let him hae his right, an I should sell my coat to pay the cost.'

The old man made no answer; and his children sat in wonder, for they inferred from his silence that he actually did intend to make a step-bairn of Watty.

'Weel;' said the Leddy emphatically, 'but I jealoused[6] something o' this;—I kent there could be nae good at the bottom o' that huggermuggering wi' Keelevin. Hows'ever, I'll see til't,[7] Watty, and I'll gar him tell what he has put intil that abomination o' a paper that ye were deluded to sign.'

Claud, at these words, started from his seat, with the dark face, and pale quivering lips of guilt and vengeance; and, giving a stamp with his foot that shook the whole house, cried,—

'If ye daur to mak or meddle[8] wi' what I hae done.'—

He paused for about the space of half a minute, and then he

added, in his wonted calm and sober voice,—'Watty, t'ou has been
provided more—I hae done mair for thee than I can weel excuse
to mysel—and I charge baith thee and thy mother never, on pain
of my curse and everlasting ill-will, to speak ony sic things again.'

'What hae ye done? canna ye tell us, and gie a bodie[1] a satisfaction?' exclaimed the Leddy.

But the wrath again mustered and lowered in his visage, and
he said, in a voice so deep and dreadful, so hollow and so troubled,
from the very innermost caverns of his spirit, that it made all
present tremble,—

'Silence, woman, silence.'

'Eh! there's Betty Bodle and her father,' exclaimed Watty, casting his eyes, at that moment, towards the window, and rushing
from his seat, with an extravagant flutter, to meet them, thus
happily terminating a scene which threatened to banish the
anticipated festivity and revels of the day.

CHAPTER XXVIII

LEDDY GRIPPY having been, as she herself observed, 'cheated
baith o' bridal and infare[2] by Charlie's moonlight marriage,' was
resolved to have all made up to her, and every jovial and auspicious
rite performed at Walter's wedding.—Accordingly, the interval
between the booking[3] and the day appointed for the ceremony
was with her all bustle and business. Nor were the preparations at
Kilmarkeckle to send forth the bride in proper trim, in any degree
less active or liberal. Among other things, it had been agreed that
each of the two families should kill a cow for the occasion, but an
accident rendered this unnecessary at Grippy.

At this time, Kilmarkeckle and Grippy kept two bulls who
cherished the most deadly hatred of each other, in so much, that
their respective herds had the greatest trouble to prevent them
from constantly fighting. And on the Thursday preceding the
wedding-day, Leddy Grippy, in the multitude of her cares and
concerns, having occasion to send a message to Glasgow, and,
unable to spare any of the other servants, called the cow-boy from
the field, and dispatched him on the errand. Bausy, as their bull
was called, taking advantage of his keeper's absence, went muttering

and growling for some time round the inclosure, till at last discovering a gap in the hedge, he leapt through, and, flourishing his tail, and grumbling as hoarse as an earthquake, he ran, breathing wrath and defiance, straight on towards a field beyond where Gurl, Kilmarkeckle's bull, was pasturing in the most conjugal manner with his sultanas.

Gurl knew the voice of his foe, and, raising his head from the grass, bellowed a hoarse and sonorous answer to the challenger, and, in the same moment, scampered to the hedge, on the outside of which Bausy was roaring his threats of vengeance and slaughter. The two adversaries glared for a moment at each other, and then galloped along the sides of the hedge in quest of an opening through which they might rush to satisfy their rage.

In the meantime, Kilmarkeckle's herd-boy had flown to the house for assistance, and Miss Betty, heading all the servants, and armed with a flail, came, at double quick time, to the scene of action. But, before she could bring up her forces, Bausy burst headlong through the hedge, like a hurricane. Gurl, however, received him with such a thundering batter on the ribs, that he fell reeling from the shock. A repetition of the blow laid him on the ground, gasping and struggling with rage, agony, and death, so that, before the bride and her allies were able to drive Gurl from his fallen antagonist, he had gored and fractured him in almost every bone with the force and strength of the beam of a steam-engine. Thus was Leddy Grippy prevented from killing the cow which she had allotted for the wedding-feast, the carcase of Bausy being so unexpectedly substituted.

But, saving this accident, nothing went amiss in the preparations for the wedding either at Grippy or Kilmarkeckle. All the neighbours were invited, and the most joyous anticipations universally prevailed; even Claud himself seemed to be softened from the habitual austerity which had for years gradually encrusted his character, and he partook of the hilarity of his family, and joked with the Leddy in a manner so facetious, that her spirits mounted, and, as she said herself, 'were flichtering¹ in the very air.'

The bridegroom alone, of all those who took any interest in the proceedings, appeared thoughtful and moody; but it was impossible that any lover could be more devoted to his mistress: from morning to night he hovered round the skirts of her father's mansion, and as often as he got a peep of her, he laughed, and then hastily retired, wistfully looking behind, as if he hoped that she would follow. Sometimes this manœuvre proved successful, and Miss Betty permitted him to encircle her waist with his arm, as they ranged the fields in amatory communion together.

This, although perfectly agreeable to their happy situation, was not at all times satisfactory to his mother; and she frequently chided Watty for neglecting the dinner hour, and 'curdooing,'[1] as she said, 'under cloud o' night.' However, at last every preparatory rite but the feet-washing[2] was performed; and that it also might be accomplished according to the most mirthful observance of the ceremony at that period, Charles and George brought out from Glasgow, on the evening prior to the wedding-day, a score of their acquaintance to assist in the operation on the bridegroom; while Miss Meg, and all the maiden friends of the bride, assembled at Kilmarkeckle to officiate there. But when the hour arrived, Watty was absent. During the mixing of a large bowl of punch, at which Charles presided, he had slily escaped, and not answering to their summons, they were for some time surprised, till it was suggested that possibly he might have gone to the bride, whither they agreed to follow him.

Meanwhile the young ladies had commenced their operations with Miss Betty. The tub, the hot water, and the ring, were all in readiness; her stockings were pulled off, and loud laughter and merry scuffling, and many a freak of girlish gambol was played, as they rubbed her legs, and winded their fingers through the water to find the ring of Fortune, till a loud exulting neigh of gladness at the window at once silenced their mirth.

The bride raised her eyes; her maidens turning round from the tub, looked towards the window, where they beheld Watty standing, his white teeth and large delighted eyes glittering in the light of the room. It is impossible to describe the consternation of the ladies at this profane intrusion on their peculiar mysteries. The bride was the first that recovered her self-possession: leaping from her seat, and over-setting the tub in her fury, she bounded to the door, and, seizing Watty by the cuff of the neck, shook him as a tygress would a buffalo.

'The deevil ride a hunting on you, Watty Walkinshaw, I'll gar you glower in at windows,' was her endearing salutation, seconded by the whole vigour of her hand in a smack on the face, so impressive, that it made him yell till the very echoes yelled again. 'Gang

hame wi' you, ye roaring bull o' Bashen, or I'll take a rung[1] to
your back,' then followed; and the terrified bridegroom instantly
fled coweringly, as if she actually was pursuing him with a staff.

'I trow,' said she, addressing herself to the young ladies who
had come to the door after her, 'I'll learn him better manners,
before he's long in my aught.'[2]

'I would be none surprised were he to draw back,' said Miss
Jenny Shortridge, a soft and diffident girl, who, instead of joining in the irresistible laughter of her companions, had continued
silent, and seemed almost petrified.

'Poo!' exclaimed the bride; 'he draw back! Watty Walkinshaw
prove false to me! He dare na, woman, for his very life; but, come,
let us gang in and finish the fun.'

But the fun had suffered a material abatement by the breach
which had thus been made in it. Miss Meg Walkinshaw, however,
had the good luck to find the ring, a certain token that she would be
the next married.

In the meantime, the chastised bridegroom, in running homeward, was met by his brothers and their companions, to whose
merriment he contributed quite as much as he had subtracted
from that of the ladies, by the sincerity with which he related
what had happened,—declaring, that he would rather stand in the
kirk[3] than tak Betty Bodle; which determination Charles, in the
heedlessness and mirth of the moment, so fortified and encouraged,
that, before they had returned back to the punch-bowl, Walter
was swearing that neither father nor mother would force him to
marry such a dragoon. The old man seemed more disturbed than
might have been expected from his knowledge of the pliancy of
Walter's disposition at hearing him in this humour, while the
Leddy said, with all the solemnity suitable to her sense of the
indignity which her favourite had suffered,—

'Biting and scarting[4] may be Scotch folks wooing; but, if that's
the gait[5] Betty Bodle means to use you, Watty, my dear, I would
see her, and a' the Kilmarkeckles that ever were cleckit,[6] doon the
water, or strung in a wooddie,[7] before I would hae ony thing to
say to ane come o' their seed or breed. To lift her hands to her
bridegroom!—The like o't was never heard tell o' in a Christian
land—Na, gudeman, nane o' your winks and glooms[8] to me,—
I will speak out. She's a perfect drum-major,—the randy cutty[9]—
deevil-do-me good o' her—it's no to seek what I'll gie her the morn.'

'Dinna grow angry, mother,' interposed Walter, thawing, in some degree, from the sternness of his resentment. 'It was na a very sair knock after a'.'

'T'ou's a fool and a sumph to say any thing about it, Watty,' said Grippy himself; 'many a brawer lad has met wi' far waur; and, if t'ou had na been egget[1] on by Charlie to mak a complaint, it would just hae passed like a pat for true love.'

'Eh na, father, it was na a pat, but a scud like the clap o' a fir deal,'[2] said the bridegroom.

'Weel, wccl, Watty,' exclaimed Charlie, 'you must just put up wi't, ye're no a penny the waur o't.'[3] By this sort of conversation Walter was in the end pacified, and reconciled to his destiny.

CHAPTER XXIX

NEVER did Nature show herself better pleased on any festival than on Walter's wedding-day. The sun shone out as if his very rays were as much made up of gladness as of light. The dew-drops twinkled as if instinct with pleasure. The birds lilted—the waters and the windows sparkled; cocks crowed as if they were themselves bridegrooms, and the sounds of laughing girls, and cackling hens, made the riant banks of the Clyde joyful for many a mile.

It was originally intended that the minister should breakfast at Kilmarkcckle, to perform the ceremony there; but this, though in accordance with newer and genteeler fashions, was overruled by the young friends of the bride and bridegroom insisting that the wedding should be celebrated with a ranting dance and supper worthy of the olden, and, as they told Leddy Grippy, better times. Hence the liberality of the preparations, as intimated in the preceding chapter.

In furtherance of this plan, the minister, and all his family, were invited, and it was arranged, that the ceremony should not take place till the evening, when the whole friends of the parties, with the bride and bridegroom at their head, should walk in procession after the ceremony from the manse to Grippy, where the barn, by the fair hands of Miss Meg and her companions, was garnished and garlanded for the ball and banquet. Accordingly, as the marriage hour drew near, and as it had been previously concerted by 'the best men' on both sides, a numerous assemblage of the guests took place, both at Grippy and Kilmarkeckle—and, at the time appointed, the two parties, respectively carrying with them the bride and bridegroom, headed by a piper playing 'Hey let us a' to the bridal,' proceeded to the manse, where they were met by their worthy parish pastor at the door.

The Reverend Doctor Denholm was one of those old estimable stock characters of the best days of the presbytery, who, to great learning and sincere piety, evinced an inexhaustible fund of couthy[1] jocularity. He was far advanced in life, an aged man, but withal hale and hearty, and as fond of an innocent ploy, such as a wedding or a christening, as the blithest spirit in its teens of any lad or lass in the parish. But he was not quite prepared to receive so numerous a company; nor, indeed, could any room in the manse have accommodated half the party. He, therefore, proposed to perform the ceremony under the great tree, which sheltered the house from the south-west wind in winter, and afforded shade and shelter to all the birds of summer that ventured to trust themselves beneath its hospitable boughs. To this, however, Walter, the bridegroom, seemed disposed to make some objection, alleging that it might be a very good place for field-preaching, or for a tent on sacramental occasions, 'but it was an unco like thing to think of marrying folk under the canopy of the heavens; adding, that he did na think it was canny[2] to be married under a tree.'

The Doctor soon, however, obviated this objection, by assuring him that Adam and Eve had been married under a tree.

'Gude keep us a' frae sic a wedding as they had,' replied Watty; 'where the deil was best-man? Howsever, Doctor, sin it's no an apple-tree, I'll mak a conformity.' At which the pipes again struck up, and, led by the worthy Doctor bare-headed, the whole assemblage proceeded to the spot.

'Noo, Doctor,' said the bridegroom, as all present were composing themselves to listen to the religious part of the ceremony— 'Noo, Doctor, dinna scrimp the prayer, but tie a sicker[3] knot; I hae nae broo o'[4] the carnality o' five minute marriages, like the Glasgowers, and ye can weel afford to gie us half an hour, 'cause ye're weel payt for the wind o' your mouth: the hat and gloves I sent you cost me four-and-twenty shillings, clean countit out to my brother Charlie, that would na in his niggerality faik[5] me a saxpence on a' the liveries I bought frae him.'

This address occasioned a little delay, but order being again restored, the Reverend Doctor, folding his hands together, and lowering his eyelids, and assuming his pulpit voice, began the prayer.

It was a calm and beautiful evening, the sun at the time appeared to be resting on the flaky amber that adorned his western throne, to look back on the world, as if pleased to see the corn and the fruits gathered, with which he had assisted to fill the wide lap of the matronly earth. We happened at the time to be walking alone towards Blantyre,[1] enjoying the universal air of contentment with which all things at the golden sunsets of autumn invites the anxious spirit of man to serenity and repose. As we approached the little gate that opened to the footpath across the glebe by which the road to the village was abridged to visitors on foot, our attention was first drawn towards the wedding party, by the kindly, pleasing, deep-toned voice of the venerable pastor, whose solemn murmurs rose softly into the balmy air, diffusing all around an odour of holiness that sweetened the very sense of life.

We paused, and uncovering, walked gently and quietly towards the spot, which we reached just as the worthy Doctor had bestowed the benediction. The bride looked blushing and expectant, but Walter, instead of saluting her in the customary manner, held her by the hand at arm's length, and said to the Doctor, 'Be served.'

'Ye should kiss her, bridegroom,' said the minister.

'I ken that,' replied Watty, 'but no till my betters be served. Help yoursel, Doctor.'

Upon which the Doctor, wiping his mouth with the back of his hand, enjoyed himself as he was requested.

'It's the last buss,' added Walter, 'it's the last buss, Betty Bodle, ye'll e'er gie to mortal man while am your gudeman.'

'I did na think,' said the Reverend Doctor aside to us, 'that the creature had sic a knowledge o' the vows.'

The pipes at this crisis being again filled, the guests, hand in hand, following the bridegroom and bride, then marched to the ornamented barn at Grippy, to which we were invited to follow; but what then ensued deserves a new Chapter.

CHAPTER XXX

HAVING accepted the invitation to come with the minister's family to the wedding, we stopped and took tea at the manse with the Reverend Doctor and Mrs Denholm,—the young ladies and their brother having joined the procession. For all our days we have been naturally of a most sedate turn of mind; and although then but in our twenty-third year,[1] we preferred the temperate good humour of the Doctor's conversation, and the householdry topics of his wife, to the boisterous blair of the bagpipes. As soon, however, as tea was over, with Mrs Denholm dressed in her best, and the pastor in his newest suit, we proceeded towards Grippy.

By this time the sun was set, but the speckless topaz of the western skies diffused a golden twilight, that tinged every object with a pleasing mellow softness. Like the wedding-ring of a bashful bride, the new moon just showed her silver rim, and the evening star was kindling her lamp, as we approached the foot of the avenue which led to the house, the windows of which sparkled with festivity; while from the barn the merry yelps of two delighted fiddles, and the good-humoured grumbling of a well pleased bass, mingling with laughter and squeaks, and the thudding of bounding feet, made every pulse in our young blood circle as briskly as the dancers in their reeling.

When we reached the door, the moment that the venerable minister made his appearance, the music stopped, and the dancing was suspended, by which we were enabled to survey the assembly for a few minutes, in its most composed and ceremonious form. At the upper end of the barn stood two arm chairs, one of which, appropriated to the bridegroom, was empty; in the other sat the bride, panting from the vigorous efforts she had made in the reel that was interrupted by our entrance. The bridegroom himself was standing near a table close to the musicians, stirring a large punch-bowl, and filling from time to time the glasses. His father sat in a corner by himself, with his hands leaning on his staff, and his lips firmly drawn together, contemplating the scene before him with a sharp but thoughtful eye. Old Kilmarkeckle, with an ivory snuff-box, mounted with gold, in his hand, was sitting with Mr Keelevin on the left hand of Claud, evidently explaining some remarkable property in the flavour of the snuff, to which the honest lawyer was paying the utmost attention, looking at the philosophical Laird, however, every now and then, with a countenance at once expressive of admiration, curiosity, and laughter. Leddy Grippy sat on the left of the bride, apparelled in a crimson satin gown, made for the occasion, with a stupendous fabric of gauze and catgut, adorned with vast convolutions of broad red ribbons for a head-dress, and a costly French shawl, primly pinned open, to show her embroidered stomacher. At her side sat the meek and beautiful Isabella, like a primrose within the shadow of a peony; and on Isabella's left the aged Lady Plealands, neatly dressed in white silk, with a close cap of black lace, black silk mittens, and a rich black apron. But we must not attempt thus to describe all the guests, who, to the number of nearly a hundred, young and old, were seated in various groups around the sides of the barn; for our attention was drawn to Milrookit, the Laird of Dirdumwhamle, a hearty widower for the second time, about forty-five—he might be older—who, cozily in a corner, was engaged in serious courtship with Miss Meg.

When the formalities of respect, with which Doctor Denholm was so properly received, had been duly performed, the bridegroom bade the fiddlers again play up, and, going towards the minister, said, 'Do ye smell ony thing gude, Sir?'

'No doubt, bridegroom,' replied the Doctor, 'I canna be insensible to the pleasant savour of the supper.'

'Come here, then,' rejoined Watty, 'and I'll show you a sight would do a hungry body good—weel I wat my mother has na spared her skill and spice.'—In saying which, he lifted aside a carpet that had been drawn across the barn like a curtain behind the seats at the upper end of the ball-room, and showed him the supper table, on which about a dozen men and maid-servants were in the act of piling joints and pyes that would have done credit to the Michaelmas dinner of the Glasgow magistrates—'Is na that a gallant banquet?' said Watty—'Look at yon braw pastry pye wi' the King's crown on't.'

The Reverend Pastor declared that it was a very edificial structure, and he had no doubt it was as good as it looked—'Would ye like to pree't,[1] Doctor? I'll just nip off ane o' the pearlies on the crown to let you taste how good it is. It'll never be missed.'

The bride, who overheard part of this dialogue, started up at these words, and as Walter was in the act of stretching forth his hand to plunder the crown, she pulled him by the coat-tail, and drew him into the chair appropriated for him, sitting down, at the same time, in her own on his left, saying, in an angry whisper,— 'Are ye fou'[1] already, Watty Walkinshaw? If ye mudge out o' that seat again this night, I'll mak you as sick o' pyes and puddings as ever a dog was o' het kail.'[2]

Nothing more particular happened before supper; and every thing went off at the banquet as mirthfully as on any similar occasion. The dancing was then resumed, and during the bustle and whirl of the reels, the bride and bridegroom were conducted quietly to the house to be bedded.

When they were undressed, but before the stocking was thrown, we got a hint from Charles to look at the bridal chamber, and accordingly ran with him to the house, and bolting into the room, beheld the happy pair sitting up in bed, with white napkins drawn over their heads like two shrouds, and each holding one of their hands, so as to conceal entirely their modest and downcast faces. But, before we had time to say a word, the minister, followed by the two pipers, and the best-men and bride's-maids, bringing posset and cake, came in,—and while the distribution, with the customary benedictions, was going forward, dancing was recommenced in the bed-room.

How it happened, or what was the cause, we know not; but the dancing continued so long, and was kept up with so much glee, that somehow, by the crowded state of the apartment, the young pair in bed were altogether forgotten, till the bridegroom, tired with sitting so long like a mummy, lost all patience, and, in a voice of rage and thunder, ordered every man and mother's son instantly to quit the room,—a command which he as vehemently repeated with a menace of immediate punishment,—putting, at the same time, one of his legs out of bed, and clenching his fist, in the act of rising. The bride cowered in giggling beneath the coverlet, and all the other ladies, followed by the men and the pipers, fled pell-mell, and hurly-burly, glad to make their escape.

CHAPTER XXXI

WHEN Claud first proposed the marriage to Kilmarkeckle, it was intended that the young couple should reside at Plealands; but an opportunity had occurred, in the meantime, for Mr Keelevin to intimate to Mr Auchincloss, the gentleman who possessed the two farms, which, with the Grippy, constituted the ancient estate of Kittlestonheugh, that Mr Walkinshaw would be glad to make an excambio[1] with him, and not only give Plealands, but even a considerable inducement in money. This proposal, particularly the latter part of it, was agreeable to Mr Auchincloss, who, at the time, stood in want of ready money to establish one of his sons in the Virginia trade;[2] and, in consequence, the negotiation was soon speedily brought to a satisfactory termination.

But, in this affair, Grippy did not think fit to confer with any of his sons. He was averse to speak to Charles on the subject, possibly from some feeling connected with the deed of entail; and, it is unnecessary to say, that, although Walter was really principal in the business, he had no regard for what his opinion might be. The consequence of which was, that the bridegroom was not a little amazed to find, next day, on proposing to ride the Brous,[3] to his own house at Plealands, and to hold the Infare[4] there, that it was intended to be assigned to Mr Auchincloss, and that, as soon as his family were removed thither, the house of Divethill, one of the exchanged farms, would be set in order for him in its stead.

The moment that this explanation was given to Walter, he remembered the parchments which he had signed, and the agitation of his father on the way home, and he made no scruple of loudly and bitterly declaring, with many a lusty sob, that he was cheated out of his inheritance by his father and Charles. The old man was confounded at this view which the Natural plausibly enough took of the arrangement; but yet, anxious to conceal from his first-born the injustice with which he had used him in the entail, he at first attempted to silence Walter by threats, and then to cajole him with promises, but without effect; at last, so high did the conflict rise between them, that Leddy Grippy and Walter's wife came into the room to inquire what had happened.

'O Betty Bodle!' exclaimed Walter, the moment he saw them;

'what are we to do? My father has beguiled me o' the Plealands, and I hae neither house nor ha' to tak you to. He has gart me wise it awa[1] to Charlie, and we'll hae nathing as lang as Kilmarkeckle lives, but scant and want and beggary. It's no my fau't, Betty Bodle, that ye'll hae to work for your daily bread, the sin o't a' is my father's. But I'll help you a' I can, Betty, and if ye turn a washerwoman on the Green of Glasgow,[2] I'll carry your boynes, and water your claes,[3] and watch them, that ye may sleep when ye're weary't, Betty Bodle,—for though he's a false father, I'll be a true gudeman.'

Betty Bodle sat down in a chair, with her back to the window, and Walter, going to her, hung over her with an air of kindness, which his simplicity rendered at once affecting and tender; while Leddy Grippy, petrified by what she heard, also sat down, and, leaning herself back in her seat, with a look of amazement, held her arms streaked[4] down by her side, with all her fingers stretched and spread to the utmost. Claud, himself, was for a moment overawed, and had almost lost his wonted self-possession, at the just accusation of being a false father; but, exerting all his firmness and fortitude, he said calmly,—

'I canna bear this at thy hand, Watty. I hae secured for thee far mair than the Plealands; and is the satisfaction that I thought to hae had this day, noo when I hae made a conquest of the lands o' my forefathers, to be turned into sadness and bitterness o' heart?'

'What hae ye secur'd?' exclaimed Leddy Grippy. 'Is na it ordaint that Charlie, by his birthright,[5] will get your lands? How is't then that ye hae wrang't Watty of his ain? the braw property that my worthy father left him both by will and testament. An he had been to the fore,[6] ye durst na, gudeman, hae played at sic jookery pookery; for he had a skill o' law, and kent the kittle points[7] in a manner that ye can never fathom; weel wat I, that your ellwand would hae been a jimp measure to the sauvendie o' his books and Latin taliations.[8] But, gudeman, ye's no get a' your ain way.[9] I'll put on my cloak, and, Betty Bodle, put on yours, and Watty, my ill-used bairn, get your hat. We'll oure for[10] Kilmarkeckle, and gang a' to Mr Keelevin together to make an interlocutor[11] about this most dreadful extortioning.'

The old man absolutely shuddered; his face became yellow, and his lips white with anger and vexation at this speech.

'Girzy Hypel,' said he, with a troubled and broken voice, 'were t'ou a woman o' understanding, or had t'at haverel get[1] o' thine the gumshion o' a sucking turkey, I could speak, and confound your injustice, were I no restrained by a sense of my own shame.'

'But what's a' this stoor[2] about?' said the young wife, addressing herself to her father-in-law. 'Surely ye'll no objek to mak me the wiser?'

'No, my dear,' replied Claud, 'I hope I can speak and be understood by thee. I hae gotten Mr Auchincloss to mak an excambio of the Divethill for the Plealands, by the whilk the whole of the Kittlestonheugh patrimony will be redeemed to the family; and I intend and wis you and Watty to live at the Divethill, our neighbours here, and your father's neighbours, that, my bairn, io the whole straemash.'[3]

'But,' said she, 'when ye're dead, will we still hae the Divethill?'

'No doubt o' that, my dawty,' said the old man delighted; 'and even far mair.'

'Then, Watty Walkinshaw, ye gaumeril,'[4] said she, addressing her husband, 'what would ye be at?—Your father's a most just man, and will do you and a' his weans[5] justice.'

'But, for a' that,' said Leddy Grippy to her husband, somewhat bamboozled by the view which her daughter-in-law seemed to take of the subject,—

'When will we hear o' you giving hundreds o' pounds to Watty, as ye did to Charlie, for a matrimonial hansel?'

'I'm sure,' replied the Laird, 'were the like o' that to quiet thy unruly member, Girzy, and be any satisfaction to thee, that I hae done my full duty to Walter, a five score pound should na be wanting to stap[6] up the gap.'

'I'll tell you what it is, father,' interrupted Walter, 'if ye'll gie the whole soom o' a hundre pound, I care na gin ye mak drammock[7] o' the Plealands.'

'A bargain be't,' said Claud, happy to be relieved from their importunity; but he added, with particular emphasis, to Watty's wife,—

'Dinna ye tak ony care about what's passed; the Divethill's a good excambio for the Plealands, and it sall be bound as stiffly as law and statute can tether to you and your heirs by Walter.'

Thus so far Grippy continued to sail before the wind, and, perhaps, in the steady pursuit of his object, he met with as few serious obstacles as most adventurers. What sacrifice of internal feeling he may have made, may be known hereafter. In the mean time, the secrets and mysteries of his bosom were never divulged; but all his thoughts and anxieties as carefully hidden from the world as if the disclosure of them would have brought shame on himself. Events, however, press; and we must proceed with the current of our history.

CHAPTER XXXII

ALTHOUGH Claud had accomplished the great object of all his strivings, and although, from the Divethill, where the little castle of his forefathers once stood, he could contemplate the whole extent of the Kittlestonheugh estate, restored, as he said, to the Walkinshaws, and by his exertions, there was still a craving void in his bosom that yearned to be satisfied. He felt as if the circumstance of Watty having a legal interest in the property, arising from the excambio for the Plealands, made the conquest less certainly his own than it might have been, and this lessened the enjoyment of the self-gratulation with which he contemplated the really proud eminence to which he had attained.

But keener feelings and harsher recollections were also mingled with that regret; and a sentiment of sorrow, in strong affinity with remorse, embittered his meditations, when he thought of the precipitancy with which he had executed the irrevocable entail, to the exclusion of Charles; to whom, prior to that unjust transaction, he had been more attached than to any other human being. It is true, that, when he adopted that novel resolution, he had, at the same time, appeased his conscience with intentions to indemnify his unfortunate first-born; but in this, he was not aware of the mysteries of the heart, nor that there was a latent spring in his breast, as vigorous and elastic in its energy, as the source of that indefatigable perseverance by which he had accomplished so much.

The constant animadversions of his wife, respecting his partiality for Charles and undisguised contempt for Watty, had the effect of first awakening the powers of that dormant engine. They galled the sense of his own injustice, and kept the memory of it so continually before him, that, in the mere wish not to give her cause to vex him for his partiality, he estranged himself from Charles in such a manner, that it was soon obvious and severely felt. Conscious that he had done him wrong,—aware that the wrong would probably soon be discovered,—and conscious, too, that this behaviour was calculated to beget suspicion, he began to dislike to see Charles, and alternately to feel in every necessary interview, as if he was no longer treated by him with the same respect as formerly. Still, however, there was so much of the leaven of original virtue in the composition of his paternal affection, and in the general frame of his character, that this disagreeable feeling never took the decided nature of enmity. He did not hate because he had injured, —he was only apprehensive of being upbraided for having betrayed hopes which he well knew his particular affection must have necessarily inspired.

Perhaps, had he not, immediately after Walter's marriage, been occupied with the legal arrangement consequent to an accepted proposal from Milrookit of Dirdumwhamle, to make Miss Meg his third wife, this apprehension might have hardened into animosity, and been exasperated to aversion; but the cares and affairs of that business came, as it were, in aid of the father in his nature, and while they seemingly served to excuse his gradually abridged intercourse with Charles and Isabella, they prevented such an incurable induration of his heart from taking place towards them, as the feelings at work within him had an undoubted tendency to produce. We shall not, therefore, dwell on the innumerable little incidents arising out of his estrangement, by which the happiness of that ill-fated pair was deprived of so much of its best essence,—contentment,—and their lives, with the endearing promise of a family, embittered by anxieties of which it would be as difficult to describe the importance, as to give each of them an appropriate name.

In the meantime, the marriage of Miss Meg was consummated, and we have every disposition to detail the rites and the revels, but they were all managed in a spirit so much more moderate than Walter's wedding, that the feast would seem made up but of the cold bake-meats of the former banquet. Indeed, Mr Milrookit, the bridegroom, being, as Leddy Grippy called him, a waster of wives, having had two before, and who knows how many more he may have contemplated to have, it would not have been reasonable to expect that he should allow such a free-handed junketting as took place on that occasion. Besides this, the dowry with Grippy's daughter was not quite so liberal as he had expected; for when the old man was stipulating for her jointure, he gave him a gentle hint not to expect too much.

'Two hundred pounds a-year, Mr Milrookit,' said Grippy, 'is a bare eneugh sufficiency for my dochter; but I'll no be overly extortionate, sin it's no in my power, even noo, to gie you meikle in hand,[1] and I would na lead you to expek any great deal hereafter, for ye ken it has cost me a world o' pains and ettling[2] to gather the needful to redeem the Kittlestonheugh, the whilk maun ay gang[3] in the male line; but failing my three sons and their heirs, the entail gangs to the heirs general o' Meg, so that ye hae a' to-look in that airt;[4] that, ye maun alloo, is worth something. Howsever, I dinna objek to the two hundred pounds; but I would like an ye could throw a bit fifty tilt,[5] just as a cast o' the hand to mak lucky measure.'

'I would na begrudge that, Grippy,' replied the gausey[6] widower of Dirdumwhamle; 'but ye ken I hae a sma' family: the first Mrs Milrookit brought me sax sons, and the second had four, wi' five dochters. It's true that the bairns o' the last clecking[7] are to be provided for by their mother's uncle, the auld General wi' the gout at Lon'on; but my first family are dependent on mysel', for, like your Charlie, I made a calf-love marriage, and my father was na sae kind as ye hae been to him, for he put a' past me[8] that he could, and had he no deet amang hands in one o' his scrieds[9] wi' the Lairds o' Kilpatrick, I'm sure I canna think what would hae come o' me and my first wife. So you see, Grippy'—

'I wis, Dirdumwhamle,' interrupted the old man, 'that ye would either ca' me by name or Kittlestonheugh, for the Grippy's but a pendicle[10] o' the family property; and though, by reason o' the castle being ta'en down when my grandfather took a wadset[11] on't frae the public, we are obligated to live here in this house that was on the land when I made a conquest o't again, yet a' gangs noo[12] by the ancient name o' Kittlestonheugh, and a dochter of the Walkinshaws o' the same is a match for the best laird in the shire, though she had na ither tocher than her snood and cockernony.'[13]

'Weel, Kittlestonheugh,' replied Dirdumwhamle, 'I'll e'en mak it better than the twa hunder and fifty—I'll make it whole three hunder, if ye'll get a paction o' consent and conneevance wi' your auld son Charles, to pay to Miss Meg, or to the off-spring o' my marriage wi' her, a yearly soom during his liferent in the property, you yoursel' undertaking in your lifetime to be as good. I'm sure that's baith fair and a very great liberality on my side.'

Claud received this proposal with a convulsive gurgle of the heart's blood. It seemed to him, that, on every occasion, the wrong which he had done Charles was to be brought in the most offensive form before him, and he sat for the space of two or three minutes without making any reply; at last he said,—

'Mr Milrookit, I ne'er rue't[1] any thing in my life but the consequence of twa three het words that ance passed between me and my gudefather Plealands, anent our properties; and I hae lived to repent my obduracy. For this cause I'll say nae mair about an augmentation of the proposed jointure, but just get my dochter to put up wi' the two hundred pounds, hoping that hereafter, an ye can mak it better, she'll be none the waur of her father's confidence in you on this occasion.'

Thus was Miss Meg disposed of, and thus did the act of injustice which was done to one child operate, through the mazy feelings of the father's conscious spirit, to deter him, even in the midst of such sordid bargaining, not only from venturing to insist on his own terms, but even from entertaining a proposal which had for its object a much more liberal provision for his daughter than he had any reason, under all the circumstances, to expect.

CHAPTER XXXIII

SOON after the marriage of Miss Meg, George, the third son, and youngest of the family, was placed in the counting-house of one of the most eminent West Indian merchants at that period in Glasgow. This incident was in no other respect important in the history of the Lairds of Grippy, than as serving to open a career to George, that would lead him into a higher class of acquaintance than his elder brothers: for it was about this time that the general merchants of the royal city began to arrogate to themselves that aristocratic superiority over the shopkeepers, which they have since established into an oligarchy,[2] as proud and sacred, in what respects the reciprocities of society, as the famous Seignories of Venice and of Genoa.

In the character, however, of George, there was nothing

ostensibly haughty, or rather his pride had not shown itself in any strong colour, when he first entered on his mercantile career. Like his father, he was firm and persevering; but he wanted something of the old man's shrewdness; and there was more of avarice in his hopes of wealth than in the sordidness of his father, for they were not elevated by any such ambitious sentiment as that which prompted Claud to strive with such constancy for the recovery of his paternal inheritance. In fact, the young merchant, notwithstanding the superiority of his education and other advantages, we may safely venture to assert, was a more vulgar character than the old pedlar. But his peculiarities did not manifest themselves till long after the period of which we are now speaking.

In the meantime, every thing proceeded with the family much in the same manner as with most others. Claud and his wife had daily altercations about their household affairs. Charles and Isabella narrowed themselves into a small sphere, of which his grandmother, the venerable Lady Plealands, now above fourscore, was their principal associate, and their mutual affection was strengthened by the birth of a son. Walter and Betty Bodle resided at the Divethill; and they, too, had the prospect of adding, as a Malthusian[1] would say, to the mass of suffering mankind. The philosophical Kilmarkeckle continued his abstruse researches as successfully as ever into the affinities between snuff and the natures of beasts and birds, while the Laird of Dirdumwhamle and his Lady struggled on in the yoke together, as well as a father and stepmother, amidst fifteen children, the progeny of two prior marriages, could reasonably be expected to do, where neither party was particularly gifted with delicacy or forbearance. In a word, they all moved along with the rest of the world during the first twelve months, after the execution of the deed of entail, without experiencing any other particular change in their relative situations than those to which we have alluded.

But the epoch was now drawing near, when Mrs Walter Walkinshaw was required to prepare herself for becoming a mother, and her husband was no less interested than herself in the event. He did nothing for several months, from morning to night, but inquire how she felt herself, and contrive, in his affectionate simplicity, a thousand insufferable annoyances to one of her disposition, for the purpose of affording her ease and pleasure; all of which were either answered by a laugh, or a slap, as the humour of the moment dictated. Sometimes, when she, regardless of her maternal state, would, in walking to Grippy or Kilmarkeckle, take short cuts across the fields, and over ditches, and through hedges, he would anxiously follow her at a distance, and when he saw her in any difficulty to pass, he would run kindly to her assistance. More than once, at her jocular suggestion, he has lain down in the dry ditches to allow her to step across on his back. Never had wife a more loving or obedient husband. She was allowed in every thing, not only to please herself, but to make him do whatever she pleased; and yet, with all her whims and caprice, she proved so true and so worthy a wife, that he grew every day more and more uxorious.

Nor was his mother less satisfied with Betty Bodle. They enjoyed together the most intimate communion of minds on all topics of household economy; but it was somewhat surprising, that, notwithstanding the care and pains which the old leddy took to instruct her daughter-in-law in all the mysteries of the churn and cheesset,[1] Mrs Walter's butter was seldom fit for market, and the huxters of the royal city[2] never gave her near so good a price for her cheese as Leddy Grippy regularly received for hers, although, in the process of the making, they both followed the same recipes.

The conjugal felicities of Walter afforded, however, but little pleasure to his father. The obstreperous humours of his daughter-in-law jarred with his sedate dispositions, and in her fun and freaks[3] she so loudly showed her thorough knowledge of her husband's defective intellects, that it for ever reminded him of the probable indignation with which the world would one day hear of the injustice he had done to Charles. The effect of this gradually led him to shun the society of his own family, and having neither from nature nor habit any inclination for general company, he became solitary and morose. He only visited Glasgow once a week, on Wednesday, and generally sat about an hour in the shop, in his old elbow chair, in the corner; and, saving a few questions relative to the business, he abstained from conversing with his son. It would seem, however, that, under this sullen taciturnity, the love which he had once cherished for Charles still tugged at his heart; for, happening to come into the shop, on the morning after Isabella had made him a grandfather, by the birth of a boy, on being informed of that happy event, he shook his son warmly by the hand, and said, in a serious and impressive manner,—

'An it please God, Charlie, to gie thee ony mair childer, I redde thee, wi' the counsel o' a father, to mak na odds among them, but remember they are a' alike thine, and that t'ou canna prefer ane aboon anither¹ without sin;'—and he followed this admonition with a gifty of twenty pounds to buy the infant a christening frock.

But from that day he never spoke to Charles of his family; on the contrary, he became dark and more obdurate in his manner to every one around him. His only enjoyment seemed to be a sort of doating delight in contemplating, from a rude bench which he had constructed on a rising ground behind the house of Grippy, the surrounding fields of his forefathers. There he would sit for hours together alone, bending forward with his chin resting on the ivory head of his staff, which he held between his knees by both hands, and with a quick and eager glance survey the scene for a moment, and then drop his eyelids, and look only on the ground.

Whatever might be the general tenor of his reflections as he sat on that spot, they were evidently not always pleasant; for one afternoon, as he was sitting there, his wife, who came upon him suddenly and unperceived, to tell him a messenger was sent to Glasgow from Divethill for the midwife, she was surprised to find him agitated and almost in tears.

'Dear me, gudeman,' said she, 'what's come o'er you, that ye're sitting here hanging your gruntel² like a sow playing on a trump? Hae na ye heard that Betty Bodle's time's come? I'm gaun ower to the crying,³ and if ye like ye may walk that length wi' me. I hope, poor thing, she'll hae an easy time o't, and that we'll hae blithes-meat⁴ before the sun gangs doun.'

'Gang the gait thysel, Girzy Hypel,' said Claud, raising his head, 'and no fash me with thy clishmaclavers.'

'Heh, gudeman! but ye hae been eating sourrocks instead o' lang-kail.⁵ But e'ens ye like, Meg dorts, as Patie and Roger⁶ says, I can gang mysel';' and with that, whisking pettishly round, she walked away.

Claud being thus disturbed in his meditations, looked after her as she moved along the footpath down the slope, and for the space of a minute or two, appeared inclined to follow her, but relapsing into some new train of thought, before she had reached the bottom, he had again resumed his common attitude, and replaced his chin on the ivory head of his staff.

CHAPTER XXXIV

THERE are times in life when every man feels as if his sympathies were extinct. This arises from various causes; sometimes from vicissitudes of fortune; sometimes from the sense of ingratitude, which, like the canker in the rose, destroys the germ of all kindness and charity; often from disappointments in affairs of the heart, which leave it incapable of ever again loving; but the most common cause is the consciousness of having committed wrong, when the feelings recoil inward, and, by some curious mystery in the nature of our selfishness, instead of prompting atonement, irritate us to repeat and to persevere in our injustice.

Into one of these temporary trances Claud had fallen when his wife left him; and he continued sitting, with his eyes rivetted on the ground, insensible to all the actual state of life, contemplating the circumstances and condition of his children, as if he had no interest in their fate, nor could be affected by any thing in their fortunes.

In this fit of apathy and abstraction, he was roused by the sound of some one approaching; and on looking up, and turning his eyes towards the path which led from the house to the bench where he was then sitting, he saw Walter coming.

There was something unwonted in the appearance and gestures of Walter, which soon interested the old man. At one moment he rushed forward several steps, with a strange wildness of air. He would then stop and wring his hands, gaze upward, as if he wondered at some extraordinary phenomenon in the sky; but seeing nothing, he dropped his hands, and, at his ordinary pace, came slowly up the hill.

When he arrived within a few paces of the bench, he halted, and looked, with such an open and innocent sadness, that even the heart of his father, which so shortly before was as inert to humanity as case-hardened iron, throbbed with pity, and was melted to a degree of softness and compassion, almost entirely new to its sensibilities.

'What's the matter wi' thee, Watty?' said he, with unusual kindliness. The poor natural, however, made no reply,—but continued to gaze at him with the same inexpressible simplicity of grief.

'Hast t'ou lost ony thing, Watty?'—'I dinna ken,' was the answer, followed by a burst of tears.

'Surely something dreadfu' has befallen the lad,' said Claud to himself, alarmed at the astonishment of sorrow with which his faculties seemed to be bound up.

'Can t'ou no tell me what has happened, Watty?'

In about the space of half a minute, Walter moved his eyes slowly round, as if he saw and followed something which filled him with awe and dread. He then suddenly checked himself, and said, 'It's naething; she's no there.'

'Sit down beside me, Watty,' exclaimed his father, alarmed; 'sit down beside me, and compose thysel.'

Walter did as he was bidden, and stretching out his feet, hung forward in such a posture of extreme listlessness and helpless despondency, that all power of action appeared to be withdrawn.

Claud rose, and believing he was only under the influence of some of those silly passions to which he was occasionally subject, moved to go away, when he looked up, and said,—

'Father, Betty Bodle's dead!—My Betty Bodle's dead!'

'Dead!' said Claud, thunderstruck.

'Aye, father, she's dead! My Betty Bodle's dead!'

'Dost t'ou ken what t'ou's saying?'[1] But Walter, without attending to the question, repeated, with an accent of tenderness still more simple and touching,—

'My Betty Bodle's dead! She's awa up aboon the skies yon'er, and left me a wee wee baby;' in saying which, he again burst into tears, and rising hastily from the bench, ran wildly back towards the Divethill-house, whither he was followed by the old man, where the disastrous intelligence was confirmed, that she had died in giving birth to a daughter.

Deep and secret as Claud kept his feelings from the eyes of the world, this was a misfortune which he was ill prepared to withstand. For although in the first shock he betrayed no emotion, it was soon evident that it had shattered some of the firmest intents and purposes of his mind. That he regretted the premature death of a beautiful young woman in such interesting circumstances, was natural to him as a man; but he felt the event more as a personal disappointment, and thought it was accompanied with something so like retribution, that he inwardly trembled as if he had been chastised by some visible arm of Providence. For he could not disguise to himself that a female heir was a contingency he had not contemplated; that, by the catastrophe which had happened to the mother, the excambio of the Plealands for the Divethill would be rendered of no avail; and that, unless Walter married again, and had a son, the re-united Kittlestonheugh property must again be disjoined, as the Divethill would necessarily become the inheritance of the daughter.

The vexation of this was, however, alleviated, when he reflected on the pliancy of Walter's character, and he comforted himself with the idea, that, as soon as a reasonable sacrifice of time had been made to decorum, he would be able to induce the natural to marry again. Shall we venture to say, it also occurred in the cogitations of his sordid ambition, that, as the infant was prematurely born, and was feeble and infirm, he entertained some hope it might die, and not interfere with the entailed destination of the general estate? But if, in hazarding this harsh supposition, we do him any injustice, it is certain that he began to think there was something in the current of human affairs over which he could acquire no control, and that, although, in pursuing so steadily the single purpose of recovering his family inheritance, his endeavours had, till this period, proved eminently successful, he yet saw, with dismay, that, from the moment other interests came to be blended with those which he considered so peculiarly his own, other causes also came into operation, and turned, in spite of all his hedging and prudence, the whole issue of his labours awry. He perceived that human power was set at nought by the natural course of things, and nothing produced a more painful conviction of the wrong he had committed against his first-born, than the frustration of his wishes by the misfortune which had befallen Walter. His reflections were also embittered from another source; by his parsimony he foresaw that, in the course of a few years, he would have been able, from his own funds, to have redeemed the Divethill without having had recourse to the excambio; and that the whole of the Kittlestonheugh might thus have been his own conquest, and, as such, without violating any of the usages of society, he might have commenced the entail with Charles. In a word, the death of Walter's wife and the birth of the daughter disturbed all his schemes, and rent from roof to foundation the castles which he had been so long and so arduously building. But it is necessary that we should return to poor Walter, on whom the loss of his beloved Betty Bodle acted with the incitement of a new impulse, and produced a change of character that rendered him a far less tractable instrument than his father expected to find.

CHAPTER XXXV

THE sorrow of Walter, after he had returned home, assumed the appearance of a calm and settled melancholy. He sat beside the corpse with his hands folded and his head drooping. He made no answer to any question; but as often as he heard the infant's cry, he looked towards the bed, and said, with an accent of indescribable sadness, 'My Betty Bodle!'

When the coffin arrived, his mother wished him to leave the room, apprehensive, from the profound grief in which he was plunged, that he might break out into some extravagance of passion, but he refused; and, when it was brought in, he assisted with singular tranquillity in the ceremonial of the coffining. But when the lid was lifted and placed over the body, and the carpenter was preparing to fasten it down for ever, he shuddered for a moment from head to foot; and, raising it with his left hand, he took a last look of the face, removing the veil with his right, and touching the sunken cheek as if he had hoped still to feel some ember of life; but it was cold and stiff.

'She's clay noo,' said he.—'There's nane o' my Betty Bodle here.'

And he turned away with a careless air, as if he had no farther interest in the scene. From that moment his artless affections took another direction; he immediately quitted the death-room, and, going to the nursery where the infant lay asleep in the nurse's lap, he contemplated it for some time, and then, with a cheerful and happy look and tone, said,—'It's a wee Betty Bodle; and it's my Betty Bodle noo.' And all his time and thoughts were thenceforth devoted to this darling object, in so much that, when the hour of the funeral was near, and he was requested to dress himself to perform the husband's customary part in the solemnity, he refused, not only to quit the child, but to have any thing to do with the burial.

'I canna understand,' said he, 'what for a' this fykerie's about a lump o' yird? Sho'elt intil a hole, and no fash me.'[1]

'It's your wife, my lad,' replied his mother; 'ye'll surely never refuse to carry her head in a gudemanlike manner to the kirk-yard.'

'Na, na, mother, Betty Bodle's my wife, yon clod in the black kist[2] is but her auld boddice; and when she flang't off, she put on this bonny wee new cleiding[3] o' clay,' said he, pointing to the baby.

The Leddy, after some farther remonstrance, was disconcerted by the pertinacity with which he continued to adhere to his resolution, and went to beg her husband to interfere.

'Ye'll hae to gang ben, gudeman,' said she, 'and speak to Watty. —I wis the poor thing hasna gane by itsel[4] wi' a broken heart. He threeps[5] that the body is no his wife's, and ca's it a hateral[6] o' clay and stones, and says we may fling't, Gude guide us, ayont the midden for him.—We'll just be affrontit if he'll no carry the head.'

Claud, who had dressed himself in the morning for the funeral, was sitting in the elbow chair, on the right side of the chimney-place, with his cheek resting on his hand, and his eyelids dropped, but not entirely shut, and on being thus addressed, he instantly rose, and went to the nursery.

'What's t'ou doing there like a hussy-fellow?'[7] said he. 'Rise and get on thy mournings, and behave wise-like, and leave the bairn to the women.'

'It's my bairn,' replied Watty, 'and ye hae naething, father, to do wi't.—Will I no tak care o' my ain baby—my bonny wee Betty Bodle?'

'Do as I bid thee, or I'll maybe gar thee fin' the weight o' my staff,' cried the old man sharply, expecting immediate obedience to his commands, such as he always found, however positively Walter, on other occasions, at first refused; but in this instance he was disappointed; for the widower looked him steadily in the face, and said,—

'I'm a father noo; it would be an awfu' thing for a decent grey-headed man like you, father, to strike the head o' a motherless family.'

Claud was so strangely affected by the look and accent with which this was expressed, that he stood for some time at a loss what to say, but soon recovering his self-possession, he replied, in a mild and persuasive manner,—

'The frien's expek, Watty, that ye'll attend the burial, and carry the head, as the use and wont is in every weel-doing family.'

'It's a thriftless custom, father, and what care I for burial-bread and services o' wine? They cost siller, father, and I'll no wrang Betty Bodle for ony sic outlay on her auld yirden[1] garment. Ye may gang, for fashion's cause, wi' your weepers and your mourning strings, and lay the black kist i' the kirk-yard hole, but I'll no mudge the ba' o' my muckle tae[2] in ony sic road.'

'T'ou's past remede, I fear,' replied his father thoughtfully; 'but, Watty, I hope in this t'ou'll oblige thy mother and me, and put on thy new black claes;—t'ou kens they're in a braw fasson, —and come ben and receive the guests in a douce and sober manner.'

'The minister, I'm thinking, will soon be here, and t'ou should be in the way when he comes.'

'No,' said Watty, 'no, do as ye like, and come wha may, it's a' ane to me: I'm positeeve.'

The old man, losing all self-command at this extraordinary opposition, exclaimed,—

'There's a judgment in this; and, if there's power in the law o' Scotland, I'll gar thee rue sic dourness.[3] Get up, I say, and put on thy mournings, or I'll hae thee cognost,[4] and sent to bedlam.'

'I'm sure I look for nae mair at your hands, father,' replied Walter simply; 'for my mither has often telt me, when ye hae been sitting sour and sulky in the nook, that ye would na begrudge crowns and pounds to mak me *compos mentis* for the benefit of Charlie.'

Every pulse in the veins of Claud stood still at this stroke, and he staggered, overwhelmed with shame, remorse, and indignation, into a seat.

'Eh!' said the Leddy, returning into the room at this juncture, 'what's come o'er you, gudeman? Pity me, will he no do your bidding?'

'Girzy Hypel,' was the hoarse and emphatic reply, 'Girzy Hypel, t'ou's the curse o' my life; the folly in thee has altered to idiotical depravity in him, and the wrong I did against my ain ·nature in marrying thee, I maun noo,[5] in my auld age, reap the fruits o' in sorrow, and shame, and sin.'

'Here's composity for a burial!' exclaimed the Leddy. 'What's the matter, Watty Walkinshaw?'

'My father's in a passion.'

Claud started from his seat, and, with fury in his eyes, and his hands clenched, rushed across the room towards the spot where Walter was sitting, watching the infant in the nurse's lap. In the same moment, the affectionate natural also sprang forward, and placed himself in an attitude to protect the child. The fierce old man was confounded, and turning round hastily, quitted the room, wringing his hands, unable any longer to master the conflicting feelings which warred so wildly in his bosom.

'This is a pretty like house o' mourning,' said the Leddy; 'a father and a son fighting, and a dead body waiting to be ta'en to the kirk-yard. O Watty Walkinshaw! Watty Walkinshaw! many a sore heart ye hae gi'en your parents,—will ye ne'er divaul¹ till ye hae brought our grey hairs wi' sorrow to the grave? There's your poor father flown demented, and a' the comfort in his cup and mine gane like water spilt on the ground. Many a happy day we hae had, till this condumacity o' thine grew to sic a head. But tak your ain way o't. Do as ye like. Let strangers carry your wife to the kirk-yard, and see what ye'll mak o't.'

But notwithstanding all these, and many more equally persuasive and commanding arguments, Walter was not to be moved, and the funeral, in consequence, was obliged to be performed without him. Yet still, though thus tortured in his feelings, the stern old man inflexibly adhered to his purpose. The entail which he had executed was still with him held irrevocable; and, indeed, it had been so framed, that, unless he rendered himself insolvent, it could not be set aside.

CHAPTER XXXVI

FOR some time after the funeral of Mrs Walter Walkinshaw, the affairs of the Grippy family ran in a straight and even current. The estrangement of the old man from his first-born suffered no describable increase, but Charles felt that it was increasing. The old Leddy, in the meanwhile, had a world of cares upon her hands in breaking up the establishment which had been formed for Walter at the house on the Divethill, and in removing him back with the infant and the nurse to Grippy. And scarcely had she accomplished these, when a letter from her daughter, Mrs Milrookit, informed her that the preparations for an addition to the 'sma family' of Dirdumwhamle were complete, and that she hoped her mother could be present on the occasion, which was expected to come to pass in the course of a few weeks from the date.

Nothing was more congenial to the mind and habits of the Leddy, than a business of this sort, or, indeed, any epochal domestic event, such as, in her own phraseology, was entitled to the epithet of a handling. But when she mentioned the subject to her husband, he objected, saying,—

'It's no possible, Girzy, for ye ken Mr and Mrs Givan are to be here next week with their dochter, Miss Peggy, and I would fain hae them to see an ony thing could be brought to a head between her and our Geordie. He's noo o' a time o' life when I would like he were settled in the world, and amang a' our frien's there's no a family I would be mair content to see him connected wi' than the Givans, who are come o' the best blood, and are, moreover, o' great wealth and property.'

'Weel, if e'er there was the like o' you, gudeman,' replied the Leddy, delighted with the news; 'an ye were to set your mind on a purpose o' marriage between a goose and a grumphie, I dinna think but ye would make it a' come to pass. For wha would hae thought o' this plot on the Givans, who, to be sure, are a most creditable family, and Miss Peggy, their dochter, is a vera genty[1] creature, although it's my notion she's no o' a capacity to do meikle in the way o' throughgality.[2] Howsever, she's a bonny playock, and noo that the stipend ye alloo't to Watty is at an end, by reason of that heavy loss which we all met wi' in his wife, ye'll can weel afford to help Geordie to keep her out in a station o' life; for times, gudeman, are no noo as when you and me cam thegither. Then a bein house, and a snod but and ben,[3] was a' that was lookit for; but sin genteelity came into fashion, lads and lasses hae grown leddies and gentlemen, and a Glasgow wife saullying[4] to the kirk wi' her muff and her mantle, looks as puckered wi' pride as my lord's leddy.'

Claud, who knew well that his helpmate was able to continue her desultory consultations as long as she could keep herself awake, here endeavoured to turn the speat[5] of her clatter into a new channel, by observing, that hitherto they had not enjoyed any great degree of comfort in the marriages of their family.

'Watty's,' said he, 'ye see, has in a manner been waur than nane;

for a' we hae gotten by't is that weakly lassie bairn; and the sumph himsel is sae ta'en up wi't, that he's a perfect obdooracy to every wis o' mine, that he would tak another wife to raise a male-heir to the family.'

'I'm sure,' replied the Leddy, 'it's just a sport to hear you, gudeman, and your male-heirs. What for can ye no be content wi' Charlie's son?'

The countenance of Grippy was instantaneously clouded, but in a moment the gloom passed, and he said,—

'Girzy Hypel, t'ou kens naething about it. Will na Watty's dochter inherit the Divethill by right o' her father, for the Plealands, and so rive the heart again out o' the Kittlestonheugh, and mak a' my ettling[1] fruitless? Noo, what I wis is, that Geordie should tak a wife to himsel as soon as a possibility will alloo, and if he has a son, by course o' nature, it might be wised[2] in time to marry Watty's dochter, and so keep the property frae ganging out o' the family.'

'Noo, gudeman, thole[3] wi' me, and no be angry,' replied the Leddy; 'for I canna but say it's a thing past ordinar, that ye never seem to refleck, that Charlie's laddie might just as weel be wised to marry Watty's dochter, as ony son that Geordie's like to get; and over and moreover, the wean's in the world already, gudeman, but a' Geordie's are as trouts in the water; so I redde you to consider weel what ye're doing, and gut nae fish till ye catch them.'

During this speech, Claud's face was again overcast; the harsh and agonizing discord of his bosom rudely jangled through all the depths of his conscience, and reminded him how futile his wishes and devices might be rendered either by the failure of issue, or the birth of daughters. Every thing seemed arranged by Providence, to keep the afflicting sense of the wrong he had done his first-born constantly galled. But it had not before occurred to him, that even a marriage between the son of Charles and Walter's daughter could not remedy the fault he had committed. The heirs-male of George had a preference in the entail; and such a marriage would, in no degree, tend to prevent the Kittlestonheugh from being again disjoined. In one sentence, the ambitious old man was miserable; but rather than yet consent to retrace any step he had taken, he persevered in his original course, as if the fire in his heart could be subdued by adding fresh piles of the same fuel. The match which he had formed for George was accordingly brought to what he deemed a favourable issue; for George, possessing but little innate delicacy, and only eager to become rich, had no scruple in proposing himself, at his father's suggestion, to Miss Peggy Givan; and the young lady being entirely under the control of her mother, who regarded a union with her relations, the Grippy family, as one of the most desirable, peaceably acquiesced in the arrangement.

Prior, however, to the marriage taking place, Mr Givan, a shrewd and worldly man, conceiving, that, as George was a younger son, his elder brother married, and Walter's daughter standing between him and the succession to the estate,—he stipulated that the bridegroom should be settled as a principal in business. A short delay in consequence occurred between the arrangement and the solemnization; but the difficulty was overcome, by the old man advancing nearly the whole of his ready money as a proportion of the capital which was required by the house that received George into partnership. Perhaps he might have been spared this sacrifice, for as such he felt it, could he have brought himself to divulge to Mr Givan the nature of the entail which he had executed; but the shame of that transaction had by this time sunk so deep, that he often wished and tried to consider the deed as having no existence.

Meanwhile, Mrs Milrookit had become the mother of a son; the only occurrence which, for some time, had given Claud any un-alloyed satisfaction. But it also was soon converted into a new source of vexation and of punishment; for Leddy Grippy, ever dotingly fond of Walter, determined, from the first hour in which she heard of the birth of Walkinshaw Milrookit, as the child was called, to match him with her favourite's Betty; and the mere possibility of such an event taking place filled her husband with anxiety and fear; the expressions of which, and the peevish and bitter accents that he used in checking her loquacity on the sub-ject, only served to make her wonderment at his prejudices the more and more tormenting.

END OF VOLUME FIRST

VOLUME II

CHAPTER I[1]

In the meantime, Charles and Isabella had enjoyed a large share of domestic felicity, rendered the more endearingly exquisite by their parental anxiety, for it had pleased Heaven at once to bless and burden their narrow circumstances with two beautiful children, James and Mary. Their income arising from the share which the old man had assigned of the business had, during the first two or three years subsequent to their marriage, proved sufficient for the supply of their restricted wants; but their expences began gradually to increase, and about the end of the third year Charles found that they had incurred several small debts above their means of payment. These, in the course of the fourth, rose to such a sum, that, being naturally of an apprehensive mind, he grew uneasy at the amount, and came to the resolution to borrow two hundred pounds to discharge them. This, he imagined, there could be no difficulty in procuring; for, believing that he was the heir of entail to the main part of the estate which his father had so entirely redeemed, he conceived that he might raise the money on his reversionary prospects, and, with this view, he called one morning on Mr Keelevin to request his agency in the business.

'I'm grieved, man,' said the honest lawyer, 'to hear that ye're in such straits; but had na ye better speak to your father? It might bring on you his displeasure if he heard ye were borrowing money to be paid at his death. It's a thing nae frien', far less a father, would like done by himsel.'

'In truth,' replied Charles, 'I am quite sensible of that; but what can I do? for my father, ever since my brother Watty's marriage, has been so cold and reserved about his affairs to me, that every thing like confidence seems as if it were perished from between us.'

Mr Keelevin, during this speech, raised his left arm on the elbow from the table at which he was sitting, and rested his chin

on his hand. There was nothing in the habitual calm of his countenance which indicated what was passing in his heart, but his
eyes once or twice glimmered with a vivid expression of pity.

'Mr Walkinshaw,' said he, 'if you dinna like to apply to your
father yoursel, could na some friend mediate for you? Let me
speak to him.'

'It's friendly of you, Mr Keelevin, to offer to do that; but really,
to speak plainly, I would far rather borrow the money from a
stranger, than lay myself open to any remarks. Indeed, for myself,
I don't much care; but ye ken my father's narrow ideas about
household charges; and may be he might take it on him to make
remarks to my wife that I would na like to hear o'.'

'But, Mr Charles, you know that money canna be borrow't without security.'

'I am aware of that; and it's on that account I want your assistance. I should think that my chance of surviving my father is
worth something.'

'But the whole estate is strictly entailed, Mr Charles,' replied
the lawyer, with compassionate regard.

'The income, however, is all clear, Mr Keelevin.'

'I dinna misdoubt that, Mr Charles, but the entail—Do you
ken how it runs?'

'No; but I imagine much in the usual manner.'

'No, Mr Charles,' said the honest writer, raising his head, and
letting his hand fall on the table, with a mournful emphasis; 'No,
Mr Charles, it does na run in the usual manner; and I hope ye'll
no put ony reliance on't. It was na right o' your father to let you
live in ignorance so long. May be it has been this to-look¹ that has
led you into the debts ye want to pay.'

The manner in which this was said affected the unfortunate first-
born more than the meaning; but he replied,—

'No doubt, Mr Keelevin, I may have been less scrupulous in my
expences than I would have been, had I not counted on the chance
of my birth-right.'

'Mr Charles, I'm sorry for you; but I would na do a frien's
part by you, were I to keep you ony langer in the dark. Your
father, Mr Charles, is an honest man; but there's a bee in his
bonnet, as we a' ken, anent his pedigree. I need na tell you how
he has warslet² to get back the inheritance o' his forefathers;
but I am wae³ to say, that in a pursuit so meritorious, he has

committed ae great fault. Really, Mr Charles, I have na hardly the heart to tell you.'

'What is it?' said Charles, with emotion and apprehension.

'He has made a deed,' said Mr Keelevin, 'whereby he has cut you off frae the succession, in order that Walter, your brother, might be in a condition to make an exchange of the Plealands for the twa mailings[1] that were wanting to make up wi' the Grippy property, a restoration of the auld estate of Kittlestonheugh; and I doubt it's o' a nature in consequence, that, even were he willing, canna be easily altered.'

To this heart-withering communication Charles made no answer. He stood for several minutes astonished; and then giving Mr Keelevin a wild look, shuddered and quitted the office.

Instead of returning home, he rushed with rapid and unequal steps down the Gallowgate, and, turning to the left hand[2] in reaching the end of the street, never halted till he had gained the dark firs which overhang the cathedral and skirt the Molindinar Burn, which at the time was swelled with rains, and pouring its troubled torrent almost as violently as the tide of feelings that struggled in his bosom. Unconscious of what he did, and borne along by the whirlwind of his own thoughts, he darted down the steep, and for a moment hung on the rocks at the bottom as if he meditated some frantic leap. Recoiling and trembling with the recollections of his family, he then threw himself on the ground, and for some time shut his eyes as if he wished to believe that he was agitated only by a dream.

The scene and the day were in unison with the tempest which shook his frame and shivered his mind. The sky was darkly overcast. The clouds were rolling in black and lowering masses, through which an occasional gleam of sunshine flickered for a moment on the towers and pinnacles of the cathedral, and glimmered in its rapid transit on the monuments and graves in the church-yard. A gloomy shadow succeeded; and then a white and ghastly light hovered along the ruins of the bishop's castle, and darted with a strong and steady ray on a gibbet which stood on the rising ground beyond. The gusty wind howled like a death dog among the firs, which waved their dark boughs like hearse plumes over him, and the voice of the raging waters encouraged his despair.

He felt as if he had been betrayed into a situation which compelled him to surrender all the honourable intents of his life, and

that he must spend the comfortless remainder of his days in a conflict with poverty, a prey to all its temptations, expedients, and
crimes. At one moment, he clenched his grasp, and gnashed his
teeth, and smote his forehead, abandoning himself to the wild and
headlong energies and instincts of a rage that was almost revenge;
at another, the image of Isabella, so gentle and so defenceless, rose
in a burst of tenderness and sorrow, and subdued him with inexpressible grief. But the thought of his children in the heedless
days of their innocence, condemned to beggary by a fraud against
nature, again scattered these subsiding feelings like the blast that
brushes the waves of the ocean into spindrift.

This vehemence of feeling could not last long without producing
some visible effect. When the storm had in some degree spent itself, he left the wild and solitary spot where he had given himself
so entirely up to his passion, and returned towards his home; but
his limbs trembled, his knees faltered, and a cold shivering
vibrated through his whole frame. An intense pain was kindled in
his forehead; every object reeled and shuddered to him as he
passed; and, before he reached the house, he was so unwell that he
immediately retired to bed. In the course of the afternoon he became delirious, and a rapid and raging fever terrified his ill-
fated wife.

CHAPTER II

MR KEELEVIN, when Charles had left him, sat for some time
with his cheek resting on his hand, reflecting on what had passed;
and in the afternoon, he ordered his horse, and rode over to Grippy,
where he found the Laird sitting sullenly by himself in the easy
chair by the fire-side, with a white night-cap on his head, and grey
worsted stockings drawn over his knees.

'I'm wae, Mr Walkinshaw,' said the honest lawyer, as he
entered the room, 'to see you in sic an ailing condition; what's
the matter wi' you, and how lang hae ye been sae indisposed?'

Claud had not observed his entrance; for, supposing the noise
in opening the door had been made by the Leddy in her manifold
household cares, or by some one of the servants, he never moved
his head, but kept his eyes ruminatingly fixed on a peeling of soot

that was ominously fluttering on one of the ribs of the grate, betokening, according to the most credible oracles of Scottish superstition, the arrival of a stranger, or the occurrence of some remarkable event. But, on hearing the voice of his legal friend, he turned briskly round.

'Sit ye doun, Mr Keelevin, sit ye doun forenent[1] me. What's brought you here the day? Man, this is sore weather for ane at your time o' life to come so far afield,' was the salutation with which he received him.

'Aye,' replied Mr Keelevin, 'baith you and me, Grippy, are beginning to be the waur o' the wear; but I didna expek to find you in sic a condition as this. I hope it's no the gout or the rheumatism.'

Claud, who had the natural horror of death as strong as most country gentlemen of a certain age, if not of all ages, did not much relish either the observation or the inquiries. He, however, said, with affected indifference,—

'No! be thankit, it's neither the t'ane nor the t'ither, but just a waff o' cauld that I got twa nights ago;—a bit towt[2] that's no worth the talking o'.'

'I'm extraordinar glad to hear't; for, seeing you in sic a frail and feckless state, I was fear't that ye were na in a way to converse on any concern o' business. No that I hae muckle to say, but ye ken a' sma' things are a great fasherie to a weakly person, and I would na discompose you, Mr Walkinshaw, unless you just felt yoursel in your right ordinar, for, at your time o' life, ony disturbance'*****[3]

'My time o' life?' interrupted the old man tartly. 'Surely I'm no sae auld that ye need to be speaking o' my time o' life? But what's your will, Mr Keelevin, wi' me?'

Whether all this sympathetic condolence, on the part of the lawyer, was said in sincerity, or with any ulterior view, we need not pause to discuss, for the abrupt question of the invalid brought it at once to a conclusion.

'In truth, Laird,' replied Mr Keelevin, 'I canna say that I hae ony thing o' a particular speciality to trouble you anent, for I came hither more in the way o' friendship than o' business,—having had this morning a visit frae your son Charles, a fine weel doing young man as can be.'

'He's weel enough,' said the old man gruffly, and the lawyer continued,—

''Deed, Mr Walkinshaw, he's mair than weel enough. He's by common,[1] and it was with great concern I heard that you and him are no on sic a footing of cordiality as I had thought ye were.'

'Has he been making a complaint o' me?' said Claud looking sharply, and with a grim and knotted brow as if he was, at the same time, apprehensive and indignant.

'He has mair sense and discretion,' replied Mr Keelevin; 'but he was speaking to me on a piece of business, and I was surprised he did na rather confer wi' you; till, in course of conversation, it fell out, as it were unawares, that he did na like to speak to you anent it; the which dislike, I jealouse,[2] could only proceed o' some lack o' confidence between you, mair than should ever be between a father and a weel-behaved son like Mr Charles.'

'And what was't?' said Grippy drily.

'I doubt that[3] his income is scant to his want, Mr Walkinshaw.'

'He's an extravagant fool; and ne'er had a hand to thraw a key[4] in a lock;—when I began the world I had na'——

'Surely,' interrupted Mr Keelevin, 'ye could ne'er think the son o' a man in your circumstances should hain and hamper[5] as ye were necessitated to do in your younger years. But no to mak a hearing or an argument concerning the same—Mr Charles requires a sma' sum to get him free o' a wee bit difficulty, for, ye ken, there are some folk, Mr Walkinshaw, that a flea-bite molests like the lash o' a whip.'

The old man made no answer to this; but sat for some time silent, drawing down his brows and twirling his thumbs. Mr Keelevin waited in patience till he should digest the reply he so evidently meditated.

'I hae ay thought Charlie honest, at least,' said Grippy; 'but I maun say that this fashes me, for if he's in sic straits, there's no telling what liberties he may be led to tak wi' my property in the shop.'

Mr Keelevin, who, in the first part of this reply, had bent eagerly forward, was so thunderstruck by the conclusion, that he threw himself back in his chair with his arms extended; but in a moment recovering from his consternation, he said, with fervour,—

'Mr Walkinshaw, I mind weel the reproof ye gave me when I remonstrated wi' you against the injustice ye were doing the poor lad in the entail, but there's no consideration on this earth will let me alloo you to gang on in a course of error and prejudice. Your

son is an honest young man. I wish I could say his father kent his
worth, or was worthy o' him—and I'll no see him wrangeously
driven to the door, without taking his part, and letting the world
ken wha's to blame. I'll no say ye hae defrauded him o' his birth-
right, for the property was your ain—but if ye drive him forth the
shop, and cast him wi' his sma family on the scrimp mercy of mankind, I would be wanting to human nature in general, if I did na
say it was most abominable, and that you yoursel, wi' a' your
trumpery o' Walkinshaws and Kittlestonheughs, ought to be
scourged by the hands o' the hangman. So do as ye like, Mr
Walkinshaw, ride to the deevil at the full gallop for ought I care,
but ye's no get out o' this world without hearing the hue and cry,
that every Christian soul canna but raise after you.'

Claud was completely cowed both by the anger and menace of
the honest lawyer, but still more by the upbraidings of his own
startled conscience—and he said, in a humiliated tone, that almost
provoked contempt,—

'Ye're owre hasty, Mr Keelevin. I did na mint[1] a word about
driving him forth the shop. Did he tell you how muckle his
defect was?'

'Twa miserable hundred pounds,' replied Mr Keelevin, somewhat subsiding into his wonted equanimity.

'Twa hundred pound o' debt!' exclaimed Claud.

'Aye,' said Mr Keelevin, 'and I marvel it's no mair, when I
consider the stinting and the sterile father o' him.'

'If I had the siller, Mr Keelevin,' replied Claud, 'to convince
baith you and him that I'm no the niggar[2] ye tak me for, I would
gi'e you't wi' hearty gude will; but the advance I made to get
Geordie into his partnership has for the present rookit[3] me o' a'
I had at command.'

'No possible!' exclaimed Mr Keelevin, subdued from his
indignation; adding, 'and heavens preserve us, Mr Walkinshaw,
an ony thing were happening on a sudden to carry you aff, ye hae
made na provision for Charlie nor your dochter.'

There was something in this observation which made the old
man shrink up into himself, and vibrate from head to heel. In the
course, however, of less than a minute, he regained his self-
possession, and said,—

''Deed your observe, Mr Keelevin, is very just, and I ought to
do something to provide for what may come to pass. I maun try

and get Watty to concur wi' me in some bit settlement that may lighten the disappointment to Charlie and Meg, should it please the Lord to tak me to himsel without a reasonable warning. Can sic a paper be made out?'

'O, yes,' replied the worthy lawyer, delighted with so successful an issue to his voluntary mission; 'ye hae twa ways o' doing the business; either by getting Watty to agree to an aliment,[1] or by making a bond of provision to Charles and Mrs Milrookit.'

Claud said he would prefer the former mode; observing, with respect to the latter, that he thought it would be a cheating o' the law to take the other course.

'As for cheating the law,' said the lawyer, 'ye need gie yoursel no uneasiness about it, provided ye do honestly by your ain bairns, and the rest o' the community.'

And it was in consequence agreed, that, in the course of a day or two, Claud should take Walter to Glasgow, to execute a deed, by which, in the event of surviving his father, he would undertake to pay a certain annuity for the behoof of Charles's family, and that of his sister, Mrs Milrookit.

CHAPTER III

In furtherance of the arrangement agreed upon, as we have described in the foregoing chapter, as soon as Mr Keelevin had retired, Claud summoned Walter into the parlour. It happened, that the Leddy, during the period of the lawyer's visit, had been so engaged in another part of the house, that she was not aware of the conference, till, by chance, she saw him riding down the avenue. We need not, therefore, say that she experienced some degree of alarm, at the idea of a lawyer having been with her husband, unknown to her; and particularly, when, so immediately after his departure, her darling was requested to attend his father.

The mother and son entered the room together. Walter came from the nursery, where he had been dandling his child, and his appearance was not of the most prepossessing kind. From the death of his wife, in whose time, under her dictation, he was brushed up into something of a gentlemanly exterior, he had become gradually more and more slovenly. He only shaved on

Saturday night, and buttoned his breeches knees on Sunday morning. Nor was the dress of Leddy Grippy at all out of keeping with
that of her hopeful favourite. Her, time-out-of-mind, red quilted
silk petticoat was broken into many holes;—her thrice dyed
double tabinet[1] gown, of bottle-green, with large ruffle cuffs, was
in need of another dip; for, in her various culinary inspections, it
had received many stains, and the superstructure of lawn and catgut, ornamented with ribbons, dyed blea[2] in ink, surmounting her
ill-toiletted toupee, had every appearance of having been smoked
into yellow, beyond all power of blanching in the bleacher's art.

'And so, gudeman,' said she, on entering the room, 'ye hae had
that auld sneck-drawer,[3] Keelevin, wi' you? I won'er what you
and him can hae to say in sic a clandestine manner, that the door
maun be ay steekit[4] when ye're thegither at your confabbles.
Surely there's nae honesty that a man can hae, whilk his wife ought
na to come in for a share of.'

'Sit down, Girzy Hypel, and haud thy tongue,' was the peevish
command which this speech provoked.

'What for will I haud my tongue? a fool posture that would be,
and no very commodious at this time; for ye see my fingers are
coomy.'[5]

'Woman, t'ou's past bearing!' exclaimed her disconcerted
husband.

'An it's nae shame to me, gudeman; for every body kens I'm a
grannie.'

The Laird smote his right thigh, and shook his left hand, with
vexation; presently, however, he said,—

'Weel, weel; but sit ye down, and Watty, tak t'ou a chair beside
her; for I want to consult you anent a paper that I'm mindit to hae
drawn out for a satisfaction to you a'; for nane can tell when their
time may come.'

'Ye ne'er made a mair sensible observe, gudeman, in a' your days,'
replied the Leddy, sitting down; 'and it's vera right to make your
will and testament; for ye ken what a straemash[6] happened in the
Glengowlmahallaghan family, by reason o' the Laird holo-
graphing his codicil; whilk, to be sure, was a dreadfu' omission,
as my cousin, his wife, fand in her widowhood; for a' the moveables
thereby gaed wi' the heritage to his auld son by the first wife—even
the vera silver pourie[7] that I gied her mysel wi' my own hands, in
a gift at her marriage—a' gaed to the heir.'

'T'ou kens,' said Claud, interrupting her oration, 'that I hae provided thee wi' the liferent o' a house o' fifteen pounds a-year, furniture, and a jointure of a hundred and twenty over and aboon the outcoming o' thy father's gathering.[1] So t'ou canna expek, Girzy, that I would wrang our bairns wi' ony mair overlay on thy account.'

'Ye're grown richer, gudeman, than when we came thegither,' replied the Leddy; 'and ne'er a man made siller without his wife's leave. So it would be a most hard thing, after a' my toiling and moiling, to make me nae better o't than the stricts o' the law in my marriage articles and my father's will; whilk was a gratus amous,[2] that made me nane behauden to you.—No, an ye mean to do justice, gudeman, I'll get my thirds o' the conquest ye hae gotten sin the time o' our marriage; and I'll be content wi' nae less.'

'Weel, weel, Girzy, we'll no cast out about a settlement for thee.'

'It would be a fearful thing to hear tell o' an we did,' replied the Leddy: 'Living as we hae lived, a comfort to ane anither for thirty years, and bringin up sic a braw family, wi' so meikle credit. No, gudeman, I hae mair confidence in you than to misdoot your love and kindness, noo that ye're drawing so near your latter end as to be seriously thinking o' making a will. But, for a' that, I would like to ken what I'm to hae.'

'Very right, Girzy; very right,' said Claud; 'but, before we can come to a clear understanding, me and Watty maun conform in a bit paper by oursels, just that there may be nae debate hereafter about his right to the excambio we made for the Plealands.'

'I'll no put hand to ony drumhead[3] paper again,' said Watty, 'for fear it wrang my wee Betty Bodle.'

Although this was said in a vacant heedless manner, it yet disturbed the mind of his father exceedingly, for the strange obstinacy with which the natural had persisted in his refusal to attend the funeral of his wife, had shown that there was something deeper and more intractable in his character than any one had previously imagined. But opposition had only the effect of making Claud more pertinacious, while it induced him to change his mode of operation. Perceiving, or at least being afraid that he might again call his obduracy into action, he accordingly shifted his ground, and, instead of his wonted method of treating Walter with commands and menaces, he dexterously availed himself of the Leddy's auxiliary assistance.

'Far be it, Watty, frae me, thy father,' said he, 'to think or wis wrang to thee or thine; but t'ou kens that in family settlements, where there's a patch't property like ours, we maun hae conjunk proceedings. Noo, as I'm fain to do something satisfactory to thy mother, t'ou'll surely never objek to join me in the needfu' instruments to gie effek to my intentions.'

'I'll do every thing to serve my mother,' replied Walter, 'but I'll no sign ony papers.'

'Surely, Watty Walkinshaw,' exclaimed the old Leddy, surprised at this repetition of his refusal, 'ye would na see me in want, and driven to a needcessity[1] to gang frae door to door, wi' a meal-pock round my neck, and an oaken rung[2] in my hand?'

'I would rather gie you my twa dollars, and the auld French half-a-crown, that I got long syne, on my birth-day, frae grannie,' said Watty.

'Then what for will ye no let your father make a rightfu' settlement?' cried his mother.

'I'm sure I dinna hinder him. He may mak fifty settlements for me; I'll ne'er fin' fau't wi' him.'

'Then,' said the Leddy, 'ye canna objek to his reasonable request.'

'I objek to no reasonable request; I only say, mother, that I'll no sign ony paper whatsomever, wheresomever, howsomever, nor ever and ever—so ye need na try to fleetch[3] me.'

'Ye're an outstrapolous ne'er-do-weel,' cried the Leddy, in a rage, knocking her neives[4] smartly together, 'to speak to thy mother in that way; t'ou sall sign the paper, an te life be[5] in thy body.'

'I'll no wrang my ain bairn for father nor mother; I'll gang to Jock Harrigals, the flesher, and pay him to hag aff[6] my right hand, afore I put pen to law-paper again.'

'This is a' I get for my love and affection,' exclaimed the Leddy, bursting into tears; while her husband, scarcely less agitated by the firmness with which his purpose was resisted, sat in a state of gloomy abstraction, seemingly unconscious of the altercation. 'But,' added Mrs Walkinshaw, 'I'm no in thy reverence,[7] t'ou unnatural Absalom, to rebel sae against thy parents. I hae may be a hoggar,[8] and I ken whan I die wha s'all get the gouden guts o't— Wilt t'ou sign the paper?'

'I'll burn aff my right hand in the lowing fire, that I may ne'er be able to write the scrape o' a pen;' and with these emphatic words, said in à soft and simple manner, he rose from his seat, and was actually proceeding towards the fire-place, when a loud knocking at the door disturbed, and put an end to the conversation. It was a messenger sent from old Lady Plealands, to inform her daughter of Charles' malady, and to say that the doctor, who had been called in, was greatly alarmed at the rapid progress of the disease.

CHAPTER IV

LEDDY GRIPPY was one of those worthy gentlewomen, who, without the slightest interest or feeling in any object or purpose with which they happen to be engaged, conceive themselves bound to perform all the customary indications of the profoundest sympathy and the deepest sensibility. Accordingly, no sooner did she receive the message of her son's melancholy condition, than she proceeded forthwith to prepare herself for going immediately to Glasgow.

'I canna expek, gudeman,' said she, 'that wi' your host[1] ye'll come wi' me to Glasgow on this very sorrowful occasion; therefore I hope ye'll tak gude care o' yoursel, and see that the servan' lasses get your water-gruel, wi' a tamarind in't, at night, if it should please Charlie's Maker, by reason o' the dangerous distemper, no to alloo me to come hame.'

The intelligence, however, had so troubled the old man, that he scarcely heard her observation. The indisposition of his son seemed to be somehow connected with the visit of Mr Keelevin, which it certainly was; and while his wife busily prepared for her visit, his mind wandered in devious conjectures, without being able to reach any thing calculated either to satisfy his wonder or to appease his apprehension.

'It's very right, Girzy, my dear,' said he, 'that ye sou'd gang in and see Charlie, poor lad; I'm extraordinar sorry to hear o' this income,[2] and ye'll be sure to tak care he wants for nothing. Hear'st t'ou; look into the auld pockct-book in the scrutoire neuk; t'ou'l aiblins fin'[3] there a five-pound note, tak it wi' thee—there's no sic an extravagant commodity in ony man's house as a delirious fever.'

'Ah!' replied the Leddy, looking at her darling and ungrateful Walter, 'ye see what it is to hae a kind father; but ill ye deserve ony attention either frae father or mother, for your condumacity is ordained to break our hearts.'

'Mother,' said Walter, 'dinna be in sic a hurry—I hae something that 'ill do Charlie good.' In saying which, he rose and went to the nursery, whence he immediately returned with a pill box.

'There, mother! tak that wi' you; it's a box o' excellent medicaments, either for the cough, or the cauld, or shortness o' breath; to say naething amang frien's o' a constipation. Gie Charlie twa at bed time and ane in the morning, and ye'll see an effek sufficient to cure every impediment in man or woman.'

Leddy Grippy, with the utmost contempt for the pills, snatched the box out of his hand, and flung it behind the fire. She then seated herself in the chair opposite her husband, and while she at the same time tied her cloak and placed on her bonnet, she said,—

'I'll alloo at last, gudeman, that I hae been a' my days in an error, for I could na hae believed that Watty was sic an idiot o' a naturalist, had I no lived to see this day. But the will o' Providence be done on earth as it is in heaven, and let us pray that he may be forgiven the sair heart he has gi'en to us his aged parents, as we forgive our debtors. I won'er, howsever, that my mother did na send word o' the nature o' this delirietness o' Charlie, for to be surely it's a very sudden come-to-pass, but the things o' time are no to be lippent to,[1] and life fleeth away like a weaver's shuttle, and no man knoweth wheresoever it findeth rest for the sole of its foot. But, before I go, ye'll no neglek to tell Jenny in the morning to tak the three spyniels[2] o' yarn to Josey Thrums, the weaver, for my Dornick[3] towelling; and ye'll be sure to put Tam Modiwart in mind that he's no to harl[4] the plough out o'er the green brae till I get my big washing out o' hand. As for t'ee, Watty, stay till this calamity's past, and I'll let ee ken what it is to treat baith father and mother wi' sae little reverence. Really, gudeman, I begin to hae a notion, that he's, as auld Elspeth Freet, the midwife, ance said to me, a ta'enawa,[5] and I would be nane surprised, that whoever lives to see him dee will find in the bed a benweed or a windlestrae,[6] instead o' a Christian corpse. But sufficient for the day is the evil thereof; and this sore news o' our auld son should mak us walk humbly, and no repine at the mercies set before us in this our sinfu' estate.'

The worthy Leddy might have continued her edifying

exhortation for some time longer, but her husband grew impatient, and harshly interrupted her eloquence, by reminding her that the day was far advanced, and that the road to Glasgow was both deep and dreigh.[1]

'I would counsel you, Girzy Hypel,' said he, 'no to put off your time wi' sic havers here, but gang intil the town, and send us out word in the morning, if ye dinna come hame, how Charlie may happen to be; for I canna but say that thir[2] news are no just what I could hae wiss'd to hear at this time. As for what we hae been saying to Watty, we baith ken he's a kind-hearted chiel,[3] and he'll think better or the morn[4] o' what we were speaking about—will na ye, Watty?'

'I'll think as muckle's ye like,' said the faithful natural; 'but I'll sign nae papers; that's a fact afore divines. What for do ye ay fash me wi' your deeds and your instruments? I'm sure baith Charlie and Geordie could write better than me, and ye ne'er troublet them. But I jealouse the cause—an my grandfather had na left me his lawful heir to the Plealands, I might hae sat at the chumley lug whistling on my thumb. We a' hae frien's anew when we hae ony thing, and so I see in a' this flyting and fleetching;[5] but ye'll flyte and ye'll fleetch till puddocks grow chucky-stanes[6] before ye'll get me to wrang my ain bairn, my bonny wee Betty Bodle, that has na ane that cares for her, but only my leafu' lane.'[7]

The Leddy would have renewed her remonstratory animadversions on his obstinacy, but the Laird again reminded her of the length of the journey in such an evening before her, and after a few half advices and half reproaches, she left the house.

Indisposed as Claud had previously felt himself, or seemed to be, she had not been long away, when he rose from his easy chair, and walked slowly across the room, with his hands behind, swinging his body heavily as he paced the floor. Walter, who still remained on his seat, appeared for some time not to notice his father's gestures; but the old man unconsciously began to quicken his steps, and at last walked so rapidly that his son's attention was roused.

'Father,' said he, 'hae ye been taking epicacco,[8] for that was just the way that I was telt to gang, when I was last no weel?'[9]

'No, no,' exclaimed the wretched old man; 'but I hae drank the bitterest dose o' life. There's nae vomit for a sick soul—nae purge for a foul conscience.'

These were, however, confessions that escaped from him

unawares, like the sparks that are elicited in violent percussions,—for he soon drew himself firmly and bravely up, as if he prepared himself to defy the worst that was in store for him; but this resolution also as quickly passed away, and he returned to his easy chair, and sat down, as if he had been abandoned of all hope, and had resigned himself into a dull and sleepy lethargy.

For about half an hour he continued in this slumbering and inaccessible state, at the end of which he called one of the servants, and bade him be ready to go to Glasgow by break of day, and bring Mr Keelevin before breakfast. 'Something maun be done,' said he as the servant, accompanied by Walter, left the room; 'the curse of God has fallen upon me, my hands are tied, a dreadfu' chain is fastened about me; I hae cheated mysel, and there's nae bail—no, not in the Heavens—for the man that has wilfully raffled away his own soul in the guilty game o' pride.'

CHAPTER V

MEANWHILE, the disease which had laid Charles prostrate was proceeding with a terrific and devastating fury. Before his mother reached the house, he had lost all sense of himself and situation, and his mind was a chaos of the wildest and most extravagant phantasies. Occasionally, however, he would sink into a momentary calm, when a feeble gleam of reason would appear amidst his ravings, like the transient glimmer of a passing light from the shore on the black waves of the stormy ocean, when the cry has arisen at midnight of a vessel on the rocks, and her crew in jeopardy. But these breathing pauses of the fever's rage were, perhaps, more dreadful than its violence, for they were accompanied with a return of the moral anguish which had brought on his malady; and as often as his eye caught the meek, but desponding countenance of Isabella, as she sat by his bed-side, he would make a convulsive effort to raise himself, and instantly relapse into the tempestuous raptures of the delirium. In this state he passed the night.

Towards morning symptoms of a change began to show themselves,—the turbulence of his thoughts subsided,—his breathing became more regular; and both Isabella and his mother were persuaded that he was considerably better. Under this impression, the old lady, at day-break, dispatched a messenger to inform his father of the favourable change, who, in the interval, had passed a night, in a state, not more calm, and far less enviable, than that of his distracted son.

Whatever was the motive which induced Claud, on the preceding evening, to determine on sending for Mr Keelevin, it would appear that it did not long maintain its influence; for, before going to bed, he countermanded the order. Indeed, his whole behaviour that night indicated a strange and unwonted degree of indecision. It was evident that he meditated some intention, which he hesitated to carry into effect; and the conflict banished sleep from his pillow. When the messenger from Glasgow arrived, he was already dressed, and, as none of the servants were stirring, he opened the door himself. The news certainly gave him pleasure, but they also produced some change in the secret workings of his mind, of no auspicious augury to the fulfilment of the parental intention which he had probably formed; but which he was as probably reluctant to realize, as it could not be carried into effect without material detriment to that one single dominant object to which his whole life, efforts, and errors, had been devoted. At least from the moment he received the agreeable intelligence that Charles was better, his agitation ceased, and he resumed his seat in the elbow chair, by the parlour fire-side, as composedly as if nothing had occurred, in any degree, to trouble the apparently even tenor of his daily unsocial and solitary reflections. In this situation he fell asleep, from which he was roused by another messenger with still more interesting intelligence to him, than even the convalescence, as it was supposed, of his favourite son.

Mrs George Walkinshaw had, for some time, given a large promise, in her appearance, of adding to the heirs of Kittlestonheugh; but, by her residence in Glasgow, and holding little intercourse with the Grippy family, owing to her own situation, and to her dislike of the members, especially after Walter had been brought back with his child; the Laird and Leddy were less acquainted with her maternal progress than might have been expected, particularly when the anxiety of the old man, with respect to male issue, is considered. Such things, however, are of common occurrence in all families; and it so happened, that, during the course of this interesting night, Mrs George had been delivered; and that her husband, as in duty bound, in the morning, dispatched a maid-servant to inform his father and mother of the joyous event.

The messenger, Jenny Purdie, had several years before been in the servitude of the Laird's house, from which she translated herself to that of George. Being something forward, at the same time sly and adroit, and having heard how much her old master had been disappointed that Walter's daughter was not a son, she made no scruple of employing a little address in communicating her news. Accordingly, when the Laird, disturbed in his slumber by her entrance, roused himself, and turned round to see who it was that had come into the room, she presented herself, as she had walked from the royal city muffled up in a dingy red cloak, her dark blue and white striped petticoat, sorely scanty, and her glowing purple legs, and well spread shoeless feet, bearing liberal proof of the speed with which she had spattered and splashed along the road.

'I wis you meikle joy,[1] Laird! I hae brought you blithesmeat,' was her salutation.

'What is't, Jenny?' said the old man.

'I'll let you guess that, unless ye promise to gi'e me half-a-crown,' was her reply.

'T'ou canna think I would ware[2] less on sic errand as t'ou's come on. Is't a laddie?'

'It's far better, Laird,' said Jenny triumphantly.

'Is't twins?' exclaimed the Laird, sympathizing with her exultation.

'A half-crown, a half-crown, Laird,' was, however, all the satisfaction he received. 'Down wi' the dust.'

'An t'ou's sae on thy peremptors,[3] I fancy I maun comply. There, take it, and welcome,' said he, pulling the money from under the flap of his waistcoat pocket; while Jenny, stretching her arm, as she hoisted it from under the cloak, eagerly bent forward and took the silver out of his hand, instantaneously affecting the greatest gravity of face.

'Laird,' said she, 'ye mauna be angry wi' me, but I did na like just to dumb-foun'er you a' at ance wi' the news; my mistress, it's very true, has been brought to bed, but it's no as ye expekit.'

'Then it's but a dochter?' replied the Laird discontentedly.

'No, Sir, it's no a dochter.—It's twa dochters, Sir!' exclaimed

Jenny, scarcely able to repress her risibility, while she endeavoured to assume an accent of condolence.

Claud sank back in his chair, and, drooping his head, gave a deep sigh.

'But,' rejoined the adroit Jenny, 'it's a gude earnest of a braw family, so keep up your heart, Laird, aiblins the neist[1] birds may be a' cocks; there ne'er was a goose without a gander.'

'Gae bot[2] the house, and fash na me wi' thy clishmaclavers. I say gae bot the house,' cried the Laird, in a tone so deep and strong, that Jenny's disposition to gossip was most effectually daunted, and she immediately retired.

For some time after she had left the room, Claud continued sitting in the same posture with which he had uttered the command, leaning slightly forward, and holding the arms of the easy-chair graspingly by both his hands, as if in the act of raising himself. Gradually, however, he relaxed his hold, and subsided slowly and heavily into the position in which he usually fell asleep. Shutting his eyes, he remained in that state for a considerable time, exhibiting no external indication of the rush of mortified feelings, which, like a subterranean stream of some acrid mineral, struggled through all the abysses of his bosom.

This last stroke—the birth of twin daughters—seemed to perfect the signs and omens of that displeasure with which he had for some time thought the disinheritance of his first-born was regarded; and there was undoubtedly something sublime in the fortitude with which he endured the gnawings of remorse.—It may be impossible to consider the course of his sordid ambition without indignation; but the strength of character which enabled him to contend at once with his paternal partiality, and stand firm in his injustice before what he awfully deemed the frowns and the menaces of Heaven, forms a spectacle of moral bravery that cannot be contemplated without emotions of wonder mingled with dread.

CHAPTER VI

THE fallacious symptoms in the progress of Charles's malady, which had deceived his wife and mother, assumed, on the third day, the most alarming appearance. Mr Keelevin, who, from the interview, had taken an uncommon interest in his situation, did not, however, hear of his illness till the doctors, from the firmest persuasion that he could not survive, had expressed some doubts of his recovery; but, from that time, the inquiries of the honest lawyer were frequent; and, notwithstanding what had passed on the former occasion, he resolved to make another attempt on the sympathies of the father. For this purpose, on the morning of the fifth day, which happened to be Sunday, he called at Charles's house, to inquire how he was, previous to the visit which he intended to pay to Grippy. But the servant who attended the door was in tears, and told him that her master was in the last struggles of life.

Any other general acquaintance would, on receiving such intelligence, however deeply he might have felt affected, have retired; but the ardent mind and simplicity of Mr Keelevin prompted him to act differently; and without replying to the girl, he softly slipped his feet from his shoes, and stepping gently to the sick chamber, entered it unobserved; so much were those around the death-bed occupied with the scene before them.

Isabella was sitting at the bed-head, holding her dying husband by both the hands, and bending over him almost as insensible as himself. His mother was sitting near the foot of the bed, with a phial in one hand, and a towel, resting on her knee, in the other, looking over her left shoulder towards her son, with an eager countenance, in which curiosity, and alarm, and pity, were, in rapid succession, strangely and vacantly expressed. At the foot of the bed, the curtains of which were drawn aside, the two little children stood wondering in solemn innocence at the mournful mystery which Nature was performing with their father. Mr Keelevin was more moved by their helpless astonishment than even by the sight of the last and lessening heavings and pantings of his dying friend; and, melted to tears, he withdrew, and wept behind the door.

In the course of three or four minutes, a rustle in the chamber roused him; and on looking round, he saw Isabella standing on the floor, and her mother-in-law, who had dropped the phial, sitting, with a look of horror, holding up her hand, which quivered with agitation. He stepped forward, and giving a momentary glance at the bed, saw that all was over; but, before he could turn round to address himself to the ladies, the children uttered a shrill piercing shriek of terror; and running to their mother, hid their little faces in her dress, and clasped her fearfully in their arms.

For some minutes he was overcome. The young, the beautiful, the defenceless widow, was the first that recovered her self-possession. A flood of tears relieved her heart; and bending down, and folding her arms round her orphans, she knelt, and said, with an upward look of supplication, 'God will protect you.'

Mr Keelevin was still unable to trust himself to say a word; but he approached, and gently assisting her to rise, led her, with the children, into the parlour, where old Lady Plealands was sitting alone, with a large psalm-book in her hand. Her spectacles lying on a table in the middle of the room, showed that she had been unable to read.

He then returned to bring Leddy Grippy also away from the body, but met her in the passage. We dare not venture to repeat what she said to him, for she was a mother; but the result was, a request from her that he would undertake to communicate the intelligence to her husband, and to beg him either to come to her in the course of the day, or send her some money: 'For,' said she, 'this is a bare house, Mr Keelevin; and Heaven only knows what's to become o' the wee orphans.'

The kind-hearted lawyer needed, however, no argument to spur him on to do all that he could in such a time, and in such circumstances, to lighten the distress and misery of a family whose necessities he so well knew. On quitting the house, he proceeded immediately towards Grippy, ruminating on the scene he had witnessed, and on the sorrows which he foresaw the desolate widow and her children were destined to suffer.

The weather, for some days before, had been unsettled and boisterous; but it was that morning uncommonly fine for the advanced state of the season. Every thing was calm and in repose, as if Nature herself had hallowed the Sabbath. Mr Keelevin walked thoughtfully along, the grief of his reflections being gradually subdued by the benevolence of his intentions; but he was a man well stricken in years, and the agitation he had undergone made the way appear to him so long, that he felt himself tired, in so much, that when he came to the bottom of the lane which led to Kilmarkeckle, he sat down to rest himself on the old dike, where Claud himself had sat, on his return from the town, after executing the fatal entail. Absorbed in the reflections to which the event of the morning naturally gave rise, he leaned for some time pensively forward, supporting his head on his hand, insensible to every object around, till he was roused by the cooing of a pigeon in the field behind him. The softness and the affectionate sound of its tones comforted his spirits as he thought of his client's harsh temper, and he raised his eyes and looked on the beautiful tranquillity of the landscape before him, with a sensation of freshness and pleasure, that restored him to confidence in the charity of his intentions. The waters of the river were glancing to the cloudless morning sun,—a clear bright cheerfulness dwelt on the foreheads of the distant hills,—the verdure of the nearer fields seemed to be gladdened by the presence of spring,—and a band of little schoolboys, in their Sunday clothes, playing with a large dog on the opposite bank of the river, was in unison with the general benevolence that smiled and breathed around, but was liveliest in his own heart.

CHAPTER VII

The benevolent lawyer found the old man in his accustomed seat by the fire-side. Walter was in the room with him, dressed for church, and dandling his child. At first Mr Keelevin felt a little embarrassment, not being exactly aware in what manner the news he had to communicate might be received; but seeing how Walter was engaged, he took occasion to commend his parental affection.

'That's acting like a father, Mr Walter,' said he; 'for a kind parent innocently pleasuring his bairn is a sight that the very angels are proud to look on. Mak muckle o' the poor wee thing, for nobody can tell how long she may be spared to you. I dare say, Mr Walkinshaw,' he added, addressing himself to Claud, 'ye hae mony a time been happy in the same manner wi' your own children?'

'I had something else to tak up my mind,' replied the old man gruffly, not altogether pleased to see the lawyer, and apprehensive of some new animadversions.

'Nae doubt, your's has been an eydent[1] and industrious life,' said Mr Keelevin, 'and hitherto it has na been without a large scare[2] o' comfort. Ye canna, however, expek a greater constancy in fortune and the favour o' Providence than falls to the common lot of man; and ye maun lay your account to meet wi' troubles and sorrows as weel as your neighbours.'

This was intended by the speaker as a prelude to the tidings he had brought, and was said in a mild and sympathetic manner; but the heart of Claud, galled and skinless by the corrosion of his own thoughts, felt it as a reproach, and he interrupted him sharply.

'What ken ye, Mr Keelevin, either o' my trumps[3] or my troubles?' And he subjoined, in his austerest and most emphatic manner, 'The inner man alone knows, whether, in the gifts o' fortune, he has gotten gude, or but only gowd.[4] Mr Keelevin, I hae lived long eneugh to mak an observe on prosperity,—the whilk is, that the doited and heedless world is very ready to mistak the smothering growth of the ivy, on a doddered stem, for the green boughs o' a sound and flourishing tree.'

To which Walter added singingly, as he swung his child by the arms,—

'Near planted by a river,
Which in his season yields his fruit,
And his leaf fadeth never.'[5]

'But no to enter upon any controversy, Mr Walkinshaw,' said Mr Keelevin,—'ye'll no hae heard the day how your son Charles is?'

'No,' replied Claud, with a peculiarly impressive accent; 'but, at the latest last night, the gudewife sent word he was very ill.'

'I'm greatly concerned about him,' resumed the lawyer, scarcely aware of the address with which, in his simplicity, he was moving on towards the fatal communication; 'I am greatly concerned about him, but mair for his young children—they'll be very helpless orphans, Mr Walkinshaw.'

'I ken that,' was the stern answer, uttered with such a dark and troubled look, that it quite daunted Mr Keelevin at the moment from proceeding.

'Ye ken that!' cried Walter, pausing, and setting down the child on the floor, and seating himself beside it; 'how do ye ken that, father?'

The old man eyed him for a moment with a fierce and strong aversion, and, turning to Mr Keelevin, shook his head, but said nothing.

'What's done, is done, and canna be helped,' resumed the lawyer; 'but reparation may yet, by some sma cost and cooking,[1] be made; and I hope Mr Walkinshaw, considering what has happened, ye'll do your duty.'

'I'll sign nae papers,' interposed Walter; 'I'll do nothing to wrang my wee Betty Bodle,'—and he fondly kissed the child.

Mr Keelevin looked compassionately at the natural, and then, turning to his father, said,—

'I hae been this morning to see Mr Charles.'

'Weel, and how is he?' exclaimed the father eagerly.

The lawyer, for about the term of a minute, made no reply, but looked at him steadily in the face, and then added solemnly,

'He's no more!'

At first the news seemed to produce scarcely any effect; the iron countenance of the old man underwent no immediate change—he only remained immoveable in the position in which he had received the shock; but presently Mr Keelevin saw that he did not fetch his breath, and that his lips began to contract asunder, and to expose his yellow teeth with the grin almost of a skull.

'Heavens preserve us, Mr Walkinshaw!' cried Mr Keelevin, rising to his assistance; but, in the same moment, the old man uttered a groan so deep and dreadful, so strange and superhuman, that Walter snatched up his child, and rushed in terror out of the room. After this earthquake-struggle, he in some degree recovered himself, and the lawyer returned to his chair, where he remained some time silent.

'I had a fear o't, but I was na prepar't, Mr Keelevin, for this,' said the miserable father; 'and noo I'll kick against the pricks nae langer. Wonderful God! I bend my aged grey head at thy footstool. O lay not thy hand heavier upon me than I am able to bear. Mr Keelevin, ye ance said the entail cou'd be broken if I were to die insolvent—mak me sae in the name of the God I have dared so long to fight against. An Charlie's dead—murdered by my devices! Weel do I mind, when he was a playing bairn, that I first

kent the blessing of what it is to hae something to be kind to;—
aften and aften did his glad and bright young face thaw the frost
that had bound up my heart, but ay something new o' the world's
pride and trash cam in between, and hardent it mair and mair.—
But a's done noo, Mr Keelevin—the fight's done and the battle
won, and the avenging God of righteousness and judgment is
victorious.'

Mr Keelevin sat in silent astonishment at this violence of sorrow.
He had no previous conception of that vast abyss of sensibility
which lay hidden and unknown within the impenetrable granite of
the old man's pride and avarice; and he was amazed and overawed
when he beheld it burst forth, as when the fountains of the great
deep were broken up, and the deluge swept away the earliest and
the oldest iniquities of man.

The immediate effect, when he began to recover from his
wonder, was a sentiment of profound reverence.

'Mr Walkinshaw,' said he, 'I have long done you great injustice;'
and he was proceeding to say something more as an apology, but
Claud interrupted him.

'You hae ne'er done me any manner of wrong, Mr Keelevin;
but I hae sinned greatly and lang against my ain nature, and it's
time I sou'd repent. In a few sorrowful days I maun follow the
lamb I hae sacrificed on the altars o' pride; speed a' ye dow[1] to
mak the little way I hae to gang to the grave easy to one that travels
wi' a broken heart. I gie you nae further instructions—your skill
and honest conscience will tell you what is needful to be done;
and when the paper's made out, come to me. For the present leave
me, and in your way hame bid Dr Denholm come hither in the
afternoon.'

'I think, Mr Walkinshaw,' replied Mr Keelevin, falling into his
professional manner on receiving these orders, 'that it would be
as weel for me to come back the morn, when ye're more composed,
to get the particulars of what ye wish done.'

'O man!' exclaimed the hoary penitent, 'ye ken little o' me.
Frae the very dawn o' life I hae done nothing but big[2] and build
an idolatrous image; and when it was finished, ye saw how I laid
my first-born on its burning and brazen altar. But ye never saw
what I saw—the face of an angry God looking constantly from
behind a cloud that darkened a' the world like the shadow of death
to me; and ye canna feel what I feel now, when His dreadful right

hand has smashed my idol into dust. I hae nae langer part interest
nor portion in the concerns of this life; but only to sign ony paper
that ye can devise, to restore their rights to the twa babies that my
idolatry has made fatherless.'

'I hope, in mercy, Mr Walkinshaw, that ye'll be comforted,'
said the worthy lawyer, deeply affected by his vehemence.

'I hope so too, but I see na whar at present it's to come frae,'
replied Claud, bursting into tears, and weeping bitterly. 'But,' he
added, 'I would fain, Mr Keelevin, be left to mysel—alack! alack!
I hae been owre lang left to mysel. Howsever, gang away the day,[1]
and remember Dr Denholm as ye pass;—but I'll ne'er hae peace
o' mind till the paper's made and signed; so, as a Christian, I beg
you to make haste, for it will be a Samaritan's act of charity.'

Mr Keelevin perceived that it was of no use at that time to offer
any farther consolation, and he accordingly withdrew.

CHAPTER VIII

DURING the remainder of the day, after Mr Keelevin had left
him, Claud continued to sit alone, and took no heed of any thing
that occurred around him.—Dinner was placed on the table at the
usual hour; but he did not join Walter.

'I won'er, father,' said the natural, as he was hewing at the joint,
'that ye're no for ony dinner the day; for ye ken if a' the folk in the
world were to die but only ae[2] man, it would behove that man to
hae his dinner.'

To this sage observation the grey-haired penitent made no
reply; and Walter finished his meal without attempting to draw
him again into conversation.

In the afternoon Claud left his elbow chair, and walked slowly
and heavily up the path which led to the bench he had constructed
on the rising ground, where he was so often in the practice of contemplating the lands of his forefathers; and on gaining the brow
of the hill, he halted, and once more surveyed the scene. For a
moment it would seem that a glow of satisfaction passed over his
heart; but it was only a hectical flush, instantly succeeded by the
nausea of moral disgust; and he turned abruptly round, and seated
himself with his back towards the view which had afforded him so

much pleasure. In this situation he continued some time, resting his forehead on his ivory-headed staff, and with his eyes fixed on the ground.

In the meantime, Mr Keelevin having called on the Reverend Dr Denholm, according to Claud's wish, to request he would visit him in the afternoon, the venerable minister was on his way to Grippy. On reaching the house, he was informed by one of the maid-servants, that her master had walked to his summer-seat on the hill, whither he immediately proceeded, and found the old man still rapt in his moody and mournful meditations.

Claud had looked up, as he heard him approach, and pointing to the bench, beckoned him to be seated. For some time they sat together without speaking; the minister appearing to wait in expectation that the penitent would address him first; but observing him still disposed to continue silent, he at last said,—

'Mr Keelevin told me, Mr Walkinshaw, that ye wished to see me under this dispensation with which the hand o' a righteous Providence has visited your family.'

'I'm greatly obligated to Mr Keelevin,' replied Claud, thoughtfully; 'he's a frien'ly and a very honest man. It would hae been happy wi' me the day, Dr Denholm, had I put mair confidence in him; but I doobt, I doobt, I hae been a' my life a sore hypocrite.'

'I was ay o' that notion,' said the Reverend Doctor, not quite sure whether the contrition so humbly expressed was sincere or affected, but the meek look of resignation with which the desolate old man replied to the cutting sarcaśm, moved the very heart of the chastiser with strong emotions of sympathy and grief; and he added, in his kindliest manner,—

'But I hope, Mr Walkinshaw, I may say to you, "Brother, be of good cheer;" for if this stroke, by which your first-born is cut off from the inheritance of the years that were in the promise of his winsome youth, is ta'en and borne as the admonition of the vanity of setting your heart on the things of carnal life, it will prove to you a great blessing for evermore.'

There was something in the words in which this was couched, that, still more painfully than the taunt, affected the disconsolate penitent, and he burst into tears, taking hold of the minister's right hand graspingly with his left, saying, 'Spare me, doctor! O spare me, an it be possible—for the worm that never dieth hath coiled itsel within my bosom, and the

fire that's never quenched is kindled around me—What an it be
for ever?'

'Ye should na, Mr Walkinshaw,' replied the clergyman, awed
by the energy and solemnity of his manner—'Ye should na
entertain such desperate thoughts, but hope for better things;
for it's a blithe thing for your precious soul to be at last sensible o'
your own unworthiness.'

'Aye, doctor, but, alack for me! I was ay sensible o' that. I hae
sinned wi' my e'en open, and I thought to mak up for't by a strict
observance o' church ordinances.'

''Deed, Mr Walkinshaw, there are few shorter roads to the pit
than through the kirk-door; and many a Christian has been
brought nigh to the death, thinking himsel cheered and guided
by the sound o' gospel preaching, when, a' the time, his ear was
turned to the sough[1] o' perdition.'

'What shall I do to be saved?' said the old man, reverentially
and timidly.

'Ye can do naething yoursel, Mr Walkinshaw,' replied the
minister; and he proceeded, with the fearlessness of a champion
and the energy of an apostle, to make manifest to his understanding the corruption of the human heart, and its utter unworthiness in the pure eyes of Him that alone can wash away the
Ethiopian hue of original sin, and eradicate the Leopard[2] spots of
personal guilt.

While he spoke the bosom of Claud was convulsed—he breathed
deeply and fearfully—his eyes glared—and the manner in which
he held his hands, trembling and slightly raised, showed that his
whole inward being was transfixed as it were, with a horrible sense
of some tremendous apocalypse.

'I fear, I fear, Doctor Denholm,' he exclaimed, 'that I can hae
no hope.'

The venerable pastor was struck with the despair of the expression, and, after a short pause, said, 'Dinna let yoursel despond;
tak comfort in the mercy of God; surely your life has na been
blacken't wi' ony great crime?'

'It has been one continued crime,' cried the penitent—'frae the
first hour that my remembrance can look back to, down to the vera
last minute, there has been no break nor interruption in the constancy of my iniquity. I sold my soul to the Evil One in my childhood, that I might recover the inheritance of my forebears. O the

pride of that mystery! and a' the time there was a voice within me that would na be pacified wi' the vain promises I made to become another man, as soon as ever my conquest was complete.'

'I see but in that,' said the pious Doctor, in a kind and consoling manner, 'I see but in a' that, Mr Walkinshaw, an inordinate love of the world; and noo that ye're awakened to a sense of your danger, the Comforter will soon come. Ye hae ay been reputed an honest man, and no deficient in your moral duties, as a husband, a parent, a master, and a friend.'

Claud clasped his hands fervently together, exclaiming, 'O God! thou hast ever seen my hypocrisy!—Dr Denholm,' and he took him firmly by the hand;—'when I was but a bairn, I kent na what it was to hae the innocence o' a young heart. I used to hide the sma' presents of siller I got frae my frien's, even when Maudge Dobbie, the auld kind creature that brought me up, could na earn a sufficiency for our scrimpit meals; I did na gang near her when I kent she was in poortith¹ and bedrid, for fear my heart would relent, and gar me gie² her something out o' the gathering I was making for the redemption o' this vile yird³ that is mair grateful than·me, for it repays with its fruits the care o' the tiller. I stiffled the very sense o' loving kindness within me; and in furtherance of my wicked avarice, I married a woman—Heaven may forgie the aversion I had to her; but my own nature never can.'

Dr Denholm held up his hands, and contemplated in silence the humbled and prostrate spirit that was thus proceeding with the frightful confession of its own baseness and depravity.

'But,' cried the penitent, 'I canna hope that ye're able to thole⁴ the sight that I would lay open in the inner sepulchre of my guilty conscience—for in a' my reprobation I had ever the right before me, when I deliberately preferred the wrang. The angel of the Lord ceased not, by night nor by day, to warsle⁵ for me; but I clung to Baal, and spurned and kicked whenever the messenger of brightness and grace tried to tak me away.'

The old man paused, and then looking towards the minister, who still continued silent, regarding him with compassionate amazement, said,—

'Doctor, what can I expek?'

'O! Mr Walkinshaw, but ye hae been a doure⁶ sinner,' was the simple and emphatic reply; 'and I hope that this sense o' the evil of your way is an admonition to a repentance that may lead you into the right road at last. Be ye, therefore, thankful for the warning ye hae now gotten of the power and the displeasure of God.'

'Many a warning,' said Claud, 'in tokens sairer than the plagues o' Egypt, which but grieved the flesh, hae I had in the spirit; but still my heart was harden't till the destroying angel slew my first-born.'

'Still I say, be thankful, Mr Walkinshaw! ye hae received a singular manifestation of the goodness of God. Your son, we're to hope, is removed into a better world. He's exposed no more to the temptations of this life—a' care wi' him is past—a' sorrow is taken from him. It's no misfortune to die, but a great risk to be born; and nae Christian should sorrow, like unto those who are without hope, when Death, frae ahint the black yett,[1] puts forth his ancient hand, and pulls in a brother or a sister by the skirts of the garment of flesh. The like o' that, Mr Walkinshaw, is naething; but when, by the removal of a friend, we are taught to see the error of our way, it's a great thing for us—it's a blithe thing; and, therefore, I say unto you again, brother, be of good cheer, for in this temporal death of your son, may be the Lord has been pleased to bring about your own salvation.'

'And what may be the token whereby I may venture to take comfort frae the hope?'

'There's nae surer sign gi'en to man than that token—when ye see this life but as a pilgrimage, then ye may set forward in your way rejoicing—when ye behold nothing in your goods and gear but trash and splendid dirt, then may ye be sure that ye hae gotten better than silver or gold—when ye see in your herds and flocks but fodder for a carnal creature like the beasts that perish, then shall ye eat of the heavenly manna—when ye thirst to do good, then shall the rock be smitten, and the waters of life, flowing forth, will follow you wheresoever you travel in the wilderness of this world.'

The venerable pastor suddenly paused, for at that moment Claud laid aside his hat, and, falling on his knees, clasped his hands together, and looking towards the skies, his long grey hair flowing over his back, he said with awful solemnity, 'Father, thy will be done!—in the devastation of my earthly heart, I accept the crls[2] of thy service.'

He then rose with a serene countenance, as if his rigid features had undergone some benignant transformation. At that moment a distant strain of wild and holy music, rising from a hundred voices, drew their attention towards a shaggy bank of natural birch and hazel, where, on the sloping ground in front, they saw a number of Cameronians[1] from Glasgow, and the neighbouring villages, assembled to commemorate in worship the persecutions which their forefathers had suffered there for righteousness sake.

After listening till the psalm was finished, Claud and Dr Denholm returned towards the house, where they found Leddy Grippy had arrived. The old man, in order to avoid any unnecessary conversation, proposed that the servants should be called in, and that the Doctor should pray—which he did accordingly, and at the conclusion retired.

CHAPTER IX

ON Monday Claud rose early, and, without waiting for breakfast, or heeding the remonstrances of his wife on the risk he ran in going afield fasting, walked to Glasgow, and went directly to the house of his mother-in-law, the aged Lady Plealands, now considerably above four-score. The natural delicacy of her constitution had received so great a shock from the death of Charles, that she was unable that morning to leave her room. Having, however, brought home with her the two orphans, until after the funeral, their grandfather found them playing in the parlour, and perhaps he was better pleased to meet with them than had she been there herself.

Although they knew him perfectly, yet the cold and distant intercourse which arose from his estrangement towards their father, had prevented them from being on those terms of familiarity which commonly subsist between children and their grandfathers; and when they saw him enter the room, they immediately left their toys on the floor, and, retiring to a corner, stood looking at him timidly, with their hands behind.

The old man, without seeming to notice their innocent reverence, walked to a chair near the window, and sat down. His demeanour was as calm, and his features as sedate, as usual, but his eyes glittered with a slight sprinkling of tears, and twice or thrice he pressed his elbows into his sides, as if to restrain some inordinate agitation of the heart. In the course of a few minutes he became

quite master of himself, and, looking for a short time compassionately at the children, he invited them to come to him. Mary, the
girl, who was the youngest, obeyed at once the summons; but
James, the boy, still kept back.

'What for wilt t'ou no[1] come to me?' said Claud.

'I'll come, if ye'll no hurt me,' replied the child. 'Hurt thee!
what for, poor thing, should I hurt thee?' inquired his grandfather,
somewhat disturbed by the proposed condition.

'I dinna ken,' said the boy, still retreating,—'but I am feart, for
ye hurt papa for naething, and mamma used to greet for't.'[2]

Claud shuddered, and in the spasmodic effort which he made to
suppress his emotion, he unconsciously squeezed the little hand
of the girl so hardly, as he held her between his knees, that she
shrieked with the pain, and flew towards her brother, who, equally
terrified, ran to shelter himself behind a chair.

For some time the old man was so much affected, that he felt
himself incapable of speaking to them. But he said to himself,—

'It is fit that I should endure this. I sowed tares, and mauna
expek wheat.'

The children, not finding themselves angrily pursued, began to
recover courage, and again to look at him.

'I did na mean to hurt thee, Mary,' said he, after a short interval.
'Come, and we'll mak it up;'—and, turning to the boy, he added,
'I'm very wae that e'er I did ony wrang to your father, my bonny
laddie, but I'll do sae nae mair.'

'That's cause ye canna help it,' replied James boldly, 'for he's
dead—he's in a soun' soun' sleep—nobody but an angel wi' the
last trumpet at his vera lug[3] is able to waken him—and Mary and
me, and mamma—we're a' gaun to lie down and die too, for there's
nobody now in the world that cares for us.'

'I care for you, my lambie, and I'll be kind to you; I'll be as kind
as your father.'

It would appear that these words had been spoken affectionately, for the little girl, forgetful of her hurt, returned, and
placed herself between his knees; but her brother still stood
aloof.

'But will ye be kind to mamma?' said the boy, with an eager and
suspicious look.

'That I will,' was the answer. 'She'll ne'er again hae to blame me
—nor hae reason to be sorrowful on my account.'

'But were nae ye ance papa's papa?' rejoined the child, still more suspiciously.

The old man felt the full force of all that was meant by these simple expressions, and he drew his hand hastily over his eyes to wipe away the rising tears.

'And will ye never trust me?' said he sorrowfully to the child, who, melted by the tone in which it was uttered, advanced two or three steps towards him.

'Ay, if ye'll say as sure's death that ye'll no hurt me.'

'Then I do say as sure's death,' exclaimed Claud fervently, and held out his hand, which the child, running forward, caught in his, and was in the same moment folded to his grandfather's bosom.

Lady Plealands had, in the meantime, been told who was her visitor, and being anxious, for many reasons, to see him at this crisis, opened the door. Feeble, pale, and delicate, the venerable gentlewoman was startled at seeing a sight she so little expected, and stood several minutes with the door in her hand before she entered.

'Come in,' said Claud to her—'come in—I hae something to say to you anent thir bairns[1]—Something maun be done for them and their mother; and I would fain tak counsel wi' you concerning 't. Bell Fatherlans is o' oure frush a heart to thole wi' the dinging and fyke o' our house,[2] or I would tak them a' hame to Grippy; but ye maun devise some method wi' her to mak their loss as light in worldly circumstances as my means will alloo; and whatsoever you and her 'gree upon Mr Keelevin will see executed baith by deed and paction.'

'Is't possible that ye're sincere, Mr Walkinshaw?' replied the old lady.

Claud made no answer, but, disconsolately, shook his head.

'This is a mercy past hope, if ye're really sincere.'

'I am sincere,' said the stern old man, severely; 'and I speak wi' humiliation and contrition. I hae borne the rebuke of thir babies, and their suspicion has spoken sermons of reproaches to my cowed spirit and broken heart.'

'What have ye done?' inquired the Lady, surprised at his vehemence—'what have ye done to make you speak in such a way, Mr Walkinshaw?'

'In an evil hour I was beguiled by the Moloch o' pride and ambition to disinherit their father, and settle a' my property on

Watty, because he had the Plealands. But, from that hour, I hae never kent what comfort is, or amaist[1] what it is to hope for heavenly mercy. But I hae lived to see my sin, and I yearn to mak atonement. When that's done, I trust that I may be permitted to lay down my head, and close my een in peace.'

Mrs Hypel did not well know what answer to make, the disclosure seemed to her so extraordinary, that she looked at Claud as if she distrusted what she heard, or was disposed to question the soundness of his mind.

'I see,' he added, 'that, like the orphans, ye dinna believe me; but, like them, Mrs Hypel, ye'll may be in time be wrought to hae compassion on a humbled and contrite heart. A', therefore, that I can say for the present is, consult wi' Bell, and confer wi' Mr Keelevin; he has full power frae me to do whatsoever he may think just and right; and what ye do, do quickly, for a heavy hand is on my shouther;[2] and there's one before me in the shape o' my braw Charlie, that waves his hand, and beckons me to follow him.'

The profound despondency with which this was uttered overwhelmed the feelings of the old Lady; even the children were affected, and, disengaging themselves from his arms, retired together, and looked at him with wonder and awe.

'Will ye go and see their mother?'—said the lady, as he rose, and was moving towards the door. He halted, and for a few seconds appeared to reflect; but suddenly looking round, he replied, with a deep and troubled voice,—

'No. I hae been enabled to do mair than I ever thought it was in my power to do; but I canna yet,—no, not this day,—I canna yet venture there.—I will, however, by and by. It's a penance I maun dree,[3] and I will go through it a'.'

And with these words he quitted the house, leaving the old gentlewoman and the children equally amazed, and incapable of comprehending the depth and mystery of a grief which, mournful as the immediate cause certainly was, undoubtedly partook in some degree of religious despair.

CHAPTER X

BETWEEN the interview described in the preceding chapter and the funeral, nothing remarkable appeared in the conduct of Claud. On the contrary, those habits of reserve and taciturnity into which he had fallen, from the date of the entail, were apparently renewed, and, to the common observation of the general eye, he moved and acted as if he had undergone no inward change. The domestics, however, began to notice, that, instead of the sharp and contemptuous manner which he usually employed in addressing himself to Walter, his voice was modulated with an accent of compassion,—and that, on the third day after the death of Charles, he, for the first time, caressed and fondled the affectionate natural's darling, Betty Bodle.

It might have been thought that this simple little incident would have afforded pleasure to her father, who happened to be out of the room, when the old man took her up in his arms; but so far from this being the case, the moment that Walter returned he ran towards him, and snatched the child away.

'What for do'st t'ou tak the bairn frae me sae frightedly, Watty?' said Claud in a mild tone of remonstrance, entirely different from any thing he had ever before addressed to him.

Walter, however, made no reply, but retiring to a distant part of the room, carefully inspected the child, and frequently inquired where she was hurt, although she was laughing and tickled with his nursery-like proceedings.

'What gars t'ee think, Watty,' rejoined his father, 'that I would hurt the wean?'[1]

''Cause I hae heard you wish that the Lord would tak the brat to himsel.'

'An I did, Watty, it was nae ill wis.'

'So I ken, or else the minister lies,' replied Walter; 'but I would na like, for a' that, to hae her sent till him;[2] and noo, as they say ye're ta'en up wi' Charlie's bairns, I jealouse[3] ye hae some end o' your ain for rooketty-cooing wi' my wee Betty Bodle. I canna understand this new kythed[4] kindness,—so, gin ye like,[5] father, we'll just be fair gude e'en and fair gude day, as we were wont.'

This sank deeper into the wounded heart of his father than even the distrust of the orphans; but the old man made no answer. Walter, however, observed him muttering something to himself, as he leant his head back, with his eyes shut, against the shoulder of the easy chair in which he was sitting; and rising softly with the child in his arms, walked cautiously behind the chair, and bent forward to listen. But the words were spoken so inwardly and thickly, that nothing could be overheard. While in this position, the little girl playfully stretched out her hand and seized her grand-father by the ear. Startled from his prayer or his reverie, Claud, yielding to the first impulse of the moment, turned angrily round at being so disturbed, and, under the influence of his old con-temptuous regard for Watty, struck him a severe blow on the face, —but almost in the same instant, ashamed of his rashness, he shudderingly exclaimed, throbbing with remorse and vexation,—

'Forgi'e me, Watty, for I know not what I do;' and he added, in a wild ejaculation, 'Lord! Lord! O lighter, lighter lay the hand o' thy anger upon me. The reed is broken—O, if it may stand wi' thy pleasure, let it not thus be trampled in the mire! But why should I supplicate for any favour?—Lord of justice and of judgment, let thy will be done!'

Walter was scarcely more confounded by the blow than by these impassioned exclamations; and hastily quitting the room, ran, with the child in his arms, to his mother, who happened at the time, as was her wont, to be in the kitchen on household cares intent, crying,—

'Mother! mother! my father's gane by himsel;[1] he's aff at the head; he's daft; and ta'en to the praising o' the Lord at this time o' day.'

But, excepting this trivial incident, nothing, as we have already stated, occurred between the interview with Lady Plealands and the funeral to indicate, in any degree, the fierce combustion of dis-tracted thoughts which was raging within the unfathomable caverns of the penitent's bosom—all without, save but for this little effusion, was calm and stable. His external appearance was as we have sometimes seen Mount Etna[2] in the sullenness of a wintry day, when the chaos and fires of its abyss uttered no sound, and an occasional gasp of vapour was heavily breathed along the grey and gloomy sky. Every thing was still and seemingly stedfast. The woods were silent in all their leaves; the convents wore an awful aspect of unsocial solemnity; and the ruins and remains of former ages appeared as if permitted to moulder in unmolested decay. The very sea, as it rolled in a noiseless swell towards the black promontories of lava, suggested strange imageries of universal death, as if it had been the pall of the former world heavily moved by the wind. But that dark and ominous tranquillity boded neither permanence nor safety—the traveller and the inhabitant alike felt it as a syncope in nature, and dreaded an eruption or a hurricane.

Such was the serenity in which Claud passed the time till Saturday, the day appointed for the funeral. On the preceding evening his wife went into Glasgow to direct the preparations, and about noon he followed her, and took his seat, to receive the guests, at the door of the principal room arranged for the company, with James, the orphan, at his knee. Nothing uncommon passed for some time; he went regularly through the ceremonial of assistant chief mourner, and in silence welcomed, by the customary shake of the hand, each of the friends of the deceased as they came in. When Dr Denholm arrived, it was observed that his limbs trembled, and that he held him a little longer by the hand than any other; but he too was allowed to pass on to his seat. After the venerable minister, Mr Keelevin made his appearance. His clothes were of an old-fashioned cut, such as even still may occasionally be seen at west country funerals among those who keep a special suit of black for the purpose of attending the burials of their friends; and the sort of quick eager look of curiosity which he glanced round the room, as he lifted his small cocked hat from off his white, well-powdered, ionic curled tie-wig,[1] which he held firm with his left forefinger, provoked a smile, in despite of the solemnity of the occasion.

Claud grasped him impatiently by the hand, and drew him into a seat beside himself. 'Hae ye made out the instrument?' said he.

'It's no just finished,' replied Mr Keelevin; 'but I was mindit to ca' on you the morn,[2] though it's Sabbath, to let you see, for approbation, what I have thought might be sufficient.'

'Ye ought to hae had it done by this time,' said Claud, somewhat chidingly.

''Deed should I,' was the answer, 'but ye ken the Lords[3] are coming to the town next week, and I hae had to prepare for the defence of several unfortunate creatures.'

'It's a judgment time indeed,' said Claud; and, after a pause of several minutes, he added, 'I would fain no be disturbed on the Lord's day, so ye need na come to Grippy, and on Monday morning I'll be wi' you betimes; I hope a' may be finished that day, for, till I hae made atonement, I can expek no peace o' mind.'

Nothing farther was allowed at that time to pass between them, for the betherils[1] employed to carry round the services of bread and wine came in with their trays, and Deacon Gardner, of the Wrights,[2] who had charge of the funeral, having nodded to the Reverend Dr John Hamilton, the minister of the Inner High Church,[3] in the district of which the house was situated, the worthy divine rose, and put an end to all farther private whispering, by commencing the prayer.

When the regular in-door rites and ceremonies were performing, and the body had, in the meantime, been removed into the street, and placed on the shoulders of those who were to carry it to the grave, Claud took his grandson by the hand, and followed at the head, with a firmly knotted countenance, but with faultering steps.

In the procession to the church-yard no particular expression of feeling took place; but when the first shovelful of earth rattled hollowly on the coffin, the little boy, who still held his grandfather by the finger, gave a shriek, and ran to stop the grave-digger from covering it up. But the old man softly and composedly drew him back, telling him it was the will of God, and that the same thing must be done to every body in the world.

'And to me too?' said the child, inquiringly and fearfully.

'To a' that live,' replied his grandfather; and the earth being, by this time, half filled in, he took off his hat, and looking at the grave for a moment, gave a profound sigh, and again covering his head, led the child home.

CHAPTER XI

IMMEDIATELY after the funeral Claud returned home to Grippy, where he continued during the remainder of the day secluded in his bed-chamber. Next morning, being Sunday, he was up and dressed earlier than usual; and after partaking slightly of breakfast, he walked into Glasgow, and went straight to the house of his daughter-in-law.

The widow was still in her own room, and not in any state or condition to be seen; but the children were dressed for church, and when the bells began to ring, he led them out, each holding him by the hand, innocently proud of their new black clothes.

In all the way up the High Street, and down the pathway from the church-yard gate to the door of the cathedral, he never raised his eyes; and during the sermon he continued in the same apparent state of stupor. In retiring from the church, the little boy drew him gently aside from the path to show his sister the spot where their father was laid; and the old man, absorbed in his own reflections, was unconsciously on the point of stepping on the grave, when James checked him,—

'It's papa—dinna tramp on him.'

Aghast and recoiling, as if he had trodden upon an adder, he looked wildly around, and breathed quickly and with great difficulty, but said nothing. In an instant his countenance underwent a remarkable change—his eyes became glittering and glassy, and his lips white. His whole frame shook, and appeared under the influence of some mortal agitation. His presence of mind did not, however, desert him, and he led the children hastily home. On reaching the door, he gave them in to the servant that opened it without speaking, and went immediately to Grippy, where, the moment he had seated himself in his elbow chair, he ordered one of the servants to go for Mr Keelevin.

'What ails you, father?' said Walter, who was in the room at the time; 'ye speak unco drumly[1]—hae ye bitten your tongue?' But scarcely had he uttered these words, when the astonished creature gave a wild and fearful shout, and, clasping his hands above his head, cried, 'Help! help! something's riving my father in picces!'

The cry brought in the servants, who, scarcely less terrified, found the old man smitten with a universal paralysis, his mouth and eyes dreadfully distorted, and his arms powerless.

In the alarm and consternation of the moment, he was almost immediately deserted; every one ran in quest of medical aid. Walter alone remained with him, and continued gazing in his face with a strange horror, which idiocy rendered terrific.

Before any of the servants returned, the violence of the shock seemed to subside, and he appeared to be sensible of his situation. The moment that the first entered the room he made an effort to speak, and the name of Keelevin was two or three times so distinctly articulated, that even Walter understood what he meant, and immediately ran wildly to Glasgow for the lawyer. Another messenger was dispatched for the Leddy, who had, during the forenoon, gone to her daughter-in-law, with the intention of spending the day.

In the meantime a Doctor was procured, but he seemed to consider the situation of the patient hopeless; he, however, as in all similar cases, applied the usual stimulants to restore energy, but without any decisive effect.

The weather, which had all day been lowering and hazy, about this time became drizzly, and the wind rose, insomuch that Leddy Grippy, who came flying to the summons, before reaching home was drenched to the skin, and was for some time, both from her agitation and fatigue, incapable of taking any part in the bustle around her husband.

Walter, who had made the utmost speed for Mr Keelevin, returned soon after his mother; and, on appearing before his father, the old man eagerly spoke to him; but his voice was so thick, that few of his words were intelligible. It was, however, evident that he inquired for the lawyer; for he threw his eyes constantly towards the door, and several times again was able to articulate his name.

At last, Mr Keelevin arrived on horseback, and came into the room, dressed in his trotcosey;[1] the hood of which, over his cocked hat, was drawn so closely on his face, that but the tip of his sharp aquiline nose was visible. But, forgetful or regardless of his appearance, he stalked with long strides at once to the chair where Claud was sitting; and taking from under the skirt of the trotcosey a bond of provision for the widow and children of Charles, and for Mrs Milrookit, he knelt down, and began to read it aloud.

'Sir,' said the Doctor, who was standing at the other side of the patient, 'Mr Walkinshaw is in no condition to understand you.'

Still, however, Mr Keelevin read on; and when he had finished, he called for pen and ink.

'It is impossible that he can write,' said the Doctor.

'Ye hae no business to mak ony sic observation,' exclaimed the benevolent lawyer. 'Ye shou'd say nothing till we try. In the name of justice and mercy, is there nobody in this house that will fetch me pen and ink?'

It was evident to all present that Claud perfectly understood what his friend said; and his eyes betokened eagerness and satisfaction; but the expression with which his features accompanied the assent in his look was horrible and appalling.

At this juncture Leddy Grippy came rushing, half dressed, into the room, her dishevelled grey hair flying loosely over her shoulders, exclaiming,—

'What's wrang noo?—what new judgment has befallen us?—Whatna fearfu' image is that like a corpse out o' a tomb, that's making a' this rippet for the cheatrie instruments[1] o' pen and ink, when a dying man is at his last gasp?'

'Mrs Walkinshaw, for Heaven's sake be quiet;—your gudeman,' replied Mr Keelevin, opening the hood of his trotcosey, and throwing it back; taking off, at the same time, his cocked hat—'Your gudeman kens very weel what I hae read to him. It's a provision for Mrs Charles and her orphans.'

'But is there no likewise a provision in't for me?' cried the Leddy.

'O, Mrs Walkinshaw, we'll speak o' that hereafter; but let us get this executed aff hand,' replied Mr Keelevin. 'Ye see your gudeman kens what we're saying, and looks wistfully to get it done. I say, in the name of God, get me pen and ink.'

'Ye's get neither pen nor ink here, Mr Keelevin, till my rights are cognost in a record o' sederunt and session.'[2]

'Hush!' exclaimed the Doctor—all was silent, and every eye turned on the patient, whose countenance was again hideously convulsed;—a troubled groan struggled and heaved for a moment in his breast, and was followed by short quivering through his whole frame.

'It is all over!' said the Doctor. At these words the Leddy rushed towards the elbow chair, and, with frantic cries and gestures, flew on the body, and acted an extravagance of sorrow ten times more outrageous than grief. Mr Keelevin stood motionless, holding the paper in his hand; and, after contemplating the spectacle before him for about two or three minutes, shook his head disconsolately, and replacing his cocked hat, drew the hood of the trotcosey again over his face, and left the house.

CHAPTER XII

As soon as the nature of the settlement which Claud had made of his property was known, Lady Plealands removed Mrs Charles and the children to her own house, and earnestly entreated her daughter the Leddy, who continued to reside at Grippy, managing the household cares there as usual, to exert her influence with Walter to make some provision for his unfortunate relations. Even George, who, engrossed by his business and his own family, cared almost as little as any man for the concerns of others, felt so ashamed of his father's conduct, that, on the Sunday after the funeral, he went to pay a visit of condolence to his mother, and to join his exhortations to hers, in the hope that something might be done. But Walter was inexorable.

'If my father,' said he, 'did sic a wicked thing to Charlie as ye a' say, what for would ye hae me to do as ill and as wrang to my bairn? Is na wee Betty Bodle my first-born, and, by course o' nature and law, she has a right to a' I hae; what for then would ye hae me to mak away wi' ony thing that pertains to her? I'll no be guilty o' ony sic sin.'

'But you know, Walter,' replied George, 'that our father did intend to make some provision both for Mrs Charles her family and our sister, and it's really a disgrace to us all if nothing be done for them. It was but a chance that the bond of provision was na signed.'

'Ye may say sae, Geordie, in your cracks at the Yarn Club,[1] o'er the punch-bowl, but I think it was the will o' Providence; for, had it been ordain't that Bell Fatherlans and her weans were to get a part o' father's gear, they would hae gotten't. But ye saw the Lord took him to Abraham's bosom before the bond was signed, which was a clear proof and testimony to me, that it does na stand wi' the pleasure o' Heaven that she should get ony thing. She'll get nothing frae me.'

'But,' again interposed George, 'if you will do nothing in consideration of our father's intention, you ought in charity to think of her distress.'

'Charity begins at hame, Geordie, and wha kens but I may be brought to want if I dinna tak care?'

'I'm sure,' replied the merchant, sharply, 'that many a one has who less deserved it.'

'How do ye ken what I deserve?' cried the natural, offended. 'It's speaking ill o' the understanding o' Providence, to say I dinna deserve what it has gi'en me. I'm thinking, Geordie, Providence kens my deserts muckle better than you.'

Leddy Grippy, who, during this conversation, was sitting at the table, in all the pomp of her new widow's weeds, with the big Bible before her, in which she was trying to read that edifying chapter, the tenth of Nehemiah,[1] here interposed.

'Wheesht, wheesht, Watty, and dinna blaspheme,' said she; 'and no be overly condumacious. Ye ken your father was a good man, and nothing but the dart o' death prevented him frae making a handsome provision for a' his family, forbye you; and no doubt, when ye hae gotten the better o' the sore stroke o' the sudden removal of the golden candlestick o' his life from among us, ye'll do every thing in a rational and just manner.'

''Deed I'll do nae sic things, mother,' was the reply; 'I'm mindit to haud[2] the grip I hae gotten.'

'But ye're a Christian, Watty,' resumed the Leddy, still preserving her well put on mourning equanimity, 'and it behoves you to reflek, that a' in your power is gi'en to you but as a steward.'

'Ye need na tell me that; but wha's steward am I? Is na the matter a trust for my bairn? I'm wee Betty Bodle's steward, and no man shall upbraid me wi' being unfaithfu',' replied Walter.

'Aye, aye, Watty, that's very true in a sense,' said she, 'but whosoever giveth to the poor lendeth to the Lord.'

'That's what I canna comprehend; for the Lord has no need to borrow; he can make a world o' gold for the poor folk, if he likes, and if he keeps them in poortith,[3] he has his ain reasons for't.'

'Ah, weel I wat!' exclaimed the Leddy pathetically; 'noo I fin' to my cost, that my cousin, Ringan Gilhaise,[4] the Mauchlin

malster, had the rights o't when he plea't[1] my father's will, on
account of thy concos montis;[2] and, but for auld pawky[3] Keelevin,
he would hae gotten the property that's sae ill waur't on thee.'[4]

All this, however, made no impression; but George, in walking
back to Glasgow, several times thought of what had fallen from his
mother respecting the attempt which had been made to set aside
her father's settlement, on the score of Walter's idiocy; and once
or twice it occurred to him that the thing was still not impracticable,
and that, being next heir of entail, and nearest male relative, it
might be of advantage to his own family to get the management of
the estate. Thus, by a conversation intended to benefit the disinherited heirs, the seed was sown of new plans and proceedings,
worthy of the father's son. From that period, George took no
farther interest in the affairs of his sister-in-law, but his visits became unusually frequent to Grippy, and he was generally always
attended by some friend, whom he led into conversation with his
brother, calculated to call forth the least equivocal disclosures of
the state of Walter's mind.

But whatever were his motives for these visits, and this kind of
conduct, he kept them close within his own breast. No one suspected him of any sinister design, but many applauded his filial
attentions to his mother; for so his visits were construed, and they
were deemed the more meritorious on account of the state of his
own family, his wife, after the birth of her twin daughters, having
fallen into ill health. Indeed, he was in general contemplated with
sentiments of compassion and respect. Every body had heard of
his anxiety, on the death of his father, to procure some provision
for his deceased brother's family, and sympathised with the regret
which he expressed at finding Walter so niggardly and intractable;
for not a word was breathed of his incapacity. The increased
thoughtfulness and reserve of his manner which began, we may
say, from the conversation quoted, was in consequence attributed
to the effect of his comfortless domestic situation, and the public
sympathy was considerably augmented, when, in the course of the
same year in which his father died, he happened to lose one of his
daughters.

There were, however, among his friends, as there are always
about most men, certain shrewd and invidious characters, and
some among them did not give him credit for so much sensibility
as their mutual acquaintance in common parlance ascribed to him.

On the contrary, they openly condemned his indelicacy, in so often exposing the fooleries of his brother; and those who had detected the well hidden sordid meanness of his disposition, wondered that he had so quietly acquiesced in Walter's succession. But they had either forgotten, or had never heard of, the circumstance to which his mother alluded with respect to her relation, the Mauchlin maltster's attempt to invalidate her father's will, and, of course, were not aware of the address requisite to prove the incapacity of a man whose situation had been already investigated, and who, by a solemn adjudication, was declared in the full possession of all his faculties. Their wonderment was not, however, allowed to continue long, for an event, which took place within a little more than three months after the death of his daughter, ended all debates and controversies on the subject.

CHAPTER XIII

DEATH, it is said, rarely enters a house without making himself familiar to the inmates. Walter's daughter, a premature child, had from her birth been always infirm and delicate. In the course of the spring after her grandfather's death, she evidently grew worse, and towards the end of summer it was the opinion of all who saw her that she could not live long. The tenderness and solicitude of her father knew no bounds. She was, indeed, the sole object that interested him in life; he doated over her with the most single and entire affection; and when she died, he would not believe, nor allow himself to think, she had expired, but sat by the bedside, preserving silence, and preventing her from being touched, lest it should awaken her from a slumber which he fondly imagined was to establish her recovery. No inducement could be contrived to draw him from his vigilant watch, nor by any persuasion could permission be obtained to dress her corpse. George, in the meanwhile, called several times at the house, and took occasion, in going there one day, to ask the Reverend Doctor Denholm to accompany him, under the pretext that perhaps he might prevail with Walter to allow the body to be removed, as it was beginning to grow offensive. But, when they reached the house, Walter was missing—he had suddenly and unobserved quitted the room where the corpse lay, and his mother, availing herself of his absence, was busily preparing for the interment.

They waited some time in expectation of his return, believing he had only walked into the fields, in consequence of the air of the chamber having become intolerable; but, after conversing upwards of an hour on general topics, some anxiety began to be expressed for his appearance, and his mother grew so alarmed, that servants were dispatched in all directions in quest of him. They had not, however, proceeded far, when he was met on the Glasgow road, coming with his niece Mary in his arms, followed by Lady Plealands' maid-servant, loudly remonstrating with him for carrying off the child, and every now and then making an attempt to snatch it from his arms.

'What hae ye been about?' cried his mother, as she saw him approaching towards the house. He, however, made no answer; but, carrying the child into the nursery, he immediately stripped it naked, and dressed her in the clothes of his own daughter, caressing and pleasing her with a thousand fond assurances—calling her his third Betty Bodle, and betraying all the artless delight and satisfaction with which a child regards a new toy.

Dr Denholm happening to be among those who wondered that his brother had permitted him to succeed his father unmolested, and on seeing this indisputable proof of idiocy according to the notions of society, said,—

'I canna refrain, Mr George, from telling you, that I think it's no right to alloo such a fine property as your father left, to be exposed to wastrie and ruination in the possession of such a haverel. It's neither doing justice to the world nor to your ain family; and I redde you look about you—for wha kens what he may do next?'

Such an admonition, the involuntary incitement of the moment, was not lost. George had, in fact, been long fishing for something of the kind, but nothing had occurred to provoke so explicit an opinion of Walter's obvious incapacity. He, however, replied cautiously,—

'Some allowance, Doctor, must be made for the consternation of his sorrow; and ye should know that it's a kittle[1] point of law to determine when a man has or has not his sufficient senses.'

''Deed, Dr Denholm,' added Leddy Grippy, who happened to be present,—'what ye say is very true; for I can ne'er abide to think that Watty's as he ought to be, since he refus't to make good his honest father's kind intents to the rest o' the family. Here am I toiling and moiling frae morning to night for his advantage; and would ye believe me, Doctor, when I tell you, that he'll no alloo a black bawbee for any needful outlay? and I'm obligated to tak frae my ain jointure money to pay the cost o' every thing the house stands in need of.'

'Not possible!' said George, with every indication of the sincerest astonishment.

'Whether it's possible, or whether it's probable, I ken best mysel,' replied the Leddy;—'and this I ken likewise, that what I say is the even-down[1] truth; and nae farther gain than Mononday was eight days,[2] I paid Deacon Paul, the Glasgow mason,[3] thirteen shillings, a groat, and a bawbee, for the count o' his sklater that pointed the skews[4] o' the house at Martinmas; and though I would supplicate, an it were on my knees, like Queen Esther, the doure Ahasuerus,[5] that he is, has no mercy. Indeed, I'll be nane surprised gin[6] he leaves me to pay a' the charge o' his bairn's burial, which will be a black shame if he does.'

'This must not be endured,' said George, gravely; 'and I am surprised, mother, ye never spoke of such treatment before. I cannot sit patient and hear that ye're used in such a cruel and unnatural manner.'

'It would be a blot on your character, Mr George,' rejoined the minister, 'if ye did. Your brother has been from his youth upward an evident idiot; and ever since the death of his wife, ony little wit he had has been daily growing less.'

'What ye say, Doctor,' resumed the Leddy, 'is no to be controverted; for, poor lad, he certainly fell intil a sore melancholic at that time; and it's my conceit he has ne'er rightly got the better o't; for he was—hegh, sirs!—he was till that time the kindest o' a' my bairns; but, frae the day and hour that his wife took her departel in childbed, he has been a changed creature. Ye'll mind how outstrapolous and constipated[7] he was at her burial; and it's wi' a heavy heart that I maun say't, when his kind father, soon after, wanted to mak a will and testament to keep us a' right and comfortable, he was just like to burn the house aboon our heads wi' his condumacity.'

'I am well aware of the truth of much that you have said; but it's a painful thing for a man to think of taking steps against the capacity of his brother,' replied George. 'For, in the event of not succeeding, he must suffer great obloquy in the opinion of the world; and you know that, with respect to Walter, the attempt was once made already.'

'And every body said,' cried the Leddy, 'that, but for the devices of auld draughty[1] Keelevin, he would hae been proven as mad as a March hare; and nae doubt, as he kens how he jookit[2] the law afore, he might be o' an instrumentality were the thing to gang to a revisidendo.[3] No that I would like to see my bairn put into bedlam; at the same time, Dr Denholm, I would na be doing a Christian and a parent's part to the lave[4] o' my family, an I were to mak a mitigation[5] against it.'

'I do not think,' replied George, looking inquiringly at the Reverend Doctor—'that when a man is proved incapable of conducting his affairs, it is necessary to confine him.'

'O, no; not at all, Mr George,' was the unsuspicious minister's answer. 'It would mak no odds to your brother; it would only oblige you to take the management of the estate.'

'That,' replied George, 'would be far from convenient, for the business of the counting-house requires my whole attention. Ye can have no notion, Dr Denholm, how much this rebellion in America has increased the anxieties of merchants.[6] At the same time, I would be greatly wanting in duty and respect towards my mother, were I to allow her to remain any longer in such an unhappy state, to say nothing of the manifest injustice of obliging her to lay out her own proper jointure in repairs and other expences of the house.'

Little more passed at that time on the subject; but, in the course of walking back to Glasgow, George was fortified in his intentions by the conversation of the Doctor—or, what is, perhaps, more correct, he appeared so doubtful and scrupulous, that the guileless pastor thought it necessary to argue with him against allowing his delicacy to carry him too far.

CHAPTER XIV

AFTER the minister and George had left the house, the cares, we should say the enjoyments, of the Leddy were considerably increased, when she had leisure to reflect on the singular transaction by which Walter had supplied himself with another child. What with the requisite preparations for the funeral of his daughter next day, and 'this new income,'¹ as she called the adopted orphan, 'that, in itself, was a handling² little short o' a birth,' she had not, from the death of her husband, found herself half so earnestly occupied as on this sorrowful occasion. The house rung with her admonitions to the servants, and her short quick steps, in consequence of walking with old shoes down the heel, clattered as cleverly as her tongue. But all this bustle and prodigality of anxieties suffered a sudden suspension, by the arrival of Mrs Charles Walkinshaw, in quest of her child. The little girl, however, was by this time so delighted with the fondling and caresses of her uncle, that she was averse to return home with her mother.

'I won'er,' said Leddy Grippy, 'how ane in your straitened circumstance, Bell Fatherlans, canna be thankfu' for sic a gratus amous³ as this. Watty's a kind-hearted creature, and ye may be sure that neither scaith nor scant⁴ will be alloo't to come near the wean while it stays in this house. For my part, I think his kidnapping her has been nothing less than an instigation o' Providence, since he would na be constrained, by any reason or understanding, to settle an aliment⁵ on you.'

'I cannot, however, part with my child to him. You know there are many little peculiarities about Mr Walter that do not exactly fit him for taking charge of children.'

'But, since he's willing to bear the cost and charge o' her,' said the Leddy, 'ye should mak no objek, but conform; for ye ken, I'll hae the direction o' her edication; and am sure ye would na wis to see her any better brought up than was our Meg, Mrs Milrookit, who could once play seven tunes and a march on the spinet, and sewed a satin piece, at Embrough,⁶ of Adam and Eve eating the forbidden fruit under the tree of life;—the like of which had na before been seen in a' this kintra side. In short, Bell, my dear, it's my advice to you to let the lassie bide wi' us; for, unless

Watty is put out o' the way, it may prove a great thing baith for her and you; for he's a most conomical[1] creature; and the siller he'll save belyve[2] will be just a portion.'

'What do you mean,' replied the young widow, eagerly, 'about putting him out of the way?'

'Ah! Bell Fatherlans,' exclaimed the Leddy, in her most pathetic manner;—'little ken ye yet what it is to hae a family. This has, indeed, been a house o' mourning the day, even though we had na a body in it waiting for interment. The minister has been here wi' Geordie, and it's his solid opinion—we a' ken what a man o' lair[3] and judgment Dr Denholm is;—he thinks that Watty's no o' a faculty to maintain the salvation of the family property; and when your gudebrother[4] heard how I hae been used, he said, that neither law nor justice should oblige him to let his mother live any longer in this house o' bondâge and land o' Egypt; so that, when we get the wean put aneath the ground, there aiblins[5] will be some terrogation as to the naturality[6] of Watty's capacity, which, ye may be sure, is a most sore heart to me, his mother, to hear tell o'. But if it's the Lord's will, I maun submit; for really, in some things, Watty's no to be thol't;[7] yet, for a' that, Bell, my dear, I would let him tak his own way wi' your bairn, till we see what's to be the upshot. For, and though I maun say it, who is his parent, that it canna be weel denied, that he's a thought daft by course o' nature; he may, nevertheless, be decreetit douce enough[8] by course o' law. Therefore, it's neither for you nor me to mak or meddle in the matter; but gather the haws afore the snaws,[9] betide whatever may betide.'

We cannot venture to say that Mrs Charles Walkinshaw was exactly what we should call surprised at this information. She knew enough of the characters of her mother-in-law and of George, to hear even more extraordinary communications from the former unmoved. We need scarcely add, however, that the Leddy's argument was not calculated with her to produce the effect intended; on the contrary, she said,—

'What you tell me only serves to convince me of the impropriety I should be guilty of in leaving my child with Walter.'

But their conversation was interrupted at this juncture by the entrance of Walter, leading Mary.

'I'm come,' said he, 'Bell Fatherlans, to tell you that ye're to gang away hame, and bring Jamie here to stay wi' us. The house is big enough to haud us a', and it'll be a grand ploy[10] to my mother—for ye ken she has such a heart for a thrangerie butt and ben,[1] that, rather than want wark, she'll mak a baby o' the beetle, and dance til't,[2] cracking her thumbs, and singing,

> Dance to your deddie, my bonny leddie;
> Jink through the reelie; jook round and wheelie;
>   Bob in the setting, my bonny lamb;
> And ye's get a slicie o' a dishie nicie—
>   Red cheekit apples and a mutton ham.

So just gang hame at ance, Bell, and bring your laddie, and we'll a' live thegither, and rookettycoo wi' ane anither like doos in a doocot.'[3]

But although Leddy Grippy certainly did like a bustle with all her heart and spirit, she had still that infirmity which ever belongs to human nature gifted with similar propensities,—namely, a throbbing apprehension at the idea of it, such as mankind in general suffer in the prospect of enjoying pleasure; and the expression of this feeling with her took commonly the form and language of repugnance and reluctance, yea sometimes it even amounted to refusal.

'What say ye?' cried she to Walter, under a strong impression of it at the moment,—'are ye utterly bereav't o' your senses, to speak o' bringing the lade[4] o' another family on my hands?'

'I'm sure,' was his answer, 'if ye dinna like to tak the pleasure o't, ye're free to set up your jointure house, and live the life o' dowager duchess, for me, mother. But Bell Fatherlans and her bairns are to come here,—for this is my house, ye ken—settlet on me and mine, past a' power o' law, by my father—and what's my ain I'll mak my ain.'

'Wha would hae thought o' sic outcoming o' kindness as this!' replied the Leddy. 'I fancy, Bell, ye'll hae to come and resident wi' us?'

'An she does na,' said Walter, 'I'll gang away where never one kent me, and tak her wee Mary on my back in a basket, like Jenny Nettles[5]—that's what I will; so put the matter to your knee and straight it.'

'I'll mak a bargain, Mr Walter,' replied Mrs Charles,—'I'll leave Mary to-night, and come, after the burial to-morrow, with James, and stay a few days.'

'Ye'll stay a' your days,' exclaimed Walter; 'and as ye're a leddy o' mair genteelity than my mother, ye shall hae the full rule and power o' the house, and mak jam and jelly;—a' the cast[1] o' her grace and skill gangs nae farther than butter and cheese.'

His mother was confounded, and unable for some time to utter a word. At last, putting her hands firmly into her sides, she said,—

'My word, but thou's no blate.[2] But it's no worth my while to gang intil a passion for a born idiot. Your reign, my lad, 's no ordaint to be lang, if there's either law or gospel among the fifteen at Embro.[3] To misliken[4] his mother! to misuse me as I were nae better than an auld bachle,[5] and, in a manner, to turn me out the house!'

'O don't disturb yourself,' interposed Mrs Charles; 'they were but words of course. You know his humour, and need not be surprised at what he says.'

The indignant mother was not, however, soon appeased,—her wrath for some time burnt fiercely, and it required no little dexterity on the part of her daughter-in-law to allay the altercation which ensued; but in the end her endeavours proved successful, and the result was an arrangement, that the child should be left for a day or two, to ascertain whether Walter's attachment was dictated by caprice or a transfer of his affections. And in order to preserve quiet, and to prevent any extravagance that might be injurious to the little girl, it was also arranged that her mother and brother should likewise spend a few weeks at Grippy.

CHAPTER XV

THE news of the arrangement, when communicated to Doctor Denholm and George, at the funeral next day, produced on them very opposite effects. The minister, who was naturally of a warm and benevolent disposition, persuaded himself that the proposal of Walter, to receive his sister-in-law and her family, was dictated by a sense of duty and of religion, and regretted that he had so hastily expressed himself so strongly respecting his incapacity. Indeed, every one who heard the story put upon it nearly the same sort of construction, and applauded the uncouth kindness of the natural as brotherly and Christian.

George, however, saw it, perhaps, more correctly; but he was exceedingly disturbed by the favourable impression which it made on the minds of his acquaintance, and hesitated to indulge his desire to obtain the management of the estate. But still he continued his visits to Grippy, and took every opportunity of drawing the attention of his friends to the imbecility of his brother. Nothing, however, occurred to further his wishes till the term of Martinmas[1] after the incident mentioned in the foregoing chapter; when, on receiving his rents, he[2] presented his sister-in-law with a ten pound note, at the same time counting out, to the calculation of a halfpenny, the balance he owed his mother of her jointure, but absolutely refusing to repay her any of the money she had, in the meantime, disbursed for different little household concerns and repairs, saying, that all she had laid out was nothing in comparison to what she was due for bed and board. This was the unkindest cut of all; for she justly and truly estimated her services to him as of far more value. However, she said nothing; but next day, on the pretext of going to see her mother, who was now very infirm, and unable to quit her chamber, she went to Glasgow and called on George, to whom she made a loud and long complaint of the insults she had received, and of the total unfitness and unworthiness of his brother to continue uncontrolled in the possession of the estate.

George sympathized with her sorrows and her sufferings like a dutiful son, and comforted her with the assurance that he would lose no time in taking some steps for her relief, and the preservation of the property. And, as she consented to remain that day to dinner, it was thought, considering the disposition Walter had shown to squander his gifts on his sister-in-law, without any consideration for the rest of the family, it might be as well to consult Mr Keelevin on the occasion. A message was, accordingly, dispatched to the honest lawyer, begging him to call after dinner; in short, every demonstration was made by George to convince his mother how much better her worth was appreciated by him than by his brother;—and she was not only consoled, but delighted with the sincerity of his attentions.

In due time Mr Keelevin made his appearance; and the Leddy began a strong representation of all the indignities which she had endured, but her son softly and mildly interposed, saying,—

'It is of no use, my dear mother, to trouble Mr Keelevin with these things; he knows the infirmities of Walter as well as we do. No doubt,' he added, turning to the lawyer, 'you have heard

of the very extraordinary manner in which my brother took Mrs
Charles and her family to Grippy.'

'I really,' replied the honest-hearted man, 'had no idea that he
possessed so muckle feeling and common sense, but I was very
happy to hear't. For, his own wean being no more, I'm sure he
can do nothing better than make up to the disinherited orphans
some portion of that which, but for your father's sudden death,
would hae been provided for them.'

George knew not what reply to make to this; but his mother,
who, like the rest of her sex, had an answer for all subjects and
occasions ever ready, said,—

'It's weel to ca't sense and feeling, but if I were obligated to
speak the truth, I would baptize it wi' another name. It's no to be
rehearsed by the tongue o' man, Mr Keelevin, what I hae borne at
the hands of the haverel idiot, since the death of him that's awa—
your auld friend, Mr Keelevin;—he was a man of a capacity, and
had he been spared a comfort to me, as he was, and aye sae couthy[1]
wi' his kindness, I would na kent[2] what it is to be a helpless widow.
But surely there maun be some way o' remedde for us a' in thir[3]
straits? It's no possible that Walter can be alloo't to riot and ravage
in sic a most rabiator-like[4] manner; for I need na tell you, that he's
gane beyond all counsel and admonition. Noo, do ye think, Mr
Keelevin, by your knowledge and skill in law, that we can get him
cognost,[5] and the rents and rule o' the property ta'en out of his
hands? for, if he gangs on at the gait he's going, I'll be herri't, and
he'll no leave himself ae bawbee[6] to rub on anither.'

'What has he done?' inquired the lawyer, a little thoughtfully.

'Done! what has he no done? He gied Bell Fatherlands a ten
pound note, and was as dour[7] as a smith's vice in the grip, when I
wantit him to refund me a pour[8] o' ready money that I was obligated to lay out for the house.'

George, who had watched the lawyer's countenance in the meantime, said,—

'I doubt, mother, few will agree in thinking of that in the way
you do. My sister-in-law stands in need of his kindness, but your
jointure is more than you require; for, after all your terrible out-
lays,' and he smiled to Mr Keelevin as he said the words, 'you have
already saved money.'

'But what's that to him?' exclaimed the Leddy. 'Is nae a just
debt a just debt—was na he bound to pay what I paid for him—

and is't no like a daft man and an idiot, to say he'll no do't? I'm
sure, Mr Keelevin, I need na tell you that Watty was ne'er truly
concos montes.[1] How ye got him made sound in his intellectuals
when the law plea was about my father's will, ye ken best yoursel;
but the straemash[2] that was thereanent is a thing to be remembered.'

Mr Keelevin gave a profound sigh, adding, in a sort of apolo-
gistic manner,—

'But Walter has maybe undergone some change since that time?'

'Yes,' said George, 'the grief and consternation into which he
was thrown by the sudden death of his wife had undoubtedly a
great effect on his mind.'

'He was clean dementit at that time,' cried the Leddy; 'he would
neither buff nor stye[3] for father nor mother, friend nor foe; a' the
King's forces would na hae gart him carry his wife's head in a wise-
like[4] manner to the kirk-yard. I'm sure, Mr Keelevin, for ye were
at the burial, ye may mind that her father, Kilmarkeckle, had to
do't, and lost his Canary snuff by a twirl o' the wind, when he was
taking a pinch, as they said, after lowering her head intil the grave;
which was thought, at the time, a most unparent-like action for
any man to be about at his only dochter's burial.'

Mr Keelevin replied, 'I will honestly confess to you, that I do
think there has of late been signs of a want about Mr Walter. But
in his kindness to his poor brother's widow and family, there's
great proof and evidence, both of a sound mind, reason, and a right
heart. Ye'll just, Mrs Walkinshaw, hae to fight on wi' him as well as
ye can, for in the conscience o' me I would, knowing what I know
of the family, be wae and sorry to disturb such a consolatory manifestation of brotherly love.'

'That's just my opinion,' said George, 'and I would fain persuade my mother to put up with the slights and ill usage to which
she is so distressingly subjected—at the same time, I cannot say,
but I have my fears, that her situation is likely to be made worse
rather than better, for Walter appears disposed, not only to treat
her in a very mean and unworthy manner, but to give the whole
dominion of the house to Mrs Charles.'

'Na,' exclaimed the Leddy, kindling at this dexterous awakening of her wrongs. 'He did far waur, he a'maist turnt me out o' the
house by the shouthers.'[5]

'Did he lay hands on you, his mother?' inquired Mr Keelevin

with his professional accent and earnestness. But George prevented her from replying, by saying that his mother naturally felt much molested in receiving so harsh a return for the particular partiality with which she had always treated his brother—and was proceeding in his wily and insidious manner to fan the flame he seemed so anxious to smother. Mr Keelevin, however, of a sudden, appeared to detect his drift, and gave him such a rebuking look, that he became confused and embarrassed, during which the honest lawyer rose and wished them good afternoon—saying to George, who accompanied him to the door,—

'The deil needs baith a syde cloak[1] and a wary step to hide his cloven-foot—I'll say nae mair, Mr George; but dinna mak your poor brother's bairns waur than they are—and your mother should na be egget[2] on in her anger, when she happens, poor body, to tak the dods[3] now and then—for the most sensible of women hae their turns o' tantrums, and need baith rein and bridle.'

CHAPTER XVI

'I HOPE and trust,' said Leddy Grippy, as George returned from conducting the lawyer to the door, 'that ye'll hae mair compassion for your mother than to be sway't by the crooked counsels o' yon quirkie bodie. I could see vera weel that he has a because[4] o' his ain for keeping his thumb on Watty's unnaturality. But Geordie, he's no surely the only lawyer in the town? I wat there are scores baith able and willing to tak the business by the hand; and if there shou'd be nane o' a sufficient capacity in Glasgow, just tak a step in til Enbro', where, I hae often heard my honest father say, there are legions o' a capacity to contest wi' Belzebub himsel.'

'I am very anxious, mother, to do every thing to promote your happiness,' was the reply; 'but the world will be apt to accuse me of being actuated by some sinister and selfish motive. It would be most disgraceful to me were I to fail.'

'It will be a black burning shame to alloo a daft man any longer to rule and govern us like a tyrant wi' a rod o' iron, pooking and rooking[5] me, his mother, o' my ain lawful jointure and honest hainings, forbye skailing[6] and scattering his inheritance in a manner, as if ten pound notes were tree-leaves at Hallowe'en.'[7]

'I am quite sensible of the truth and justice of all you say; but you know the uncertainty of the law,' said George, 'and the consequences would be fatal to me were we not to succeed.'

'And what will be the consequences if he were taking it in his head to marry again? He would mak nae scruple of sending me off frae Grippy at an hour's warning.'

This touched the keenest nerve of her son's anxieties; and he was immediately alarmed by a long visionary vista of unborn sons, rising between him and the succession to the estate;—but he only appeared to sympathise with his mother.

'It's not possible,' said he, 'even were he to marry again, that he could be so harsh. You have lived ever since your marriage with my father at Grippy. It's your home, and endeared to you by many pleasing recollections. It would be extreme cruelty now, in your declining years, to force you to live in the close air, and up the dirty turnpike stairs o' Glasgow.'[1]

'It would soon be the death o' me,' exclaimed the Leddy, with a sigh, wiping one of her eyes with the corner of her apron. 'In short, Geordie, if ye dinna step out and get him put past the power o' marrying, I'll regard you as little better than art and part[2] in his idiocety. But it's time I were taking the road, for they'll a' be marvelling what keeps me. There's, however, ae thing I would advise you, and that is, to take gude care and no mint[3] what we hae been speaking o' to living creature, for nobody can tell what detriment the born idiot might do to us baith, were he to get an inkling before a's ready to put the strait waiscot o' the law on him; so I redde you set about it in a wary and wily manner, that he may hae nae cause to jealouse[4] your intent.'

There was, however, no great occasion for the latter part of this speech, George being perfectly aware of all the difficulties and delicacies of the case; but he said,—

'Did he ever attempt actually to strike you?'

'O, no,' replied his mother; 'to do the fool thing justice, it's kindly enough in its manner; only it will neither be governed nor guided by me as it used to be; which is a sore trial.'

'Because,' rejoined George, 'had he ever dared to do so, there would then have been less trouble or scruple in instituting proceedings against him.'

'Na; an it's ony way to commode the business, we might soon provoke him to lift his hand; but it's a powerful creature, and I'm fear't. However, Geordie, ye might lay yoursel out for a bit slaik o' its paw;[1] so just come o'er the morn's morning and try; for it'll no do to stand shilly-shallying, if we hope to mak a right legality o't.'

Cowardice is the best auxiliary to the police, and George had discretion enough not to risk the danger of rousing the sleeping lion of his brother's Herculean sinews. But, in other respects, he took his mother's advice; and, avoiding the guilt of causing an offence, in order that he might be able to prosecute the offender, he applied to Gabriel Pitwinnoch, the writer,[2] from whose character he expected to encounter fewer scruples and less scrutiny than with Mr Keelevin.

In the meantime, the Leddy, who had returned home to Grippy, preserved the most entire reserve upon the subject to all the inmates of the family, and acted her part so well, that even a much more suspicious observer than her daughter-in-law would never have suspected her of double dealing. Indeed, any change that could be perceived in her manner was calculated to lull every suspicion,— for she appeared more than usually considerate and attentive towards Walter, and even condescended to wheedle and coax him on different occasions, when it would have been more consonant to her wonted behaviour had she employed commands and reproaches.

In the course of a week after the interview with Mr Keelevin, George went to Edinburgh, and he was accompanied in his journey by the wary Gabriel Pitwinnoch. What passed between them on the road, and who they saw, and what advice they received in the intellectual city, we need not be particular in relating; but the result was, that, about a week after their return, Gabriel came to Grippy, accompanied by a stranger, of whose consequence and rank it would appear the Leddy had some previous knowledge, as she deported herself towards him with a degree of ceremonious deference very unusual to her habits. The stranger, indeed, was no less a personage than Mr Threeper the advocate, a gentleman of long standing and great practice in the Parliament House,[3] and much celebrated for his shrewd perception of technical flaws, and clever discrimination of those nicer points of the law that are so often at variance with justice.

It happened, that, when this learned doctor of the Caledonian Padua[4] arrived with his worthy associate, Mrs Charles Walkinshaw was in the fields; but, the moment her son James saw him, he was

so struck with his appearance, that he ran to tell her. Walter also
followed him, under the influence of the same feeling, and said,—

'Come in, Bell Fatherlans, and see what a warld's won'er
Pitwinnoch the writer has brought to our house. My mother says
it's a haudthecat,[1] and that it gangs about the town o' Embro,
walking afore the Lords, in a black gown, wi' a wig on'ts head. I
marvel what the creature's come here for. It has a silver snuff-
box, that it's ay pat patting; and ye would think, to hear it speak,
that King Solomon, wi' a' his hundreds o' wives and concubines,
was but a fool to him.'

Mrs Charles was alarmed at hearing of such a visitor; for the
journey of George and Pitwinnoch to Edinburgh immediately
occurred to her, and a feeling of compassion, mingled with gratitude for the kindness which Walter had lately shown to herself and
her children, suggested that she ought to put him on his guard.

'Walter,' said she, 'I would not advise you to go near the house
while the two lawyers are there,—for who knows what they may
do to you? But go as fast as ye can to Glasgow, and tell Mr Keelevin
what has happened; and say that I have some reason to fear it's a
visit that bodes you no good, and therefore ye'll stand in need of
his advice and assistance.'

The natural, who had an instinctive horror of the law, made no
reply, but, with a strong expression of terror in his countenance,
immediately left her, and went straight to Glasgow.

CHAPTER XVII

DURING the journey of George and Pitwinnoch to Edinburgh,
a Brief of Chancery[2] had been quietly obtained, directing the
Sheriff of the county to summon a jury, to examine into the alleged
fatuity of Walter; and the visit of the latter with Mr Threeper, the
advocate, to Grippy, was to meet George, for the purpose of determining with respect to the evidence that it might be requisite to
adduce before the inquest. All this was conducted, as it was
intended to appear, in a spirit of the greatest delicacy towards the
unfortunate *fatuus*, consistent with the administration of public
justice.

'I can assure you,' said our friend Gabriel to Mr Threeper, as they walked towards the house—the advocate perusing the ground as he poked his way along with his cane, and occasionally taking snuff; 'I can assure you, that nothing but the most imperious necessity could have induced Mr George Walkinshaw to institute these proceedings; for he is a gentleman of the utmost respectability; and to my knowledge has been long and often urged in vain to get his brother cognost; but, until the idiot's conduct became so intolerable, that his mother could no longer endure it, he was quite inexorable.'

'Is Mr George in affluent circumstances?' said the advocate, dryly.

'He is but a young man; the house, however, in which he is a partner is one of the most flourishing in Glasgow,' was the answer.

'He has, perhaps, a large family?'

'O dear no; only one daughter; and his wife,' said Gabriel, 'is, I understand, not likely to have any more.'

'She may, however, have sons, Pitwinnoch,' rejoined the advocate, wittily—at the same time taking snuff. 'But you say it is the mother that has chiefly incited Mr Walkinshaw to this action.'

'So he told me,' replied the writer.

'Her evidence will be most important; for it is not natural that a mother would urge a process of such a nature, without very strong grounds indeed, unless she has some immediate or distinct prospective interest in the result. Have you any idea that such is the case?'

'I should think not,' said Gabriel.

'Do you imagine that such allowance as the Court might grant for the custody of the *fatuus* would have any influence with her?' inquired Mr Threeper, without raising his eyes from the road.

'I have always understood,' was the reply, 'that she is in the possession, not only of a handsome jointure, but of a considerable provision, specially disponed to her by the will of old Plealands, her father.'

'Ah! was she the daughter of old Plealands?' said the advocate. 'It was in a cause of his that I was first retained. He had the spirit of litigation in a very zealous degree.'

In this manner the two redressers of wrongs chattingly proceeded towards Grippy, by appointment, to meet George; and they arrived, as we have related in the foregoing chapter, a few minutes before he made his appearance.

In the meantime, Watty hastened with rapid steps, goaded by a mysterious apprehension of some impending danger, to the counting-house of Mr Keelevin, whom he found at his desk.

'Weel, Mr Walter,' said the honest writer, looking up from a deed he was perusing, somewhat surprised at seeing him—'What's the best o' your news the day,[1] and what's brought you frae Grippy?'

'Mr Keelevin,' replied Walter, going towards him on tiptoe, and whispering audibly in his ear, 'I'll tell you something, Mr Keelevin:—twa gleds[2] o' the law hae lighted yonder; and ye ken, by your ain ways, that the likes o' them dinna flee afield for naething.'

'No possible!' exclaimed Mr Keelevin; and the recollection of his interview with George and the Leddy flashing upon him at the moment, he at once divined the object of their visit; and added, 'It's most abominable;—but ken ye what they're seeking, Mr Walter?'

'No,' said he. 'But Bell Fatherlans bade me come and tell you; for she thought I might need your counsel.'

'She has acted a true friend's part; and I'm glad ye're come,' replied the lawyer; 'and for her and her bairns' sake, I hope we'll be able to defeat their plots and devices. But I would advise you, Mr Walter, to keep out o' harm's way, and no gang in the gate o' the gleds,[3] as ye ca' them.'

'Hae ye ony ark or amrie,[4] Mr Keelevin, where a body might den himsel[5] till they're out o' the gate and away?' cried Walter timidly, and looking anxiously round the room.

'Ye should na speak sic havers, Mr Walter, but conduct yourself mair like a man,' said his legal friend grievedly. 'Indeed, Mr Walter, as I hae some notion that they're come to tak down your words—may be to spy your conduct, and mak nae gude report thereon to their superiors—tak my advice, and speak as little as possible.'

'I'll no say ae word—I'll be a dumbie—I'll sit as quiet as ony ane o' the images afore Bailie Glassford's house at the head o' the Stockwell.[6] King William himsel,[7] on his bell-metal horse at the Cross, is a popular preacher, Mr Keelevin, compared to what I'll be.'

The simplicity and sincerity with which this was said moved the kind-hearted lawyer at once to smile and sigh.

'There will, I hope, Mr Walter,' said he, 'be no occasion to put any restraint like that upon yoursel; only it's my advice to you as a friend, to enter into no conversation with any one you do not well know, and to dress in your best clothes, and shave yoursel,—and in a' things demean and deport yoursel, like the laird o' Kittleston-heugh, and the representative of an ancient and respected family.'

'O, I can easily do that,' replied the natural; 'and I'll tak my father's ivory-headed cane, with the golden virl,[1] and the silver e'e[2] for a tassel, frae ahint the scrutoire, where it has ay stood since his death, and walk up and down the front of the house like a Glasgow magistrate.'

'For the love o' Heaven, Mr Walter,' exclaimed the lawyer, 'do nae sic mad like action! The like o' that is a' they want.'

'In whatna other way, then,' said Walter helplessly, 'can I behave like a gentleman, or a laird o' yird and stane,[3] wi' the retinue o' an ancient pedigree like my father's Walkinshaws o' Kittleston-heugh?'

''Deed,' said Mr Keelevin compassionately, 'I'm wae to say't— but I doot, I doot, it's past the compass o' my power to advise you.'

'I'm sure,' exclaimed Walter despairingly, 'that THE MAKER was ill aff for a turn when he took to the creating o' lawyers. The deils are but prentice work compared to them. I dinna ken what to do, Mr Keelevin—I wish that I was dead, but I'm no like to dee, as Jenny says in her wally-wae about her father's cow and auld Robin Gray.'[4]

'Mr Walter,' said his friend, after a pause of several minutes, 'go you to Mrs Hypel, your grandmother, for the present, and I'll out to Grippy, and sift the meaning o' this visitation. When I have gathered what it means, we'll hae the better notion in what way we ought to fight with the foe.'

'I'll smash them like a fore hammer,'[5] exclaimed Walter proudly. 'I'll stand ahint a dike, and gie them a belter wi' stanes,[6] till I hae na left the souls in their bodies—that's what I will,—if ye approve o't, Mr Keelevin.'

'Weel, weel, Mr Walter,' was the chagrined and grieved reply, 'we'll see to that when I return; but it's a terrible thing to think o' proving a man non compos mentis for the only sensible action he ever did in all his life. Nevertheless, I will not let myself despond; and I have only for the present to exhort you to get yoursel in an order and fitness to appear as ye ought to be;—for really, Mr Walter, ye alloo yoursel to gang sae like a divor,[1] that I dinna wonder ye hae been ta'en notice o'. So I counsel you to mak yoursel trig, and no to play ony antics.'

Walter assured him, that his advice would in every respect be followed; and, leaving the office, he went straight to the residence of his grandmother, while Mr Keelevin, actuated at once by his humanity and professional duty, ordered his horse, and reached Grippy just as the advocate, Mr Pitwinnoch, and George, were on the point of coming away, after waiting in vain for the return of Walter, whom Mr Threeper was desirous of conversing with personally.

CHAPTER XVIII

THE triumvirate and Leddy Grippy were disconcerted at the appearance of Mr Keelevin—for, at that moment, the result of Mr Threeper's inquiries among the servants had put them all in the most agreeable and unanimous opinion with respect to the un-doubted certainty of poor Watty's fatuity.—'We have just to walk over the course,' the advocate was saying; when George, happen-ing to glance his eye towards the window, beheld the benevolent lawyer coming up the avenue.

'Good Heavens!' said he, 'what can that old pest, Keelevin, want here?'

'Keelevin!' exclaimed the Leddy,—'that's a miracle to me. I think, gentlemen,' she added, 'ye had as weel gang away by the back door—for ye would na like, may be, to be fashed wi' his con-fabbles. He's no a man, or I'm far mista'en, that kens muckle about the prejinketties o' the law, though he got the poor daft creature harl't[2] through the difficulties o' the plea wi' my cousin Gilhaise, the Mauchlin maltster. I'm very sure, Mr Threeper, he's no an acquaintance ye would like to cultivate, for he has na the talons[3] o' an advocate versed in the devices o' the courts, but is a quirkie bodie, capable o' making law no law at a', according to the best o' my discernment, which, to be sure, in matters o' locutories and decreets, is but that o' a hamely household woman, so I would advise you to eschew his company at this present time.'

Mr Threeper, however, saw farther into the lady's bosom than she suspected; and as it is never contrary, either to the interest of advocate or agent, to avoid having causes contested, especially when there is, as was in this case, substance enough to support a long and zealous litigation, that gentleman said,—

'Then Mr Keelevin is the agent who was employed in the former action?'

'Just sae,' resumed the Leddy, 'and ye ken he could na, wi' ony regard to himsel, be art and part[1] on this occasion.'

'Ah, but, madam,' replied the advocate, earnestly, 'he may be agent for the *fatuus*. It is, therefore, highly proper we should set out with a right understanding respecting that point; for, if the allegations are to be controverted, it is impossible to foresee what obstacles may be raised, although, in my opinion, from the evidence I have heard, there is no doubt that the fatuity of your son is a fact which cannot fail to be in the end substantiated. Don't you think, Mr Pitwinnoch, that we had as well see Mr Keelevin?'

'Certainly,' said Gabriel. 'And, indeed, considering that, by the brief to the Sheriff, the Laird is a party, perhaps, even though Mr Keelevin should not have been employed, it would be but fair, and look well towards the world, were he instructed to take up this case on behalf of the *fatuus*. What say you, Mr Walkinshaw?'

George did not well know what to say, but he replied, that, for many reasons, he was desirous the whole affair should be managed as privately as possible. 'If, however, the forms of the procedure required that an agent should act for Walter, I have no objection; at the same time, I do not think Mr Keelevin the fittest person.'

'Heavens and earth!' exclaimed the Leddy, 'here's a respondent-ing and a hearing, and the Lord Ordinary and a' the fifteen Lords frae Embro' come to herry us out o' house and hall. Gentlemen, an ye'll tak my advice, who, in my worthy father's time, had some inkling o' what the cost o' law pleas are, ye'll hae naething to do wi' either Keelevin, Gardevine,[2] or ony other Vines in the shape o' pro forma agents: but settle the business wi' the Sheriff in a douce and discreet manner.'

Mr Threeper, looking towards Mr Pitwinnoch and George, rapped his ivory snuff-box, rimmed and garnished with gold, and smiling, took a pinch as Mr Keelevin was shown into the room.

'Mr George,' said Mr Keelevin sedately, after being seated; 'I am not come here to ask needless questions, but as Man of

Business[1] for your brother, it will be necessary to serve me with the proper notices as to what you intend.'

Mr Threeper again had recourse to his box, and Gabriel looked inquiringly at his client—who could with difficulty conceal his confusion, while the old lady, who had much more presence of mind, said,—

'May I be sae bold, Mr Keelevin, as to speer[2] wha sent you here, at this time?'

'I came at Mr Walter's own particular and personal request,' was the reply; and he turned at the same time towards the advocate, and added, 'That does not look very like fatuity.'

'He never could hae done that o' his own free will. I should na wonder if the interloper, Bell Fatherlans, sent him—but I'll soon get to the bottom o't,' exclaimed the Leddy, and she immediately left the room in quest of Mrs Charles, to inquire. During her absence, Mr Keelevin resumed,—

'It is not to be contested, Mr Threeper,' for he knew the person of the advocate, 'that the Laird is a man o' singularities and oddities—we a' hae our foibles; but he got a gude education, and his schoolmaster bore testimony on a former occasion to his capacity; and if it can be shown that he does not manage his estate so advantageously as he might do, surely that can never be objected against him, when we every day see so many o' the wisest o' our lairds, and lords, and country gentry, falling to pigs and whistles, frae even doun[3] inattention or prodigality. I think it will be no easy thing to prove Mr Walter incapable o' managing his own affairs, with his mother's assistance.'

'Ah! Mr Keelevin, with his mother's assistance!' exclaimed the acute Mr Threeper. 'It's time that he were out of leading-strings, and able to take care of himself, without his mother's assistance—if he's ever likely to do so.'

At this crisis, the Leddy returned into the room flushed with anger. 'It's just as I jealoused,' cried she; 'it's a' the wark o' my gude-dochter—it was her that sent him; black was the day she e'er came to stay here; many a sore heart in the watches o' the night hae I had sin syne,[4] for my poor weak misled lad; for if he were left to the freedom o' his own will, he would na stand on stepping stanes, but, without scrupulosity, would send me, his mother, to crack sand,[5] or mak my leaving[6] where I could, after wastering a' my jointure.'

This speech made a strong impression on the minds of all the lawyers present. Mr Keelevin treasured it up, and said nothing. Our friend Gabriel glanced the tail of his eye at the advocate, who, without affecting to have noticed the interested motive which the Leddy had betrayed, said to Mr Keelevin,—

'The case, Sir, cannot but go before a jury; for, although the *fatuus* be of a capacity to repeat any injunction which he may have received, and which is not inconsistent with a high degree of fatuity—it does not therefore follow that he is able to originate such motions or volitions of the mind as are requisite to constitute what may be denominated a legal modicum of understanding, the possession of which in Mr Walter Walkinshaw is the object of the proposed inquiry to determine.'

'Very well, gentlemen, since such is the case,' replied Mr Keelevin, rising, 'as I have undertaken the cause, it is unnecessary for us to hold any further conversation on the subject. I shall be prepared to protect my client.'

With these words he left the room, in some hope that possibly they might induce George still to stay proceedings. But the cupidity of George's own breast, the views and arguments of his counsel, and the animosity of his mother, all co-operated to weaken their effect; so that, in the course of as short a time as the forms of the judicature permitted, a jury was impannelled before the Sheriff, according to the tenor of the special brief of Chancery which had been procured for the purpose, and evidence as to the state of poor Watty's understanding and capacity regularly examined;—some account of which we shall proceed to lay before our readers, premising, that Mr Threeper opened the business in a speech replete with eloquence and ingenuity, and all that metaphysical refinement for which the Scottish bar was then, as at present, so justly celebrated. Nothing, indeed, could be more subtle, nor less applicable to the coarse and daily tear and wear of human concerns, than his definition of what constituted 'the minimum of understanding, or of reason, or of mental faculty in general, which the law, in its wisdom, required to be enjoyed by every individual claiming to exercise the functions that belong to man, as a subject, a citizen, a husband, a father, a master, a servant,—in one word, to enable him to execute those different essential duties, which every gentleman of the jury so well knew, and so laudably, so respectably, and so meritoriously performed.'—

But we regret that our limits do not allow us to enter upon the subject; and the more so, as it could not fail to prove highly interesting to our fair readers, in whose opinion the eloquence of the Parliament House of Edinburgh, no doubt, possesses many charming touches of sentiment, and amiable pathetic graces.

CHAPTER XIX

THE first witness examined was Jenny Purdie, servant to Mr George Walkinshaw. She had previously been several years in the service of his father, and is the same who, as our readers will perhaps recollect, contrived so femininely to seduce half-a-crown from the pocket of the old man, when she brought him the news of the birth of his son's twin daughters.

'What is your opinion of Mr Walter Walkinshaw?' inquired Mr Threeper.

''Deed, Sir,' said Jenny, 'I hae but a sma' opinion o' him—he's a daft man, and has been sae a' his days.'

'But what do you mean by a daft man?'

'I thought every body kent what a daft man is,' replied Jenny; 'he's just silly, and tavert,[1] and heedless, and o' an inclination to swattle in the dirt like a grumphie[2]'

'Well, but do you mean to say,' interrupted the advocate, 'that, to your knowledge, he has been daft all his days?'

'I never kent him ony better.'

'But you have not known him all his days—therefore, how can you say he has been daft all his days?—He might have been wise enough when you did not know him.'

'I dinna think it,' said Jenny;—'I dinna think it was ever in him to be wise—he's no o' a nature to be wise.'

'What do you mean by a nature?—Explain yourself.'

'I canna explain mysel ony better,' was the answer; 'only I ken that a cat's no a dog, nor o' a nature to be,—and so the Laird could ne'er be a man o' sense.'

'Very ingenious, indeed,' said Mr Threeper; 'and I am sure the gentlemen of the jury must be satisfied that it is not possible to give a clearer—a more distinctive impression of the deficiency of Mr Walkinshaw's capacity, than has been given by this simple and innocent country girl.—But, Jenny, can you tell us of any instance of his daftness?'

'I can tell you o' naething but the sic like[1] about him.'

'Cannot you remember any thing he said or did on any particular day?'

'O aye, atweel I wat[2] I can do that—on the vera day when I gaed hame, frae my service at the Grippy to Mr George's, the sheep were sheared, and Mr Watty said they were made sae naked, it was a shame to see them, and took one o' his mother's flannen polonies, to mak a hap[3] to Mall Loup-the-Dike, the auld ewe, for decency.'

Jenny was then cross-questioned by Mr Queerie, the able and intelligent advocate employed for the defence by Mr Keelevin; but her evidence was none shaken, nor did it appear that her master had in any way influenced her. Before she left the box, the Sheriff said jocularly,—

'I'm sure, from your account, Jenny, that Mr Walkinshaw's no a man ye would like to marry?'

'There's no saying,' replied Jenny,—'the Kittlestonheugh's a braw estate; and mony a better born than me has been blithe to put up wi' houses and lan's, though wit and worth were baith wanting.'

The first witness thus came off with considerable eclat, and indeed gained the love and affections, it is said, of one of the jurors, an old bien carle, a bonnet-laird,[4] to whom she was, in the course of a short time after, married.

The next witness was Mr Mordecai Saxheere, preses[5] and founder of that renowned focus of sosherie[6] the Yarn Club, which held its periodical libations of the vintage of the colonies in the buxom Widow Sheid's tavern, in Sour-milk John's Land, a stately pile[7] that still lifts its lofty head in the Trongate. He was an elderly, trim, smooth, Quaker-faced gentleman, dressed in drab, with spacious buckram-lined skirts, that came round on his knees, giving to the general outline of his figure the appearance of a cone supported on legs in white worsted hose. He wore a highly powdered horse-hair wig, with a long queue; buckles at the knees and in his shoes, presenting, in the collective attributes of his dress and appearance, a respect-bespeaking epitome of competency, good-eating, honesty, and self-conceit. He was one of several gentlemen whom the long-forecasting George had carried with him to Grippy on those occasions when he was desirous to provide witnesses, to be available when the era should arrive that had now come to pass.

'Well, Mr Saxheere,' said the Edinburgh advocate, 'what have you to say with respect to the state of Mr Walter Walkinshaw?'

'Sir,' replied the preses of the Yarn Club, giving that sort of congratulatory smack with which he was in the practice of swallowing and sending round the dram that crowned the substantials, and was herald to what were called the liquidities of the club,— 'Sir,' said Mordecai Saxheere, 'I have been in no terms of intromission with Mr Walkinshaw of Grippy, cept and except in the way of visitation; and on those occasions I always found him of a demeanour more sportive to others than congenial.'

'You are a merchant, I believe, Mr Saxheere,' said Mr Threeper; 'you have your shop in the High Street, near the Cross. On the market day you keep a bottle of whisky and a glass on the counter, from which, as I understand, you are in the practice of giving your customers a dram—first preeing¹ or smelling the liquor yourself, and then handing it to them.—Now, I would ask you, if Mr Walkinshaw were to come to your shop on the market day, would you deal with him?—would you, on your oath, smell the glass, and then hand it across the counter, to be by him drunk off?'

The advocate intended this as a display of his intimate knowledge of the local habits and usages of Glasgow, though himself but an Edinburgh man,—in order to amaze the natives by his cleverness.

'Sir,' replied Mr Saxheere, again repeating his habitual congratulatory smack, 'much would rely on the purpose for which he came to custom. If he offered me yarn for sale, there could be no opponency on my side to give him the fair price of the day; but, if he wanted to buy, I might undergo some constipation of thought before compliance.'

'The doubtful credit of any wiser person might produce the same astringency,' said the advocate, slyly.

'No doubt it would,' replied the preses of the Yarn Club; 'but the predicament of the Laird of Grippy would na be under that denominator, but because I would have a suspicion of him in the way of judgment and sensibility.'

'Then he is not a man that you would think it safe to trade with as a customer?' said the Sheriff, desirous of putting an end to his prosing.

'Just so, Sir,' replied Mordecai; 'for, though it might be safe in the way of advantage, I could not think myself, in the way of character, free from an imputation, were I to intromit with him.'

It was not deemed expedient to cross question this witness; and another was called, a celebrated Professor of Mathematics[1] in the University, the founder and preses of a club, called the 'Anderson Summer Saturday's.' The scientific attainments and abstract genius of this distinguished person were undisputed; but his simplicity of character and absence of mind were no less remarkable. The object that George probably had in view in taking him, as an occasional visitor, to see his brother, was, perhaps, to qualify the Professor to bear testimony to the arithmetical incapacity of Walter; and certainly the Professor had always found him sufficiently incapable to have warranted him to give the most decisive evidence on that head; but a circumstance had occurred at the last visit, which came out in the course of the investigation, by which it would appear the opinion of the learned mathematician was greatly shaken.

'I am informed, Professor, that you are acquainted with Mr Walter Walkinshaw. Will you have the goodness to tell the Court what is your opinion of that gentleman?' said the advocate.

'My opinion is, that he is a very extraordinary man; for he put a question to me when I last saw him, which I have not yet been able to answer.'

The advocate thought the Professor said this in irony,—and inquired, with a simper,—

'And, pray, what might that question be?'

'I was trying if he could calculate the aliquot parts of a pound; and he said to me, could I tell him the reason that there were but four and twenty bawbees in a shilling?'

'You may retire,' said the advocate, disconcerted; and the Professor immediately withdrew; for still the counsel in behalf of Walter declined to cross question.

'The next witness that I shall produce,' resumed Mr Threeper, 'is one whom I call with extreme reluctance. Every man must sympathise with the feelings of a mother on such an occasion as this,—and will easily comprehend, that, in the questions which my duty obliges me to put to Mrs Walkinshaw, I am, as it were, obliged, out of that sacred respect which is due to her maternal sensibility, to address myself in more general terms than I should otherwise do.'

The Leddy was then called,—and the advocate, with a solemn voice and pauses of lengthened sadness and commiseration, said,—

'Madam, the Court and the jury do not expect you to enter into any particular description of the state of your unfortunate son. They only desire to know if you think he is capable of conducting his affairs like other men.'

'Him capable!' exclaimed the Leddy. 'He's no o' a capacity to be advised.'

She would have proceeded farther,—but Mr Threeper interposed, saying, 'Madam, we shall not distress you farther; the Court and the jury must be satisfied.'

Not so was Mr Keelevin, who nodded to Mr Queerie, the counsel for Walter; and he immediately rose.

'I wish,' said he, 'just to put one question to the witness. How long is it since your son has been so incapable of acting for himself?'

'I canna gie[1] you day nor date,' replied the Leddy; 'but he has been in a state of condumacity ever since his dochter diet.'[2]

'Indeed!' said Mr Queerie; 'then he was not always incapable?'

'O no,' cried the Leddy; 'he was a most tractable creature, and the kindliest son,' she added, with a sigh; 'but since that time he's been neither to bind nor to haud, threatning to send me, his mother, a garsing[3]—garing me lay out my own lawful jointure on the house, and using me in the most horridable manner—wastring his income in the most thoughtless way.'

Mr Threeper began to whisper to our friend Gabriel, and occasionally to look, with an afflicted glance, towards the Leddy.

Mr Queerie resumed,—

'Your situation, I perceive, has been for some time very unhappy—but, I suppose, were Mr Walkinshaw to make you a reasonable compensation for the trouble you take in managing his house, you would have no objections still to continue with him.'

'O! to be surely,' said the Leddy;—'only it would need to be something worth while; and my gude-dochter and her family would require to be obligated to gang hame.'

'Certainly, what you say, Madam, is very reasonable,' rejoined Mr Queerie;—'and I have no doubt that the Court perceives that a great part of your distress, from the idiotry of your son, arises from his having brought in the lady alluded to and her family.'

'It has come a' frae that,' replied the witness, unconscious of the force of what she was saying;—'for, 'cepting his unnaturality to me about them, his idiocety is very harmless.'

'Perhaps not worse than formerly?

A look from George at this crisis put her on her guard; and she instantly replied, as if eager to redeem the effects of what she had just said,—

''Deed, Sir, it's no right to let him continue in the rule and power o' the property; for nobody can tell what he may commit.'

At this juncture, Mr Queerie, perceiving her wariness, sat down; and the Reverend Dr Denholm being called by Mr Threeper, stated, in answer to the usual question,—

'I acknowledge, that I do not think Mr Walkinshaw entirely of a sound mind; but he has glaiks and gleams o' sense about him, that mak me very dootful if I could judicially swear, that he canna deport himsel wi' sufficient sagacity.'

'But,' said the advocate, 'did not you yourself advise Mr George Walkinshaw to institute these proceedings.'

'I'll no disown that,' replied the Doctor; 'but Mr Walter has since then done such a humane and a Christian duty to his brother's widow, and her two defenceless and portionless bairns, that I canna, in my conscience, think now so lightly of him as I once did.'

Here the jury consulted together; and, after a short conference, the foreman inquired if Mr Walkinshaw was in Court. On being answered in the negative, the Sheriff suggested an adjournment till next day, that he might be brought forward.

CHAPTER XX

WHEN the Leddy returned from the Court to Grippy, Walter, who had in the meantime been somehow informed of the nature of the proceedings instituted against him, said to his mother,—

'Weel, mother, so ye hae been trying to mak me daft? but I'm just as wise as ever.'

'Thou's ordaint to bring disgrace on us a',' was her answer, dictated under a feeling of vague apprehension, arising from the uncertainty which seemed to lower upon the issue of the process by the evidence of Dr Denholm.

'I'm sure I hae nae hand in't,' said Walter; 'an ye had na meddlet

wi' me, I would ne'er hae spoken to Keelevin, to vex you. But I
suppose, mother, that you and that wily headcadab¹ Geordie hae
made naething o' your fause witnessing.'

'Haud thy fool tongue, and insult na me,' exclaimed the Leddy
in a rage at the simpleton's insinuation, which was uttered without the slightest sentiment of reproach. 'But,' she added, 'ye'll
see what it is to stand wi' a het face afore the Court the morn.'²

'I'll no gang,' replied Walter; 'I hae nae broo³ o' Courts and
law-pleas.'

'But ye shall gang, if the life be in your body.'

'I'll do nothing but what Mr Keelevin bids me.'

'Mr Keelevin,' exclaimed the Leddy, 'ought to be drum't out
o' the town for bringing sic trebalation intil my family.—What
business had he, wi' his controversies, to gumle⁴ law and justice
in the manner he has done the day?' And while she was thus speaking, George and Mr Pitwinnoch made their appearance.

'Hegh man, Geordie!' said Watty,—'I'm thinking, instead o'
making me daft, ye hae demented my mother, poor bodie; for she's
come hame wi' a flyte⁵ proceeding out of her mouth like a two-
edged sword.'

'If you were not worse than ye are,' said his brother, 'you would
have compassion on your mother's feelings.'

'I'm sure,' said Watty, 'I hae every compassion for her; but
there was nae need o' her to wis to mak me daft. It's a foul bird
that files its ain nest; and really, to speak my mind, I think,
Geordie, that you and her were na wise, but far left to yoursels,⁶
to put your heads intil the hangman's halter o' a law-plea anent
my intellectuals.'

Gabriel Pitwinnoch, who began to distrust the effect of the
evidence, was troubled not a little at this observation; for he
thought, if Walter spoke as well to the point before the Court, the
cause must be abandoned. As for George, he was scarcely in a
state to think of any thing, so much was he confounded and vexed
by the impression of Dr Denholm's evidence, the tenor of which
was so decidedly at variance with all he had flattered himself it
would be. He, however, said,—

'Ye're to be examined to-morrow, and what will you say for
yourself?'

'I hae mair modesty,' replied Walter, 'than to be my ain trumpeter—I'll say naething but what Mr Keelevin bids me.'

Gabriel smiled encouragingly to George at this, who continued,—

'You had better tak care what ye say.'

'Na,' cried Watty, 'an that's the gait o't, I'll keep a calm sough[1]—least said's soonest mendit—I'll haud my tongue.'

'But you must answer every question.'

'Is't in the Shorter or the Larger Catechism?'[2] said Walter. 'I can say till the third petition o' the t'ane, and frae end to end o' the t'ither.'

'That's quite enough,' replied Gabriel, 'and more than will be required of you.'

But the satisfaction which such an agreeable exposure of the innocency of the simpleton was calculated to afford to all present, was disturbed at this juncture by the entrance of Mr Keelevin.

'I'm glad, gentlemen,' said he, the moment he came in, 'that I have found you here. I think you must all be convinced that the investigation should na gang farther. I'm sure Mr Walter will be willing to grant a reasonable consideration to his mother for her care and trouble in the house, and even to assign a moitie o' his income to you, Mr George. Be counselled by me:—let us settle the matter in that manner quietly.'

Pitwinnoch winked to his client,—and Watty said,—

'What for should I gie my mother ony more? Has na she bed, board, and washing, house-room and chattels, a' clear aboon her jointure? and I'm sure Geordie has nae lawful claim on me for ony aliment.—Od, Mr Keelevin, it would be a terrible wastrie o' me to do the like o' that. They might weel mak me daft if I did sae.'

'But it will be far decenter and better for a' parties to enter into some agreement of that sort. Don't you think so, Mrs Walkinshaw, rather than to go on with this harsh business of proving your son an idiot?'

'I'm no an idiot, Mr Keelevin,' exclaimed Walter—'though it seems to me that there's a thraw[3] in the judgment o' the family, or my mother and brother would ne'er hae raised this straemash[4] about my capacity to take care o' the property. Did na I keep the cows frae the corn a' the last Ruglen fair-day, when Jock, the herd, got leave to gang in to try his luck and fortune at the roley-poleys?'[5]

Honest Mr Keelevin wrung his hands at this.

'I'm sure, Sir,' said George, in his sleekiest manner, 'that you must yourself, Mr Keelevin, be quite sensible that the inquiry ought to proceed to a verdict.'

'I'm sensible o' nae sic things, Mr George,' was the indignant answer. 'Your brother is in as full possession of all his faculties as when your father executed the cursed entail, or when he was married to Kilmarkeckle's dochter.'

''Deed, Mr Keelevin,' replied Walter, 'ye're mista'en there; for I hae had twa teeth tuggit out for the toothache since syne; and I hae grown deaf in the left lug.'

'Did na I tell you,' said the worthy man, angrily, 'that ye were na to open your mouth?'

'Really, Mr Keelevin, I won'er to hear you,' replied the natural, with great sincerity; 'the mouth's the only trance-door¹ that I ken to the belly.'

'Weel, weel,' again exclaimed his friend; 'mak a kirk and a mill o't;² but be ruled by me, and let us draw up a reasonable agreement.'

'I'm thinking, Mr Keelevin, that ye dinna ken that I hae made a paction with mysel to sign nae law-papers, for fear it be to the injury of Betty Bodle.'

'Betty Bodle!' said Gabriel Pitwinnoch, eagerly; 'she has been long dead.'

'Ah!' said Walter, 'that's a' ye ken about it. She's baith living and life like.'

Mr Keelevin was startled and alarmed at this; but abstained from saying any thing. Gabriel also said nothing; but looked significantly to his client, who interposed, and put an end to the conversation.

'Having gone so far,' said he, 'I could, with no respect for my own character, allow the proceedings to be now arrested. It is, therefore, unnecessary either to consider your suggestion, or to hold any further debate here on the subject.'

Mr Keelevin made no reply to this; but said, as he had something to communicate in private to his client, he would carry him to Glasgow for that night. To so reasonable and so professional a proposal no objection was made. Walter himself also at once acquiesced, on the express condition, that he was not to be obliged to sign any law-papers.

CHAPTER XXI

NEXT day, when the Court again assembled, Walter was there, seated beside his agent, and dressed in his best. Every eye was directed towards him; and the simple expression of wonder, mingled with anxiety, which the scene around him occasioned, gave an air of so much intelligence to his features, which were regular, and, indeed, handsome, that he excited almost universal sympathy; even Mr Threeper was perplexed, when he saw him, at the proper time, rise from beside his friend, and, approaching the bottom of the table, make a slow and profound bow, first to the Sheriff and then to the jury.

'You are Mr Walkinshaw, I believe?' said Mr Threeper.

'I believe I am,' replied Walter, timidly.

'What are you, Mr Walkinshaw?'

'A man, Sir.—My mother and brother want to mak me a daft ane.'

'How do you suspect them of any such intention?'

'Because ye see I'm here—I would na hae been here but for that.'

The countenance of honest Keelevin began to brighten, while that of George was clouded and overcast.

'Then you do not think you are a daft man?' said the advocate.

'Nobody thinks himsel daft. I dare say ye think ye're just as wise as me.'

A roar of laughter shook the Court, and Threeper blushed and was disconcerted; but he soon resumed, tartly,—

'Upon my word, Mr Walkinshaw, you have a good opinion of yourself. I should like to know for what reason?'

'That's a droll question to speer at[1] a man,' replied Walter. 'A poll parrot thinks weel o' itsel, which is but a feathered creature, and short o' the capacity of a man by twa hands.'

Mr Keelevin trembled and grew pale; and the advocate, recovering full possession of his assurance, proceeded,—

'And so ye think, Mr Walkinshaw, that the two hands make all the difference between a man and a parrot?'

'No, no, Sir,' replied Walter, 'I dinna think that,—for ye ken the beast has feathers.'

'And why have not men feathers?'

'That's ne a right question, Sir, to put to the like o' me, a weak human creature;—ye should ask their Maker,' said Walter gravely.

The advocate was again repulsed; Pitwinnoch sat doubting the intelligence of his ears, and George shivering from head to foot: a buzz of satisfaction pervaded the whole Court.

'Well, but not to meddle with such mysteries,' said Mr Threeper, assuming a jocular tone, 'I suppose you think yourself a very clever fellow?'

'At some things,' replied Walter modestly; 'but I dinna like to make a roos¹ o' mysel.'

'And pray now, Mr Walkinshaw, may I ask what do you think you do best?'

'Man! and ye could see how I can sup curds and ream²—there's no ane in a' the house can ding me.'

The sincerity and exultation with which this was expressed convulsed the Court, and threw the advocate completely on his beam-ends. However, he soon righted, and proceeded,—

'I don't doubt your ability in that way, Mr Walkinshaw; and I dare say you can play a capital knife and fork.'

'I'm better at the spoon,' replied Walter laughing.

'Well, I must confess you are a devilish clever fellow.'

'Mair sae, I'm thinking, than ye thought, Sir.—But noo, since,' continued Walter, 'ye hae speer't so many questions at me, will ye answer one yoursel?'

'O, I can have no possible objection to do that, Mr Walkinshaw.'

'Then,' said Walter, 'how muckle are ye to get frae my brother for this job?'

Again the Court was convulsed, and the questioner again disconcerted.

'I suspect, brother Threeper,' said the Sheriff, 'that you are in the wrong box.'

'I suspect so too,' replied the advocate laughing; but, addressing himself again to Walter, he said,—

'You have been married, Mr Walkinshaw?'

'Aye, auld Doctor Denholm married me to Betty Bodle.'

'And pray where is she?'

'Her mortal remains, as the headstone says, lie in the kirkyard.'

The countenance of Mr Keelevin became pale and anxious—George and Pitwinnoch exchanged smiles of gratulation.

'You had a daughter?' said the advocate, looking knowingly to the jury, who sat listening with greedy ears.

'I had,' said Walter, and glanced anxiously towards his trembling agent.

'And what became of your daughter?'

No answer was immediately given—Walter hung his head, and seemed troubled; he sighed deeply, and again turned his eye inquiringly to Mr Keelevin. Almost every one present sympathised with his emotion, and ascribed it to parental sorrow.

'I say,' resumed the advocate, 'what became of your daughter?'

'I canna answer that question.'

The simple accent in which this was uttered interested all in his favour still more and more.

'Is she dead?' said the pertinacious Mr Threeper.

'Folk said sae; and what every body says maun be true.'

'Then you don't, of your own knowledge, know the fact?'

'Before I can answer that, I would like to ken what a fact is?'

The counsel shifted his ground, without noticing the question; and said,—

'But I understand, Mr Walkinshaw, you have still a child that you call your Betty Bodle?'

'And what business hae ye wi' that?' said the natural, offended. 'I never saw sic a stock o' impudence as ye hae in my life.'

'I did not mean to offend you, Mr Walkinshaw; I was only anxious, for the ends of justice, to know if you consider the child you call Betty Bodle as your daughter?'

'I'm sure,' replied Walter, 'that the ends o' justice would be meikle better served an ye would hae done wi' your speering.'

'It is, I must confess, strange that I cannot get a direct answer from you, Mr Walkinshaw. Surely, as a parent, you should know your child!' exclaimed the advocate, peevishly.

'An I was a mother ye might say sae.'

Mr Threeper began to feel, that, hitherto, he had made no impression; and forming an opinion of Walter's shrewdness far beyond what he was led to expect, he stooped, and conferred a short time with Mr Pitwinnoch. On resuming his wonted posture, he said,—

'I do not wish, Mr Walkinshaw, to harass your feelings; but I am not satisfied with the answer you have given respecting your child; and I beg you will be a little more explicit. Is the little girl that lives with you your daughter?'

'I dinna like to gie you any satisfaction on that head; for Mr Keelevin said, ye would bother me if I did.'

'Ah!' exclaimed the triumphant advocate, 'have I caught you at last?'

A murmur of disappointment ran through all the Court; and Walter looked around coweringly and afraid.

'So, Mr Keelevin has primed you, has he? He has instructed you what to say?'

'No,' said the poor natural; 'he instructed me to say nothing.'

'Then, why did he tell you that I would bother you?'

'I dinna ken, speer at himsel; there he sits.'

'No, Sir! I ask you,' said the advocate, grandly.

'I'm wearied, Mr Keelevin,' said Walter, helplessly, as he looked towards his disconsolate agent. 'May I no come away?'

The honest lawyer gave a deep sigh; to which all the spectators sympathisingly responded.

'Mr Walkinshaw,' said the Sheriff, 'don't be alarmed—we are all friendly disposed towards you; but it is necessary, for the satisfaction of the jury, that you should tell us what you think respecting the child that lives with you.'

Walter smiled and said, 'I hae nae objection to converse wi' a weel-bred gentleman like you; but that barking terrier in the wig, I can thole[1] him no longer.'

'Well, then,' resumed the judge, 'is the little girl your daughter?'

''Deed is she—my ain dochter.'

'How can that be, when, as you acknowledged, every body said your dochter was dead?'

'But I kent better mysel—my bairn and dochter, ye see, Sir, was lang a weakly baby, ay bleating like a lambie that has lost its mother; and she dwin't and dwinlet, and moant and grew sleepy sleepy, and then she clos'd her wee bonny een, and lay still; and I sat beside her three days and three nights, watching her a' the time, never lifting my een frae her face, that was as sweet to look on as a gowan in a lown[2] May morning. But I ken na how it came to pass—I thought, as I look't at her, that she was change't, and there began to come a kirkyard smell frae the bed, that was just as if the hand o' Nature was wising[3] me to gae away; and then I saw, wi' the eye o' my heart, that my brother's wee Mary was grown my wee Betty Bodle, and so I gaed and brought her hame in my arms, and she is noo my dochter. But my mother has gaen on like a randy at me ever sin syne,[1] and wants me to put away my ain bairn, which I will never, never do—No, Sir, I'll stand by her, and guard her, though fifty mothers, and fifty times fifty brother Geordies, were to flyte at me frae morning to night.'

One of the jury here interposed, and asked several questions relative to the management of the estate; by the answers to which it appeared, not only that Walter had never taken any charge whatever, but that he was totally ignorant of business, and even of the most ordinary money transactions.

The jury then turned round and laid their heads together; the legal gentlemen spoke across the table, and Walter was evidently alarmed at the bustle.—In the course of two or three minutes, the foreman returned a verdict of Fatuity.

The poor Laird shuddered, and, looking at the Sheriff, said, in an accent of simplicity that melted every heart, 'Am I found guilty?—O surely, Sir, ye'll no hang me, for I cou'dna help it?'

CHAPTER XXII

THE scene in the parlour of Grippy, after the inquiry, was of the most solemn and lugubrious description.—The Leddy sat in the great chair, at the fire-side, in all the pomp of woe, wiping her eyes, and, ever and anon, giving vent to the deepest soughs[2] of sorrow. Mrs Charles, with her son leaning on her knee, occupied another chair, pensive and anxious. George and Mr Pitwinnoch sat at the table, taking an inventory of the papers in the scrutoire, and Walter was playfully tickling his adopted daughter on the green before the window, when Mrs Milrookit, with her husband, the Laird of Dirdumwhamle, came to sympathise and condole with their friends, and to ascertain what would be the pecuniary consequences of the decision to them.

'Come awa, my dear,' said the Leddy to her daughter, as she entered the room;—'Come away and tak a seat beside me. Your poor brother, Watty, has been weighed in the balance o' the Sheriff, and found wanting; and his vessels o' gold and silver, as I may say in the words o' Scripture, are carried away into captivity; for I understand that George gets no proper right to them, as I expeckit, but is obligated to keep them in custody, in case Watty

should hereafter come to years o' discretion. Hegh Meg! but this
is a sair day for us a'—and for nane mair sae than your afflicted
gude-sister there and her twa bairns. She'll be under a needcessity
to gang back and live again wi' my mother, now in her ninety-third
year, and by course o' nature drawing near to her latter end.'

'And what's to become of you?' replied Mrs Milrookit.

'O I'll hae to bide here, to tak care o' every thing; and an aliment
will be alloot[1] to me for keeping poor Watty. Hegh Sirs! Wha
would hae thought it, that sic a fine lad as he ance was, and preferred by his honest father as the best able to keep the property
right, would thus hae been, by decreet o' court, proven a born
idiot?'

'But,' interrupted Mrs Milrookit, glancing compassionately
towards her sister-in-law, 'I think, since so little change is to be
made, that ye might just as weel let Bell and her bairns bide wi'
you—for my grandmother's income is little enough for her ain
wants, now that she's in a manner bedrid.'

'It's easy for you, Meg, to speak,' replied her mother;—'but if
ye had an experiment o' the heavy handfu' they hae been to me, ye
would hae mair compassion for your mother. It's surely a dispensation sair enough, to hae the grief and heart-breaking sight
before my eyes of a demented lad, that was so long a comfort to
me in my widowhood. But it's the Lord's will, and I maun bend
the knee o' resignation.'

'Is't your intent, Mr George,' said the Laird o' Dirdumwhamle,
'to mak any division o' what lying money there may hae been saved
since your father's death?'

'I suspect there will not be enough to defray the costs of the
process,' replied George; 'and if any balance should remain, the
house really stands so much in need of repair, that I am persuaded
there will not be a farthing left.'

''Deed,' said the Leddy, 'what he says, Mr Milrookit, is oure
true;[2] the house is in a frail condition, for it was like pu'ing the
teeth out o' the head o' Watty to get him to do what was needful.'

'I think,' replied the Laird o' Dirdumwhamle, 'that since ye hae
so soon come to the property, Mr George, and no likelihood o' any
molestation in the possession, that ye might let us a' share and
share alike o' the gethering,[3] and be at the outlay o' the repairs frae
the rental.'

'To this suggestion Mr George, however, replied, 'It will be time enough to consider that, when the law expences are paid.'

'They'll be a heavy soom, Mr Milrookit,' said the Leddy; 'weel do I ken frae my father's pleas what it is to pay law expences. The like o' Mr Pitwinnoch there, and Mr Keelevin, are men o' moderation and commonality in their charges—but yon awfu' folk wi' the cloaks o' darkness and the wigs o' wisdom frae Edinbro'—they are costly commodities.—But now that we're a' met here, I think it would be just as weel an we waur to settle at ance[1] what I'm to hae, as the judicious curator o' Watty—for, by course o' law and nature, the aliment will begin frae this day.'

'Yes,' replied George, 'I think it will be just as well; and I'm glad, mother, that you have mentioned it. What is your opinion, Mr Milrookit, as to the amount that she should have?'

'All things considered,' replied the Laird of Dirdumwhamle, prospectively contemplating some chance of a reversionary interest to his wife in the Leddy's savings, 'I think you ought not to make it less than a hundred pounds a-year.'

'A hundred pounds a-year!' exclaimed the Leddy, 'that'll no buy saut to his kail.[2] I hope and expek no less than the whole half o' the rents; and they were last year weel on to four hunder.'

'I think,' said George to Mr Pitwinnoch, 'I would not be justified to the Court were I to give any thing like that; but if you think I may, I can have no objection to comply with my mother's expectations.'

'O, Mr Walkinshaw,' replied Gabriel, 'you are no at a' aware o' your responsibility,—you can do no such things. Your brother has been found a *fatuus*, and, of course, entitled but to the plainest maintenance. I think that you will hardly be permitted to allow his mother more than fifty pounds; if, indeed, so much.'

'Fifty pounds! fifty placks,'[3] cried the indignant Leddy. 'I'll let baith you and the Sheriff ken I'm no to be frauded o' my rights in that gait. I'll no faik[4] a farthing o' a hundred and fifty.'

'In that case, I fear,' said Gabriel, 'Mr George will be obliged to seek another custodier for the *fatuus*, as assuredly, Mem, he'll ne'er be sanctioned to allow you any thing like that.'

'If ye think sae,' interposed Mrs Milrookit, compassionating the forlorn estate of her sister-in-law,—'I dare say Mrs Charles will be content to take him at a very moderate rate.'

'Megsty me!' exclaimed the Leddy. 'Hae I been buying a pig

in a pock like that? Is't a possibility that he can be ta'en out o' my
hands, and no reasonable allowance made to me at a'? Surely,
Mr Pitwinnoch, surely, Geordie, this can never stand either by
the laws of God or man.'

'I can assure you, Mrs Walkinshaw,' replied the lawyer, 'that
fifty pounds a-year is as much as I could venture to advise Mr
George to give; and seeing it is sae, you had as well agree to it
at once.'

'I'll never agree to ony such thing.' I'll gang intil Embro mysel,
and hae justice done me frae the Fifteen. I'll this very night consult Mr Keelevin, who is a most just man, and o' a right partiality.'

'I hope, mother,' said George, 'that you and I will not cast out
about this; and to end all debates, if ye like, we'll leave the aliment
to be settled by Mr Pitwinnoch and Mr Keelevin.'

'Nothing can be fairer,' observed the Laird of Dirdumwhamle,
in the hope Mr Keelevin might be so wrought on as to insist, that
at least a hundred should be allowed; and after some further
altercation, the Leddy grudgingly assented to this proposal.'

'But,' said Mrs Milrookit, 'considering now the altered state of
Watty's circumstances, I dinna discern how it is possible for my
mother to uphold this house and the farm?'

The Leddy looked a little aghast at this fearful intimation, while
George replied,—

'I have reflected on that, Margaret, and I am quite of your
opinion; and, indeed, it is my intention, after the requisite repairs
are done to the house, to flit¹ my family; for I am in hopes the
change of air will be advantageous to my wife's health.'

The Leddy was thunderstruck, and unable to speak; but her
eyes were eloquent with indignation.

'Perhaps, after all, it would be as well for our mother,' continued George, 'to take up house at once in Glasgow; and as I mean
to settle an annuity of fifty pounds on Mrs Charles, they could not
do better than all live together.'

All present but his mother applauded the liberality of George.
To the young widow the intelligence of such a settlement was as
fresh air to the captive; but before she could express her thankfulness, Leddy Grippy started up, and gave a tremendous stamp with
her foot. She then resumed her seat, and appeared all at once calm
and smiling; but it was a calm betokening no tranquillity, and a
smile expressive of as little pleasure. In the course of a few seconds

the hurricane burst forth, and alternately, with sobs and supplica-
tions, menaces, and knocking of nieves,[1] and drumming with her
feet, the hapless Leddy Grippy divulged and expatiated on the
plots and devices of George. But all was of no avail—her destiny
was sealed; and long before Messrs Keelevin and Pitwinnoch
adjusted the amount of the allowance, which, after a great struggle
on the part of the former, was settled at seventy-five pounds, she
found herself under the painful necessity of taking a flat up a turnpike stair[2] in Glasgow, for herself and the *fatuus*.

CHAPTER XXIII

FOR some time after the decision of Walter's fatuity, nothing
important occurred in the history of the Grippy family. George
pacified his own conscience, and gained the approbation of the
world, by fulfilling the promise of settling fifty pounds per annum
on his sister-in-law. The house was enlarged and adorned, and the
whole estate, under the ancient name of Kittlestonheugh, began to
partake of that general spirit of improvement[3] which was then
gradually diffusing itself over the face of the west country.

In the meantime, Mrs Charles Walkinshaw, who had returned
with her children to reside with their grandmother, found her
situation comparatively comfortable; but an acute anxiety for the
consequences that would ensue by the daily expected death of that
gentlewoman, continued to thrill through her bosom, and chequer
the sickly gleam of the uncertain sunshine that glimmered in her
path. At last the old lady died, and she was reduced, as she had long
foreseen, with her children, to the parsimonious annuity. As it was
impossible for her to live in Glasgow, and educate her children, on
so small a stipend, there, she retired to one of the neighbouring
villages, where, in the family of the Reverend Mr Eadie, the
minister, she found that kind of quiet intelligent society which her
feelings and her misfortunes required.

Mrs Eadie was a Highland lady, and, according to the living
chronicles of the region of clans and traditions, she was of scarcely
less than illustrious birth. But for the last attempt to restore the
royal line of the Stuarts, she would, in all probability, have moved
in a sphere more spacious and suitable to the splendour of her

pedigree than the humble and narrow orbit of a country clergy-man's wife. Nor in her appearance did it seem that Nature and Fortune were agreed about her destiny; for the former had adorned her youth with the beauty, the virtues, and the dignity, which command admiration in the palace,—endowments but little consonant to the lowly duties of the rural manse.

At the epoch of which we are now speaking she was supposed to have passed her fiftieth year; but something in her air and manner gave her the appearance of being older—a slight shade of melancholy, the pale cast of thought, lent sweetness to the benign composure of her countenance; and she was seldom seen without inspiring interest, and awakening sentiments of profound and reverential respect. She had lost her only daughter about a year before; and a son, her remaining child, a boy about ten years of age, was supposed to have inherited the malady which carried off his sister. The anxiety which Mrs Eadie, in consequence, felt as a mother, partly occasioned that mild sadness of complexion to which we have alluded; but there was still a deeper and more affecting cause.

Before the ruin of her father's fortune, by the part he took in the Rebellion,[1] she was betrothed to a youth who united many of the best Lowland virtues with the gallantry and enthusiasm peculiar to the Highlanders of that period. It was believed that he had fallen in the fatal field of Culloden; and, after a long period of virgin widowhood, on his account, she was induced, by the amiable manners and gentle virtues of Mr Eadie, to consent to change her life. He was then tutor in the family of a relation, with whom, on her father's forfeiture and death, she had found an asylum,—and when he was presented to the parish of Camrachle, they were married.

The first seven years, from the date of their union, were spent in that temperate state of enjoyment which is the nearest to perfect happiness; during the course of which their two children were born. In that time no symptom of the latent poison of the daughter's constitution appeared; but all around them, and in their prospects, was calm, and green, and mild, and prosperous.

In the course of the summer of the eighth year, in consequence of an often repeated invitation, they went, at the meeting of the General Assembly,[2] to which Mr Eadie was returned a member, to spend a short time with a relation in Edinburgh, and among the strangers with whom they happened to meet at the houses of their friends were several from France, children and relations of some of those who had been out in the Forty-five.

A young gentleman belonging to these expatriated visitors, one evening interested Mrs Eadie, to so great a degree, that she requested to be particularly introduced to him, and, in the course of conversation, she learnt that he was the son of her former lover, and that his father was still alive, and married to a French woman, his mother. The shock which this discovery produced was so violent that she was obliged to leave the room, and falling afterwards into bad health, her singular beauty began to fade with premature decay.

Her husband, to whom she disclosed her grief, endeavoured to soften it by all the means and blandishments in his power; but it continued so long inveterate, that he, yielded himself to the common weakness of our nature, and growing peevish at her sorrow, chided her melancholy till their domestic felicity was mournfully impaired.

Such was the state in which Mrs Charles Walkinshaw found Mrs Eadie at their first acquaintance; and the disappointments and shadows which had fallen on the hopes of her own youth, soon led to an intimate and sympathetic friendship between them, the influence of which contributed at once to alleviate their reciprocal griefs, and to have the effect of reviving, in some degree, the withered affections of the minister. The gradual and irremediable progress of the consumption which preyed on his son, soon, however, claimed from that gentle and excellent man efforts of higher fortitude than he had before exerted, and from that inward exercise, and the sympathy which he felt for his wife's maternal solicitude, Mrs Walkinshaw had the satisfaction, in the course of a year, to see their mutual confidence and cordiality restored. But in the same period the boy died; and though the long foreseen event deeply affected his parents, it proved a fortunate occurrence to the widow. For the minister, to withdraw his reflections from the contemplation of his childless state, undertook the education of James, and Mrs Eadie, partly from the same motives, but chiefly to enjoy the society of her friend, proposed to unite with her in the education of Mary. 'We cannot tell,' said she to Mrs Walkinshaw, 'what her lot may be; but let us do our best to prepare her for the world, and leave her fortunes, as they ever must be, in the hands of Providence. The penury and obscurity of her present condition ought to be no objection to bestowing on her all the accomplishments we have it in our power to give. How little likely was it, in my father's time, that I should have been in this comparative poverty, and yet, but for those acquirements, which were studied for brighter prospects, how dark and sad would often have been my residence in this sequestered village?'

CHAPTER XXIV

IN the meantime, the fortunes of George, whom we now regard as the third Laird of Grippy, continued to flourish. The estate rose in value, and his mercantile circumstances improved; but still the infirmities of his wife's health remained the same, and the want of a male heir was a craving void in his bosom, that no prosperity could supply.

The reflections, connected with this subject, were rendered the more afflicting, by the consideration, that, in the event of dying without a son, the estate would pass from his daughter to James, the son of his brother Charles—and the only consolation that he had to balance this was a hope that, perhaps, in time he might be able to bring to pass a marriage between them. Accordingly, after a suspension of intercourse for several years, actuated by a perspective design of this kind, he, one afternoon, made his appearance in his own carriage, with his lady and daughter, at the door of Mrs Charles' humble dwelling, in the village of Camrachle.

'I am afraid,' said he, after they were all seated in her little parlour, the window of which was curtained without with honey-suckle and jessamine—and the grate filled with flowers;—'I am afraid, my dear sister, unless we occasionally renew our intercourse, that the intimacy will be lost between our families, which it ought to be the interest of friends to preserve. Mrs Walkinshaw and I have, therefore, come to request that you and the children will spend a few days with us at Kittlestonheugh, and if you do not object, we shall invite our mother and Walter to join you—you would be surprised to hear how much the poor fellow still dotes on the recollection of your Mary, as Betty Bodle, and bewails, because the law, as he says, has found him guilty of being daft, that he should not be allowed to see her.'

This visit and invitation were so unexpected, that even Mrs Charles, who was of the most gentle and confiding nature, could not avoid suspecting they were dictated by some unexplained purpose; but adversity had long taught her that she was only as a reed in the world, and must stoop as the wind blew. She, therefore, readily agreed to spend a few days at the mansion-house, and the children who were present, eagerly expressing a desire to see their uncle Walter, of whose indulgence and good nature they retained the liveliest recollection, it was arranged that, on the Monday following, the carriage should be sent for her and them, and that the Leddy and Walter should also be at Kittlestonheugh to meet them.

In the evening after this occurrence, Mrs Charles went to the manse, and communicated to the minister and Mrs Eadie what had happened. They knew her story, and were partly acquainted with the history of the strange and infatuated Entail. Like her, they believed that her family had been entirely cut off from the succession, and, like her too, they respected the liberality of George, in granting her the annuity, small as it was. His character, indeed, stood fair and honourable with the world; he was a partner in one of the most eminent concerns in the royal city;[1] his birth and the family estate placed him in the first class of her sons and daughters, that stately class who, though entirely devoted to the pursuit of lucre, still held their heads high as ancestral gentry. But after a suspension of intercourse for so long a period, so sudden a renewal of intimacy, and with a degree of cordiality never before evinced, naturally excited their wonder, and awakened their conjectures. Mrs Eadie, superior and high-minded herself, ascribed it to the best intentions. 'Your brother-in-law,' said she, 'is feeling the generous influence of prosperity, and is sensible that it must redound to his personal advantage with the world to continue towards you, on an enlarged scale, that friendship which you have already experienced.'

But the minister, who, from his humbler birth, and the necessity which it imposed on him to contemplate the movements of society from below, together with that acquired insight of the hidden workings of the heart, occasionally laid open in the confessional moments of contrition, when his assistance was required at the death-beds of his parishioners, appeared to entertain a different opinion.

'I hope his kindness proceeds,' said he, 'from so good a source; but I should have been better satisfied had it run in a constant stream, and not, after such an entire occultation, burst forth so suddenly. It is either the result of considerations with respect to things already past, recently impressed upon him, in some new manner, or springs from some sinister purpose that he has in view; and, therefore, Mrs Walkinshaw, though it may seem harsh in me to suggest so ill a return for such a demonstration of brotherly regard, I would advise you, on account of your children, to observe to what it tends.'

In the meantime, George, with his lady and daughter, had proceeded to his mother's residence in Virginia Street, to invite her and Walter to join Mrs Charles and the children.

His intercourse with her, after her domiciliation in the town had been established, was restored to the freest footing; for although, in the first instance, and in the most vehement manner, she declared, 'He had cheated her, and deprived Walter of his lawful senses; and that she ne'er would open her lips to him again,' he had, nevertheless, contrived to make his peace, by sending her presents, and paying her the most marked deference and respect; lamenting that the hard conditions of his situation as a trustee did not allow him to be in other respects more liberal. But still the embers of suspicion were not extinguished; and when, on this occasion, he told her where he had been, and the immediate object of his visit, she could not refrain from observing, that it was a very wonderful thing.

'Dear keep me, Geordie!' said she, 'what's in the wind noo, that ye hae been galloping awa in your new carriage¹ to invite Bell Fatherlans and her weans to Grippy?'

George, eager to prevent her observations, interrupted her, saying,—

'I am surprised, mother, that you still continue to call the place Grippy. You know it is properly Kittlestonheugh.'

'To be sure,' replied the Leddy, 'since my time and your worthy father's time, it has undergone a great transmogrification; what wi' your dining-rooms, and what wi' your drawing-rooms, and your new back jams² and your wings.'

'Why, mother, I have but as yet built only one of the wings,' said he.

'And enough too,' exclaimed the Leddy. 'Geordie, tak my word for't, it'll a' flee fast enough away wi' ae wing.[1] Howsever, I'll no objek to the visitation, for I hae had a sort o' wis to see my grand-childer, which is very natural I shou'd hae. Nae doot, by this time they are grown braw bairns; and their mother was ay a genty bodie,[2] though, in a sense, mair for ornament than use.'

Walter, who, during this conversation, was sitting in his father's easy chair, that had, among other chattels, been removed from Grippy,—swinging backward and forwards, and occasionally throwing glances towards the visitors, said,—

'And is my Betty Bodle to be there?'

'O, yes,' replied George, glad to escape from his mother's remarks, 'and you'll be quite delighted to see her. She is un-commonly tall for her age.'

'I dinna like that,' said Walter; 'she should na hae grown ony bigger,—for I dinna like big folk.'

'And why not?'

''Cause ye ken, Geordie, the law's made only for them; and if you and me had ay been twa wee brotherly laddies, playing on the gowany brae,[3] as we used to do, ye would ne'er hae thought o' bringing yon Cluty's[4] claw frae Enbro' to prove me guilty o' daftness.'

'I'm sure, Watty,' said George, under the twinge which he suffered from the observation, 'that I could not do otherwise. It was required from me equally by what was due to the world and to my mother.'

'It may be sae,' replied Walter; 'but, as I'm daft, ye ken I dinna understand it;' and he again resumed his oscillations.

After some further conversation on the subject of the proposed visit, in which George arranged that he should call on Monday for his mother and Walter in the carriage, and take them out to the country with him, he took his leave.

CHAPTER XXV

ON the same evening on which George and his family visited Mrs Charles at Camrachle, and while she was sitting in the manse parlour, Mrs Eadie received a letter by the post. It was from her cousin Frazer, who, as heir-male of Frazer of Glengael, her father's house, would, but for the forfeiture,[1] have been his successor, and it was written to inform her, that, among other forfeited properties, the Glengael estate was to be soon publicly sold, and that he was making interest, according to the custom of the time, and the bearing in the minds of the Scottish gentry in general towards the unfortunate adherents of the Stuarts, to obtain a private preference at the sale; also begging that she would come to Edinburgh and assist him in the business, some of their mutual friends and relations having thought that, perhaps, she might herself think of concerting the means to make the purchase.

At one time, undoubtedly, the hereditary affections of Mrs Eadie would have prompted her to have made the attempt; but the loss of her children extinguished all the desire she had ever cherished on the subject, and left her only the wish that her kinsman might succeed. Nevertheless, she was too deeply under the influence of the clannish sentiments peculiar to the Highlanders, not to feel that a compliance with Frazer's request was a duty. Accordingly, as soon as she read the letter, she handed it to her husband, at the same time saying,—

'I am glad that this has happened when we are about to lose for a time the society of Mrs Walkinshaw. We shall set out for Edinburgh on Monday, the day she leaves this, and perhaps we may be able to return about the time she expects to be back. For I feel,' she added, turning towards her, 'that your company has become an essential ingredient to our happiness.'

Mr Eadie was so much surprised at the decision with which his wife spoke, and the firmness with which she proposed going to Edinburgh, without reference to what he might be inclined to do, that, instead of reading the letter, he looked at her anxiously for a moment, perhaps recollecting the unpleasant incident of their former visit to the metropolis, and said, 'What has occurred?'

'Glengael is to be sold,' she replied, 'and my cousin, Frazer, is using all the influence he can to prevent any one from bidding against him. Kindness towards me deters some of our mutual friends from giving him their assistance; and he wishes my presence in Edinburgh to remove their scruples, and otherwise to help him.'

'You can do that as well by letter as in person,' said the minister, opening the letter; 'for, indeed, this year we cannot so well afford the expences of such a journey.'

'The honour of my father's house is concerned in this business,' replied the lady, calmly but proudly; 'and there is no immediate duty to interfere with what I owe to my family as the daughter of Glengael.'

Mrs Walkinshaw had, from her first interview, admired the august presence and lofty sentiments of Mrs Eadie; but nothing had before occurred to afford her even a glimpse of her dormant pride and sleeping energies, the sinews of a spirit capable of heroic and masculine effort; and she felt for a moment awed by the incidental disclosure of a power and resolution, that she had never once imagined to exist beneath the calm and equable sensibility which constituted the general tenor of her friend's character.

When the minister had read the letter, he again expressed his opinion that it was unnecessary to go to Edinburgh; but Mrs Eadie, without entering into any observation on his argument, said,—

'On second thoughts, it may not be necessary for you to go— but I must. I am summoned by my kinsman; and it is not for me to question the propriety of what he asks, but only to obey. It is the cause of my father's house.'

The minister smiled at her determination, and said, 'I suppose there is nothing else for me but also to obey. I do not, however, recollect who this Frazer is—Was he out with your father in the Forty-five?'

'No; but his father was,' replied Mrs Eadie, 'and was likewise executed at Carlisle. He, himself, was bred to the bar, and is an advocate in Edinburgh.' And, turning suddenly round to Mrs Walkinshaw, she added solemnly, 'There is something in this—There is some mysterious link between the fortunes of your family and mine. It has brought your brother-in-law here to-day, as if a new era were begun to you, and also this letter of auspicious omen to the blood of Glengael.'

Mr Eadie laughingly remarked, 'That he had not for a long time heard from her such a burst of Highland lore.'

But Mrs Walkinshaw was so affected by the solemnity with which it had been expressed, that she inadvertently said, 'I hope in Heaven it may be so.'

'I am persuaded it is,' rejoined Mrs Eadie, still serious; and emphatically taking her by the hand, she said, 'The minister dislikes what he calls my Highland freats,[1] and believes they have their source in some dark remnants of pagan superstition; on that account, I abstain from speaking of many things that I see, the signs and forecoming shadows of events—nevertheless, my faith in them is none shaken, for the spirit has more faculties than the five senses, by which, among other things, the heart is taught to love or hate, it knows not wherefore—Mark, therefore, my words, and bear them in remembrance—for this day the fortunes of Glengael are mingled with those of your house.—The lights of both have been long set; but the time is coming, when they shall again shine in their brightness.'

'I should be incredulous no more,' replied the minister, 'if you could persuade her brother-in-law, Mr George Walkinshaw, to help Frazer with a loan towards the sum required for the purchase of Glengael.'

Perceiving, however, that he was treading too closely on a tender point, he turned the conversation, and nothing more particular occurred that evening. The interval between and Monday was occupied by the two families in little preparations for their respective journeys; Mr Eadie, notwithstanding the pecuniary inconvenience, having agreed to accompany his wife.

In the meantime, George, for some reason best known to himself, it would appear, had resolved to make the visit of so many connections a festival; for, on the day after he had been at Camrachle, he wrote to his brother-in-law, the Laird of Dirdumwhamle, to join the party with Mrs Milrookit, and to bring their son with them,—a circumstance which, when he mentioned it to his mother, only served to make her suspect that more was meant than met either the eye or ear in such extraordinary kindness; and the consequence was, that she secretly resolved to take the advice of Mr Keelevin, as to how she ought to conduct herself; for, from the time of his warsle, as she called it, with Pitwinnoch for the aliment,[2] he had regained her good opinion. She had also another

motive for being desirous of conferring with him, no less than a
laudable wish to have her will made, especially as the worthy
lawyer, now far declined into the vale of years, had been for some
time in ill health, and unable to give regular attendance to his
clients at the office: 'symptoms,' as the Leddy said when she heard
it 'that he felt the cauld hand o' Death muddling about the root
o' life, and a warning to a' that wanted to profit by his skill, no to
slumber and sleep like the foolish virgins, that alloo't their cruises
to burn out, and were wakened to desperation, when the shout got
up that the bridegroom and the musickers were coming.'

But the worthy lawyer, when she called, was in no condition to
attend any longer to worldly concerns,—a circumstance which she
greatly deplored, as she mentioned it to her son George, who, however, was far from sympathising with her anxiety; on the contrary,
the news, perhaps, afforded him particular satisfaction. For he
was desirous that the world should continue to believe his elder
brother had been entirely disinherited, and Mr Keelevin was the
only person that he thought likely to set the heirs in that respect
right.

CHAPTER XXVI

ON the day appointed, the different members of the Grippy
family assembled at Kittlestonheugh. Mrs Charles and her two
children were the last that arrived; and during the drive from
Camrachle, both James and Mary repeated many little instances
of Walter's kindness, so lasting are the impressions of affection
received in the artless and heedless hours of childhood; and they
again anticipated, from the recollection of his good nature, a long
summer day with him of frolic and mirth.

But they were now several years older, and they had undergone that unconscious change, by which, though the stores of
memory are unaltered, the moral being becomes another creature,
and can no longer feel towards the same object as it once felt.
On alighting from the carriage, they bounded with light steps and
jocund hearts in quest of their uncle; but, when they saw him
sitting by himself in the garden, they paused, and were disappointed.

They recognised in him the same person whom they formerly knew, but they had heard he was daft; and they beheld him stooping forward, with his hands sillily hanging between his knees; and he appeared melancholy and helpless.

'Uncle Watty,' said James, compassionately, 'what for are ye sitting there alone?'

Watty looked up, and gazing at him vacantly for a few seconds, said, ''Cause naebody will sit wi' me, for I'm a daft man.' He then drooped his head, and sank into the same listless posture in which they had found him.

'Do ye no ken me?' said Mary.

He again raised his eyes, and alternately looked at them both, eagerly and suspiciously. Mary appeared to have outgrown his recollection, for he turned from her; but, after some time, he began to discover James; and a smile of curious wonder gradually illuminated his countenance, and developed itself into a broad grin of delight, as he said,—

'What a heap o' meat, Jamie Walkinshaw, ye maun hae eaten to mak you sic a muckle laddie;' and he drew the boy towards him to caress him as he had formerly done; but the child, escaping from his hands, retired several paces backward, and eyed him with pity, mingled with disgust.

Walter appeared struck with his look and movement; and again folding his hands, dropped them between his knees, and hung his head, saying to himself,—'But I'm daft; naebody cares for me noo; I'm a cumberer o' the ground, and a' my Betty Bodles are ta'en away.'

The accent in which this was expressed touched the natural tenderness of the little girl; and she went up to him, and said,— 'Uncle, I'm your wee Betty Bodle; what for will ye no speak to me?'

His attention was again roused, and he took her by the hand, and, gently stroking her head, said, 'Ye're a bonny flower, a lily-like leddy, and leil[1] in the heart and kindly in the e'e; but ye're no my Betty Bodle.' Suddenly, however, something in the cast of her countenance reminded him so strongly of her more childish appearance, that he caught her in his arms, and attempted to dandle her; but the action was so violent that it frightened the child, and she screamed, and struggling out of his hands, ran away. James followed her; and their attention being soon drawn to other objects, poor Walter was left neglected by all during the remainder of the forenoon.

At dinner he was brought in and placed at the table, with one of the children on each side; but he paid them no attention.

'What's come o'er thee, Watty?' said his mother. 'I thought ye would hae been out o' the body[1] wi' your Betty Bodle; but ye ne'er let on ye see her.'

''Cause she's like a' the rest,' said he sorrowfully. 'She canna abide me; for ye ken I'm daft—It's surely an awfu' leprosy this daftness, that it gars every body flee me; but I canna help it—It's no my fau't, but the Maker's that made me, and the laws that found me guilty. But, Geordie,' he added, turning to his brother, 'What's the use o' letting me live in this world, doing nothing, and gude for naething?'

Mrs Charles felt her heart melt within her at the despondency with which this was said, and endeavoured to console him; he, however, took no notice of her attentions, but sat seemingly absorbed in melancholy, and heedless to the endeavours which even the compassionate children made to induce him to eat.

'No,' said he; 'I'll no eat ony mair—it's even down wastrie for sic a useless set-by thing[2] as the like o' me to consume the fruits o' the earth. The cost o' my keep would be a braw thing to Bell Fatherlans, so I hope, Geordie, ye'll mak it o'er to her; for when I gae hame I'll lie doun and die.'

'Haud thy tongue, and no fright folk wi' sic blethers,' exclaimed his mother; 'but eat your dinner, and gang out to the green and play wi' the weans.'

'An I were na a daft creature, naebody would bid me play wi' weans—and the weans ken that I am sae, and mak a fool o' me for't—I dinna like to be every body's fool. I'm sure the law, when it found me guilty, might hae alloot me a mair merciful punishment. Meg Wilcat, that stealt Provost Murdoch's cocket-hat, and was whippit for't at the Cross, was pitied wi' many a watery e'e; but every body dauds and dings[3] the daft Laird o' Grippy.'

'Na! as I'm to be trusted,' exclaimed the Leddy, 'if I dinna think, Geordie, that the creature's coming to its senses again;' and she added laughing, 'and what will come o' your braw policy, and your planting and plenishing? for ye'll hae to gie't back, and count in the Court to the last bawbee for a' the rental besides.'

George was never more at a loss than for an answer to parry this thrust; but, fortunately for him, Walter rose and left the room, and, as he had taken no dinner, his mother followed to remonstrate with him against the folly of his conduct. Her exhortations and her menaces were, however, equally ineffectual; the poor natural was not to be moved; he felt his own despised and humiliated state; and the expectation which he had formed of the pleasure he was to enjoy, in again being permitted to caress and fondle his Betty Bodle, was so bitterly disappointed, that it cut him to the heart. No persuasion, no promise, could entice him to return to the dining-room; but a settled and rivetted resolution to go back to Glasgow obliged his mother to desist, and allow him to take his own way. He accordingly quitted the house, and immediately on arriving at home went to bed. Overpowered by the calls of hunger, he was next day allured to take some food; and from day to day after, for several years, he was in the same manner tempted to eat; but all power of volition, from the period of the visit, appeared to have become extinct within him. His features suffered a melancholy change, and he never spoke—nor did he seem to recognize any one; but gradually, as it were, the whole of his mind and intellect ebbed away, leaving scarcely the merest instincts of life. But the woeful form which Nature assumes in the death-bed of fatuity admonishes us to draw the curtain over the last scene of poor Watty.

CHAPTER XXVII

In the foregoing Chapter we were led, by our regard for the simple affections and harmless character of the second Laird, to overstep a period of several years. We must now, in consequence, return, and resume the narrative from the time that Walter retired from the company; but, without entering too minutely into the other occurrences of the day, we may be allowed to observe, in the sage words of the Leddy, that the party enjoyed themselves with as much insipidity as is commonly found at the formal feasts of near relations.

Mrs Charles Walkinshaw, put on her guard by the conjectures of the minister of Camrachle, soon perceived an evident partiality on the part of her brother-in-law towards her son, and that he took particular pains to make the boy attentive to Robina, as his daughter was called. Indeed, the design of George was so obvious, and the whole proceedings of the day so peculiarly marked, that even the Leddy could not but observe them.

'I'm thinking,' said she, 'that the seeds of a matrimony are sown among us this day, for Geordie's a far-before looking soothsayer, and a Chaldee excellence[1] like his father; and a bodie does na need an e'e in the neck to discern that he's just wising and wiling[2] for a purpose of marriage hereafter between Jamie and Beenie. Gude speed the wark![3] for really we hae had but little luck among us since the spirit o' disinheritance got the upper hand; and it would be a great comfort if a' sores could be salved and healed in the fulness of time, when the weans can be married according to law.'

'I do assure you, mother,' replied her dutiful son, 'that nothing would give me greater pleasure; and I hope, that, by the frequent renewal of these little cordial and friendly meetings, we may help forward so desirable an event.'

'But,' replied the old Leddy piously, 'marriages are made in Heaven; and, unless there has been a booking[4] among the angels above, a' that can be done by man below, even to the crying, for the third and last time, in the kirk, will be only a thrashing the water and a raising of bells.[5] Howsever, the prayers of the righteous availeth much; and we should a' endeavour, by our walk and conversation, to compass a work so meet for repentance until it's brought to a come-to-pass. So I hope, Bell Fatherlans, that ye'll up and be doing in this good work, watching and praying, like those who stand on the tower of Siloam looking towards Lebanon[6].'

'I think,' said Mrs Charles smiling, 'that you are looking far forward. The children are still but mere weans, and many a day must pass over their green heads before such a project ought even to be thought of.'

'It's weel kent, Bell,' replied her mother-in-law, 'that ye were ne'er a queen of Sheba, either for wisdom or forethought; but I hae heard my friend that's awa[7]—your worthy father, Geordie— often say, that as the twig is bent the tree's inclined, which is a fine sentiment, and should teach us to set about our undertakings with a knowledge of better things than of silver and gold, in order that we may be enabled to work the work o' Providence.'

But just as the Leddy was thus expatiating away in high solemnity, a dreadful cry arose among the pre-ordained lovers.

The children had quarrelled; and, notwithstanding all the admonitions which they had received to be kind to one another, Miss Robina had given James a slap on the face, which he repaid with such instantaneous energy, that, during the remainder of the visit, they were never properly reconciled.

Other causes were also in operation destined to frustrate the long-forecasting prudence of her father. Mr and Mrs Eadie, on their arrival at Edinburgh, took up their abode with her relation Mr Frazer, the intending purchaser of Glengael; and they had not been many days in his house, till they came to the determination to adopt Ellen, his eldest daughter, who was then about the age of James. Accordingly, after having promoted the object of their journey, when they returned to the manse of Camrachle, they were allowed to take Ellen with them; and the intimacy which arose among the children in the progress of time ripened into love between her and James. For although his uncle, in the prosecution of his own purpose, often invited the boy to spend several days together with his cousin at Kittlestonheugh, and did every thing in his power during those visits to inspire the children with a mutual affection, their distaste for each other seemed only to increase.

Robina was sly and demure, observant, quiet, and spiteful. Ellen, on the contrary, was full of buoyancy and glee, playful and generous, qualities which assimilated much more with the dispositions of James than those of his cousin, so that, long before her beauty had awakened passion, she was to him a more interesting and delightful companion.

The amusements, also, at Camrachle, were more propitious to the growth of affection than those at Kittlestonheugh, where every thing was methodized into system, and where, if the expression may be allowed, the genius of design[1] and purpose controlled and repressed nature. The lawn was preserved in a state of neatness too trim for the gambols of childhood; and the walks were too winding for the straightforward impulses of its freedom and joy. At Camrachle the fields were open, and their expanse unbounded. The sun, James often thought, shone brighter there than at Kittlestonheugh; the birds sung sweeter in the wild broom than in his uncle's shrubbery, and the moonlight glittered like gladness in the burns; but on the wide water of the Clyde it was always dull and silent.

There are few situations more congenial to the diffusion of tenderness and sensibility—the elements of affection—than the sunny hills and clear waters of a rural neighbourhood, and few of all the beautiful scenes of Scotland excel the environs of Camrachle. The village stands on the slope of a gentle swelling ground, and consists of a single row of scattered thatched cottages, behind which a considerable stream carries its tributary waters to the Cart.[1] On the east end stands the little church, in the centre of a small cemetery, and close to it the modest mansion of the minister. The house which Mrs Walkinshaw occupied was a slated cottage near the manse. It was erected by a native of the village, who had made a moderate competency as a tradesman in Glasgow, and, both in point of external appearance and internal accommodation, it was much superior to any other of the same magnitude in the parish. A few ash trees rose among the gardens, and several of them were tufted with the nests of magpies, the birds belonging to which had been so long in the practice of resorting there, that they were familiar to all the children of the village.

But the chief beauty in the situation of Camrachle is a picturesque and extensive bank, shaggy with hazel, along the foot of which runs the stream already mentioned. The green and gowany brow of this romantic terrace commands a wide and splendid view of all the champaign district of Renfrewshire. And it was often observed, by the oldest inhabitants, that whenever any of the natives of the clachan[2] had been long absent, the first spot they visited on their return was the crown of this bank, where they had spent the sunny days of their childhood. Here the young Walkinshaws and Ellen Frazer also instinctively resorted, and their regard for each other was not only ever after endeared by the remembrance of their early pastimes there, but associated with delightful recollections of glorious summer sunshine, the fresh green mornings of spring, and the golden evenings of autumn.

CHAPTER XXVIII

As James approached his fourteenth year, his uncle, still with a view to a union with Robina, proposed, that, when Mr Eadie thought his education sufficient for the mercantile profession, he should be sent to his counting-house. But the early habits and the tenor of the lessons he had received were not calculated to insure success to James as a merchant. He was robust, handsome, and adventurous, fond of active pursuits, and had imbibed, from the Highland spirit of Mrs Eadie, a tinge of romance and enthusiasm. The bias of his character, the visions of his reveries, and the cast of his figure and physiognomy, were decidedly military. But the field of heroic enterprise was then vacant,—the American war was over, and all Europe slumbered in repose,[1] unconscious of the hurricane that was then gathering; and thus, without any consideration of his own inclinations and instincts, James, like many of those who afterwards distinguished themselves in the great conflict, acceded to the proposal.

He had not, however, been above three or four years settled in Glasgow when his natural distaste for sedentary and regular business began to make him dislike the place; and his repugnance was heightened almost to disgust by the discovery of his uncle's sordid views with respect to him; nor, on the part of his cousin, was the design better relished; for, independent of an early and ungracious antipathy, she had placed her affections on another object; and more than once complained to the old Leddy of her father's tyranny in so openly urging on a union that would render her miserable, especially, as she said, when her cousin's attachment to Ellen Frazer was so unequivocal. But Leddy Grippy had set her mind on the match as strongly as her son; and, in consequence, neither felt nor showed any sympathy for Robina.

'Never fash your head,' she said to her one day, when the young lady was soliciting her mediation,—'Never fash your head, Beenie, my dear, about Jamie's calf-love for yon daffodil; but be an obedient child, and walk in the paths of pleasantness that ye're ordain't to, both by me and your father; for we hae had oure lang a divided family; and it's full time we were brought to a cordial understanding with one another.'

'But,' replied the disconsolate damsel, 'even though he had no previous attachment, I'll ne'er consent to marry him, for really I can never fancy him.'

'And what for can ye no fancy him?' cried the Leddy—'I would like to ken that? But, to be plain wi' you, Beenie, it's a shame to hear a weel educated miss like you, brought up wi' a Christian principle, speaking about fancying young men. Sic a thing was never alloo't nor heard tell o' in my day and generation. But that comes o' your ganging to see Douglas tragedy, at that kirk o' Satan in Dunlop Street; where, as I am most creditably informed, the play-actors[1] court ane another afore a' the folk.'

'I am sure you have yourself experienced,' replied Robina, 'what it is to entertain a true affection, and to know that our wishes and inclinations are not under our own control.—How would you have liked had your father forced you to marry a man against your will?'

'Lassie, lassie!' exclaimed the Leddy, 'if ye live to be a grand-mother like me, ye'll ken the right sense o' a lawful and tender affection. But there's no sincerity noo like the auld sincerity, when me and your honest grandfather, that was in mine, and is noo in Abraham's bosom, came thegither—we had no foistring[2] and parley-vooing, like your novelle[3] turtle-doves—but discoursed in a sober and wise-like manner anent the cost and charge o' a family; and the upshot was a visibility of solid cordiality and kindness, very different, Beenie, my dear, frae the puff-paste love o' your Clarissy Harlots.'[4]

'Ah! but your affection was mutual from the beginning—you were not perhaps devoted to another?'

'Gude guide us, Beenie Walkinshaw! are ye devoted to another? —Damon and Phillis,[5] pastorauling at hide and seek wi' their sheep, was the height o' discretion, compared wi' sic curdooing. My lass, I'll let no grass grow beneath my feet, till I hae gi'en your father notice o' this loup-the-window, and hey cockalorum-like[6] love.'

'Impossible!' exclaimed the young lady; 'you will never surely be so rash as to betray me?'

'Wha is't wi'?[7] But I need na speer; for I'll be none surprised to hear that it's a play-actor, or a soldier officer, or some other clandestine poetical.'

Miss possessed more shrewdness than her grandmother gave

her credit for, and perceiving the turn and tendency of their conversation, she exerted all her address to remove the impression which she had thus produced, by affecting to laugh, saying,—

'What has made you suppose that I have formed any improper attachment? I was only anxious that you should speak to my father, and try to persuade him that I can never be happy with my cousin.'

'How can I persuade him o' ony sic havers? or how can ye hope that I would if it was in my power—when ye know what a comfort it will be to us a', to see such a prudent purpose o' marriage brought to perfection?—Na, na, Beenie, ye're an instrument in the hands o' Providence to bring aboot a great blessing to your family; and I would be as daft as your uncle Watty, when he gaed out to shoot the flees, were I to set mysel an adversary to such a righteous ordinance—so you maun just mak up your mind to conform. My word, but ye're weel aff to be married in your teens— I was past thirty before man speer't my price.'

'But,' said Robina, 'you forget that James himself has not yet consented—I am sure he is devoted to Ellen Frazer—and that he will never consent.'

'Weel, I declare if e'er I heard the like of sic upsetting.—I won'er what business either you or him hae to consenting or none consenting.—Is't no the pleasure o' your parentage that ye're to be married, and will ye dare to commit the sin of disobedient children? Beenie Walkinshaw, had I said sic a word to my father, who was a man o' past-ordinar sense, weel do I ken what I would hae gotten— I only just ance in a' my life, in a mistak, gied him a contradiction, and he declared that, had I been a son as I was but a dochter, he would hae grippit me by the cuff o' the neck and the back o' the breeks,[1] and shuttled me through the window. But the end o' the world is drawing near, and corruption's working daily to a head; a' modesty and maidenhood has departed frae womankind, and the sons of men are workers of iniquity—priests o' Baal, and transgressors every one—a', therefore, my leddy, that I hae to say to you is a word o' wisdom, and they ca't conform—Beenie, conform—and obey the fifth commandment.'

Robina was, however, in no degree changed by her grandmother's exhortations and animadversions; on the contrary, she was determined to take her own way, which is a rule that we would recommend to all young ladies, as productive of the happiest consequences in cases of the tender passion. But scarcely had she left the house, till Leddy Grippy, reflecting on what had passed, was not quite at ease in her mind, with respect to the sentimental insinuation of being devoted to another. For, although, in the subsequent conversation, the dexterity and address of the young lady considerably weakened the impression which it had at first made, still enough remained to make her suspect it really contained more than was intended to have been conveyed. But, to avoid unnecessary disturbance, she resolved to give her son a hint to observe the motions of his daughter, while, at the same time, she also determined to ascertain how far there was any ground to suppose that from the attachment of James to Ellen Frazer, there was reason to apprehend that he might likewise be as much averse to the projected marriage as Robina. And with this view she sent for him that evening—but what past will furnish matter for another Chapter.

CHAPTER XXIX

THE Leddy was seated at her tea-table when young Walkinshaw arrived, and, as on all occasions when she had any intention in her head, she wore an aspect pregnant with importance. She was now an old woman,[1] and had so long survived the sorrows of her widowhood, that even the weeds were thrown aside, and she had resumed her former dresses, unchanged from the fashion in which they were originally made. Her appearance, in consequence, was at once aged and ancient.

'Come your ways, Jamie,' said she, 'and draw in a chair and sit down; but, afore doing sae, tell the lass to bring ben the treck-pot,' —which he accordingly did; and as soon as the treck-pot, alias tea-pot, was on the board, she opened her trenches.[2]

'Jamie,' she began, 'your uncle George has a great notion of you, and has done muckle for your mother, giving her, o' his own free will, a handsome 'nuity; by the which she has brought you, and Mary your sister, up wi' great credit and confort. I would therefore fain hope, that, in the way o' gratitude, there will be no slackness on your part.'

James assured her that he had a very strong sense of his uncle's kindness; and that, to the best of his ability, he would exert himself to afford him every satisfaction; but that Glasgow was not a place which he much liked, and that he would rather go abroad, and push his fortune elsewhere, than continue confined to the counting-house.

'There's baith sense and sadness, Jamie, in what ye say,' replied the Leddy; 'but I won'er what ye would do abroad, when there's sic a bein beild biggit[1] for you at home. Ye ken, by course o' nature, that your uncle's ordaint to die, and that he has only his ae dochter Beenie, your cousin, to inherit the braw conquest o' your worthy grandfather—the whilk, but for some mistak o' law, and the sudden o'ercome o' death amang us, would hae been yours by right o' birth. So that it's in a manner pointed out to you by the forefinger o' Providence to marry Beenie.'

James was less surprised at this suggestion than the old lady expected, and said, with a degree of coolness that she was not prepared for,—

'I dare say what you speak of would not be disagreeable to my uncle, for several times he has himself intimated as much, but it is an event that can never take place.'

'And what for no? I'm sure Beenie's fortune will be a better bargain than a landless lad like you can hope for at ony other hand.'

'True, but I'll never marry for morey.'

'And what will ye marry for, then?' exclaimed the Leddy. 'Tak my word o' experience for't, my man,—a warm downseat's o' far mair consequence in matrimony than the silly low[2] o' love; and think what a bonny business your father and mother made o' their gentle-shepherding.[3] But, Jamie, what's the reason ye'll no tak Beenie?—there maun surely be some because[4] for sic unnaturality?'

'Why,' said he laughing, 'I think it's time enough for me yet to be dreaming o' marrying.'

'That's no a satisfaction to my question; but there's ae thing I would fain gie you warning o', and that's, if ye'll no marry Beenie, I dinna think ye can hae ony farther to-look,[5] in the way o' patronage, frae your uncle.'

'Then,' said James indignantly, 'if his kindness is only given on such a condition as that, I ought not to receive it an hour longer.'

'Here's a tap o' tow!'[6] exclaimed the Leddy. 'Aff and awa wi' you to your mother at Camrachle, and gallant about the braes and dyke-sides wi' that lang windlestrae-legget tawpie,[7] Nell Frizel—

She's the because o' your rebellion. 'Deed ye may think shame o't, Jamie; for it's a' enough to bring disgrace on a' manner o' affection to hear what I hae heard about you and her.'

'What have you heard?' cried he, burning with wrath and indignation.

'The callan's[1] gaun aff at the head, to look at me as if his e'en were pistols—How dare ye, Sir?—But it's no worth my while to lose my temper wi' a creature that doesna ken the homage and honour due to his aged grandmother. Howsever, I'll be as plain as I'm pleasant wi' you my man; and if there's no an end soon put to your pastoraulity wi' yon Highland heron, and a sedate and dutiful compliancy vouchsafed to your benefactor, uncle George, there will be news in the land or lang.'[2]

'You really place the motives of my uncle's conduct towards me in a strange light, and you forget that Robina is perhaps as strongly averse to the connection as I am.'

'So she would fain try to gar me true,'[3] replied the Leddy; 'the whilk is a most mystical thing; but, poor lassie, I needna be surprised at it, when she jealouses that your affections are set on a loup-the-dyke Jenny Cameron[4] like Nell Frizel. Howsever, Jamie, no to make a confabble about the matter, there can be no doubt if ye'll sing "We'll gang nae mair to yon toun,' wi' your back to the manse o' Camrachle, that Beenie, who is a most sweet-tempered and obedient fine lassie, will soon be wrought into a spirit of conformity wi' her father's will and my wishes.'

'I cannot but say,' replied Walkinshaw, 'that you consider affection as very pliant. Nor do I know why you take such liberties with Miss Frazer; who, in every respect, is infinitely superior to Robina.'

'Her superior!' cried the Leddy; 'but love's blin' as well as fey,[5] or ye would as soon think o' likening a yird tead to a patrick[6] or a turtle-dove, as Nell Frizel to Beenie Walkinshaw. Eh man! Jamie, but ye hae a poor taste; and I may say, as the auld sang sings, "Will ye compare a docken till a tansie?" I would na touch her wi' the tangs.'[7]

'But you know,' said Walkinshaw, laughing at the excess of her contempt, 'that there is no accounting for tastes.'

'The craw thinks it's ain bird the whitest,' replied the Leddy; 'but, for a' that, it's as black as the back o' the bress;[8] and, therefore, I would advise you to believe me, that Nell Frizel is just as ill-far't a creature as e'er came out the Maker's hand. I hae lived threescore and fifteen years in the world, and surely, in the course o' nature, should ken by this time what beauty is, and ought to be.'

How far the Leddy might have proceeded with her argument is impossible to say; for it was suddenly interrupted by her grandson bursting into an immoderate fit of laughter, which had the effect of instantly checking her eloquence, and turning the course of her ideas and animadversions into another channel. In the course, however, of a few minutes, she returned to the charge, but with no better success; and Walkinshaw left her, half resolved to come to some explanation on the subject with his uncle. It happened, however, that this discussion, which we have just related, took place on a Saturday night; and the weather next day being bright and beautiful, instead of going to his uncle's at Kittlestonheugh, as he commonly did on Sunday, from the time he had been placed in the counting-house, he rose early, and walked to Camrachle, where he arrived to breakfast, and afterwards accompanied his mother and sister to church.

The conversation with the old Leddy was still ringing in his ears, and her strictures on the beauty and person of Ellen Frazer seemed so irresistibly ridiculous, when he beheld her tall and elegant figure advancing to the minister's pew, that he could with difficulty preserve the decorum requisite to the sanctity of the place. Indeed, the effect was so strong, that Ellen herself noticed it; insomuch, that, when they met after sermon in the churchyard, she could not refrain from asking what had tickled him. Simple as the question was, and easy as the explanation might have been, he found himself, at the moment, embarrassed, and at a loss to answer her. Perhaps, had they been by themselves, this would not have happened; but Mrs Eadie, and his mother and sister, were present. In the evening, however, when he accompanied Mary and her to a walk, along the brow of the hazel bank, which overlooked the village, he took an opportunity of telling her what had passed, and of expressing his determination to ascertain how far his uncle was seriously bent on wishing him to marry Robina; protesting, at the same time, that it was a union which could never be—intermingled with a thousand little tender demonstrations, infinitely more delightful to the ears of Ellen than it is possible to make them to our readers. Indeed, Nature plainly shows, that the conversations of lovers are not fit for the public, by the care which she takes to tell the gentle parties, that they must speak in whispers, and choose retired spots and shady bowers, and other sequestered poetical places, for their conferences.

CHAPTER XXX

THE conversations between the Leddy and her grandchildren were not of a kind to keep with her. On Monday morning she sent for her son, and, without explaining to him what had passed, cunningly began to express her doubts if ever a match would take place between James and Robina; recommending that the design should be given up, and an attempt made to conciliate a union between his daughter and her cousin Dirdumwhamle's son, by which, as she observed, the gear would still be kept in the family.

George, however, had many reasons against the match, not only with respect to the entail, but in consideration of Dirdumwhamle having six sons by his first marriage, and four by his second, all of whom stood between his nephew and the succession to his estate. It is, therefore, almost unnecessary to say, that he had a stronger repugnance to his mother's suggestion than if she had proposed a stranger rather than their relation.

'But,' said he, 'what reason have you to doubt that James and Robina are not likely to gratify our hopes and wishes? He is a very well-behaved lad; and though his heart does not appear to lie much to the business of the counting-house, still he is so desirous, apparently, to give satisfaction, that I have no doubt in time he will acquire steadiness and mercantile habits.'

'It would na be easy to say,' replied the Leddy, 'a' the whys and wherefores that I hae for my suspicion. But, ye ken, if the twa hae na a right true love and kindness for ane anither, it will be a doure job to make them happy in the way o' matrimonial felicity; and, to be plain wi' you, Geordie, I would be nane surprised if something had kittled between Jamie and a Highland lassie, anc Nell Frizel, that bides wi' the new-light minister[1] o' Camrachle.'

The Laird had incidentally heard of Ellen, and once or twice, when he happened to visit his sister-in-law, he had seen her, and was struck with her beauty. But it had never occurred to him that there was any attachment between her and his nephew. The moment, however, that the Leddy mentioned her name, he acknowledged to himself its probability.

'But do you really think,' said he anxiously, 'that there is any thing of the sort between her and him?'

'Frae a' that I can hear, learn, and understand,' replied the Leddy, 'though it may na be probable-like, yet I fear it's oure true; for when he gangs to see his mother, and it's ay wi' him as wi' the saints,—"O mother dear Jerusalem, when shall I come to thee?"—I am most creditably informed that the twa do nothing but sauly[1] forth hand in hand to walk in the green vallies, singing, "Low down in the broom," and "Pu'ing lilies both fresh and gay,"—which is as sure a symptom o' something very like love, as the hen's cackle is o' a new-laid egg.'

'Nevertheless,' said the Laird, 'I should have no great apprehensions, especially when he comes to understand how much it is his interest to prefer Robina.'

'That's a' true, Geordie; but I hae a misdoot that a's no right and sound wi' her mair than wi' him; and when we reflek how the mim maidens now-a-days hae delivered themselves up to the Little-gude[2] in the shape and glamour o' novelles and Thomson's Seasons, we need be nane surprised to fin' Miss as headstrong in her obdooracy as the lovely young Lavinia[3] that your sister Meg learnt to 'cite at the boarding-school.'

'It is not likely, however,' said the Laird, 'that she has yet fixed her affections on any one; and a very little attention on the part of James would soon overcome any prejudice that she may happen to have formed against him,—for now, when you bring the matter to mind, I do recollect that I have more than once observed a degree of petulance and repugnance on her part.'

'Then I mak no doot,' exclaimed the old lady, 'that she is in a begoted[4] state to another, and it wou'd be wise to watch her. But, first and foremost, you should sift Jamie's tender passion—that's the novelle name for calf-love; and if it's within the compass o' a possibility, get the swine driven through't, or it may work us a' muckle dule, as his father's moonlight marriage did to your ain, worthy man!—That was indeed a sair warning to us a', and is the because to this day o' a' the penance o' vexation and tribulation that me and you, Geordie, are sae obligated to dree.'[5]

The admonition was not lost; on the contrary, George, who was a decisive man of business, at once resolved to ascertain whether there were indeed any reasonable grounds for his mother's suspicions. For this purpose, on returning to the counting-house, he requested Walkinshaw to come in the evening to Kittlestonheugh, as he had something particular to say. The look and tone with which the communication was made convinced James that he could not be mistaken with respect to the topic intended, which, he conjectured, was connected with the conversation he had himself held with the Leddy on the preceding Saturday evening; and it was the more agreeable to him, as he was anxious to be relieved from the doubts which began to trouble him regarding the views and motives of his uncle's partiality. For, after parting from Ellen, he had, in the course of his walk back to Glasgow, worked himself up into a determination to quit the place, if any hope of the suggested marriage with Robina was the tenure by which he held her father's favour. His mind, in consequence, as he went to Kittlestonheugh in the evening, was occupied with many plans and schemes—the vague and aimless projects which fill the imagination of youth, when borne forward either by hopes or apprehensions. Indeed, the event contemplated, though it was still contingent on the spirit with which his uncle might receive his refusal, he yet, with the common precipitancy of youth, anticipated as settled, and his reflections were accordingly framed and modified by that conclusion. To leave Glasgow was determined; but where to go, and what to do, were points not so easily arranged; and ever and anon the image of Ellen Frazer rose in all the radiance of her beauty, like the angel to Balaam,[1] and stood between him and his purpose.

The doubts, the fears, and the fondness, which alternately predominated in his bosom, received a secret and sympathetic energy from the appearance and state of external nature. The weather was cloudy but not lowering—a strong tempest seemed, however, to be raging at a distance; and several times he paused and looked back at the enormous masses of dark and troubled vapour, which were drifting along the whole sweep of the northern horizon, from Ben Lomond to the Ochils, as if some awful burning was laying waste the world beyond them; while a long and splendid stream of hazy sunshine, from behind the Cowal mountains, brightened the rugged summits of Dumbuck, and, spreading its golden fires over Dumbarton moor, gilded the brow of Dumgoin, and lighted up the magnificent vista which opens between them of the dark and distant Grampians.[1]

The appearance of the city was also in harmony with the general sublimity of the evening. Her smoky canopy was lowered almost to a covering—a mist from the river hovered along her skirts and scattered buildings, but here and there some lofty edifice stood proudly eminent, and the pinnacles of the steeples glittering like spear-points through the cloud, suggested to the fancy strange and solemn images of heavenly guardians, stationed to oppose the adversaries of man.

A scene so wild, so calm, and yet so troubled and darkened, would, at any time, have heightened the enthusiasm of young Walkinshaw, but the state of his feelings made him more than ordinarily susceptible to the eloquence of its various lights and shadows. The uncertainty which wavered in the prospects of his future life, found a mystical reflex in the swift and stormy wrack of the carry,[2] that some unfelt wind was silently urging along the distant horizon. The still and stationary objects around—the protected city and the everlasting hills, seemed to bear an assurance, that, however obscured the complexion of his fortunes might at that moment be, there was still something within himself that ought not to suffer any change, from the evanescent circumstances of another's frown or favour. This confidence in himself, felt perhaps for the first time that evening, gave a degree of vigour and decision to the determination which he had formed; and by the time he had reached the porch of his uncle's mansion,[3] his step was firm, his emotions regulated, and a full and manly self-possession had succeeded to the fluctuating feelings, with which he left Glasgow, in so much that even his countenance seemed to have received some new impress, and to have lost the softness of youth, and taken more decidedly the cast and characteristics of manhood.

CHAPTER XXXI

WALKINSHAW found his uncle alone, who, after some slight inquiries, relative to unimportant matters of business, said to him,—

'I have been desirous to see you, because I am anxious to make some family arrangements, to which, though I do not anticipate any objection on your part, as they will be highly advantageous to your interests, it is still proper that we should clearly understand each other respecting. It is unnecessary to inform you, that, by the disinheritance of your father, I came to the family estate, which, in the common course of nature, might have been yours—and you are quite aware, that, from the time it became necessary to cognosce your uncle, I have uniformly done more for your mother's family than could be claimed or was expected of me.'

'I am sensible of all that, Sir,' replied Walkinshaw, 'and I hope there is nothing which you can reasonably expect me to do, that I shall not feel pleasure in performing.'

His uncle was not quite satisfied with this; the firmness with which it was uttered, and the self-reservation which it implied— were not propitious to his wishes, but he resumed,—

'In the course of a short time, you will naturally be looking to me for some establishment in business, and certainly if you conduct yourself as you have hitherto done, it is but right that I should do something for you—much, however, will depend, as to the extent of what I may do, on the disposition with which you fall in with my views. Now, what I wish particularly to say to you is, that having but one child, and my circumstances enabling me to retire from the active management of the house,[1] it is in my power to resign a considerable share in your favour—and this it is my wish to do in the course of two or three years; if'—and he paused, looking his nephew steadily in the face.

'I trust,' said Walkinshaw, 'it can be coupled with no condition that will prevent me from availing myself of your great liberality.'

His uncle was still more damped by this than by the former observation, and he replied peevishly,—

'I think, young man, considering your destitute circumstances, you might be a little more grateful for my friendship. It is but a cold return to suppose I would subject you to any condition that you would not gladly agree to.'

This, though hastily conceived, was not so sharply expressed as to have occasioned any particular sensation; but the train of Walkinshaw's reflections, with his suspicion of the object for which he was that evening invited to the country, made him feel it acutely, and his blood mounted at the allusion to his poverty. Still without petulance, but in an emphatic manner, he replied,—

'I have considered your friendship always as disinterested, and as such I have felt and cherished the sense of gratitude which it naturally inspired; but I frankly confess, that, had I any reason to believe it was less so than I hope it is, I doubt I should be unable to feel exactly as I have hitherto felt.'

'And in the name of goodness!' exclaimed his uncle, at once surprised and apprehensive; 'what reason have you to suppose that I was not actuated by my regard for you as my nephew?'

'I have never had any, nor have I said so,' replied Walkinshaw; 'but you seem to suspect that I may not be so agreeable to some purpose you intend as the obligations you have laid me under, perhaps, entitle you to expect.'

'The purpose I intend,' said the uncle, 'is the strongest proof that I can give you of my affection. It is nothing less than founded on a hope that you will so demean yourself, as to give me the pleasure, in due time, of calling you by a dearer name than nephew.'

Notwithstanding all the preparations which Walkinshaw had made to hear the proposal with firmness, it overcame him like a thunder-clap—and he sat some time looking quickly from side to side, and unable to answer.

'You do not speak,' said his uncle, and he added, softly and inquisitively, 'Is there any cause to make you averse to Robina?— I trust I may say to you, as a young man of discretion and good sense, that there is no green and foolish affection which ought for a moment to weigh with you against the advantages of a marriage with your cousin—Were there nothing else held out to you, the very circumstance of regaining so easily the patrimony, which your father had so inconsiderately forfeited, should of itself be sufficient. But, besides that, on the day you are married to Robina, it is my fixed intent to resign the greatest part of my concern in the house to you, thereby placing you at once in opulence.'

While he was thus earnestly speaking, Walkinshaw recovered

his self-possession; and being averse to give a disagreeable answer, he said, that he could not but duly estimate, to the fullest extent, all the advantages which the connection would insure; but, said he, 'Have you spoken to Robina herself?'

'No,' replied his uncle, with a smile of satisfaction, anticipating from the question something like a disposition to acquiesce in his views. 'No; I leave that to you—that's your part. You now know my wishes; and I trust and hope you are sensible that few proposals could be made to you so likely to promote your best interests.'

Walkinshaw saw the difficulties of his situation. He could no longer equivocate with them. It was impossible, he felt, to say that he would speak on the subject to Robina, without being guilty of duplicity towards his uncle. Besides this, he conceived it would sully the honour and purity of his affection for Ellen Frazer to allow himself to seek any declaration of refusal from Robina, however certain of receiving it. His uncle saw his perplexity, and said,—

'This proposal seems to have very much disconcerted you—but I will be plain; for, in a matter on which my heart is so much set, it is prudent to be candid. I do not merely suspect, but have some reason to believe, that you have formed a schoolboy attachment to Mrs Eadie's young friend. Now, without any other remark on the subject, I will only say, that, though Miss Frazer is a very fine girl, and of a most respectable family, there is nothing in the circumstances of her situation compared with those of your cousin, that would make any man of sense hesitate between them.'

So thought Walkinshaw; for, in his opinion, the man of sense would at once prefer Ellen.

'However,' continued his uncle,—'I will not at present press this matter farther. I have opened my mind to you, and I make no doubt, that you will soon see the wisdom and propriety of acceding to my wishes.'

Walkinshaw thought he would be acting unworthy of himself if he allowed his uncle to entertain any hope of his compliance; and, accordingly, he said, with some degree of agitation, but not so much as materially to affect the force with which he expressed himself,—

'I will not deny that your information with respect to Miss Frazer is correct; and the state of our sentiments renders it impossible that I should for a moment suffer you to expect I can ever look on Robina but as my cousin.'

'Well, well, James,' interrupted his uncle,—'I knew all that; and I calculated on hearing as much, and even more; but take time to reflect on what I have proposed; and I shall be perfectly content to see the result in your actions. So, let us go to your aunt's room, and take tea with her and Robina.'

'Impossible!—never!' exclaimed Walkinshaw, rising;—'I cannot allow you for a moment longer to continue in so fallacious an expectation. My mind is made up; my decision was formed before I came here; and no earthly consideration will induce me to forego an affection that has grown with my growth, and strengthened with my strength.'

His uncle laughed, and rubbed his hands, exceedingly amused at this rhapsody, and said, with the most provoking coolness,—

'I shall not increase your flame by stirring the fire—you are still but a youth—and it is very natural that you should have a love fit —all, therefore, that I mean to say at present is, take time—consider—reflect on the fortune you may obtain, and contrast it with the penury and dependence to which your father and mother exposed themselves by the rash indulgence of an inconsiderate attachment.'

'Sir,' exclaimed Walkinshaw, fervently, 'I was prepared for the proposal you have made, and my determination with respect to it was formed and settled before I came here.'

'Indeed!' said his uncle coldly; 'and pray what is it?'

'To quit Glasgow; to forego all the pecuniary advantages that I may derive from my connection with you—if'—and he made a full stop and looked his uncle severely in the face,—'if,' he resumed, 'your kindness was dictated with a view to this proposal.'

A short silence ensued, in which Walkinshaw still kept his eye brightly and keenly fixed on his uncle's face; but the Laird was too much a man of the world not to be able to endure this scrutiny.

'You are a strange fellow,' he at last said, with a smile, that he intended should be conciliatory; 'but as I was prepared for a few heroics I can forgive you.'

'Forgive!' cried the hot and indignant youth; 'what have I done to deserve such an insult? I thought your kindness merited my gratitude. I felt towards you as a man should feel towards a great benefactor; but now it would almost seem that you have in all your kindness but pursued some sinister purpose. Why am I selected to be your instrument? Why are my feelings and affections to be sacrificed on your sordid altars?'

He found his passion betraying him into irrational extravagance, and, torn by the conflict within him, he covered his face with his hands, and burst into tears.

'This is absolute folly, James,' said his uncle soberly.

'It is not folly,' was again his impassioned answer. 'My words may be foolish, but my feelings are at this moment wise. I cannot for ten times all your fortune, told a hundred times, endure to think I may be induced to barter my heart. It may be that I am ungrateful; if so, as I can never feel otherwise upon the subject than I do, send me away, as unworthy longer to share your favour; but worthy I shall nevertheless be of something still better.'

'Young man, you will be more reasonable to-morrow,' said his uncle contemptuously, and immediately left the room. Walkinshaw at the same moment also took his hat, and, rushing towards the door, quitted the house; but in turning suddenly round the corner, he ran against Robina, who, having some idea of the object of his visit, had been listening at the window to their conversation.

CHAPTER XXXII

THE agitation in which Walkinshaw was at the moment when he encountered Robina, prevented him from being surprised at meeting her, and also from suspecting the cause which had taken her to that particular place so late in the evening. The young lady was more cool and collected, as we believe young ladies always are on such occasions, and she was the first who spoke.

'Where are you running so fast?' said she. 'I thought you would have staid tea. Will you not go back with me? My mother expects you.'

'Your father does not,' replied Walkinshaw tersely; 'and I wish it had been my fortune never to have set my foot within his door.'

'Dear me!' exclaimed Miss Robina, as artfully as if she had known nothing, nor overheard every word which had passed. 'What has happened? I hope nothing has occurred to occasion any quarrel between you. Do think, James, how prejudicial it must be to your interests to quarrel with my father.'

'Curse that eternal word interests!' was the unceremonious answer. 'Your father seems to think that human beings have nothing but interests; that the heart keeps a ledger, and values every thing in pounds sterling. Our best affections, our dearest feelings, are with him only as tare,[1] that should pass for nothing in the weight of moral obligations.'

'But stop,' said Robina, 'don't be in such a hurry; tell me what all this means—what has affections and dear feelings to do with your counting-house affairs?—I thought you and he never spoke of any thing but rum puncheons and sugar cargoes.'

'He is incapable of knowing the value of any thing less tangible and vendible!' exclaimed her cousin—'but I have done with both him and you.'

'Me!' cried Miss Robina, with an accent of the most innocent admiration, that any sly and shrewd miss of eighteen could possibly assume.—'Me! what have I to do with your hopes and your affections, and your tangible and vendible commodities?'

'I beg your pardon, I meant no offence to you, Robina—I am overborne by my feelings,' said Walkinshaw; 'and if you knew what has passed, you would sympathise with me.'

'But as I do not,' replied the young lady coolly, 'you must allow me to say that your behaviour appears to me very extravagant— surely nothing has passed between you and my father that I may not know?'

This was said in a manner that instantly recalled Walkinshaw to his senses. The deep and cunning character of his cousin he had often before remarked—with, we may say plainly, aversion—and he detected at once in the hollow and sonorous affectation of sympathy with which her voice was tuned, particularly in the latter clause of the sentence, the insincerity and hypocrisy of her conduct.—He did not, however, suspect that she had been playing the eaves-dropper; and, therefore, still tempered with moderation his expression of the sentiments she was so ingeniously leading him on to declare.

'No,' said he calmly, 'nothing has passed between your father and me that you may not know, but it will come more properly from him, for it concerns you, and in a manner that I can never take interest or part in.'

'Concerns me! concerns me!' exclaimed the actress; 'it is impossible that any thing of mine could occasion a misunderstanding between you.'

'But it has,' said Walkinshaw; 'and to deal with you, Robina, as you ought to be dealt with, for affecting to be so ignorant of your father's long evident wishes and intents—he has actually declared that he is most anxious we should be married.'

'I can see no harm in that,' said she, adding drily, 'provided it is not to one another.'

'But it is to one another,' said Walkinshaw, unguardedly, and in the simplicity of earnestness, which Miss perceiving, instantly with the adroitness of her sex turned to account—saying with well feigned diffidence,—

'I do not see why that should be so distressing to you.'

'No!' replied he. 'But the thing can never be, and it is of no use for us to talk of it—so good night.'

'Stay,' cried Robina,—'what you have told me deserves consideration.—Surely I have given you no reason to suppose that in a matter so important, I may not find it my interest to comply with my father's wishes.'

'Heavens!' exclaimed Walkinshaw, raising his clenched hands in a transport to the skies.

'Why are you so vehement?' said Robina.

'Because,' replied he solemnly, 'interest seems the everlasting consideration of our family—interest disinherited my father—interest made my uncle Walter consign my mother to poverty—interest proved the poor repentant wretch insane—interest claims the extinction of all I hold most precious in life,—and interest would make me baser than the most sordid of all our sordid race.'

'Then I am to understand you dislike me so much, that you have refused to accede to my father's wishes, for our mutual happiness?'

'For our mutual misery, I have refused to accede,' was the abrupt reply—'and if you had not some motive for appearing to feel otherwise—which motive I neither can penetrate nor desire to know, you would be as resolute in your objection to the bargain as I am—match I cannot call it, for it proceeds in a total oblivion of all that can endear or ennoble such a permanent connection.'

Miss was conscious of the truth of this observation, and with all her innate address, it threw her off her guard, and she said,—

'Why do you suppose that I am so insensible? My father may

intend what he pleases, but my consent must be obtained before he can complete his intentions.' She had, however, scarcely said so much, when she perceived she was losing the 'vantage-ground that she had so dexterously occupied, and she turned briskly round and added, 'But, James, why should we fall out about this? —there is time enough before us to consider the subject dispassionately—my father cannot mean that the marriage should take place immediately.'

'Robina, you are your father's daughter, and the heiress of his nature as well as of his estate—no such marriage ever can or shall take place; nor do you wish it should—but I am going too far—it is enough that I declare my affections irrevocably engaged, and that I will never listen to a second proposition on that subject, which has to-night driven me wild. I have quitted your father—I intend it for ever—I will never return to his office. All that I built on my connection with him is now thrown down—perhaps with it my happiness is also lost—but no matter, I cannot be a dealer in such bargaining as I have heard to-night. I am thankful to Providence that gave me a heart to feel better, and friends who taught me to think more nobly. However, I waste my breath and spirits idly; my resolution is fixed, and when I say Good night, I mean Farewell.'

With these words he hurried away, and, after walking a short time on the lawn, Robina returned into the house; and going up to her mother's apartment, where her father was sitting, she appeared as unconcerned and unconscious of the two preceding conversations, as if she had neither been a listener to the one, nor an actress in the other.

On entering the room, she perceived that her father had been mentioning to her mother something of what had passed between himself and her cousin; but it was her interest, on account of the direction which her affections had taken, to appear ignorant of many things, and studiously to avoid any topic with her father that might lead him to suspect her bent; for she had often observed, that few individuals could be proposed to him as a match for her, that he entertained so strong a prejudice against; although really, in point of appearance, relationship, and behaviour, it could hardly be said that the object of her preference was much inferior to her romantic cousin. The sources and motives of that prejudice she was, however, regardless of discovering. She considered it in fact as an unreasonable and unaccountable antipathy, and was only anxious for the removal of any cause that might impede the consummation she devoutly wished. Glad, therefore, to be so fully mistress of Walkinshaw's sentiments as she had that night made herself, she thought, by a judicious management of her knowledge, she might overcome her father's prejudice;—and the address and dexterity with which she tried this we shall attempt to describe in the following Chapter.

CHAPTER XXXIII

'I THOUGHT,' said she, after seating herself at the tea-table, 'that my cousin would have stopped to-night; but I understand he has gone away.'

'Perhaps,' replied her father, 'had you requested him, he might have staid.'

'I don't think he would for me,' was her answer.—'He does not appear particularly satisfied when I attempt to interfere with any of his proceedings.'

'Then you do sometimes attempt to interfere?' said her father, somewhat surprised at the observation, and not suspecting that she had heard one word of what had passed, every syllable of which was carefully stored in the treasury of her bosom.

The young lady perceived that she was proceeding a little too quickly, and drew in her horns.

'All,' said she, 'that I meant to remark was, that he is not very tractable, which I regret;' and she contrived to give a sigh.

'Why should you regret it so particularly?' inquired her father, a little struck at the peculiar accent with which she had expressed herself.

'I cannot tell,' was her adroit reply; and then she added, in a brisker tone,—'But I wonder what business I have to trouble myself about him?'

For some time her father made no return to this; but, pushing back his chair from the tea-table till he had reached the chimney-corner, he leant his elbow on the mantle-piece, and appeared for several minutes in a state of profound abstraction. In the meantime, Mrs Walkinshaw had continued the conversation with her

daughter, observing to her that she did, indeed, think her cousin
must be a very headstrong lad; for he had spoken that night to
her father in such a manner as had not only astonished but distressed him. 'However,' said she,—'he is still a mere boy; and, I
doubt not, will, before long is past, think better of what his uncle
has been telling him.'

'I am extremely sorry,' replied Robina, with the very voice of
the most artless sympathy, though, perhaps, a little more accen-
tuated than simplicity would have employed—'I am very sorry,
indeed, that any difference has arisen between him and my father.
I am sure I have always heard him spoken of as an amiable and very
deserving young man. I trust it is of no particular consequence.'

'It is of the utmost consequence,' interposed her father; 'and
it is of more to you than to any other besides.'

'To me, Sir! how is that possible?—What have I to do with him,
or he with me? I am sure, except in being more deficient in his
civilities than those of most of my acquaintance, I have had no
occasion to remark any thing particular in his behaviour or conduct towards me.'

'I know it—I know it,' exclaimed her father; 'and therein lies
the source of all my anxiety.'

'I fear that I do not rightly understand you,' said the cunning girl.

'Nor do I almost wish that you ever should; but, nevertheless,
my heart is so intent on the business, that I think, were you to
second my endeavours, the scheme might be accomplished.'

'The scheme—What scheme?' replied the most unaffected
Robina.

'In a word, child,' said her father, 'How would you like James
as a husband?'

'How can I tell?' was her simple answer. 'He has never given me
any reason to think on the subject.'

'You cannot, however, but long have seen that it was with me a
favourite object?'

'I confess it;—and, perhaps, I have myself,' she said, with a
second sigh—'thought more of it than I ought to have done; but
I have never had any encouragement from him.'

'How unhappy am I,' thought her father to himself—'The poor
thing is as much disposed to the match as my heart could hope
for.—Surely, surely, by a little address and perseverance, the

romantic boy may be brought to reason and to reflect;' and he then said to her—'My dear Robina, you have been the subject of my conversation with James this evening; but I am grieved to say, that his sentiments, at present, are neither favourable to your wishes nor to mine.—He seems enchanted by Mrs Eadie's relation, and talked so much nonsense on the subject that we almost quarrelled.'

'I shall never accept of a divided heart,' said the young lady despondingly; 'and I entreat, my dear father, that you will never take another step in the business; for, as long as I can recollect, he has viewed me with eyes of aversion—and in all that time he has been the playmate, and the lover, perhaps, of Ellen Frazer.— Again I implore you to abandon every idea of promoting a union between him and me: It can never take place on his part but from the most sordid considerations of interest; nor on mine without feeling that I have been but as a bale bargained for.'

Her father listened with attention to what she said—it appeared reasonable—it was spirited; but there was something, nevertheless, in it which did not quite satisfy his mind, though the sense was clear and complete.

'Of course,' he replied guardedly; 'I should never require you to bestow your hand where you had not already given your affections; but it does not follow, that because the headstrong boy is at this time taken up with Miss Frazer, that he is always to remain of the same mind. On the contrary, Robina, were you to exert a little address, I am sure you would soon draw him from that unfortunate attachment.'

'What woman,' said she, with an air of supreme dignity, 'would submit to pilfer the betrothed affections of any man? No—Sir, I cannot do that—nor ought I; and pardon me when I use the expression, nor will I. Had my cousin made himself more agreeable to me, I do not say that such would have been my sentiments; but having seen nothing in his behaviour that can lead me to hope from him any thing but the same constancy in his dislike which I have ever experienced, I should think myself base, indeed, were I to allow you to expect that I may alter my opinion.'

Nothing farther passed at that time; for to leave the impression which she intended to produce as strong as possible, she immediately rose and left the room. Her father soon after also quitted his seat, and after taking two or three turns across the floor, went to his own apartment.

'I am the most unfortunate of men,' said he to himself, 'and my poor Robina is no less frustrated in her affections. I cannot, however, believe that the boy is so entirely destitute of prudence as not to think of what I have told him. I must give him time. Old heads do not grow on young shoulders. But it never occurred to me that Robina was attached to him; on the contrary, I have always thought that the distaste was stronger on her part than on his. But it is of no use to vex myself on the subject. Let me rest satisfied to-night with having ascertained that at least on Robina's part there is no objection to the match. My endeavours hereafter must be directed to detach James from the girl Frazer. It will, however, be no easy task, for he is ardent and enthusiastic, and she has undoubtedly many of those graces which readiest find favour in a young man's eye.'

He then hastily rose, and hurriedly paced the room.

'Why am I cursed,' he exclaimed, 'with this joyless and barren fate? Were Robina a son, all my anxieties would be hushed; but with her my interest in the estate of my ancestors terminates. Her mother, however, may yet'—and he paused. 'It is very weak,' he added, in a moment after, 'to indulge in these reflections. I have a plain task before me, and instead of speculating on hopes and chances, I ought to set earnestly about it, and leave no stone unturned till I have performed it thoroughly.'

With this he composed his mind for the remainder of the evening, and when he again joined Robina and her mother, the conversation by all parties was studiously directed to indifferent topics.

CHAPTER XXXIV

THERE are few things more ludicrous, and at the same time more interesting, than the state of a young man in love, unless, perhaps, it be that of an old man in the same unfortunate situation. The warmth of the admiration, the blindness of the passion, and the fond sincerity of the enthusiasm, which gives grace and sentiment to the instinct, all awaken sympathy, and even inspire a degree of compassionate regard; but the extravagance of feeling beyond what any neutral person can sympathise with, the ostrich-like simplicity of the expedients resorted to in assignations, and that self-approved sagacity and prudence in concealing what every body with half an eye can see, afford the most harmless and diverting spectacles of human absurdity. However, as we are desirous of conciliating the reverence of the young and fair, perhaps it may be as well to say nothing more on this head, but allow them to enjoy, in undisturbed faith, the amiable anticipation of that state of beatitude which Heaven, and all married personages, know is but a very very transient enchantment.

But we cannot, with any regard to the fidelity of circumstantial history, omit to relate what passed in young Walkinshaw's bosom, after he parted from his cousin.—To render it in some degree picturesque, we might describe his appearance; but when we spoke of him as a handsome manly youth for his inches and his eild,[1] we said perhaps as much as we could well say upon that head, unless we were to paint the colour and fashion of his clothes, —a task in which we have no particular relish;—and, therefore, we may just briefly mention, that they were in the style of the sprucest clerks of Glasgow; and every body knows, that if the bucks of the Trongate would only button their coats, they might pass for gentlemen of as good blood and breeding as the best in Bond Street. But, even though Walkinshaw had been in the practice of buttoning his, he was that night in no condition to think of it. His whole bosom was as a flaming furnace—raging as fiercely as those of the Muirkirk Iron Works[2] that served to illuminate his path.

He felt as if he had been held in a state of degradation; and had been regarded as so destitute of all the honourable qualities of a young man, that he would not scruple to barter himself in the most sordid manner. His spirit then mounting on the exulting wings of youthful hope, bore him aloft into the cloudy and meteoric region of romance, and visions of fortune and glory almost too splendid for the aching sight of his fancy, presented themselves in a thousand smiling forms, beckoning him away from the smoky confines and fœtid airs of Glasgow, and pointing to some of the brightest and beaming bubbles that allure fantastic youth. But, in the midst of these glittering visions of triumphant adventure, 'a change came o'er the spirit of his dream,' and he beheld Ellen Frazer in the simple and tasteful attire in which she appeared so beautiful at Camrachle church. In the back ground of the sunny scene was a pretty poetical cottage, with a lamb tethered by the foot on the

green, surrounded by a flock of snowy geese, enjoying their noon-
tide siesta, and on the ground troops of cocks and hens, with
several gabbling bandy-legged ducks; at the sight of which another
change soon came o'er the spirit of his dream; and the elegant
mansion that his uncle had made of the old house of Grippy, with
all its lawns and plantations, and stately gate and porter's lodge,
together with an elegant carriage in the avenue, presented a most
alluring picture.[1]—But it, too, soon vanished; and in the next
change, he beheld Robina converted into his wife, carping at all
his little pranks and humours, and studious only of her own enjoyments, without having any consideration for those that might be
his. Then all was instantly darkened; and after a terrible burst of
whirlwinds, and thunder and lightning, the cloud again opened,
and he saw in its phantasmagorial mirror—a calm and summer
sunset, with his beautiful Ellen Frazer in the shape of a venerable
matron, partaking of the temperate pleasures of an aged man,
seated on a rustic seat, under a tree, on the brow of Camrachlebank,
enjoying the beauties of the view, and talking of their children's
children; and in the visage of that aged man, he discovered a most
respectable resemblance of himself.—So fine a close of a life, un-
troubled by any mischance, malady, or injustice, could not fail to
produce the most satisfactory result. Accordingly, he decidedly
resolved, that it should be his; and that, as he had previously determined, the connection with his uncle should thenceforth be cut
for ever.

By the time that imagination rather than reason had worked him
into this decision, he arrived at Glasgow; and being resolved to
carry his intention into immediate effect, instead of going to the
house where he was boarded, at his uncle's expence, he went to
the Leddy's, partly with the intention of remaining there, but
chiefly to remonstrate with her for having spoken of his attachment to Ellen Frazer; having concluded, naturally enough, that
it was from her his uncle had received the information.

On entering the parlour he found the old lady seated alone, in
her elbow chair, at the fireside. A single slender candle stood at
her elbow, on a small claw-foot table; and she was winding the
yarn from a pirn,[2] with a hand-reel, carefully counting the turns.
Hearing the door open, she looked round, and seeing who it was,
said,—

'Is that thee, Jamie Walkinshaw?—six and thirty—where came

ye frae—seven and thirty—at this time o'night?—eight and thirty —sit ye down—nine and thirty—snuff the candle—forty.'

'I'll wait till ye're done,' said he, 'as I wish to tell you something —for I have been out at Kittlestonheugh, where I had some words with my uncle.'

'No possible!—nine and forty,'—replied the Leddy;—'what hast been about?—fifty.'——

'He seems to regard me as if I had neither a will nor feelings, neither a head nor a heart.'

'I hope ye hae baith—five and fifty—but hae ye been con-dumacious?—seven and—plague tak the laddie, I'm out in my count, and I'll hae to begin the cutt[1] again; so I may set by the reel. What were you saying, Jamie, anent an outcast[2] wi' your uncle?'

'He has used me exceedingly ill—ripping up the obligations he has laid me under, and taunting me with my poverty.'

'And is't no true that ye're obligated to him, and that, but for the uncly duty he has fulfilled towards you, ye would this night hae been a bare lad?—gude kens an ye would na hae been as scant o' cleeding[3] as a salmon in the river.'

'It may be so, but when it is considered that he got the family estate by a quirk of law, he could scarcely have done less than he did for my unfortunate father's family. But I could have forgiven all that, had he not, in a way insulting to my feelings, intimated that he expected I would break with Ellen Frazer, and offer myself to Robina.'

'And sure am I, Jamie,' replied the Leddy, 'that it will be lang before you can do better.'

'My mind, however, is made up,' said he; 'and to-morrow morning I shall go to Camrachle, and tell my mother that I have resolved to leave Glasgow.—I will never again set my foot in the counting-house.'

'Got ye ony drink, Jamie, in the gait hame, that ye're in sic a wud[4] humour for dancing "Auld Sir Simon the King,"[5] on the road to Camrachle?—Man, an I had as brisk a bee in the bonnet, I would set aff at ance, cracking my fingers at the moon and seven stars as I gaed louping alang.[6]—But, to speak the words of sober-ness, I'm glad ye hae discretion enough to tak a night's rest first.'

'Do not think so lightly of my determination—It is fixed—and, from the moment I quitted Kittlestonheugh, I resolved to be no longer under any obligation to my uncle—He considers me as a mere passive instrument for his own ends.'

'Hegh, Sirs! man, but ye hae a great share o' sagacity,' exclaimed the Leddy; 'and because your uncle is fain that ye should marry his only dochter, and would, if ye did sae, leave you for dowry and tocher a braw estate and a bank o' siller,[1] ye think he has pookit[2] you by the nose.'

'No—not for that; but because he thinks so meanly of me, as to expect that, for mercenary considerations, I would bargain away both my feelings and my principles.'

'Sure am I he would ne'er mint[3] ony sic matter,' replied the Leddy; 'and if he wantit you to break wi' yon galloping nymph o' the Highland heather, and draw up wi' that sweet primrose-creature, your cousin Beenie, wha is a lassie o' sense and composity, and might be a match to majesty, it was a' for your honour and exaltation.'

'Don't distress me any farther with the subject,' said he. 'Will you have the goodness to let me stay here to-night? for, as I told you, there shall never now be any addition made to the obligations which have sunk me so low.'

''Deed my lad, an ye gang on in that deleerit manner, I'll no only gie you a bed, but send baith for a doctor and a gradawa,[4] that your head may be shaved, and a' proper remedies—outwardly and inwardly—gotten to bring you back to a right way o' thinking.—But to end a' debates, ye'll just pack up your ends and your awls[5] and gang hame to Mrs Spruil's, for the tow's to spin and the woo's to card[6] that 'ill be the sheets and blankets o' your bed in this house the night—tak my word for't.'

'In that case, I will at once go to Camrachle. The night is fine, and the moon's up.'

'Awa wi' you, and show how weel ye hae come to years o' discretion, by singing as ye gang,—

> 'Scotsman ho! Scotsman lo!
> Where shall this poor Scotsman go?
> Send him east, send him west,
> Send him to the craw's next.'[7]

Notwithstanding the stern mood that Walkinshaw was in, this latter sally of his grandmother's eccentric humour compelled him to laugh, and he said gaily, 'But I shall be none the worse of a little supper before I set out. I hope you will not refuse me that?'

The old Lady, supposing that she had effectually brought him, as she said, round to himself, cheerfully acquiesced; but she was not a little disappointed, when, after some light and ludicrous conversation on general topics, he still so persisted either to remain in the house or to proceed to his mother's, that she found herself obliged to order a bed to be prepared for him—at the same time she continued to express her confidence, that he would be in a more docile humour next morning. 'I hope,' said she, 'nevertheless, that the spirit of obedience will soople that stiff neck o' thine, in the slumbers and watches of the night, or I ne'er would be consenting to countenance such outstrapulous rebellion.'

END OF VOLUME SECOND

VOLUME III

CHAPTER I

WALKINSHAW passed a night of 'restless ecstasy.' Sometimes he reflected on the proposition with all the coolness that the Laird himself could have desired; but still and anon the centripetal movement of the thoughts and feelings which generated this prudence was suddenly arrested before they had gravitated into any thing like resolution, and then he was thrown as wild and as wide from the object of his uncle's solicitude as ever.

In the calmer, perhaps it may therefore be said, in the wiser course of his reflections, Robina appeared to him a shrewd and sensible girl, with a competent share of personal beauty, and many other excellent household qualities, to make her a commendable wife. With her he would at once enter on the enjoyment of opulence, and with it independence; and, moreover, and above all, have it in his power to restore his mother and sister to that state in society, to which, by birth and original expectations, they considered themselves as having some claim. This was a pleasing and a proud thought; and not to indulge it at the expence of a little sacrifice of personal feeling, seemed to him selfish and unmanly. But then he would remember with what high-toned bravery of determination he had boasted to his uncle of his pure and unalterable affections; how contemptuously he had spoken of pecuniary inducements, and in what terms, too, he had told Robina herself, that she had nothing to hope from him. It was, therefore, impossible that he could present himself to either with any expression of regret for what had passed, without appearing, in the eyes of both, as equally weak and unworthy. But the very thought of finding that he could think of entertaining the proposition at all, was more acute and mortifying than even this; and he despised himself when he considered how Ellen Frazer would look upon him, if she knew he had been so base as, for a moment, to calculate the sordid advantages of preferring his cousin.

But what was to be done? To return to the counting-house, after his resolute declaration; to embark again in that indoor and tame drudgery which he ever hated, and which was rendered as vile as slavery, by the disclosures which had taken place, could not be. He would be baser than were he to sell himself to his uncle's purposes, could he yield to such a suggestion.

To leave Glasgow was his only alternative; but how? and where to go? and where to obtain the means? were stinging questions that he could not answer; and then what was he to gain? To marry Robina was to sacrifice Ellen Frazer; to quit the country entailed the same consequence. Besides all that, in so doing, he would add to the sorrows and the disappointments of his gentle-hearted and affectionate mother, who had built renewed hopes on his success under the auspices of his uncle, and who looked eagerly forward to the time when he should be so established in business as to bring his sister before the world in circumstances befitting his father's child; for the hereditary pride of family was mingled with his sensibility; and even the beautiful and sprightly Ellen Frazer herself, perhaps, owed something of her superiority over Robina to the Highland pedigrees and heroic traditions which Mrs Eadie delighted to relate of her ancestors.

While tossing on these troubled and conflicting tides of the mind, he happened to recollect, that a merchant, a school-fellow of his father, and who, when he occasionally met him, always inquired, with more than common interest, for his mother and sister, had at that time a vessel bound for New York, where he intended to establish a store, and was in want of a clerk; and it occurred to him, that, perhaps, through that means, he might accomplish his wishes. This notion was as oil to his agitation, and hope restored soon brought sleep and soothing dreams to his pillow; but his slumbers were not of long duration, for before sunrise he awoke; and, in order to avoid the garrulous remonstrances of the Leddy, he rose and went to Camrachle for the purpose, as he persuaded himself, to consult his mother; but, for all that we have been able to understand, it was in reality only to communicate his determination. But these sort of self-delusions are very common to youths under age.

The morning air, as he issued from Glasgow, was cold and raw. Heavy blobs of water, the uncongenial distillations of the midnight fogs, hung so dully on the hoary hedges, that even Poesy would be guilty of downright extravagance, were she, on any occasion, to call such gross uncrystalline knobs of physic glass by any epithet implying dew. The road was not miry, but gluey, and reluctant, and wearisome to the tread. The smoke from the farmhouses rolled listlessly down the thatch, and lazily spread itself into a dingy azure haze, that lingered and lowered among the stacks of the farm-yards. The cows, instead of proceeding, with their ordinary sedate common sense, to the pastures, stood on the loans, looking east and west, and lowing to one another—no doubt concerning the state of the weather. The birds chirped peevishly, as they hopped from bough to bough. The ducks walked in silence to their accustomed pools. The hens, creatures at all times of a sober temperament, condoled in actual sadness together under sheds and bushes; and chanticleer himself wore a paler crest than usual, and was so low in spirits, that he only once had heart enough to wind his bugle-horn. Nature was sullen—and the herd-boy drew his blanket-mantle closer round him, and snarlingly struck the calf as he grudgingly drove the herd a-field. On the ground, at the door of the toll-bar house,[1] lay a gill-stoup on its side, and near it, on a plate, an empty glass and a bit of bread, which showed that some earlier traveller had, in despite of the Statute,[2] but in consideration of the damp and unwholesome morning, obtained a dram from the gudewife's ain bottle.

In consequence of these sympathetic circumstances, before Walkinshaw reached Camrachle, his heart was almost as heavy as his limbs were tired. His mother, when she saw him pass the parlour window, as he approached the door, was surprised at his appearance, and suffered something like a shock of fear when she perceived the dulness of his eye and the dejection of his features.

'What has brought you here?' was her first exclamation; 'and what has happened?'

But, instead of replying, he walked in, and seated himself at the fireside, complaining of his cold and uncomfortable walk, and the heaviness of the road. His sister was preparing breakfast, and happening not to be in the room, his mother repeated her anxious inquiries with an accent of more earnest solicitude.

'I fear,' said Walkinshaw, 'that I am only come to distress you;' and he then briefly recapitulated what had passed between himself and his uncle respecting Robina. But a sentiment of tenderness for his mother's anxieties, blended with a wish to save her from the

disagreeable sensation with which he knew his determination to
quit Glasgow would affect her, made him suppress the communication that he had come expressly to make.

Mrs Walkinshaw had been too long accustomed to the occasional anticipations in which her brother-in-law had indulged on
the subject, to be surprised at what had taken place on his part;
and both from her own observations, and from the repugnance her
son expressed, she had no doubt that his attachment to Ellen
Frazer was the chief obstacle to the marriage. The considerations
and reflections to which this conclusion naturally gave rise, held
her for some time silent. The moment, however, that Walkinshaw,
encouraged by the seeming slightness of her regret at his declama-
tions against the match, proceeded to a fuller disclosure of his
sentiments, and to intimate his resolution to go abroad, her
maternal fears were startled, and she was plunged into the profoundest sorrow. But still during breakfast she said nothing—misfortune and disappointment had indeed so long subdued her gentle
spirit into the most patient resignation, that, while her soul
quivered in all its tenderest feelings, she seldom even sighed, but,
with a pale cheek and a meek supplication, expressed only by a
heavenward look of her mild and melancholy eyes, she seemed to
say, 'Alas! am I still doomed to suffer?' That look was ever
irresistible with her children: in their very childhood it brought
them, with all their artless and innocent caresses, to her bosom;
and, on this occasion, it so penetrated the very core of Walkinshaw's heart, that he took her by the hand and burst into tears.

CHAPTER II

WE are no casuists, and therefore cannot undertake to determine
whether Jenny did right or wrong in marrying Auld Robin Gray[1]
for the sake of her poor father and mother; especially as it has been
ever held by the most approved moralists, that there are principles
to be abided by, even at the expence of great and incontrovertible
duties. But of this we are quite certain, that there are few trials to
which the generous heart can be subjected more severe than a
contest between its duties and its affections—between the claims
which others have upon the conduct of the man for their advantage,

and the desires that he has himself to seek his own gratification. In this predicament stood young Walkinshaw; and at the moment when he took his mother by the hand, the claims of filial duty were undoubtedly preferred to the wishes of love.

'I am,' said he, 'at your disposal, mother—do with me as you think fit.—When I resented the mean opinion that my uncle seemed to hold of me, I forgot you—I thought only of myself. My first duties, I now feel, are due to the world, and the highest of them to my family.—But I wish that I had never known Ellen Frazer.'

'In that wish, my dear boy, you teach me what I ought myself to do.—No, James, I can never desire nor expect that my children will sacrifice themselves for me—for I regard it as no less than immolation when the heart revolts at the tasks which the hand performs. But my life has long been one continued sorrow; and it is natural that I should shrink at the approach of another and a darker cloud. I will not, however, ask you to remain with your uncle, nor even oppose your resolution to go abroad. But be not precipitate—consider the grief, the anxieties, and the humiliations, that both your father and I have endured, and think, were you united to Ellen Frazer, supposing her father and friends would consent to so unequal a match, what would be her fate were you cut early off, as your father was?—It is the thought of that—of what I myself, with you and for you, have borne, which weighs so grievously at this moment on my spirits.'

'Do you wish me to return to Glasgow?' said Walkinshaw with an anxious and agitated voice.

'Not unless you feel yourself that you can do so without humiliation—for bitter, James, as my cup has been, and ill able as I am to wrestle with the blast, I will never counsel child of mine to do that which may lessen him in his own opinion. Heaven knows that there are mortifications ready enough in the world to humble us— we do not need to make any for ourselves—no, unless you can meet your uncle with a frank face and a free heart, do not return.'

'I am sure, then, that I never can,' replied Walkinshaw. 'I feel as if he had insulted my nature, by venturing to express what he seems to think of me; and a man can forgive almost any injury but a mean opinion of him.'

'But if you do not go to him, perhaps you will not find it difficult to obtain a situation in another counting-house?'

'If I am not to return to his, I would rather at once leave the place—I never liked it, and I shall now like it less than ever. In a word, my intention is to go, if possible, to America.'

'Go where you will, my blessing and tears is all, my dear boy, that I can give you.'

'Then you approve of my wish to go to America?'

'I do not object to it, James—It is a difficult thing for a mother to say that she approves of her son exposing himself to any hazard.'

'What would you have said, could I have obtained a commission in the army and a war raging?'

'Just what I say now—nor should I have felt more sorrow in seeing you go to a campaign than I shall feel when you leave me to encounter the yet to you untried perils of the world. Indeed, I may say, I should almost feel less, for, in the army, with all its hazard, there is a certain degree of assurance, that a young man, if he lives, will be fashioned into an honourable character.'

'I wish that there was a war,' said Walkinshaw with such sincere simplicity, that even his mother could scarcely refrain from smiling.

The conversation was, at this juncture, interrupted by the entrance of Mrs Eadie, who immediately perceived that something particular had occurred to disturb the tranquillity of her friend, and, for a moment, she looked at Walkinshaw with an austere and majestic eye. His mother observed the severity of her aspect, and thought it as well at once to mention what had happened.

Mrs Eadie listened to the recital of his uncle's proposal, and his resolution to go abroad, with a degree of juridical serenity, that lent almost as much solemnity to her appearance as it derived dignity from her august form; and, when Mrs Walkinshaw concluded, she said,—

'We have foreseen all this—and I am only surprised that now, when it has come to pass, it should affect you so much. I dreamt, last night, Mrs Walkinshaw, that you were dead, and laid out in your winding-sheet. I thought I was sitting beside the corpse, and that, though I was sorrowful, I was, nevertheless, strangely pleased. In that moment, my cousin, Glengael, came into the room, and he had a large ancient book, with brazen clasps on it, under his arm. That book he gave to Ellen Frazer, whom I then saw was also in the room, and she undid the brazen clasps, and opening it, showed her father a particular passage, which he read aloud, and, when he paused, I saw you rise, and, throwing aside the winding-sheet, you appeared richly dressed, with a chearful countenance, and on your hands were wedding-gloves. It was to tell you this auspicious dream that I came here this morning, and I have no doubt it betokens some happy change in your fortunes, to come by the agency of Glengael. Therefore, give yourself no uneasiness about this difference between James and his uncle; for, you may rest assured, it will terminate in some great good to your family; but there will be a death first, that's certain.'

Although Walkinshaw was familiar with the occasional gleams of the sybiline pretensions of Mrs Eadie, and always treated them with reverence, he could not resist from smiling at the earnestness with which she delivered her prediction, saying, 'But I do not see in what way the dream has any thing to do with my case.'

'You do not see,' replied the Lady sternly, 'nor do I see; but it does not, therefore, follow, that there is no sympathy between them. The wheels of the world work in darkness, James, and it requires the sight of the seer to discern what is coming round, though the auguries of their index are visible to all eyes. But,' and she turned to Mrs Walkinshaw, 'it strikes me, that, in the present state of your circumstances, I might write to my cousin. The possession of Glengael gives him weight with Government, and, perhaps, his influence might be of use to your son.'

This afforded a ray of hope to Walkinshaw, of which he had never entertained the slightest notion, and it also, in some degree, lightened the spirits of his mother. They both expressed their sense of her kindness; and James said gaily, that he had no doubt the omens of her dream would soon be verified; but she replied solemnly,—

'No! though Glengael may be able, by his interest, to serve you, the agency of death can alone fulfil the vision; but, for the present, let us say no more on that head. I will write to-day to Mr Frazer, and inquire in what way he can best assist all our wishes.'

In the meantime, the Leddy had been informed by her maid of Walkinshaw's early departure for Camrachle; and, in consequence, as soon as she had breakfasted, a messenger was dispatched to the counting-house, to request that the Laird might be sent to her when he came to town; but this was unnecessary, for he had scarcely passed a more tranquil night than his nephew; and, before her messenger came back, he was in the parlour with Robina, whom he had brought with him in the carriage to spend the day with one of her friends. Why the young lady should have chosen so unpleasant a day for her visit, particularly as it was a volunteer,[1] and had been, as she said, only concerted with herself after the conversation of the preceding evening, we must allow the sagacity of the reader to discover; but she appeared flurried, and put out of countenance, when her grandmother told her, that she expected Dirdumwhamle and Mrs Milrookit to dinner, and 'I think,' said she, 'Beenie, that ye ought to bide wi' me to meet them, for I expect Walky,' so she styled Walkinshaw, their son; 'and if ye're no to get the ae[2] cousin, I dinna see but ye might set your cap for the other.'

'I trust and hope,' exclaimed the Laird, 'that she has more sense. Walkinshaw Milrookit has nothing.'

'And what has Jamie Walkinshaw?' said the Leddy. ''Deed, Geordie, though I canna but say ye're baith pawkie and auld farrant,[3] it's no to be controversed that ye hae gotten your father's bee in the bonnet, anent ancestors and forbears, and nae gude can come out o' ony sic havers. Beenie, my Leddy, ne'er fash your head wi' your father's dodrums;[4] but, an ye can hook Walky's heart wi' the tail o' your ee, ye's no want my helping hand at the fishing.'

'Mother,' said George vehemently, 'I am astonished that you can talk so lightly to the girl. I have my own reasons for being most decidedly averse to any such union. And though I do feel that James has used me ill, and that his headstrong conduct deserves my severest displeasure, I not only think it a duty to bring about a marriage between Robina and him, but will endeavour to act in it as such. Perhaps, had she been entirely free, I might have felt less interest in the business; but knowing, as I now do, that his coldness alone has prevented her from cherishing towards him a just and proper affection, I should be wanting in my obligations as a father, were I not to labour, by all expedient means, to promote the happiness of my child.'

During this speech the young lady appeared both out of countenance and inwardly amused, while her grandmother, placing her hands to her sides, looked at her with a queer and inquisitive eye, and said,—

'It's no possible, Beenie Walkinshaw, that thou's sic a masquerading cutty as to hae beguilt[5] baith thy father and me? But, if ever I had an ee in my head, and could see wi' that ee, it's as true as the deil's in Dublin city, that I hae had a discernment o' thy heart-hatred to Jamie Walkinshaw. But let your father rin to the woody[1] as he will—they're no to be born that'ill live to see that I hae a judgment and an understanding o' what's what. Howsever, Geordie, what's to be done wi' that ne'er-do-well water-wag-tail that's flown awa to its mother? Poor woman, she canna afford to gie't drammock.[2] Something maun be done, and wi' your wis for a fresh clecking of the pedigrees o' the Walkinshaws o' Kittlestonheugh, that I hae been sae lang deaved and driven doited wi',[3] "for the space of forty years," I may say, in the words of the Psalmist,[4] "the race hae grieved me." Ye canna do better than just tak a hurl[5] in your chaise to Camrachle, and bring him in by the lug and horn, and nail him to the desk wi' a pin to his nose.'

There was worse advice, the Laird thought, than this; and, after some farther remarks to the same effect, he really did set off for Camrachle with the express intention of doing every thing in his power to heal the breach, and to conciliate again the affection and gratitude of his nephew.

CHAPTER III

As soon as the carriage had left the door, the Leddy resumed the conversation with her grand-daughter.

'Noo, Beenie Walkinshaw,' said she, 'I maun put you to the straights o' a question. Ye'll no tell me, lassie, that ye hae na flung stoor in your father's een,[6] after the converse that we had thegither by oursels the other day; therefore and accordingly, I requeesht to know, what's at the bottom o' this black art and glamour that ye hae been guilty o'?—whatna scamp or hempy[7] is't that the cutty has been gallanting wi', that she's trying to cast the glaiks in a' our een[8] for?—Wha is't?—I insist to know—for ye'll ne'er gar me believe that there's no a because for your jookery pawkrie.'

'You said,' replied Miss, half blushing, half laughing, 'that you would lend a helping hand to me with Walkinshaw Milrookit.'

'Eh! Megsty me! I'm sparrow-blasted!'[9] exclaimed the Leddy, throwing herself back in the chair, and lifting both her hands and eyes in wonderment.—'But thou, Beenie Walkinshaw, is a soople fairy;[10] and so a' the time that thy father, as blin' as the silly blind bodie that his wife gart believe her gallant's horse was a milch cow sent frae her minny,[1]—was wising and wyling[2] to bring about a matrimony, or, as I should ca't, a matter-o'-money conjugality wi' your cousin Jamie, hae ye been linking by the dyke-sides,[3] out o' sight, wi' Walky Milrookit? Weel, that beats print! Whatna novelle gied[4] you that lesson, lassie? Hey Sirs! auld as I am, but I would like to read it. Howsever, Beenie, as the ae oe's as sib to me as the ither,[5] I'll be as gude as my word; and when Dirdumwhamle and your aunty, wi' your joe,[6] are here the day, we'll just lay our heads thegither for a purpose o' marriage, and let your father play the Scotch measure or shantruse,[7] wi' the bellows and the shank o' the besom, to some warlock wallop o' his auld papistical and pater-nostering ancestors,[8] that hae been—Gude preserve us!—for ought I ken to the contrary, suppin' brimstone broth wi' the deil lang afore the time o' Adam and Eve. Methuselah himself, I verily believe, could be naething less than half a cousin to the nine hundred and ninety-ninth Walkinshaw o' Kittlestonheugh. Howsever, Beenie, thou's a—thou's a—I'll no say what—ye little dooble cutty, to keep me in the dark, when I could hae gi'en you and Walky sae muckle convenience for courting. But, for a' that, I'll no be devoid o' grace, but act the part of a kind and affectionate grandmother, as it is well known I hae ay been to a' my bairns' childer; only I never thought to hae had a finger in the pye o' a Clarissy Harlot wedding.'[9]

'But,' said Robina, 'what if my father should succeed in per-suading James still to fall in with his wishes? My situation will be dreadful.'

''Deed, an that come to a possibility, I ken na what's to be done,' replied the Leddy; 'for ye know it will behove me to tak my ain son, your father's part; and as I was saying, Jamie Walkinshaw being as dear to me as Walky Milrookit, I can do no less than help you to him, which need be a matter of no diffeequalty,[10] 'cause ye hae gart your father trow that ye're out o' the body for Jamie;[11] so, as I said before, ye maun just conform.'

Miss looked aghast for a moment, and exclaimed, clasping her hands, at finding the total contempt with which her grandmother seemed to consider her affections,—

'Heaven protect me! I am ruined and undone!'[12]

'Na, if that's the gait o't, Beenie, I hae nothing to say, but to help to tak up the loupen-steek[13] in your stocking wi' as much brevity as is consistent wi' perspicuity, as the minister o' Port Glasgow says.'

'What do you mean? to what do you allude?' cried the young lady terrified.

'Beenie Walkinshaw, I'll be calm; I'll no lose my composity. But it's no to seek what I could say, ye Jerusalem concubine, to bring sic a crying sin into my family. O woman, woman! but ye're a silly nymph, and the black stool o' repentance is oure gude for you!'[1]

Robina was so shocked and thunderstruck at the old lady's imputations and kindling animadversions, that she actually gasped with horror.

'But,' continued her grandmother,—'since it canna be helped noo, I maun just tell your father, as well as I can, and get the minister when we're a' thegither in the afternoon, and declare an irregular marriage,[2] which is a calamity that never happened on my side of the house.'

Unable any longer to control her agitation, Robina started from her seat, exclaiming, 'Hear me, in mercy! spare such horrible—'

'Spare!' interrupted the Leddy, with the sharpest tone of her indignation,—'An' ye were my dochter as ye're but my grand-dochter, I would spare you, ye Israelitish handmaid, and randy o' Babylon. But pride ne'er leaves its master without a fa'— your father's weel serv't—he would tak nane o' my advice in your education; but instead o' sending you to a Christian school, got down frae Manchester, in England, a governess for miss, my leddy, wi' gumflowers[3] on her head, and paint on her cheeks, and speaking in sic high English,[4] that the Babel babble o' Mull and Moydart[5] was a perfection o' sense when compar't wi't.'

'Good heavens! how have you fallen into this strange mistake?' said Robina, so much recovered, that she could scarcely refrain from laughing.

'Beenie, Beenie! ye may ca't a mistake; but I say it's a shame and a sin. O sic a blot to come on the 'scutcheon of my old age; and wha will tell your poor weakly mother, that, since the hour o' your luckless clecking,[6] has ne'er had a day to do weel. Lang, lang has she been sitting on the brink o' the grave, and this sore stroke will surely coup[7] her in.'

'How was it possible,' at last exclaimed Robina, in full

self-possession, 'that you could put such an indelicate con-struction on any thing that I have said?'

The Leddy had by this time melted into a flood of tears, and was searching for her handkerchief to wipe her eyes; but, sur-prised at the firmness with which she was addressed, she looked up as she leant forward, with one hand still in her pocket, and the other grasping the arm of the elbow chair in which she was seated.

'Yes,' continued Robina, 'you have committed a great error; and though I am mortified to think you could for a moment entertain so unworthy an opinion of me, I can hardly keep from laughing at the mistake.'

But although the Leddy was undoubtedly highly pleased to learn that she had distressed herself without reason, still, for the sake of her own dignity, which she thought somehow compromised by what she had said, she seemed as if she could have wished there had been a little truth in the imputation; for she said,—

'I'm blithe to hear you say sae, Beenie; but it was a very natural delusion on my part, for ye ken in thir[1] novelle and play-actoring times nobody can tell what might happen. Howsever, I'm glad it's no waur;[2] but ye maun alloo that it was a very suspectionable situa-tion for you to be discovered colleaguing wi' Walky Milrookit in sic a clandestine manner; and, therefore, I see that na better can be made o't, but to bring a purpose o' marriage to pass between you, as I was saying, without fashing your father about it till it's by hand;[3] when, after he has got his ramping and stamping over, he'll come to himsel, and mak us a' jocose.'

The conversation was continued with the same sort of con-sistency as far as the old lady was concerned, till Mrs Milrookit and Dirdumwhamle, with their son, arrived.

Young Milrookit, as we have already intimated, was, in point of personal figure, not much inferior to James; and though he certainly was attached to his cousin, Robina, with unfeigned affec-tion, he had still so much of the leaven of his father in him, that her prospective chance of succeeding to the estate of Kittleston-heugh had undoubtedly some influence in heightening the glow of his passion.

A marriage with her was as early and as ardently the chief object of his father's ambition, as the union with his cousin Walkinshaw had been with her's; and the hope of seeing it consummated made the old gentleman, instead of settling him in any town business,

resolve to make him a farmer, that he might one day be qualified
to undertake the management of the Kittlestonheugh estate. It is,
therefore, unnecessary to mention, that, when Robina and her
lover had retired, on being told by their grandmother they might
'divert themselves in another room,' Dirdumwhamle engaged,
with the most sympathetic alacrity, in the scheme, as he called it,
to make the two affectionate young things happy. But what passed
will be better told in a new Chapter.

CHAPTER IV

'INDEED, Leddy,' said the Laird of Dirdumwhamle, when she
told him of the detection, as she called it, of Robina's notion of his
son—'Blood ye ken's thicker than water; and I have na been without a thought mysel that there was something by the common o'
cousinship[1] atween them. But hearing, as we often a' have done, of
the great instancy that my gude-brother was in for a match tweesh[2]
her and James, I could na think of making mysel an interloper.
But if it's ordaint that she prefers Walky, I'm sure I can see nae
harm in you and me giving the twa young things a bit canny
shove[3] onward in the road to a blithesome bridal.'

'I am thinking,' rejoined his wife, 'that, perhaps, it might be as
prudent and more friendly to wait the upshot o' her father's
endeavours wi' James,—for even although he should be worked
into a compliancy, still there will be no marriage, and then Robina
can avow her partiality for Walky.'

'Meg,' replied the Leddy, 'ye speak as one of the foolish women
—ye ken naething about it; your brother Geordie's just his father's
ain gett,[4] and winna be put off frae his intents by a' the powers of
law and government—let him ance get Jamie to conform, and he'll
soon thraw[5] Beenie into an obedience, and what will then become
o' your Walky?—Na, na, Dirdumwhamle, heed her not, she lacketh
understanding—it's you and me, Laird, that maun work the wherry
in this breeze—ye're a man o' experience in the ways o' matrimony, having been, as we all know, thrice married,—and I am
an aged woman, that has na travelled the world for sax-and-
seventy years without hearing the toast o' "Love and opportunity."
Now, have na we the love ready-made to our hands in the fond

affection of Beenie and Walky?—and surely neither o' us is in such
a beggary o' capacity, that we're no able to conceit a time and place
for an opportunity. Had it been, as I had at ae time this very day,
a kind of a because to jealouse,[1] I'll no say what—it was my purpose to hae sent for a minister or a magistrate, and got an un-
regular marriage declared outright—though it would hae gi'en us
a' het hearts and red faces for liveries. Noo, Laird, ye're a man o'
sagacity and judgment, dinna ye think, though we hae na just sic
an exploit to break our hearts wi' shame and tribulation, that we
might ettle[2] at something o' the same sort?—and there can be no
sin in't, Meg; for is't no commanded in Scripture to increase and
multiply? and what we are wising[3] to bring about is a purpose o'
marriage, which is the natural way o' plenishing the earth, and
raising an increase o' the children of men.'

Much and devoutly as the Laird of Dirdumwhamle wished for
such a consummation, he was not quite prepared for proceedings
of so sudden and hasty a character. And being a personage of some
worldly prudence, eagerly as he longed for the match, he was averse
to expose himself to any strictures for the part he might take in
promoting it. Accordingly, instead of acquiescing at once in his
mother-in-law's suggestion, he said jocularly,

'Hooly,[4] hooly, Leddy; it may come vera weel off Walky and
Robina's hands to make a private marriage for themselves, poor
young things, but it never will do for the like o' you and me to
mess or mell[5] in the matter, by ony open countenancing o' a ceremony. It's vera true that I see nae objection to the match, and
would think I did nae ill in the way o' a quiet conneevance to help
them on in their courtship, but things are no ripe for an aff-hand
ploy.'[6]

'I'm glad to hear you say sae,' interposed Mrs Milrookit; 'for
really my mother seems fey[7] about this connection; and nae gude
can come o' ony thing sae rashly devised. My brother would, in
my opinion, have great cause to complain, were the gudeman to be
art or part in ony such conspiracy.'

The Leddy never liked to have her judgment called in question;
(indeed, what ladies do?) and still less by a person so much her
inferior in point of understanding (so she herself thought,) as her
daughter.

'My word, Meg,' was her reply, 'but t'ou has a stock o' impudence, to haud up thy snout in that gait[8] to the she that bore

thee.—Am I one of these that hae, by reason of more strength, amaist attain't to the age of fourscore, without learning the right frae the wrang o' a' moral conduct, as that delightful man, Dr Pringle o' Garnock,¹ said in his sermon on the Fast Day, when he preached in the Wynd Kirk, that t'ou has the spirit o' sedition, to tell me that I hae lost my solid judgment, when I'm labouring in the vineyard o' thy family?—Dirdumwhamle, your wife there, she's my dochter, and sorry am I to say't, but it's well known, and I dinna misdoot ye hae found it to your cost, that she is a most un-reasonable, narrow, contracted woman, and wi' a' her 'conomical throughgality²—her direction-books to mak grozette wine for deil-be-lickit, and her Katy Fisher's cookery, whereby she would gar us trow she can mak fat kail o' chucky stanes and an auld horse shoe—we a' ken, and ye ken, Laird, warst o' a', that she flings away the pease, and mak's her hotch-potch wi' the shawps, or, as the auld bye-word says, tyne's bottles gathering straes.³ So what need the like o' you and me sit in council, and the Shanedrims of the people, wi' ane o' the stupidest bawkie birds⁴ that e'er the Maker o't took the trouble to put the breath o' life in? Fey, did ye say?—that's a word o' discretion to fling at the head o' your aged parent. Howsever, it's no worth my condescendence to lose my temper wi' the like o' her. But, Meg Walkinshaw, or Mrs Milrookit, though ye be there afore your gudeman, the next time ye diminish my under-standing, I'll may be let ye ken what it is to blaspheme your mother, so tak heed lest ye fall. And now to wind up the thread o' what we were discoursing anent—It's my opinion, Dirdumwhamle, we should put no molestation in the way o' that purpose o' mar-riage. So, if ye dinna like to tell your son to gang for a minister, I'll do it myself; and the sooner it's by hand and awa, as the sang sings, the sooner we'll a' be in a situation to covenant and gree again wi' Beenie's father.'

The Laird was delighted to see the haste and heartiness with which the Leddy was resolved to consummate the match; but he said,—

'Do as ye like, Leddy—do as ye like; but I'll no coom⁵ my fingers wi' meddling in ony sic project. The wark be a' your ain.'

'Surely neither you nor that unreverent and misleart tumphy⁶ your wife, our Meg, would refuse to be present at the occasion?'

''Deed, Leddy, I'm unco sweert;⁷ I'll no deny that,' replied Dirdumwhamle.

'If it is to take place this day, and in this house, gudeman, I'm sure it will be ill put on blateness,[1] both on your part and mine, no to be present,' said Mrs Milrookit.

'Noo, that's a word o' sense, Meg,' cried her mother, exultingly; 'that's something like the sagacity o' a Christian parent. Surely it would be a most Pagan-like thing, for the father and mother o' the bridegroom to be in the house, to ken o' what was going on, and fidging fain,[2] as ye baith are, for the comfort it's to bring to us a', to sit in another room wi' a cloud on your brows, and your hands in a mournful posture. Awa, awa, Dirdumwhamle, wi' the like o' that; I hae nae brow[3] o' sic worldly hypocrisy. But we hae nae time to lose, for your gude-brother will soon be back frae Camrachle, and I would fain hae a' o'er before he comes. Hey, Sirs! but it will be a sport if we can get him to be present at the wedding-dinner, and he ken naething about it. So I'll just send the lass at ance for Dr De'ilfear; for it's a great thing, ye ken, to get a bridal blessed wi' the breath o' a sound orthodox;[4] and I'll gae ben and tell Beenie and Walky, that they maun mak some sort o' a preparation.'

'But, when they are married, what's to become o' them?— where are they to bide?[5]—and what hae they to live upon?'—said Mrs Milrookit, anxiously.

'Dinna ye fash your head, Meg,' said her mother, about ony sic trivialities. They can stay wi' me till after the reconciliation, when, nae doot, her father will alloo a genteel aliment; so we need na vex oursels about taking thought for to-morrow; sufficient for the day is the evil thereof. But ye hae bonny gooses and a' manner o' poultry at the Dirdumwhamle. So, as we'll need something to keep the banes green,[6] ye may just send us a tasting; na, for that matter, we'll no cast out wi' the like o' a sooking grumphie;[7] or, if ye were chancing to kill a sheep, a side o' mutton's worth house-room; and butter and eggs, I'm no a novice, as the Renfrew Doctor said, butter and eggs may dine a provice, wi' the help o' bread for kitchen.'[8]

In concluding this speech, the Leddy, who had, in the mean time, risen, gave a joyous geck[9] with her head, and swept triumphantly out of the room.

CHAPTER V

In the meantime, Kittlestonheugh, as, according to the Scottish fashion, we should denominate Squire Walkinshaw, had proceeded to Camrachle, where he arrived at his sister-in-law's door just as Mrs Eadie was taking her leave, with the intention of writing to her relation Mr Frazer in behalf of James. As the carriage drove up, Mrs Charles, on seeing it approach, begged her to stop; but, upon second thoughts, it was considered better that she should not remain, and also that she should defer her letter to Glengael until after the interview. She was accordingly at the door when the Laird alighted, who, being but slightly acquainted with her, only bowed, and was passing on without speaking into the house, when she arrested him by one of her keen and supreme looks, of which few could withstand the searching brightness.

'Mr Walkinshaw,' said she, after eyeing him inquisitively for two or three seconds, 'before you go to Mrs Charles, I would speak with you.'

It would not be easy to explain the reason which induced Mrs Eadie so suddenly to determine on interfering, especially after what had just passed; but still, as she did so, we are bound, without investigating her motives too curiously, to relate the sequel.

Mr Walkinshaw bowed, thereby intimating his acquiescence; and she walked on towards the manse with slow steps and a majestic altitude, followed by the visitor in silence. But she had not advanced above four or five paces, when she turned round, and touching him emphatically on the arm, said,—

'Let us not disturb the minister, but go into the churchyard; we can converse there—the dead are fit witnesses to what I have to say.'

Notwithstanding all his worldliness, there was something so striking in her august air, the impressive melancholy of her countenance, and the solemn Siddonian[1] grandeur of her voice, that Kittlestonheugh was awed, and could only at the moment again intimate his acquiescence by a profound bow. She then proceeded with her wonted dignity towards the churchyard, and entering the stile which opened into it, she walked on to the south side of the church. The sun by this time had exhaled away the morning mists, and was shining brightly on the venerable edifice, and on the humble tombs and frail memorials erected nigh.

'Here,' said she, stopping when they had reached the small turfless space which the feet of the rustic Sabbath pilgrims had trodden bare in front of the southern door,—'Here let us stop—the sun shines warmly here, and the church will shelter us from the cold north-east wind. Mr Walkinshaw, I am glad that we have met, before you entered yon unhappy house. The inmates are not in circumstances to contend with adversity: your sister loves her children too well not to wish that her son may obtain the great advantages which your proposal to him holds out; and he has too kind and generous a heart, not to go far, and willingly to sacrifice much on her account. You have it therefore in your power to make a family, which has hitherto known little else but misfortune, miserable or happy.'

'It cannot, I hope, Madam,' was his reply, 'be thought of me, that I should not desire greatly to make them happy.—Since you are acquainted with what has taken place, you will do me the justice to admit, that I could do nothing more expressive of the regard I entertain for my nephew, and of the esteem in which I hold his mother, than by offering him my only child in marriage, and with such a dowry, too, as no one in his situation could almost presume to expect.'

Mrs Eadie did not make any immediate answer, but again fixed her bright and penetrating eye for a few seconds so intensely on his countenance, that he turned aside from its irresistible ray.

'What you say, Sir, sounds well; but if, in seeking to confer that benefit, you mar for ever the happiness you wish to make, and know before that such must be the consequence, some other reason than either regard for your nephew, or esteem for his mother, must be the actuating spring that urges you to persevere.'

Firm of purpose, and fortified in resolution, as Kittlestonheugh was, something both in the tone and the substance of this speech made him thrill from head to foot.

'What other motive than my affection can I have?' said he.

'Interest,' replied Mrs Eadie, with a look that withered him to the heart, 'Interest; nothing else ever made a man force those to be unhappy whom he professed to love.'

'I am sorry, Madam, that you think so ill of me,' was his reply, expressed coldly and haughtily.

'I did not wish you to come here, that we should enter into any debate; but only to entreat that you will not press your wish for the marriage too urgently; because, out of the love and reverence which your nephew has for his mother, I fear he may be worked on to comply.'

'Fear! Madam—I cannot understand your meaning.'

The glance that Mrs Eadie darted at these words convinced him it was in vain to equivocate with her.

'Mr Walkinshaw,' said she, after another long pause, and a keen and suspicious scrutiny of his face—'It has always been reported, that some of my mother's family possessed the gift of a discerning spirit.[1] This morning, when I saw you alight from your carriage I felt as if the mantle of my ancestors had fallen upon me. It is a hallowed and oracular inheritance; and, under its mysterious inspirations, I dare not disguise what I feel.—You have come to-day——'

'Really, Madam,' interrupted the merchant testily, 'I come for some better purpose than to listen to Highland stories about the second-sight. I must wish you good morning.'

In saying this, he turned round, and was moving to go away, when the lady, throwing back her shawl, magnificently raised her hand, and took hold of him by the arm—

'Stop, Mr Walkinshaw, this is a place of truth—There is no deceit in death and the grave—Life and the living may impose upon us; but here, where we stand, among the sincere—the dead— I tell you, and your heart, Sir, knows that what I tell you is true, there is no affection—no love for your nephew—nor respect for his mother, in the undivulged motives of that seeming kindness with which you are, shall I say plainly, seeking their ruin?'

The impassioned gestures and the suppressed energy with which this was said, gave an awful and mysterious effect to expressions that were in themselves simple, in so much that the astonished man of the world regarded her, for some time, with a mingled sentiment of wonder and awe. At last he said, with a sneer,—

'Upon my word, Mrs Eadie, the minister himself could hardly preach with more eloquence. It is a long time since I have been so lectured; and I should like to know by what authority I am so brought to book?'

The sarcastic tone in which this was said provoked the pride and Highland blood of the lady, who, stepping back, and raising her right arm with a towering grandeur, shook it over him as she said,—

'I have no more to say;—the fate of the blood of Glengael is twined and twisted with the destiny of Mrs Charles Walkinshaw's family; but at your dying hour you will remember what I have said, and, trembling, think of this place—of these tombs, these doors that lead into the judgment-chamber of Heaven, and of yon sun, that is the eye of the Almighty's chief sentinel over man.'

She then dropped her hand, and, walking slowly past him, went straight towards the manse, the door of which she had almost reached before he recovered himself from the amazement and apprehension with which he followed her with his eye. His feelings, however, he soon so far mastered in outward appearance, that he even assumed an air of ineffable contempt; but, nevertheless, an impression had been so stamped by her mystery and menace, that, in returning towards the dwelling of Mrs Charles, he gradually fell into a moody state of thoughtfulness and abstraction.

CHAPTER VI

MRS CHARLES WALKINSHAW had been a good deal surprised by the abrupt manner in which Mrs Eadie had intercepted her brother-in-law. Her son, not a little pleased of an opportunity to avoid his uncle, no sooner saw them pass the window than he made his escape from the house. Observing that they did not go to the manse, but turned off towards the churchyard, he hastened to take refuge with his old preceptor, the minister, possibly to see Ellen Frazer. The relation, however, of what passed in the manse does not fall within the scope of our narrative, particularly as it will be easily comprehended and understood by its effects. We have, therefore, only at present to mention, that Mrs Charles, in the meantime, sat in wonder and expectation, observing to her daughter, a mild and unobtrusive girl, who seldom spoke many sentences at a time, that she thought of late Mrs Eadie seemed unusually attentive to her Highland superstitions. 'She has been, I think, not so well of late,—her nerves are evidently in a high state of excitement. It is much to be regretted that she is so indisposed at this time, when we stand so much in need of her advice.'

Mary replied that she had noticed with sorrow a very great change indeed in their friend,—and she added,—

'Ellen says that she often walks out at night to the churchyard, and sits moaning over the graves of her children. It is strange after they have been so long dead, that her grief should have so unexpectedly broken out afresh. The minister, I am sure, is very uneasy—for I have noticed that he looks paler than he used to do, and with a degree of sadness that is really very affecting.'

While they were thus speaking Mr Walkinshaw came in, and the first words he said, before taking a seat, were,—

'Is the minister's wife in her right mind? She seems to me a little touched. I could with difficulty preserve my gravity at her fantastical nonsense.'

Mrs Charles, out of respect for her friend, did not choose to make any reply to this observation, so that her brother-in-law found himself obliged to revert to the business which had brought him to Camrachle.

'I thought James was here,' said he; 'what has become of him?'

'He has just stepped out.—I suspect he was not exactly prepared to meet you.'

'He is hot and hasty,' rejoined the uncle; 'we had rather an unpleasant conversation last night. I hope, since he has had time to reflect on what I said, he sees things differently.'

'I am grieved,' replied Mrs Charles with a sigh, 'that any thing should have arisen to mar the prospects that your kindness had opened to him. But young men will be headstrong; their feelings often run away with their judgment.'

'But,' said Kittlestonheugh, 'I can forgive him. I never looked for any conduct in him different from that of others of his own age. Folly is the superfluous blossoms of youth: They drop off as the fruit forms. I hope he is not resolute in adhering to his declaration about leaving Glasgow.'

'He seems at present quite resolved,' replied his mother, with a deep and slow sigh, which told how heavily that determination lay upon her heart.

'Perhaps, then,' said his uncle, 'it may just be as well to leave him to himself for a few days; and I had better say nothing more to him on the subject.'

'I think,' replied Mrs Charles, timidly, as if afraid that she might offend,—'it is needless at present to speak to him about Robina: he must have time to reflect.'—She would have added, 'on the great advantages of the match to him;' but knowing, as she did, the decided sentiments of her son, she paused in the unfinished sentence, and felt vexed with herself for having said so much.

'But,' inquired her brother-in-law, in some degree solaced by the manner in which she had expressed herself—'But, surely, the boy will not be so ridiculous as to absent himself from the counting-house?'

'He speaks of going abroad,' was the soft and diffident answer.

'Impossible! he has not the means.'

She then told him what he had been considering with respect to his father's old acquaintance, who had the vessel going to America.

'In that case,' said his uncle, with an off-hand freedom that seemed much like generosity,—'I must undertake the expence of his outfit. He will be none the worse of seeing a little of the world; and he will return to us in the course of a year or two a wiser and a better man.'

'Your kindness, Sir, is truly extraordinary, and I shall be most happy if he can be persuaded to avail himself of it; but his mind lies towards the army, and, if he could get a cadetcy[1] to India, I am sure he would prefer it above all things.'

'A cadetcy to India!' exclaimed the astonished uncle.—'By what chance or interest could he hope for such an appointment?'

'Mrs Eadie's cousin, who bought back her father's estate, she says, has some Parliamentary interest, and she intends to write him to beg his good offices for James.'

Kittlestonheugh was thunderstruck:—this was a turn in the affair that he had never once imagined within the scope and range of possibility. 'Do you think,' said he, 'that he had any view to this in his ungrateful insolence to me last night? If I thought so, every desire I had to serve him should be henceforth suppressed and extinguished.'

At this crisis the door was opened, and Mr Eadie, the minister, came in, by which occurrence the conversation was interrupted, and the vehemence of Mr Walkinshaw was allowed to subside during the interchange of the common reciprocities of the morning.

'I am much grieved, Mr Walkinshaw,' said the worthy clergy-man, after a short pause, 'to hear of this unfortunate difference with your nephew. I hope the young man will soon come to a more considerate way of thinking.'

Mr Walkinshaw thought Mr Eadie a most sensible man, and could not but express his confidence, that, when the boy came to see how much all his best friends condemned his conduct, and were so solicitous for his compliance, he would repent his pre-cipitation. 'We must, however,' said he, 'give him time. His mother tells me that he has resolved to go to America. I shall do all in my power to assist his views in that direction, not doubting in the end to reap the happiest effects.'

'But before taking any step in that scheme,' said the minister, 'he has resolved to wait the issue of a letter which I have left my wife writing to her relation—for he would prefer a military life to any other.'

'From all that I can understand,' replied the uncle, 'Mr Frazer, your friend, will not be slack in using his interests to get him to India; for he cannot but be aware of the pennyless condition of my nephew, and must be glad to get him out of his daughter's way.'

There was something in this that grated the heart of the mother, and jarred on the feelings of the minister.

'No,' said the latter; 'on the contrary, the affection which Glengael bears to his daughter would act with him as a motive to lessen any obstacles that might oppose her happiness. Were Mrs Eadie to say—but, for many reasons, she will not yet—that she believes her young friend is attached to Ellen, I am sure Mr Frazer would exert himself, in every possible way, to advance his fortune.'

'In that he would but do as I am doing,' replied the merchant with a smile of self-gratulation; and he added briskly, addressing himself to his sister-in-law, 'Will James accept favours from a stranger, with a view to promote a union with that stranger's daughter, and yet scorn the kindness of his uncle?'

The distressed mother had an answer ready; but long depen-dence on her cool and wary brother-in-law, together with her natural gentleness, made her bury it in her heart. The minister, however, who owed him no similar obligations, and was of a more courageous nature, did more than supply what she would have said.

'The cases, Mr Walkinshaw, are not similar. The affection between your nephew and Ellen is mutual; but your favour is to get him to agree to a union at which his heart revolts.'

'Revolts! you use strong language unnecessarily,' was the indignant retort.

'I beg your pardon, Mr Walkinshaw,' said the worthy Presbyter, disturbed at the thought of being so unceremonious; 'I am much interested in your nephew—I feel greatly for his present unhappy situation. I need not remind you that he has been to me, and with me, as my own son; and therefore you ought not to be surprised that I should take his part, particularly as, in so doing, I but defend the generous principles of a very noble youth.'

'Well, well,' exclaimed the Laird peevishly, 'I need not at present trouble myself any farther—I am as willing as ever to befriend him as I ought; but, from the humour he is in, it would serve no good purpose for me at present to interfere. I shall therefore return to Glasgow; and, when Mrs Eadie receives her answer, his mother will have the goodness to let me know.'

With these words he hastily bade his sister-in-law good morning, and hurried into his carriage.

'His conduct is very extraordinary,' said the minister as he drove off. 'There is something more than the mere regard and anxiety of an uncle in all this, especially when he knows that the proposed match is so obnoxious to his daughter. I cannot understand it; but come, Mrs Walkinshaw, let us go over to the manse—James is to dine with me to-day, and we shall be the better of all being together; for Mrs Eadie seems much out of spirits, and her health of late has not been good. Go, Mary, get your bonnet too, and come with us.'

So ended the pursuit to Camrachle; and we shall now beg the courteous reader to return with us to Glasgow, where we left the Leddy in high spirits, in the act of sending for the Reverend Dr De'ilfear to marry her grandchildren.

CHAPTER VII

LONG before Kittlestonheugh returned to Glasgow, the indissoluble knot was tied between his daughter and her cousin, Walkinshaw Milrookit. The Laird of Dirdumwhamle was secretly enjoying this happy consummation of a scheme which he considered as securing to his son the probable reversion of an affluent fortune, and a flourishing estate. Occasional flakes of fear floated, however, in the sunshine of his bosom, and fell cold for a moment on his heart. His wife was less satisfied. She knew the ardour with which her brother had pursued another object; she respected the consideration that was due to him as a parent in the disposal of his daughter; and she justly dreaded his indignation and reproaches. She was, therefore, anxious that Mr Milrookit should return with her to the country before he came back from Camrachle. But her mother, the Leddy, was in high glee, and triumphant, at having so cleverly, as she thought, accomplished a most meritorious stratagem, she would not for a moment listen to the idea of their going away before dinner.

'Na; ye'll just bide where ye are,' said she. 'It will be an unco like[1] thing no to partake o' the marriage feast, though ye hae come without a wedding garment, after I hae been at the cost and outlay o' a jigot o' mutton, a fine young poney cock, and a florentine pye;[2] dainties that the like o' hae na been in my house since Geordie, wi' his quirks o' law, wheedled me to connive wi' him to deprive uncle Watty o' his seven lawful senses, forbye[3] the property. But I trow I hae now gotten the blin side o' him at last: he'll no daur to say a word to me about a huggery muggery matrimonial, take my word for't; for he kens the black craw I hae to pluck wi' him anent the prank he played me in the deevelry o' the concos mentos, whilk ought in course o' justice to have entitled me to a full half of the income o' the lands; and a blithe thing, Dirdumwhamle, that would hae been to you and your wife, could we hae wrought it into a come-to-pass; for sure am I, that, in my experience and throughgality, I would na hae tied my talent in a napkin, nor hid it in a stroopless[4] tea-pot, in the corner o' the press, but laid it out to usury wi' Robin Carrick.[5] Howsever, may be, for a' that, Meg, when I'm dead and gone, ye'll find, in the bonny pocket-book ye sewed lang syne[1] at the boarding-school for your father, a testimony o' the advantage it was to hae had a mother. But, Sirs, a wedding-day is no a time for molloncholious moralizing; so I'll mak a skip and a passover o' a matter and things pertaining to sic Death and the Leddy's confabbles[2] as legacies, and kittle up your notions wi' a wee bit spree and sprose o' jocosity,[3] afore the old man comes; for so, in course o' nature, it behoves us to ca' the bride's father, as he's now, by the benison o' Dr De'ilfear, on the lawfu' toll-road[4] to become, in due season, an ancestor. Nae doubt, he would hae liked better had it been to one of his ain Walkinshaws o' Kittlestonheugh; but when folk canna get the gouden goun,[5] they should be thankful when they get the sleeve.'

While the Leddy was thus holding forth to the Laird and his wife, the carriage with George stopped at the door. Dirdumwhamle, notwithstanding all his inward pleasure, changed colour. Mrs Milrookit fled to another room, to which the happy pair had retired after the ceremony, that they might not be visible to any accidental visitors; and even the Leddy was for a time smitten with consternation. She, however, was the first who recovered her self-possession; and, before Mr Walkinshaw was announced, she was seated in her accustomed elbow chair with a volume of Mathew Henry's Commentary[6] on her lap, and her spectacles on her nose, as if she had been piously reading. Dirdumwhamle sat opposite to her, and apparently in a profound sleep, from which he was not roused until some time after the entrance of his brother-in-law.

'So, Geordie,' said the Leddy, taking off her spectacles, and shutting the book, as her son entered; 'what's come o' Jamie?—hae ye no brought the Douglas-tragedy-like mountebank, back wi' you?'

'Let him go to the devil,' was the answer.

'That's an ill wis, Geordie.—And so ye hae been a gouk's errant?[7] But how are they a' at Camrachle?' replied the Leddy; 'and, to be sober, what's the callan[8] gaun to do? And what did he say for himsel, the kick-at-the-benweed foal that he is? If his mother had laid on the taws[9] better, he would nae hae been sae skeigh.[10] But, sit down, Geordie, and tell me a' about it.—First and foremost, howsever, gie that sleepy bodie, Dirdumwhamle, a shoogle[11] out o' his dreams. What's set the man a snoring like the bars o' Ayr,[12] at this time o' day, I won'er?'

But Dirdumwhamle did not require to be so shaken; for, at this juncture, he began to yawn and stretch his arms till, suddenly seeing his brother-in-law, he started wide awake.

'I am really sorry to say, mother,' resumed Kittlestonheugh, 'that my jaunt to Camrachle has been of no avail. The minister's wife, who, by the way, is certainly not in her right mind, has already written to her relation, Glengael, to beg his interest to procure a cadetship to India for James; and, until she receives an answer, I will let the fellow tak his own way.'

'Vera right, Geordie, vera right; ye could na act a more prudential and Solomon-like part,' replied his mother. 'But, since he will to Cupar,[1] let him gang, and a' sorrow till him;[2] and just compose your mind to approve o' Beenie's marriage wi' Walky, who is a lad of a methodical nature, and no a hurly-burly ramstam, like yon flea-luggit[3] thing, Jamie.'

Dirdumwhamle would fain have said amen, but it stuck in his throat. Nor had he any inducement to make any effort farther, by the decisive manner in which his brother-in-law declared, that he would almost as soon carry his daughter's head to the churchyard as see that match.

'Weel, weel; but I dare say, Geordie, ye need na mair waste your bir[4] about it,' exclaimed the Leddy; 'for, frae something I hae heard the lad himsel say, this very day, it's no a marriage that ever noo is likely to happen in this warld;' and she winked significantly to the bridegroom's father.—'But, Geordie,' she continued, 'there is a because that I would like to understand. How is't that ye're sae doure[5] against Walky Milrookit? I'm sure he's a very personable lad—come o' a gude family—sib to us a'; and, failing you and yours, heir o' entail to the Kittlestonheugh. Howsever, no to fash you[6] wi' the like o' that, as I see ye're kindling, I would, just by way o' diversion, be blithe to learn how it would gang wi' you, if Beenie, after a' this straemash,[7] was to loup the window under cloud o' night wi' some gaberlunzie o' a crookit and blin' soldier-officer, or, wha kens, maybe a drunken drammatical divor[8] frae the play-house, wi' ill-colour't darnt silk stockings; his coat out at the elbows, and his hat on ajee?[9] How would you like that, Geordie?—Sic misfortunes are no uncos[10] noo-a-days.'

Her son, notwithstanding the chagrin he suffered, was obliged to smile, saying, 'I have really a better opinion, both of Beenie's taste and her sense, than to suppose any such adventure possible.'

'So hae I,' replied the Leddy. 'But ye ken, if her character were to get sic a claut by a fox paw, ye would be obligated to tak her hame, and mak a genteel settlement befitting your only dochter.'

'I think,' said George, 'in such a case as you suppose, a genteel settlement would be a little more than could in reason be expected.'

'So think I, Geordie—I am sure I would ne'er counsel you into ony conformity; but, though we hae nae dread nor fear o' soldier-officers or drammaticals, it's o' the nature o' a possibility that she will draw up wi' some young lad o' very creditable connections and conduct; but wha, for some thraw[1] o' your ain, ye would na let her marry.—What would ye do then, Geordie? Ye would hae to settle, or ye would be a most horridable parent.'

'My father, for so doing, disinherited Charles,' said George gravely, and the words froze the very spirit of Dirdumwhamle.

'That's vera true, Geordie,' resumed the Leddy; 'a bitter business it was to us a', and was the because o' your worthy father's sore latter end. But ye ken the property's entail't; and, when it pleases the Maker to take you to Himsel, by consequence Beenie will get the estate.'

'That's not so certain,' replied George, jocularly looking at Dirdumwhamle;—'my wife has of late been more infirm than usual, and were I to marry again, and had male heirs—'

'Hoot, wi' your male heirs, and your snuffics;' I hate the vera name o' sic things—they hae been the pests o' my life.—It would hae been a better world without them,' exclaimed the Leddy, and then she added—'But we need na cast out about sic unborn babes o' Chevy Chase.[3] Beenie's a decent lassie, and will, nae doubt, make a prudent conjugality; so a' I hae for the present is to say that I expek ye'll tak your dinner wi' us. Indeed, considering what has happened, it would na be pleasant to you to be seen on the plane-stanes[4] the day,—for I'm really sorry to see, Geordie, that ye're no just in your right jocularity. Howsever, as we're to hae a bit ploy, I request and hope ye'll bide wi' us, and help to carve the bubbly-jock,[5] whilk is a beast, as I hae heard your father often say, that requir't the skill o' a doctor, the strength o' a butcher, and the practical hand o' a Glasgow Magistrate to diject.'[6]

Nothing more particular passed before dinner, the hour of which was drawing near; but a wedding-feast is, at any time, worthy of a chapter.

CHAPTER VIII

THE conversation which the Leddy, to do her justice, had, considering her peculiar humour and character, so adroitly managed with the bride's father, did not tend to produce the happiest feelings among the conscious wedding-guests. Both the Laird of Dirdumwhamle and his wife were uneasy, and out of countenance, and the happy pair were as miserable as ever a couple of clandestine lovers, in the full possession of all their wishes, could possibly be. But their reverend grandmother, neither daunted nor dismayed, was in the full enjoyment of a triumph, and, eager in the anticipation of accomplishing, by her dexterous address, the felicitous work which, in her own opinion, she had so well begun. Accordingly, dinner was served, with an air of glee and pride, so marked, that Kittlestonheugh was struck with it, but said nothing; and, during the whole of the dijection of the dinner, as his mother persisted in calling the carving, he felt himself frequently on the point of inquiring what had put her into such uncommon good humour. But she did not deem the time yet come for a disclosure, and went on in the most jocund spirits possible, praising the dishes, and cajoling her guests to partake.

'It's extraordinar to me, Beenie,' said she to the bride, 'to lo and behold you sitting as mim as a May puddock,[1] when you see us a' here met for a blithesome occasion—and, Walky, what's come o'er thee, that thou's no a bit mair brisk than the statute[2] o' marble-stane, that I ance saw in that sink o' deceitfulness, the Parliament House o' Embrough? As for our Meg, thy mother, she was ay one of your Moll-on-the-coals,[3] a sigher o' sadness, and I'm none surprised to see her in the hypocondoricals; but for Dirdumwhamle, your respecit father, a man o' property, family, and connections—the three cardinal points o' gentileety—to be as one in doleful dumps, is sic a doolie doomster,[4] that uncle Geordie, there whar he sits, like a sow playing on a trump, is a perfect beautiful Absalom in a sense o' comparison. Howsever, no to let us just fa' knickitty-knock, frae side to side, till our harns are splattered[5] at the bottom o' the well o' despair—I'll gie you a toast, a thing which, but at an occasion, I ne'er think o' minting, and this toast ye maun a' mak a lippy[6]—Geordie, my son and bairn, ye ken as weel as I ken, what

a happy matrimonial your sister has had wi' Dirdumwhamle—
and, Dirdumwhamle, I need na say to you, ye hae found her a
winsome helpmate; and, surely Meg, Mr Milrookit has been to
you a most cordial husband. Noo, what I would propose for a
propine,[1] Geordie, is, Health and happiness to Mr and Mrs
Milrookit, and may they long enjoy many happy returns o' this
day.'

The toast was drank with great glee; but, without entering into
any particular exposition of the respective feelings of the party,
we shall just simply notice, as we proceed, that the Leddy gave a
significant nod and a wink both to the bride and bridegroom, while
the bride's father was seized with a most immoderate fit of laughing, at, what he supposed, the ludicrous eccentricity of his mother.

'Noo, Geordie, my man,' continued the Leddy, 'seeing ye're in
sic a state o' mirth and jocundity, and knowing, as we a' know,
that life is but a weaver's shuttle, and Time a wabster, that works
for Death, Eternity, and Co. great whole merchants;[2] but for
a' that, I am creditably informed they'll be obligated, some day,
to mak a sequester—Howsever, that's nane o' our concern just
now,—but, Geordie, as I was saying, I would fain tell you o' an
exploit.'

'I am sure,' said he laughing, 'you never appeared to me so
capable to tell it well,—what is it?'

The Leddy did not immediately reply, but looking significantly
round the table, she made a short pause, and then said,—

'Do you know that ever since Adam and Eve ate the forbidden
fruit, the life o' man has been growing shorter and shorter? To me
—noo sax-and-seventy year auld—the monthly moon's but as a
glaik[3] on the wall—the spring but as a butterflee that taks the wings
o' the morning—and a' the summer only as the tinkling o' a
cymbal—as for hairst[4] and winter, they're the shadows o' death;
the whilk is an admonishment, that I should not be overly gair
anent[5] the world, but mak mysel and others happy, by taking the
santified use o' what I hae—so, Geordie and Sirs, ye'll fill another
glass.'

Another glass was filled, and the Leddy resumed, all her guests,
save her son, sitting with the solemn aspects of expectation. The
countenance of Kittlestonheugh alone was bright with admiration
at the extraordinary spirits and garrulity of his mother.

'Noo, Geordie,' she resumed, 'as life is but a vapour, a puff out o' the stroop[1] o' the tea-kettle o' Time—let us a' consent to mak one another happy—and there being nae likelihood that ever Jamie Walkinshaw will colleague wi' Beenie, your dochter; I would fain hope ye'll gie her and Walky there baith your benison and an aliment to mak them happy.'

George pushed back his chair, and looked as fiercely and as proudly as any angry and indignant gentleman could well do; but he said nothing.

'Na,' said the Leddy, 'if that's the gait o't, ye shall hae't as ye will hae't.[2]—It's no in your power to mak them unhappy.'

'Mother, what do you mean?' was his exclamation.

'Just that I hae a because for what I mean; but, unless ye compose yoursel, I'll no tell you the night[3]—and, in trouth, for that matter, if ye dinna behave wi' mair reverence to your aged parent, and no bring my grey hairs wi' sorrow to the grave, I'll no tell you at a'.'

'This is inexplicable,' cried her son. 'In the name of goodness, to what do you allude?—of what do you complain?'

'Muckle, muckle hae I to complain o',' was the pathetic reply. 'If your worthy father had been to the fore, ye would na daur't to hae spoken wi' sic unreverence[4] to me. But what hae I to expek in this world noo?—when the Laird lights[5] the Leddy, so does a' the kitchen boys; and your behaviour, Geordie, is an unco warrandice[6] to every one to lift the hoof against me in my auld days.'

'Good Heavens!' cried he, 'what have I done?'

'What hae ye no done?' exclaimed his mother.—'Was na my heart set on a match atween Beenie and Walky there—my ain grandchilder, and weel worthy o' ane anither; and hae na ye sworn, for ought I ken, a triple vow that ye would ne'er gie your consent?'

'And if I have done so—she is my daughter, and I have my own reasons for doing what I have done,' was his very dignified reply.

'Reasons here, or reasons there,' said his mother, 'I hae gude reason to know that it's no in your power to prevent it.—Noo, Beenie, and noo, Walky, down on your knees baith o' you, and mak a novelle confession that ye were married the day;[7] and beg your father's pardon, who has been so jocose at your wedding feast, that for shame he canna refuse to conciliate, and mak a handsome aliment down on the nail.'

The youthful pair did as they were desired—George looked at them for about a minute, and was unable to speak. He then threw a wild and resentful glance round the table, and started from his seat.

'Never mind him,' said the Leddy, with the most perfect equanimity; 'rise, my bairns, and tak your chairs—he'll soon come to himsel.'

'He'll never come to himself—he is distracted—he is ruined—his life is blasted, and his fortune destroyed,' were the first words that burst from the astonished father; and he subjoined impatiently, 'This cannot be true—it is impossible!—Do you trifle with me, mother?—Robina, can you have done this?'

''Deed, Geordie, I doubt it's o'er true,' replied his mother; 'and it cannot be helped noo.'

'But it may be punished!' was his furious exclamation.—'I will never speak to one of you again! To defraud me of my dearest purpose—to deceive my hopes—O you have made me miserable!'

'Ye'll be muckle the better o' your glass o' wine, Geordie—tak it, and compose yoursel like a decent and sedate fore-thinking man, as ye hae been ay reputed.'

He seized the glass, and dashed it into a thousand shivers on the table. All by this time had risen but the Leddy—she alone kept her seat and her coolness.

'The man's gaen by himsel,' said she with the most matronly tranquillity.—'He has scartit and dintit[1] my gude mahogany table past a' the power o' bees-wax and elbow grease to smooth. But, Sirs, sit down—I expekit far waur than a' this—I did na hope for ony thing like sic composity and discretion. Really, Geordie, it's heart salve to my sorrows to see that ye're a man o' a Christian meekness and resignation.'

The look with which he answered this was, however, so dark, so troubled, and so lowering, that it struck terror and alarm even into his mother's bosom, and instantly silenced her vain and vexatious attempt to ridicule the tempest of his feelings.—She threw herself back in her chair, at once overawed and alarmed; and he suddenly turned round and left the house.

CHAPTER IX

THE shock which the delicate frame of Mrs Walkinshaw of Kittlestonheugh received on hearing of her daughter's precipitate marriage, and the distress which it seemed to give her husband, acted as a stimulus to the malady which had so long undermined her health, and the same night she was suddenly seized with alarming symptoms. Next day the disease evidently made such rapid progress, that even the Doctors ventured to express their apprehensions of a speedy and fatal issue.

In the meantime, the Leddy was doing all in her power to keep up the spirits of the young couple, by the reiterated declaration, that, as soon as her son 'had come to himsel',' as she said, 'he would come down with a most genteel settlement;' but day after day passed, and there was no indication of any relenting on his part; and Robina, as we still must continue to call her, was not only depressed with the thought of her rashness, but grieved for the effect it had produced on her mother.

None of the party, however, suffered more than the Laird of Dirdumwhamle. He heard of the acceleration with which the indisposition of Mrs Walkinshaw was proceeding to a crisis, and, knowing the sentiments of his brother-in-law with respect to male heirs, he could not disguise to himself the hazard that he ran of seeing his son cut out from the succession to the Kittlestonheugh estate; and the pang of this thought was sharpened and barbed by the reflection, that he had himself contributed and administered to an event which, but for the marriage, would probably have been procrastinated for years, during which it was impossible to say what might have happened.

At Camrachle, the news of the marriage diffused unmingled satisfaction. Mrs Charles Walkinshaw saw in it the happy escape of her son from a connection that might have embittered his life; and cherished the hope that her brother-in-law would still continue his friendship and kindness.

Walkinshaw himself was still more delighted with the event than his mother. He laughed at the dexterity with which his grandmother had brought it about; and, exulting in the feeling of liberty which it gave to himself, he exclaimed, 'We shall now see whether, indeed, my uncle was actuated towards me by the affection he professed, or by some motive of which the springs are not yet discovered.'

The minister, who was present at this sally, said little; but he agreed with his young friend, that the event would soon put his uncle's affections to the test. 'I cannot explain to myself,' was his only observation, 'why we should all so unaccountably distrust the professions of your uncle, and suppose, with so little reason, in truth against the evidence of facts, that he is not actuated by the purest and kindest motives.'

'That very suspicion,' said Mrs Eadie mysteriously, 'is to me a sufficient proof that he is not so sincere in his professions as he gets the credit of being. But I know not how it is, that, in this marriage, and in the sudden illness of his wife, I perceive the tokens of great good to our friends.'

'In the marriage,' replied the minister, 'I certainly do see something which gives me reason to rejoice; but I confess that the illness of Mrs Walkinshaw does not appear to me to bode any good. On the contrary, I have no doubt, were she dying, that her husband will not be long without a young wife.'

'Did not I tell you,' said Mrs Eadie, turning to Mrs Charles, 'that there would be a death before the good to come by Glengael, to you or yours, would be gathered? Mrs Walkinshaw of Kittleston-heugh is doomed to die soon; when this event comes to pass, let us watch the issues and births of Time.'

'You grow more and more mystical every day,' said her husband pensively. 'I am sorry to observe how much you indulge yourself in superstitious anticipations; you ought to struggle against them.'

'I cannot,' replied the majestic Leddy, with solemnity—'The mortal dwelling of my spirit is shattered, and lights and glimpses of hereafter are breaking in upon me. It has been ever so with all my mother's race. The gift is an ancient inheritance of our blood; but it comes not to us till earthly things begin to lose their hold on our affections. The sense of it is to me an assurance that the bark of life has borne me to the river's mouth. I shall now soon pass that headland, beyond which lies the open sea:—from the islands therein no one ever returns.'

Mr Eadie sighed; and all present regarded her with compassion, for her benign countenance was strangely pale; her brilliant eyes shone with a supernatural lustre; and there was a wild and incommunicable air in her look, mysteriously in unison with the oracular enthusiasm of her melancholy.

At this juncture a letter was handed in. It was the answer from Glengael to Mrs Eadie's application respecting Walkinshaw; and it had the effect of changing the painful tenor of the conversation. The contents were in the highest degree satisfactory. Mr Frazer not only promised his influence, declaring that he considered himself as the agent of the family interests, but said, that he had no doubt of procuring at once the cadetcy, stating, at the same time, that the progress and complexion of the French Revolution rendered it probable that Government would find it expedient to augment the army; in which case, a commission for young Walkinshaw would be readily obtained; and he concluded with expressions of his sorrow at hearing his kinswoman had of late been so unwell, urging her to visit him at Glengael Castle, to which the family was on the point of removing for the summer, and where her native air might, perhaps, essentially contribute to her recovery.

'Yes,' said she, after having read the letter aloud, and congratulated Walkinshaw on the prospect which had opened.— 'Yes; I will visit Glengael. The spirits of my fathers hover in the silence of those mountains, and dwell in the loneliness of the heath. A voice within has long told me, that my home is there, and I have been an exile since I left it.'

'My dear Gertrude,' said Mr Eadie,—'you distress me exceedingly this morning. To hear you say so pains me to the heart. It seems to imply that you have not been happy with me.'

'I was happy with you,' was her impressive answer. 'I was happy; but then I thought the hopes of my youth had perished.— The woeful discovery that rose like a ghost upon me withered my spirit; and the death of my children has since extinguished the love of life. Still, while the corporeal tenement remained in some degree entire, I felt not as I now feel; but the door is thrown open for my departure. I feel the airs of the world of spirits blowing in upon me; and as I look round to see if I have set my house in order, all the past of life appears in a thousand pictures; and the most vivid in the series are the sunny landscapes of my early years.'

Mr Eadie saw that it was in vain to reason with his wife in such a mood; and the Walkinshaws sympathised with the tenderness that dictated his forbearance, while James turned the conversation, by proposing to his sister and Ellen, that they should walk into Glasgow next day, to pay their respects to the young couple.

Doubtless there was a little waggery at the bottom of this proposition; but there was also something of a graver feeling.—He was desirous to ascertain what effect the marriage of Robina had produced on his uncle with respect to himself, and also to communicate, through the medium of his grandmother, the favourable result of the application to Glengael, in the hope, that, if there was any sincerity in the professions of partiality with which he had been flattered, that his uncle would assist him in his outfit either for India or the army. Accordingly, the walk was arranged as he proposed; but the roads in the morning were so deep and sloughy, that the ladies did not accompany him; a disappointment which, however acute it might be to him, was hailed as a God-send by the Leddy, whose troubles and vexations of spirit had, from the wedding-day, continued to increase, and still no hope of alleviation appeared.

CHAPTER X

'REALLY,' said the Leddy, after Walkinshaw had told her the news, and that only the wetness of the road had prevented his sister and Ellen from coming with him to town,—'Really, Jamie, to tell you the gude's truth, though I would hae been blithe to see Mary, and that weel-bred lassie, your joe[1] Nell Frizel—I'm very thankful they hae na come—for, unless I soon get some relief, I'll be herrit out o' house and hall wi' Beenie and Walky,—twa thoughtless wantons,—set them up wi' a clandestine marriage, in their teens! it's enough to put marriages out of fashion.'

'I thought,' replied Walkinshaw, playing with her humours, 'that the marriage was all your own doing.'

'My doing, Jamie Walkinshaw! wha daurs to say the like o' that? I'm as clear o't as the child unborn—to be sure they were married here, but that was no fault o' mine—my twa grandchildren, it could ne'er be expected that I would let them be married on the crown-o'-the-causey[2]—But, wasna baith his mother and father present, and is that no gospel evidence, that I was but an innocent on-looker?—No, no, Jamie, whomsoever ye hear giving me the wyte o' ony sic Gretna Green job,[1] I redde ye put your foot on the spark, and no let it singe my character.—I'm abundantly and overmuch punished already, for the harmless jocosity, in the cost and cumbering o' their keeping.'

'Well, but unless you had sanctioned their marriage, and approved o't beforehand, they would never have thought of taking up their residence with you.'

'Ye're no far wrang there, Jamie; I'll no deny that I gied my approbation, and I would hae done as muckle for your happiness, had ye been o' a right conforming spirit and married Beenie, by the whilk a' this hobbleshaw[2] would hae been spare't; but there's a awful difference between approving o' a match, and providing a living and house-room, bed, board, and washing, for two married persons—and so, although it may be said in a sense, that I had a finger in the pye, yet every body who kens me, kens vera weel that I would ne'er hae meddled wi' ony sic gunpowder plot, had there been the least likelihood that it would bring upon me sic a heavy handful. In short, nobody, Jamie, has been more imposed upon than I hae been—I'm the only sufferer. De'il-be-lickit[3] has it cost Dirdumwhamle, but an auld Muscovy duck, that he got sent him frae ane o' your uncle's Jamaica skippers[4] two year ago, and it was then past laying—we smoor't it wi' ingons[5] the day afore yesterday, but ye might as soon hae tried to mak a dinner o' a hesp o' seven heere yarn,[6] for it was as teugh[7] as the grannie of the cock that craw't to Peter.'

'But surely,' said Walkinshaw, affecting to condole with her, 'surely my uncle, when he has had time to cool, will come forward with something handsome.'

'Surely—Na, an he dinna do that, what's to become o' me?—Oh! Jamie, your uncle's no a man like your worthy grandfather,—he was a saint o' a Christian disposition—when your father married against both his will and mine, he did na gar the house dirl[8] wi' his stamp to the quaking foundation; but on the Lord's day thereafter, took me by the arm—O! he was o' a kindly nature—and we gaed o'er thegither, and wis'd[9] your father and mother joy, wi' a hunder pound in our hand—that was acting the parent's part!'

'But, notwithstanding all that kindness, you know he disinherited my father,' replied Walkinshaw seriously, 'and I am still suffering the consequences.'

'The best o' men, Jamie,' said the Leddy, sympathisingly, 'are no perfect, and your grandfather, I'll ne'er maintain, was na a no mere man[1]—so anent the disinheritance, there was ay something I could na weel understand; for, although I had got an inkling o' the law frae my father, who was a deacon[2] at a plea—as a' the Lords in Embro' could testificate, still there was a because in that act of sederunt and session, the whilk, in my opinion, required an inter-locutor frae the Lord Ordinary[3] to expiscate[4] and expone, and, no doubt, had your grandfather been spare't, there would hae been a rectification.—But, waes me, the Lord took him to himsel; in the very hour when Mr Keelevin, the lawyer, was doun on his knees reading a scantling[5] o' a new last will and settlement.—Eh! Jamie, that was a moving sight,   before I could get a pen, to put in your dying grandfather's hand, to sign the paper, he took his departal to a better world, where, we are taught to hope, there are neither lawyers nor laws.'

'But if my uncle will not make a settlement on Robina, what will you do?' said Walkinshaw, laughing.

'Haud your tongue, and dinna terrify folk wi' ony sic impossi-bility!' exclaimed the Leddy—'Poor man, he has something else to think o' at present. Is na your aunty brought nigh unto the gates o' death? Would ye expek him to be thinking o' marriage settle-ments and wedding banquets, when death's so busy in his dwell-ing? Ye're an unfeeling creature, Jamie—But the army's the best place for sic graceless getts,[6] Whan do ye begin to spend your half-crown out o' saxpence a-day? And is Nell Frizel to carry your knapsack? Weel, I ay thought she was a cannonading character, and I'll be none surprised o' her fighting the French or the Yanky Doodles belyve,[7] wi' a stone in the foot of a stocking, for I am most creditably informed, that that's the conduct o' the soldier's wives in the field o' battle.'

It was never very easy to follow the Leddy, when she was on what the sailors call one of her jawing tacks; and Walkinshaw, who always enjoyed her company most when she was in that humour, felt little disposed to interrupt her. In order, however, to set her off in a new direction, he said,—'But, when I get my appointment, I hope you'll give me something to buy a sword, which is the true bride o' a soldier.'

'And a poor tocher he gets wi' her,' said the Leddy;—'wounds and bruises, and putrefying sores, to make up a pack for beggary. No doubt, howsever, but I maun break the back o' a guinea for you.'

'Nay, I expect you'll give your old friend, Robin Carrick,[1] a forenoon's call. I'll not be satisfied if you don't.'

'Well, if e'er I heard sic a stand-and-deliver-like speech since ever I was born,'—exclaimed his grandmother. 'Did I think, when I used to send the impudent smytcher, wi' my haining[2] o' twa three pounds to the bank, that he was contriving to commit sic a highway robbery on me at last?'

'But,' said Walkinshaw, 'I have always heard you say, that there should be no stepbairns in families. Now, as you are so kind to Robina and Walky, it can never be held fair if you tie up your purse to me.'

'Thou's a wheedling creature, Jamie,' replied the Leddy, 'and nae doubt I maun do my duty, as every body knows I hae ay done, to a' my family; but I'll soon hae little to do't wi', if the twa new married eating moths are ordain't to devour a' my substance. But there's ae thing I'll do for thee, the whilk may be far better than making noughts in Robin Carrick's books. I'll gang out to the Kittlestonheugh, and speir for thy aunty;[3] and though thy uncle, like a bull of Bashan, said he would not speak to me, I'll gar him fin' the weight o' a mother's tongue, and maybe, through my persuadgeon, he may be wrought to pay for thy sword and pistols, and other sinews o' war. For, to speak the truth, I'm wearying to mak a clean breast wi' him, and to tell him o' his unnaturality to his own dochter; and what's far waur, the sin, sorrow, and iniquity, of allooing me, his aged parent, to be rookit o' plack and bawbee by twa glaikit jocklandys[4] that dinna care what they burn, e'en though it were themselves.'

But, before the Leddy got this laudable intention carried into effect, her daughter-in-law, to the infinite consternation of Dirdumwhamle, died; and, for some time after that event, no opportunity presented itself, either for her to be delivered of her grudge, or for any mutual friend to pave the way to a reconciliation. Young Mrs Milrookit saw her mother, and received her last blessing; but it was by stealth, and unknown to her father. So that, altogether, it would not have been easy, about the period of the funeral, to have named in all the royal city a more constipated family, as the Leddy assured all her acquaintance, the Walkinshaws and Milrookits, were baith in root and branch, herself being the wizent and forlorn trunk o' the tree.

CHAPTER XI

ON the day immediately after the funeral of her sister-in-law, Mrs Charles Walkinshaw was surprised by a visit from the widower.

'I am come,' said he, 'partly to relieve my mind from the weight that oppresses it, arising from an occurrence to which I need not more particularly allude, and partly to vindicate myself from the harsh insinuations of James. He will find that I have not been so sordid in my views as he so unaccountably and so unreasonably supposed, and that I am still disposed to act towards him in the same liberal spirit I have ever done. What is the result of the application to Mrs Eadie's friend? And is there any way by which I can be rendered useful in the business?'

This was said in an off-hand man-of-the-world way. It was perfectly explicit. It left no room for hesitation; but still it was not said in such a manner as to bring with it the comfort it might have done to the meek and sensitive bosom of the anxious mother.

'I know not in what terms to thank you,' was her answer, diffidently and doubtingly expressed. 'Your assistance certainly would be most essential to James, for, now that he has received a commission in the King's army,[1] I shall be reduced to much difficulty.'

'In the King's army! I thought he was going to India?' exclaimed her brother-in-law, evidently surprised.

'So it was originally intended; but,' said the mother, 'Mr Frazer thought, in the present state of Europe, that it would be of more advantage for him to take his chance in the regular army; and has in consequence obtained a commission in a regiment that is to be immediately increased. He has, indeed, proved a most valuable friend; for, as the recruiting is to be in the Highlands, he has invited James to Glengael, and is to afford him his countenance to recruit among his dependants, assuring Mrs Eadie that, from the attachment of the adherents of the family, he has no doubt that, in the course of the summer, James may be able to entitle himself to a Company, and then'——

This is very extraordinary friendship, thought the Glasgow merchant to himself. These Highlanders have curious ideas about friendship and kindred; but, nevertheless, when things are reduced to their money price, they are just like other people. 'But,' said he aloud, 'what do you mean is to take place when James has obtained a Company?'

'I suppose,' replied the gentle widow timidly, she knew not wherefore, 'that he will then not object to the marriage of James and Ellen.'

'I think,' said her brother-in-law, 'he ought to have gone to India. Were he still disposed to go there, my purse shall be open to him.'

'He could not hope for such rapid promotion as he may obtain through the means of Glengael,' replied Mrs Charles somewhat firmly; so steadily, indeed, that it disconcerted the Laird; still he preserved his external equanimity, and said,—

'Nevertheless, I am willing to assist his views in whichever way they lie. What has become of him?'

Mrs Charles then told him that, in consequence of the very encouraging letter from Mr Frazer, Walkinshaw had gone to mention to his father's old friend, who had the vessel fitting out for New York, the change that had taken place in his destination, and to solicit a loan to help his outfit.

Her brother-in-law bit his lips at this information. He had obtained no little reputation among his friends for the friendship which he had shown to his unfortunate brother's family; and all those who knew his wish to accomplish a match between James and his daughter, sympathised in sincerity with his disappointment. But something, it would not be easy to say what, troubled him when he heard this, and he said,—

'I think James carries his resentment too far. I had certainly done him no ill, and he might have applied to me before going to a stranger.'

'Favours,' replied the widow, 'owe all their grace and gratitude to the way in which they are conferred. James has peculiar notions, and perhaps he has felt more from the manner in which you spoke to him than from the matter you said.'

'Let us not revert to that subject—it recals[1] mortifying reflections, and the event cannot be undone. But do you then think Mr Frazer will consent to allow his daughter to marry James? She is an uncommonly fine girl, and, considering the family connections, surely might do better.'

This was said in an easy disengaged style, but it was more

assumed than sincere; indeed, there was something in it implying
an estimate of considerations, independent of affections, which
struck so disagreeably on the feelings, that his delicate auditor did
not very well know what to say; but she added,—

'James intends, as soon as we are able to make the necessary
arrangements, to set out for Glengael Castle, which, being in a
neighbourhood where there are many old officers, he will be able
to procure some information with respect to the best mode of
proceeding with his recruiting; and Mr Frazer has kindly said that
it will be for his advantage to start from the castle.'

'I suppose Miss Frazer will accompany him?' replied the
widower drily.

'No,' said his sister-in-law, 'she does not go till she accompanies
Mrs Eadie, who intends to pass the summer at Glengael.'

'I am glad of that; her presence might interfere with his duty.'

'Whom do you mean?' inquired Mrs Charles, surprised at the
remark; 'whose presence?' and she subjoined smilingly, 'You are
thinking of Ellen; and you will hardly guess that we are all of
opinion here that both she and Mrs Eadie might be of great use to
him on the spot. Mrs Eadie is so persuaded of it, that the very
circumstance of their marriage being dependent on his raising a
sufficient number of men to entitle him to a company, would, she
says, were it known, make the sons of her father's clansmen flock
around him.'

'It is to be deplored, that a woman, who still retains so many
claims, both on her own account, and the high respectability of
her birth, should have fallen into such a decay of mind,' said the
merchant, at a loss for a more appropriate comment on his sister-
in-law's intimation.— 'But,' continued he, 'do not let James apply
to any other person. I am ready and willing to advance all he may
require; and, since it is determined that he ought immediately
to avail himself of Mr Frazer's invitation, let him lose no time in
setting off for Glengael. This, I trust,' said he in a gayer humour,
which but ill suited with his deep mourning, 'will assure both him
and Miss Frazer, that I am not so much their enemy as perhaps
they have been led to imagine.'

Soon after this promise the widower took his leave; but, although his whole behaviour during the visit was unexpectedly
kind and considerate, and although it was impossible to withhold
the epithet of liberality—nay more, even of generosity—from his

offer, still it did not carry that gladness to the widow's heart which the words and the assurance were calculated to convey. On the contrary, Mrs Charles sat for some time ruminating on what had passed; and when, in the course of about an hour after, Ellen Frazer, who had been walking on the brow of the hazel bank with Mary, came into the parlour, she looked at her for some time without speaking.

The walk had lent to the complexion of Ellen a lively rosy glow. The conversation which she had held with her companion related to her lover's hopes of renown, and it had excited emotions that at once sparkled in her eyes and fluctuated on her cheek. Her lips were vivid and smiling; her look was full of intelligence and naivéte—simple at once and elegant—gay, buoyant, and almost as sly as artless, and a wreath, if the expression may be allowed, of those nameless graces in which the charms of beauty are mingled with the allurements of air and manners, garlanded her tall and blooming form.

She seemed to the mother of her lover a creature so adorned with loveliness and nobility, that it was impossible to imagine she was not destined for some higher sphere than the humble fortunes of Walkinshaw. But in that moment the mother herself forgot the auspices of her own youth, and how seldom it is that even beauty, the most palpable of all human excellence, obtains its proper place, or the homage of the manly heart that Nature meant it should enjoy.

CHAPTER XII

MR WALKINSHAW had not left Camrachle many minutes when his nephew appeared. James had in fact returned from Glasgow, while his uncle was in the house, but, seeing the carriage at the door, he purposely kept out of the way till it drove off.

His excursion had not been successful. He found his father's old acquaintance sufficiently cordial in the way of inquiries, and even disposed to sympathise with him, when informed of his determination to go abroad; but when the army was mentioned the merchant's heart froze; and after a short pause, and the expression of some frigiverous observations with respect to the licentiousness of the military life, it was suggested that his uncle was the proper quarter to apply to. In this crisis, their conversation was interrupted by the entrance of a third party, when Walkinshaw retired.

During his walk back to Camrachle, his heart was alternately sick and saucy, depressed and proud.

He could not conceive how he had been so deluded, as to suppose that he had any right to expect friendship from the gentleman he had applied to. He felt that in so doing he acted with the greenness of a boy, and he was mortified at his own softness. Had there been any reciprocity of obligations between his father and the gentleman, the case would have been different. 'Had they been for forty or fifty years,' thought he, 'in the mutual interchange of mercantile dependance, then perhaps I might have had some claim, and, no doubt, it would have been answered, but I was a fool to mistake civilities for friendship.' Perhaps, however, had the case been even as strong as he put it, he might still have found himself quite as much deceived.

'As to making any appeal to my uncle, that was none of his business,' said he to himself. 'I did not ask the fellow for advice, I solicited but a small favour. There is no such heart-scalding insolence as in refusing a solicitation, to refer the suppliant to others, and with prudential admonitions too—curse him who would beg, were it not to avoid doing worse.'

This brave humour lasted for the length of more than a mile's walk, during which the young soldier marched briskly along, whistling courageous tunes, and flourishing his stick with all the cuts of the broadsword, lopping the boughs of the hedges, as if they had been the limbs of Frenchmen, and switching away the heads of the thistles and benweeds in his path, as if they had been Parisian carmagnols,[1] against whom, at that period, the loyalty of the British bosom was beginning to grow fretful and testy.

But the greater part of the next mile was less animated—occasionally, cowardly thoughts glimmered paly through the glorious turbulence of youthful heroism, and once or twice he paused and looked back towards Glasgow, wondering if there was any other in all that great city, who might be disposed to lend him the hundred pounds he had begged for his outfit.

'There is not one,' said he, and he sighed, but in a moment after he exclaimed, 'and who the devil cares? It does not do for soldiers to think much; let them do their duty at the moment; that's all they have to think of; I will go on in the track I have chosen, and trust to fortune for a windfall;' again 'In the Garb of Old Gaul'[1] was gallantly whistled, and again the hedges and thistles felt the weight of his stick.

But as he approached Camrachle, his mood shifted into the minor key, and when the hazel-bank and the ash-trees, with the nests of the magpies in them, appeared in sight, the sonorous bravery of the Highland march became gradually modulated into a low and querulous version of 'Lochaber no more,'[2] and when he discovered the carriage at his mother's door, his valour so subsided into boyish bashfulness, that he shrunk away, as we have already mentioned, and did not venture to go home, till he saw that his uncle had left the house.

On his entrance, however, he received a slight sensation of pleasure, at seeing both his mother and sister with more comfort in their looks than he had expected, and he was, in consequence, able to tell them, with comparative indifference, the failure of his mission. His mother then related what had passed with his uncle.

The news perplexed Walkinshaw; they contradicted the opinion he had so warmly felt and expressed of his uncle; they made him feel he had acted rashly and ungratefully—but still such strange kindness occasioned a degree of dubiety, which lessened the self-reproaches of his contrition.

'However,' said he, with a light and joyous heart, 'I shall not again trouble either myself or him, as I have done; but in this instance, at least, he has acted disinterestedly, and I shall cheerfully avail myself of his offer, because it is generous—I accept it also as encouragement—after my disappointment, it is a happy omen; I will take it as a brave fellow does his bounty-money—a pledge from Fortune of some famous "all hail hereafter." '[3]

What his sentiments would have been, had he known the tenor of his uncle's mind at that moment,—could he even but have suspected that the motive which dictated such seeming generosity, so like an honourable continuance of his former partiality, was prompted by a wish to remove him as soon as possible from the company of Ellen Frazer, in order to supplant him in her affections, we need not attempt to imagine how he would have felt. It is happy for mankind, that they know so little of the ill said of them behind their backs, by one another, and of the evil that is often meditated in satire and in malice, and still oftener undertaken

from motives of interest and envy. Walkinshaw rejoicing in the
good fortune that had so soon restored the alacrity of his spirits—
so soon wiped away the corrosive damp of disappointment from
its brightness—did not remain long with his mother and sister,
but hastened to communicate the inspiring tidings to Ellen Frazer.

She was standing on the green in front of the manse, when she
saw him coming bounding towards her, waving his hat in triumph
and exultation, and she put on a grave face, and looked so rebuk-
ingly, that he halted abruptly, and said—'What's the matter?'

'It's very ridiculous to see any body behaving so absurdly,' was
her cool and solemn answer.

'But I have glorious news to tell you; my uncle has come forward in the handsomest manner, and all's clear for action.'

This was said in an animated manner, and intended to upset her
gravity, which, from his knowledge of her disposition, he suspected, was a sinless hypocrisy, put on only to teaze him. But she
was either serious or more resolute in her purpose than he expected;
for she replied with the most chastising coolness,—

'I thought you were never to have any thing to say again to
your uncle?'

Walkinshaw felt this pierce deeper than it was intended to do,
and he reddened exceedingly, as he said, awkwardly.

'True! but I have done him injustice; and had he not been one
of the best dispositioned men, he would never have continued his
kindness to me as he has done; for I treated him harshly.'

'It says but little for you, that, after enjoying his good-will so
long, you should have thrown his favours at him, and so soon after
be obliged to confess you have done him wrong.'

Walkinshaw hung his head, still more and more confused. There
was too much truth in the remark not to be felt as a just reproach;
and, moreover, he thought it somewhat hard, as his folly had been
on her account, that she should so taunt him. But Ellen, perceiving
she had carried the joke a little too far, threw off her disguise, and,
with one of her most captivating looks and smiles, said,—'Now,
that I have tamed you into rational sobriety, let's hear what you
have got to say. Men should never be spoken to when they are
huzzaing. Remember the lesson when you are with your regiment.'

What further followed befits not our desultory pen to rehearse;
but, during this recital of what had taken place at Glasgow, and
the other incidents of the day, the lovers unconsciously strayed into

the minister's garden, where a most touching and beautiful
dialogue ensued, of which having lost our notes, we regret, on
account of our fair readers, and all his Majesty's subalterns, who
have not yet joined, that we cannot furnish a transcript.—The
result, however, was, that, when Ellen returned into the manse,
after parting from Walkinshaw, her beautiful eyes looked red and
watery, and two huge tears tumbled out of them, when she told her
aunt that he intended to set off for Glengael in the course of two
or three days.

CHAPTER XIII

NEXT day Walkinshaw found himself constrained, by many
motives, to go into Glasgow, in order to thank his uncle for the
liberality of his offer, and, in accepting it, to ask pardon for the
rudeness of his behaviour.

His reception in the counting-house was all he could have
wished; it was even more cordial than the occasion required, and
the cheque given, as the realization of the promise, considerably
exceeded the necessary amount. Emboldened by so much kindness, Walkinshaw, who felt for his cousins, and really sympathised
with the Leddy under the burden of expence which she had
brought upon herself, ventured to intercede in their behalf, and
he was gratified with his uncle's answer.

'I am pleased, James,' said he, 'that you take so great an interest
in them; but, make your mind easy, for, although I have been
shamefully used, and cannot but long resent it, still, as a man, I
ought not to indulge my anger too far. I, therefore, give you
liberty to go and tell them, that, although I do not mean to hold
any intercourse with Robina and her husband, I have, nevertheless,
ordered my man of business[1] to prepare a deed of settlement on
her, such as I ought to make on my daughter.'

Walkinshaw believed, when he heard this, that he possessed no
faculty whatever to penetrate the depths of character, so bright
and shining did all the virtues of his uncle at that moment appear;
—virtues of which, a month before, he did not conceive he possessed a single spark. It may, therefore, be easily imagined, that he
hastened with light steps and long strides towards his grandmother's

house, to communicate the generous tidings. But, on reaching the door, he met the old lady, wrapped up, as it seemed, for a journey, with her maid, coming out, carrying a small trunk under her arm. On seeing him, she made a movement to return; but, suddenly recollecting herself, she said,—'Jamie, I hae nae time, for I'm gaun to catch the Greenock flying coach at the Black Bull,[1] and ye can come wi' me.'

'But, what has become o' Robina?' cried he, surprised at this intelligence and sudden movement.

His grandmother took hold of him by the arm, and giving it an indescribable squeeze of exultation, said,—'I'll tell you, it's just a sport. They would need long spoons that sup parridge wi' the de'il, or the like o' me, ye maun ken. I was just like to be devour't into beggary by them. Ae frien' after another calling, glasses o' wine ne'er devauling;[2] the corks playing clunk in the kitchen frae morning to night, as if they had been in a change-house[3] on a fair-day. I could stand it no longer. So yesterday, when that nabal,[4] Dirdumwhamle, sent us a pair o' his hunger't hens, I told baith Beenie and Walky, that they were obligated to go and thank their parents, and to pay them a marriage visit for a day or twa, although we're a' in black for your aunty, her mother; and so this morning I got them off, Lord be praised; and I am noo on my way to pay a visit to Miss Jenny Purdie, my cousin, at Greenock.'

'Goodness! and is this to throw poor Beenie and Walky adrift?' exclaimed Walkinshaw.

'Charity, Jamie, my bairn, begins at hame, and they hae a nearer claim on Dirdumwhamle, who is Walky's lawful father, than on me; so e'en let them live upon him till I invite them back again.'

Walkinshaw, though really shocked, he could not tell why, was yet so tickled by the Leddy's adroitness, that he laughed most immoderately, and was unable for some time in consequence to communicate the message, of which he was the joyous bearer; but when he told her, she exclaimed,—

'Na, if that's the turn things hae ta'en, I'll defer my visit to Miss Jenny for the present; so we'll return back. For surely, baith Beenie and Walky will no be destitute of a' consideration when they come to their kingdom, for the dreadfu' cost and outlay that I hae been at the last five weeks. But, if they're guilty o' sic niggerality,[5] I'll mak out a count—bed, board, and washing, at five and twenty

shillings a-week, Mrs Scrimpit, the minister's widow of Toomgarnels,[1] tells me, would be a charge o' great moderation;—and
if they pay't, as pay't they shall, or I'll hae them for an affront to
the Clerk's Chambers;[2] ye's get the whole half o't, Jamie, to buy
yoursel a braw Andrew Ferrara.[3] But I marvel, wi' an exceeding
great joy, at this cast o' grace that's come on your uncle. For, frae
the hour he saw the light, he was o' a most voracious nature for
himsel; and while the fit lasts, I hope ye'll get him to do something
for you.'

Walkinshaw then told her not only what his uncle had done,
but with the ardour in which the free heart of youth delights to
speak of favours, he recapitulated all the kind and friendly things
that had been said to him.

'Jamie, Jamie, I ken your uncle Geordie better than you,—for
I hae been his mother. It's no for a courtesy o' causey clash that he's
birling his mouldy pennies in sic firlots;[4]—tak my word for't.'

'There is no possible advantage can arise to him from his kindness to me.'

'That's to say, my bairn, that ye hae na a discerning spirit[5] to
see't; but if ye had the second sight o' experience as I hae, ye
would fin' a whaup[6] in the nest, or I am no a Christian sister,
bapteesed Girzel.'

By this time they had returned to the house, and the maid having
unlocked the door, and carried in the trunk, Walkinshaw followed
his grandmother into the parlour, with the view of enjoying what
she herself called, the observes of her phlosification; but the moment
she had taken her seat, instead of resuming the wonted strain of
her jocular garrulity, she began to sigh deeply, and weep bitterly,
a thing which he never saw her do before, but in a way that seldom
failed to amuse him; on this occasion, however, her emotion was
unaffected, and it moved him to pity her. 'What's the matter with
you?' said he, kindly;—she did not, however, make any answer for
some time, but at last she said,—

'Thou's gaun awa to face thy faes,—as the sang sings, "far far
frae me and Logan braes,"[7]—and I am an aged person, and may
ne'er see thee again; and I am wae to let thee gang, for though thou
was ay o' a nature that had nae right reverence for me, a deevil's
buckie, my heart has ay warm't to thee mair than to a' the lave[8]
o' my grandchildren; but it's no in my power to do for thee as thy
uncle has done, though it's well known to every one that kens me,

that I hae a most generous heart,—far mair than e'er he had,—and I would na part wi' thee without hanselling thy knapsack.[1] Hegh, Sirs! little did I think whan the pawkie[2] laddie spoke o' my bit gathering wi' Robin Carrick, that it was in a sincerity; but thou's get a part. I'll no let thee gang without a solid benison, so tak the key, and gang into the scrutoire and bring out the pocket-book.'

Walkinshaw was petrified, but did as he was desired; and, having given her the pocket-book, sewed by his aunt, Mrs Milrookit, at the boarding-school, she took several of Robin's promissory-notes out, and looking them over, presented him with one for fifty pounds.

'Now, Jamie Walkinshaw,' said she, 'if ye spend ae plack o' that like a prodigal son,—it's no to seek what I will say whan ye come back,—but I doot I doot, lang before that day I'll be deep and dumb aneath the yird,[3] and naither to see nor hear o' thy weel or thy woe.'

So extraordinary and unlooked-for an instance of liberality on the part of his grandmother, together with the unfeigned feeling by which she was actuated, quite overwhelmed Walkinshaw, and he stood holding the bill in his hand, unable to speak. In the meantime, she was putting up her other bills, and, in turning them over, seeing one for forty-nine pounds, she said, 'Jamie, forty-nine pounds is a' the same as fifty to ane that pays his debts by the roll of a drum, so tak this, and gie me that back.'

CHAPTER XIV

THE time between the visit to Glasgow and the departure of Walkinshaw for Glengael was the busiest period that had occurred in the annals of Camrachle from the placing of Mr Eadie in the cure of the parish. To the young men belonging to the hamlet, who had grown up with Walkinshaw, it was an era of great importance; and some of them doubted whether he ought not to have beaten up for recruits in a neighbourhood where he was known rather than in the Highlands. But the elder personages, particularly the matrons, were thankful that the Lord was pleased to order it differently.

His mother and sister, with the assistance of Ellen Frazer, were more thriftily engaged in getting his baggage ready; and although the sprightliness of Ellen never sparkled more brilliantly for the amusement of her friends, there were moments when her bosom echoed in a low soft murmur to the sigh of anxiety that frequently burst from his mother's breast.

Mr Eadie was not the least interested in the village. He seemed as if he could not give his pupil advice enough, and Walkinshaw thought he had never before been so tiresome. They took long walks together, and ever and anon the burden of the worthy minister's admonition was the sins and deceptions of the world, and the moral perils of a military life.

But no one—neither tutor, mother, nor amorosa—appeared so profoundly occupied with the event as Mrs Eadie, whose majestic intellect was evidently touched with the fine frenzy of a superstition at once awful and elevated. She had dreams of the most cheering augury, though all the incidents were wild and funereal; and she interpreted the voices of the birds and the chattering of the magpies in language more oriental and coherent than Macpherson's Ossian.[1]

The moon had changed on the day on which Walkinshaw went into Glasgow, and she watched the appearance of its silver rim with the most mysterious solicitude. Soon after sun-set on the third evening, as she was sitting on a tombstone in the church-yard with Mr Eadie, she discovered it in the most favourable aspect of the Heavens, and in the very position which assured the most fortunate issues to all undertakings commenced at its change.

'So it appears,' said she, 'like a boat, and it is laden with the old moon—that betokens a storm.'

'But when?' said her husband with a sigh, mournfully disposed to humour the aberrations of her fancy.

'The power is not yet given to me to tell,' was her solemn response. 'But the sign is a witness that the winds of the skies shall perform some dreadful agency in the fortunes of all enterprises ruled by this lunar influence. Had the moon been first seen but as a portion of a broken ring, I would have veiled my face, and deplored the omen. She comes forth, however, in her brightness— a silver boat sailing the azure depths of the Heavens, and bearing a rich lading of destiny to the glorious portals of the sun.'

At that moment a cow looked over the churchyard wall, and

lowed so close to Mr Eadie's ear, that it made him start and laugh. Instead, however, of disturbing the Pythian[1] mood of his lady, it only served to deepen it; but she said nothing, though her look intimated that she was offended by his levity.

After a pause of several minutes she rose, and moved towards the gate without accepting his proffered arm.

'I am sorry,' said he, 'that you are displeased with me; but really the bathos of that cow was quite irresistible.'

'Do you think,' was her mystical reply, 'that an animal, which, for good reasons, the wise Egyptians hardly erred in worshipping, made to us but an inarticulate noise? It was to me a prophetic salutation. On the morning before my father left Glengaol to join the royal standard, I heard the same sound. An ancient woman, my mother's nurse, and one of her own blood, told me that it was a fatal enunciation for then the moon was in the wane; but heard, she said, when the new moon is first seen, it is the hail of a victory or a bridal.'

'It is strange,' replied the minister, unguardedly attempting to reason with her, 'that the knowledge of these sort of occurrences should be almost exclusively confined to the inhabitants of the Highlands.'

'It is strange,' said she; 'but no one can expound the cause. The streamers of the northern light shine not in southern skies.'

At that moment she shuddered, and, grasping the minister wildly by the arm, she seemed to follow some object with her eye that was moving past them.

'What's the matter—what do you look at?' he exclaimed with anxiety and alarm.

'I thought it was Walkinshaw's uncle,' said she with a profound and heavy sigh, as if her very spirit was respiring from a trance.

'It was nobody,' replied the minister thoughtfully.

'It was his wraith,' said Mrs Eadie.

The tone in which this was expressed curdled his very blood, and he was obliged to own to himself, in despite of the convictions of his understanding, that there are more things in the heavens and the earth than philosophy can yet explain; and he repeated the quotation from Hamlet, partly to remove the impression which his levity had made.

'I am glad to hear you allow so much,' rejoined Mrs Eadie; 'and I think you must admit that of late I have given you many proofs in confirmation. Did I not tell you when the cock crowed on the roof of our friend's cottage, that we should soon hear of some cheerful change in the lot of the inmates? and next day came Walkinshaw from Glasgow with the news of the happy separation from his uncle. On the evening before I received my letter from Glengael, you may well remember the glittering star that announced it in the candle. As sure as the omen in the crowing of the cock, and the shining of that star, were fulfilled, will the auguries which I have noted be found the harbingers of events.'

Distressing as these shadows and gleams of lunacy were to those by whom Mrs Eadie was justly beloved and venerated, to herself they afforded a high and holy delight. Her mind, during the time the passion lasted, was to others obscure and oracular. It might be compared to the moon in the misty air when she is surrounded with a halo, and her light loses its silveryness, and invests the landscape with a shroudy paleness and solemnity. But Mrs Eadie felt herself as it were ensphered in the region of spirits, and moving amidst marvels and mysteries sublimer than the faculties of ordinary mortals could explore.

The minister conducted his wife to the house of Walkinshaw's mother, where she went to communicate the agreeable intelligence, as she thought, of the favourable aspect of the moon, as it had appeared to her Highland astrology.[1] But he was so distressed by the evident increase of her malady, that he did not himself immediately go in. Indeed, it was impossible for him not to acknowledge, even to the most delicate suggestions of his own mind towards her, that she was daily becoming more and more fascinated by her visionary contemplations; and in consequence, after taking two or three turns in the village, he determined to advise her to go with Walkinshaw to Glengael, in the hope that the change of circumstances, and the interest that she might take once more in the scenes of her youth, would draw her mind from its wild and wonderful imaginings, and fix her attention again on objects calculated to inspire more sober, but not less affecting, feelings.

CHAPTER XV

THE result of Mr Eadie's reflections was a proposition to Walkinshaw to delay his journey for a day or two, until Mrs Eadie could be prepared to accompany him; but, when the subject was mentioned to her, she declared the most decided determination not to trouble the tide of his fortune by any interposition of hers which had been full of disappointments and sorrows. From whatever sentiment this feeling arose, it was undoubtedly dictated by magnanimity; for it implied a sense of sacrifice on her part, nevertheless, it was arranged, that, although Walkinshaw should set out at the time originally fixed, Mrs Eadie, accompanied by Ellen Frazer, should follow him to Glengael as soon after as possible.

To the lovers this was no doubt delightful; but, when the Laird of Kittlestonheugh heard of it in Glasgow, it disturbed him exceedingly. The departure of Ellen Frazer from Camrachle to Glengael, where his nephew was for a time to fix his headquarters, was an occurrence that he had not contemplated, and still less, if any degree can exist in an absolute negative, that the minister's insane wife should accompany her.

A circumstance, however, occurred at the time,[1] which tended materially to diminish his anxieties: A number of gentlemen belonging to the royal city had projected a sea excursion in Allan M'Lean's pilot boat, and one of the party proposed to Kittlestonheugh that he should be of their party—for they were all friends, and sympathised, of course, with the most heartfelt commiseration, for the loss he had sustained in his wife, who had been nearly twenty years almost as much dead as alive, and particularly in the grief he suffered by the injudicious marriage of his daughter. George, with his habitual suavity, accepted the invitation; and on the selfsame day that our friend and personal acquaintance Walkinshaw set off in the coach from the classical and manufacturing town (as we believe Gibbon the historian yclyped the royal city) for the soi-disant intellectual metropolis and modern Athens of Edinburgh, his uncle embarked at the stair of the west quay of Greenock.

What stores were laid in by those Glasgow Argonautics—what

baskets of limes, what hampers of wine and rum, and loaves of sugar, and cheese and bacon hams, with a modicum of biscuit, we must leave for some more circumstantial historian to describe. Sufficient for us, and for all acquainted with the munificent consideration of the Glottiani[1] for themselves, is the fact, that seven of the primest magnates of the royal city embarked together to enjoy the sea air, and the appetite consequent thereon, in one of the best sailing and best navigated schooners at that time on the west of Scotland. Whether any of them, in the course of the voyage, suffered the affliction of sea-sickness, we have never heard; but from our own opinion, believing the thing probable, we shall not enter into any controversy on the subject. There was, to be sure, some rumour shortly after, that, off Ailsa, they did suffer from one kind of malady or another; but whether from eating of that delicious encourager of appetite, solan goose—the most savoury product of the rocky pyramid—or from a stomatique inability to withstand the tossings of the sea, we have never received any satisfactory explanation. Be this, however, as it may, no jovial free-hearted, good kind of men, ever enjoyed themselves better than the party aboard the pilot boat.

They traversed the picturesque Kyles of Bute—coasted the shores of Cantyre—touched at the beautiful port of Campbelton—doubled the cliffy promontory—passed Gigha—left Isla on the left—navigated the sound of Jura—prudently kept along the romantic coast of Lorn and Appin—sailed through the sound of Mull—drank whisky at Rum—and, afraid of the beds and bowls of the hospitable Skye, cast anchor in Gareloch. What more they did, and where they farther navigated the iron shores and tusky rocks of the headlands, that grin in unsatiated hunger upon the waves and restless waters of the Minch, we shall not here pause to describe. Let it be enough that they were courageously resolved to double Cape Wrath, and to enjoy the midnight twilights, and the smuggled gin of Kirkwall;—the aurora borealis of the hyperborean region, with the fresh ling of Tamy Tomson's cobble boat at Hoy, and the silvery glimpses of Ursa Major; together with the tasty whilks and lampets that Widow Calder o' the Foul Anchor at Stromness, assured her customers in all her English—were pickled to a concupiscable state of excellence. Our immediate duty is to follow the steps of the Laird's nephew; and without entering upon any unnecessary details,—our readers, we trust, have remarked,

that we entertain a most commendable abhorrence of all circum-
stantiality,—we shall allow Allan M'Lean and his passengers to
go where it pleased themselves, while we return to Camrachle; not
that we have much more to say respecting what passed there, than
that Walkinshaw, as had been previously arranged, set out alone
for Glengael Castle, in Inverness-shire; the parting from his
mother and sister being considerably alleviated by the reflection,
that Ellen Frazer, in attendance on Mrs Eadie, was soon to follow
him. Why this should have given him any particular pleasure, we
cannot understand; but, as the young man, to speak prosaically,
was in love, possibly there are some juvenile persons capable of
entering into his feelings. Not, however, knowing, of our own
knowledge, what is meant by the phrase—we must just thus simply
advert to the fact; expressing, at the same time, a most philosophical curiosity to be informed what it means, and why it is that
young gentlemen and ladies, in their teens, should be more liable
to the calamity than personages of greater erudition in the practices
of the world.

CHAPTER XVI

IN the summer of the year 1793, we have some reason to believe
that the rugging and riving times of antiquity were so well over in
the north of Scotland, that, not only might any one of his Majesty's
subalterns travel there on the recruiting service, but even any
spinster, not less than threescore, without let, hindrance, or
molestation, to say nothing of personal violence; we shall not,
therefore, attempt to seduce the tears of our fair readers, with a
sentimental description of the incidents which befell our friend
Walkinshaw, in his journey from Camrachle to Glengael, except
to mention, in a parenthetical way, that, when he alighted from the
Edinburgh coach at the canny twa and twae toun of Aberdeenawa,[1]
he had some doubt if the inhabitants spoke any Christian language.

Having remained there a night and part of a day, to see the place,
and to make an arrangement with the host of an hostel, for a man
and gig, to take him to Glengael Castle, he turned his face towards
the north-west, and soon entered, what to him appeared, a new
region. Mrs Eadie had supplied him with introductory letters to

all her kith and kin, along the line of his route, and the recommenda-
tions of the daughter of the old Glengael were billets on the
hospitality and kindness of the country. They were even received
as the greatest favours by those who knew her least, so cherished
and so honoured was the memory of the ill-fated chieftain, among
the descendants of that brave and hardy race, who suffered in the
desolation of the clans at Culloden.

The appearance and the natural joyous spirits of Walkinshaw
endeared him to the families at the houses where he stopped on
his way to Glengael, and his journey was, in consequence, longer
and happier than he expected. On the afternoon of the ninth day
after leaving Aberdeen, he arrived at the entrance of the rugged
valley, in which the residence of Mr Frazer was situated.

During the morning, he had travelled along the foot of the
mountains and patches of cultivation, and here and there small
knots of larches, recently planted, served to vary the prospect and
enliven his journey; but as he approached the entrance to Glengael,
these marks of civilization and improvement gradually became
rarer. When he entered on the land that had been forfeited, they
entirely disappeared, for the green spots that chequered the heath
there were as the graves of a race that had been rooted out or
slaughtered. They consisted of the scites[1] of cottages, which the
soldiers of the Duke of Cumberland's army had plundered and
burnt in the year Forty-five.

The reflections which these monuments of fidelity awakened in
the breast of the young soldier, as the guide explained to him what
they were, saddened his spirit, and the scene which opened, when
he entered the cliffy pass that led into Glengael, darkened it more
and more. It seemed to him as if he was quitting the habitable
world, and passing into the realms, not merely of desolation, but
of silence and herbless sterility. A few tufts of heath and fern
among the rocks, in the bottom of the glen, showed that it was not
absolutely the valley of death.

The appearance of the lowering steeps, that hung their loose
crags over the road, was as if some elder mountains had been
crushed into fragments, and the wreck thrown in torrents, to fill
up that dreary, soundless, desolate solitude, where nature appeared
a famished skeleton, pining amidst poverty and horror.

But, after travelling for two or three miles through this inter-
dicted chasm, the cliffs began to recede, and on turning a lofty

projecting rock, his ears were gladdened with the sound of a small
torrent that was leaping in a hundred cascades down a ravine
fringed with birch and hazel. From that point verdure began to
reappear, and as the stream in its course was increased by other
mountain rivulets, the scenery of the glen gradually assumed a
more refreshing aspect. The rocks became again shaggy with intermingled heath and brambles, and the stately crimson foxglove, in
full blossom, rose so thickly along the sides of the mountains, that
Walkinshaw, unconscious that it was from the effect of their
appearance, began to dream in his reverie of guarded passes, and
bloody battles, and picquets of red-coated soldiers bivouacking on
the hills.

But his attention was soon roused from these heroical imaginings
by a sudden turn of the road, laying open before him the glassy
expanse of an extensive lake, and on the summit of a lofty rocky
peninsula, which projected far into its bosom, the walls and turrets
of Glengael.

From the desolate contrast of the pass he had travelled, it seemed
to him that he had never beheld a landscape so romantic and
beautiful. The mountains, from the margin of the water, were
green to their summits, and a few oaks and firs around the castle
enriched the picturesque appearance of the little promontory on
which it stood. Beyond a distant vista of the dark hills of Ross, the
sun had retired, but the clouds, in glorious masses of golden fires,
rose in a prodigality of splendid forms, in which the military
imagination of the young enthusiast had no difficulty in discovering the towers, and domes, and pinnacles of some airy Babylon,
with burnished chariots on the walls, and brazen warriors in
clusters on the battlements.

This poetical enchantment, however, was soon dissolved. The
road along the skirt of the lake, as it approached the castle, was
rugged and steep, and where it turned off into the peninsula,
towards the gate, it literally lay on the cornice of a precipice, which,
with all his valour, made Walkinshaw more than once inclined to
leap from the gig. Here and there a fragment of an old wall showed
that it had once been fenced, and where the rains had scooped
hollows on the edge of the cliff, a few stakes had recently been put
up; but there was an air of decay and negligence around, that prepared the mind of the visitor for the ruinous aspect of the castle.

Mr Frazer, owing to his professional avocations, had seldom

resided there, and he was too ambitious to raise the means to redeem the bonds he had granted for the purchase, to lay any thing out in improvements. The state and appearance of the place was, in consequence, lone and dismal. Not only were the outer walls mantled with ivy, but the arch of the gateway was broken. Many of the windows in the principal edifice were rudely filled up with stones. The slates in several places had fallen from the extinguisher-less[1] desolate roofed turrets, and patches of new lime on different places of the habitable buildings, bore testimony to the stinted funds which the proprietor allowed for repairs.

Within the gate the scene was somewhat more alluring. The space inclosed by the walls had been converted into a garden, which Mrs Frazer and her daughters superintended, and had ornamented with evergreens and flowers. The apartments of the family were also neatly repaired, and showed, in the midst of an evident parsimony, a degree of taste that bespoke a favourable opinion of the inhabitants, which the reception given to Walkinshaw confirmed.

Mr Frazer, an elderly gentleman, of an acute and penetrating look, met him at the door, and, heartily shaking him by the hand, led him into a parlour, where Mrs Frazer, with two daughters, the sisters of Ellen, were sitting. The young ladies and their mother received him even with more frankness than the advocate. It was, indeed, not difficult to perceive, that they had previously formed an agreeable opinion of him, which they were pleased to find his prepossessing appearance confirm. But after the first congratulatory greetings were over, a slight cloud was cast on the spirits of the family by his account of the health of their relation Mrs Eadie. It, however, was not of very long duration, for the intelligence that she might be daily expected with Ellen soon chased it away.

CHAPTER XVII

As Mr Eadie found he could not conveniently get away from his parish, and the health of his lady requiring that she should travel by easy stages, it was arranged, after Walkinshaw's departure, that his sister should take the spare corner of the carriage. Accordingly, on the day following his arrival at Glengael, they all made their appearance at the castle.

Mrs Eadie's malady had, in the meantime, undergone no change. On the contrary, she was become more constantly mystical, and the mournful feelings, awakened by the sight of her early home, desolated by time and the ravages of war, rather served to increase her superstitious reveries. Every feature of the landscape recalled some ancient domestic tradition; and as often as she alluded to the ghostly stories that were blended with her ancestral tales, she expatiated in the loftiest and wildest flights of seeming inspiration and prophecy.

But still she enjoyed lucid intervals of a serene and tender melancholy. On one occasion, while she was thus walking with the young ladies in the environs of the castle, she stopped abruptly, and, looking suddenly around, burst into tears.

'It was here,' said she—'on this spot, that the blossoms of my early hopes fell, and were scattered for ever.'

At that moment, a gentleman, some ten or twelve years older than Walkinshaw, dressed in the Highland garb, was seen coming towards the castle, and the majestic invalid uttered a terrific shriek, and fainted in the arms of her companions. The stranger, on hearing the scream, and seeing her fall, ran to the assistance of the ladies.

When Mrs Eadie was so far recovered as to be able to look up, the stranger happened to be standing behind Ellen, on whose lap her head was laid, and, not seeing him, she lay, for some time after the entire restoration of her faculties, in a state of profound solemnity and sorrow. 'O Frazer!' she exclaimed pathetically.

'I have seen him,' she added; 'and my time cannot now be long.'

At that instant her eye lighted on the stranger as he moved into another position. She looked at him for some time with startled amazement and awe; and, turning round to one of the young ladies, said, with an accent of indescribable grief, 'I have been mistaken.' She then rose, and the stranger introduced himself. He was the same person in whom, on his arrival from France, she had fourteen years before discovered the son of her early lover.[1] Seeing him on the spot where she had parted from his father, and dressed in the garb and tartan of the clan which her lover wore on that occasion, she had, in her visionary mood, believed he was an apparition.

Saving these occasional hallucinations, her health certainly received new energy from her native air; and, by her presence at the castle, she was of essential service to the recruiting of her young friend.

In the meantime, Glengael being informed of the attachment between Walkinshaw and Ellen, had espoused his interests with great ardour; and French Frazer, as the stranger was called, also raising men for promotion, the castle became a scene of so much bustle as materially to disturb the shattered nerves of the invalid. With a view, therefore, to change the scene, and to enable Mrs Eadie to enjoy the benefit of sea-bathing, an excursion was proposed to Caithness and Sutherland, where Glengael was desirous of introducing the officers to certain political connections which he had in these counties, and it was proposed that, while the gentlemen went to pay their visits, the ladies should take up their residence at the little town of Wick.

The weather had, for some days before their departure from Glengael, been bright and calm, and the journey to Wick was performed with comparative ease and comfort. The party had, however, scarcely alighted at the house, which a servant sent on before had provided for their accommodation, when the wind changed, and the skies were overcast. For three days it raged a continual tempest; the rain fell in torrents, and the gentlemen, instead of being able to proceed on their visit, were confined to the house. At the end of the third day the storm subsided, and, though the weather was broken, there were intervals which allowed them to make little excursions in the neighbourhood.

The objects they visited, and the tales and traditions of the country, were alike new and interesting to the whole party; and it was agreed, that, before leaving Wick, the gentlemen should conduct the ladies to some of the remarkable spots which they had themselves visited;—among other places, Girnigo Castle, the ancient princely abode of the Earls of Caithness, the superb remains of which still obtain additional veneration in the opinion of the people, from the many guilty and gloomy traditions that fear and fancy have exaggerated in preserving the imperfect recollections of its early history.

Mrs Eadie had agreed to accompany them, the walk not exceeding three or four miles; but on the evening preceding the day which they had fixed for the excursion, when the weather had all the appearance of being settled, she saw, or imagined that she saw, at sunset, some awful prodigy which admonished her not to go.

'I beheld,' said she, 'between me and the setting-sun, a shadowy hand bearing an hour-glass, run out; and when I looked again, I saw the visionary semblance of Walkinshaw's uncle pass me with a pale countenance. Twice have I witnessed the same apparition of his wraith, and I know from the sign, that either his time is not to be long, or to-morrow we shall hear strange tidings.'

It was useless to reason or to argue with her sublime and incomprehensible pretensions; but as it was deemed not prudent to leave her alone, Glengael and Mrs Frazer agreed to remain at Wick, while French Frazer and the young ladies, with Walkinshaw and his sister, went to inspect the ruins of Girnigo, and the rocks, caverns, and precipices of Noss-head.

Of all places in the wild and withered region of Caithness, the promontory of Noss-head presents, alike to the marine voyager and the traveller by land, one of the most tremendous objects. The waves of the universal sea have, from the earliest epochs, raged against it. Huge rocks, torn from the cliffs, stand half hid in the waters, like the teeth and racks of destruction grinning for shipwrecks. No calm of the ocean is there without a swell, and no swell without horror. The sea-birds, that love to build on the wildest cliffs and precipices of that coast of ruins, shun Noss-head, for the ocean laves against it in everlasting cataracts, and the tides, whether in ebb or flow, hurl past in devouring whirlpools. To the pilots afar at sea it is a lofty landmark and a beacon,—but the vessel embayed either within its northern or its southern cliffs, may be known by the marks on her sails, or the name on the pieces of her stern,—but none of her crew ever escape to tell the circumstances of her fate. Even there the miserable native earns no spoils from the waves;—whatever reaches the shore consists of fragments, or splinters, or corses, or limbs,—all are but the crumbs and the surfeit-relics of destruction.

CHAPTER XVIII

MR DONALD GUNN, the worthy Dominie of Wick, who had agreed to act as a guide to Girnigo, was, soon after sunrise, at the door, summoning the party to make ready for the journey; for, although the morning was fair and bright, he had seen signs in the preceding evening, which made him apprehensive of another storm.[1] 'The wind,' said he to Walkinshaw, who was the first that obeyed the call, 'often, at this time of the year, rises about noon, when the waves jump with such agility against the rocks, that the most periculous points of view cannot be seen in their proper elegance, without the risk of breaking your neck, or at least being washed away, and drowned for ever.'

Walkinshaw, accordingly, upon Gunn's report, as he called it, roused the whole party, and they set out for Staxigo, preceded by the Dominie, who, at every turn of the road, 'indexed,' as he said, 'the most interesting places.'

During the walk to the village, the weather still continued propitious; but the schoolmaster observed, that a slight occasional breeze from the north-east, the wildest wind that blows on that coast, rippled the glassy sea, as it undulated among the rocks below their path; a sure indication, so early in the morning, of a tempestuous afternoon. His companions, however, unacquainted with the omens of that ravenous shore, heard his remark without anxiety.

After breakfasting at Elspeth Heddle's public in Staxigo on milk, and ham and eggs, a partan,[2] and haddocks, they went on to the ruins of Girnigo. The occasional fetching of the wind's breath, which the Dominie had noticed in their morning walk, was now become a steady gale, and the waves began to break against the rugged cliffs and headlands to the southward, insomuch, that, when the party reached the peninsula on which the princely ruins of the united castles of Girnigo and Sinclair are situated, they found several fishermen, belonging to Wick, who had gone out to sea at day-break, busily drawing their boats on shore, in the little port, on the south side of the cliffs, under the walls. The visitors inquired why they were so careful in such bright and summer weather; but they directed the attention of the Dominie to long

flakes of goat's beard in the skies, and to the sea-birds flying towards the upland.

By this time the billows were breaking white and high, on the
extremities of Noss-head, and the long grass on the bartisans[1] and
window-sills of the ruins streamed and hissed in the wind. The
sun was bright; but the streaks of hoary vapour that veined the
pure azure of the heavens retained their position and menacing
appearance. There was, however, nothing in the phenomena of the
skies to occasion any apprehension; and the party, without thinking of the immediate horrors of a storm, sympathised with their
guide, as he related to them the mournful legends[2] of those solitary
towers. But, although he dwelt, with particular emphasis, on the
story of the Bishop, whom one of the Earls of Caithness had
ordered his vassals to boil in a cauldron, on account of his extor-
tions, their sympathy was more sorrowfully awakened by the woeful fate of the young Master of Caithness, who, in 1572, fell a
victim to the jealousy of his father.

'George, the Earl at that time,' said the schoolmaster, 'with his
son the Master of Caithness, was on the leet of the lovers of
Euphemia, the only daughter of an ancestor of Lord Reay. The
lady was young and beautiful, and naturally preferred the son to
the father; but the Earl was a haughty baron, and, in revenge for
his son proving a more thriving wooer, was desirous of putting him
for a season out of the way—but not by the dirk, as the use and
wont of that epoch of unrule might have justified. Accordingly, one
afternoon, as they were sitting together in the hall at yonder archi-
traved window in the second story, the wrathful Earl clapped his
hands thrice, and in came three black-aviced kerns in rusted
armour, who, by a signal harmonized between them and Earl
George, seized the lawful heir, and dragged him to a dampish
captivity in yon vault, of which you may see the yawning hungry
throat in the chasm between the two principal lumps of the
buildings.'

The learned Dominie then proceeded to relate the sequel of this
strange story—by which it appeared, that, soon after the imprison-
ment of his son, the Earl being obliged to render his attendance at
the court of Stirling, left his son in the custody of Murdow Mackean
Roy, who, soon after the departure of his master, was persuaded
by the prisoner to connive at a plan for his escape. But the plot was
discovered by William, the Earl's second son, who apprehended

Murdow, and executed him in the instant. Immediately after, he went down into the dungeon, and threatened his brother also with immediate punishment, if he again attempted to corrupt his keepers. The indignant young nobleman, though well ironed, sprung upon Lord William, and bruised him with such violence, that he soon after died. David and Inghrame Sinclair were then appointed custodiers of the prisoner; but, availing themselves of the absence of the Earl, and the confusion occasioned by the death of William, they embezzled the money in the castle, and fled, leaving their young lord in the dungeon, a prey to the horrors of hunger, of which he died.

About seven years after, the Earl, while he lamented the fatal consequences of his own rash rivalry, concealed his thirst for revenge. Having heard that Inghrame Sinclair, who had retired with his booty to a distant part of the country, intended to celebrate the marriage of his daughter by a great feast—resolved to make the festival the scene of punishment. Accordingly, with a numerous retinue, he proceeded to hunt in the neighbourhood of Inghrame Sinclair's residence; and, availing himself of the hospitable courtesies of the time, he entered the banquet-hall, and slew the traitor in the midst of his guests.—

While the visitors in the lee of the ruins were listening to the Dominie's legend, the wind had continued to increase and the sea to rise, and the spray of the waves was springing in stupendous water-spouts and spires of foam over all the headlands in view to the south.

'Aye,' said the Dominie, pointing out to them the ruins of Clyth Castle, over which the sea was breaking white in the distance, 'we may expect a dry storm, for Clyth has got on its shroud. Look where it stands like a ghost on the shore. It is a haunted and unhallowed monument.'

'In olden and ancient times the Laird of Clyth went over to Denmark, and, being at the court of Elsineur, counterfeited, by the help of a handsome person, and a fine elocution, the style and renown of the most prosperous gentleman in all Caithness, by which he beguiled a Prince of Copenhagen to give him his daughter in marriage, a lady of rare and surpassing beauty. After his marriage he returned to Scotland to prepare for the reception of his gorgeous bride; but, when he beheld his own rude turret amidst the spray of the ocean's sea, and thought of the golden palaces and sycamore gardens of Denmark, he was shocked at the idea of a magnificent princess inhabiting such a bleak abode, and overwhelmed with the dread of the indignation that his guilt would excite among her friends. So when the Danish man-of-war, with the lady on board, was approaching the coast, he ordered lights and fires along the cliffs of Ulbster, by which the pilots were bewildered, and the ship was dashed in pieces. The princess and her maids of honour, with many of the sailors, were drowned; but her body was found, beautiful in death, with rings on her fingers, and gems in her ears; and she was interred, as became a high-born lady of her breeding, in the vault where she now lies, among the ancestors of Sir John Sinclair of Ulbster; and ever since that time, the Castle of Clyth has been untenanted, and as often as the wind blows from the north-east, it is covered with a shroud as if doing penance for the maiden of Denmark.'

Notwithstanding the pedantry in the Dominie's language in relating this tradition, the unaffected earnestness with which he expressed himself, moved the compassion of his auditors, and some of the ladies shed tears; which the gentlemen observing, Walkinshaw, to raise their spirits, proposed they should go forward towards Noss-head to view the dreadful turbulency of the breakers. But, before they had approached within half a mile of the promontory, the violence of the gale had increased to such a degree, that they found themselves several times obliged to take refuge in the hollows of the rocks, unable to withstand the fury of the wind, and the lavish showers of spray, that rose in sheets from the waves, and came heavier than rain on the blast.

CHAPTER XIX

In the meantime, the Glasgow party on board Allan M'Lean's pilot-boat was enjoying their sail and sosherie.[1] Enticed by the beauty of the sunny weather, which had preceded the arrival of our Glengael friends at Wick, they had made a long stretch as far to the north as the Mainland of Shetland, and after enjoying fresh ling and stockfish in the highest perfection there, and laying in a capital assortment of worsted hose for winter, they again weighed anchor, with the intention of returning by the Pentland Firth.

Being, however, overtaken by the boisterous weather, which obliged Mr Frazer and his two recruiting guests to stop at Wick, they went into Kirkwall Bay, where they were so long detained, that the thoughts of business and bills began to deteriorate their pleasure.

To none of the party was the detention so irksome as to Mr Walkinshaw, for, independent of the cares of his mercantile concerns, his fancy was running on Ellen Frazer, and he was resolved, as soon as he returned to the Clyde, to sound her father with a proposal, to solicit her for his second wife. Why a gentleman, so well advanced in life, should have thought of offering himself as a candidate for a lady's love, against his nephew, we must leave to be accounted for by those who are able to unravel the principles of the Earl of Caithness's enmity to his son, particularly as we are in possession of no reasonable theory, adequate to explain how he happened to prefer Ellen Frazer to the numerous beauties of the royal city. It is sufficient for us, as historians, simply to state the fact, and narrate the events to which it gave rise.

Mr Walkinshaw then being rendered weary of the Orkneys, and, perhaps, also of the joviality of his companions, by the mingled reflections of business, and the tender intention of speedily taking a second wife, resolved, rather than again incur the uncertainties of the winds and waves, to leave the pilot-boat at Kirkwall, and embark for Thurso, in order to return home over land; a vessel belonging to that port being then wind-bound in the bay. Accordingly, on the same morning that the party from Wick went to visit Girnigo Castle, and the magnificent horrors of Noss-head, he embarked.

For some time after leaving Kirkwall, light airs and summer breezes enabled the sloop in which he had taken his passage to work pleasantly round Moulhead. But before she had passed the spiky rocks and islets of Copinshaw, the master deemed it prudent to stand farther out to sea; for the breeze had freshened, and the waves were dashing themselves into foam on Roseness and the rugged shores of Barra.

The motion of the sloop, notwithstanding the experience which the passenger had gained in the pilot-boat, overwhelmed him with unutterable sickness, and he lay on the deck in such affliction, that he once rashly wished he was drowned. The cabin-boy who attended him was so horror-struck at hearing so profane a wish at sea, while the wind was rising on a lee shore, that he left him to shift for himself.

For some time the master did not think it necessary to shorten sail, but only to stretch out towards the south-east; but, as the sun mounted towards the meridian, the gale so continued to increase, that he not only found it necessary to reef, but in the end to hand almost all his canvas save the foresail. Still, as there were no clouds, no rain, no thunder nor lightning, the seasick Glasgow merchant dreamt of no danger.

'May be,' said the cabin-boy in passing, as the Laird happened to look up from his prostrate situation on the deck, 'ye'll get your ugly wish oure soon.'[1]

The regardless manner and serious tone in which this was said had an immediate and restorative effect. Mr Walkinshaw roused himself, and, looking round, was surprised to see the sails taken in; and, casting his eyes to leeward, beheld, with a strong emotion of consternation, the ocean boiling with tremendous violence, and the spindrift rising like steam.

'It blows a dreadful gale?' said he inquiringly to the master.

'It does,' was the emphatic reply.

'I hope there is no danger,' cried the merchant, alarmed, and drawing himself close under the larboard gunnel.

The master, who was looking anxiously towards Duncansby-head, which presented a stupendous tower of foaming spray, over the starboard bow, replied,

'I hope we shall be able to weather Noss-head.'

'And if we do not,' said Mr Walkinshaw, 'what's to be done?'

'You'll be drowned,' cried the cabin-boy, who had seated himself on the lea-side of the companion; and the bitterness of the reproachful accent with which this was said stung the proud merchant to the quick—but he said nothing; his fears were, however, now all awake, and he saw, with a feeling of inexpressible alarm, that the crew were looking eagerly and sorrowfully towards the roaring precipices of Caithness.

Still the vessel kept bravely to her helm, and was working slowly outward; but, as she gradually wore round, her broadside became more and more exposed to the sea, and once or twice her decks were washed fore and aft.

'This is terrible work, Captain,' said Mr Walkinshaw.

'It is,' was all the answer he received.

'Is there no port we can bear away for?'

'None.'

'Good Heavens! Captain, if this continues till night?'

The master eyed him for a moment, and said with a shudder,—

'If it does, Sir, we shall never see night.'

'You'll be drowned,' added the little boy, casting an angry look from behind the companion.

'Almighty Powers!—surely we are not in such danger?' exclaimed the terrified merchant.

'Hold your tongue,' again cried the boy.

Mr Walkinshaw heard him, and for a moment was petrified, for the command was not given with insolence, but solemnity.

A cry of 'Hold fast,' in the same instant, came from the forecastle, and, after a momentary pause, a dreadful sea broke aboard, and swept the deck. The master, who had himself taken the helm, was washed overboard, and the tiller was broken.

'We are gone!' said the little boy, as he shook the water from his jacket, and crawled on towards the mast, at the foot of which he seated himself, for the loss of the tiller, and the damage the rudder had sustained, rendered the vessel unmanageable, and she drifted to her fate before the wind.

'Is there indeed no hope?' cried Mr Walkinshaw to one of the sailors, who was holding by the shrouds.

'If we get into Sinclair's Bay, there is a sandy beach,' replied the sailor.

'And if we do not?' exclaimed the passenger in the accent of despair.

'We'll a' be drowned,' replied the boy with a scowling glance, as he sat cowering with his head between his knees, at the foot of the mast.

'We shall not get into Sinclair's Bay,' said the sailor, firmly; 'but we may pass Noss-head.'

'Do you think so?' said Mr Walkinshaw, catching something like hope and fortitude from the sedate courage of the sailor.

Another cry of 'Hold fast' prepared him for a second breach of the sea, and he threw himself on the deck, and took hold of a ringbolt, in which situation he continued, though the vessel rose to the wave. In the meantime, the resolute sailor, after looking calmly and collectedly around for some time, went from the larboard to the starboard, and mounted several rattlings of the shrouds, against which he leant with his back, while the vessel was fast driving towards Noss-head.

CHAPTER XX

THE party from Glengael, who had, as we have described, been obliged to take refuge from the wind in the lee of the rocks, stood contemplating the scene in silence. The sky was without a cloud—but the atmosphere was nevertheless almost like steam, through which the sun shone so sickly, that, even without hearing the hiss of the wind, or the rage of the ocean, no shelter could have prevented the spectator from being sensible that some extraordinary violence agitated and troubled the whole air. Every shrub and bramble not only bent before the wind, but it may be said their branches literally streamed in the blast. There was a torrent which ran towards the sea, near the spot where the party stood; but the wind caught its waters as they fell in a cataract, and blew them over the face of the hill like a wreath of 'mist. A few birch trees, that skirted the dell through which this stream ran, brushed the ground before the breeze; and the silver lining of their leaves was so upturned in the constant current of the storm, that they had the appearance of being covered with hoar frost. Not a bee was abroad on the heath, and the sea birds were fluttering and cowering in the lee of the rocks—a bernacle,[1] that attempted to fly from behind a block of granite, was whirled screaming away in the wind, and flung with such resistless impetuosity against the precipice, behind a corner of which the party were sheltering, that it was killed on the spot. The landscape was bright in the hazy sunshine; but the sheep lay in the hollows of the ground, unable to withstand the deluge of the dry tempest that swept all before it, and a wild and lonely lifelessness reigned on the mountains.

The appearance of the sea was awful. It was not because the waves rolled in more tremendous volumes than any of the party had ever before seen, and burst against the iron precipices of Nosshead with the roar and the rage of the falls of Niagara—the whole expanse of the ocean was enveloped with spindrift, and, as it occasionally opened, a vessel was seen. At first it was thought she was steering for the bay of Wick, but it soon appeared that she drifted at random towards Sinclair's Bay, and could, by nothing less than some miraculous change of the wind, reach the anchorage opposite to Kiess Castle.

Ellen Frazer was the first who spoke of the sloop's inevitable fate.—'It is dreadful,' said she, 'for us to stand in safety here, like spectators at a tragedy, and see yon unfortunate bark rushing without hope to destruction. Let us make an attempt to reach the beach —she may be driven on the shore, and we may have it in our power to assist the poor wretches, if any should escape.'

They, accordingly, endeavoured to reach the strand; but before they could wrestle with the wind half-way towards it, they saw that the vessel could not attain Sinclair's Bay, and that her only chance of salvation was in weathering Noss-head, to which she was fast nearing. They, in consequence, changed their course, and went towards the promontory; but, by the time they had gained the height, they saw it was hopeless to think they could render any assistance, and they halted under the ledge of an overhanging rock, to see if she would be able to weather that dreadful headland.

The place where they took shelter was to the windward of the spray, which rose like a furious cataract against the promontory; and in pyramids of foam, that were seen many leagues off at sea, deluged the land to a great extent far beyond Castle Girnigo. It happened that Ellen Frazer had a small telescope in her hand, which they had brought with them, and, when they were under cover, she applied it to her eye.

'The sailors,' said she, 'seem to have abandoned themselves to despair—I see two prostrate on the deck. There is one standing on the shrouds, as if he hopes to be able to leap on the rocks when she strikes. The dog is on the end of the bowsprit—I can look at them no more.'

She then handed the telescope to Mary, and, retiring to a little distance, seated herself on a stone, and, covering her face with her handkerchief, could no longer control her tears. The vessel, in the mean time, was fast drifting towards the rocks, with her broadside to the wave.

'I think,' said Mary, 'that she must have lost her helm; nobody is near where it should be.—They have no hope.—One of the men, who had thrown himself on the deck, is risen. He is tying himself to the shrouds.—There is a boy at the foot of the mast, sitting cowering on the deck, holding his head between his hands.'

Walkinshaw, without speaking, took the telescope from his sister, who went and sat down in silence beside Ellen. By this time, the vessel had drifted so near, that every thing on her deck was distinct to the naked eye.

'The person on the deck,' said Walkinshaw, after looking through the glass about the space of a minute, 'is not a sailor—he has long clothes, and has the appearance of a gentleman, probably a passenger. That poor little boy!—he is evidently covering his ears, as if he could shut out the noise of the roaring death that awaits him. What a brave and noble fellow that is on the shrouds, —if coolness and courage can save, he is safe.'

At this moment, a shriek from Mary roused Ellen, and they both ran to the spot where Walkinshaw was standing. A tremendous wave had covered the vessel, as it were, with a winding-sheet of foam, and before it cleared away, she was among the breakers that raged against the headland.

'She is gone!' said Walkinshaw, and he took his sister and Ellen by the hands.—'Let us leave these horrors.' But the ladies trembled so much, that they were unable to walk; and Ellen became so faint, that she was obliged to sit down on the ground, while her lover ran with his hat to find, if possible, a little fresh water to revive her. He had not, however, been absent many minutes, when another shriek from his sister called him back, and, on returning, he found that a large dog, dripping wet, and whimpering and moaning, had laid himself at the feet of the ladies with a look of the most piteous and helpless expression. It was the dog they had seen on the bowsprit of the vessel, and they had no doubt her fate was consummated; but three successive enormous billows coming, with all the force of the German Ocean, from the Baltic, rolled into the bay. The roar with which they broke as they hurled by the cliff, where the party were standing, drew the attention of Walkinshaw even from Ellen; and, to his surprise, he saw that the waves had, in their sweep, drawn the vessel into the bay, and that she was coming driving along the side of the precipice, and, if not dashed in pieces before, would pass within a few yards of where they stood. Her bowsprit was carried away, which showed how narrowly she had already escaped destruction.

The ladies, roused again into eager and anxious sympathy by this new incident, approached with Walkinshaw as near as possible to the brink of the cliff—to the very edge of which the raging waters raised their foamy crests as they passed in their might and majesty from the headland into the bay. Another awful wave was

soon after seen rising at a distance, and, as it came rolling onward
nearer and nearer, it swallowed up every lesser billow. When it
approached the vessel, it swept her along so closely to the rocks that
Walkinshaw shouted unconsciously, and the dog ran barking to
the edge of the precipice,—all on board were for a moment animated with fresh energy,—the little boy stood erect; and the sailor
on the shrouds, seeing Walkinshaw and the ladies, cried bravely, as
the vessel rose on the swell in passing, 'It will not do yet.' But the
attention of his admiring spectators was suddenly drawn from him
to the gentleman. 'Good Heavens!' exclaimed Ellen Frazer, 'it is
your uncle!'

It was even so. Mr Walkinshaw, on raising his head to look up,
saw and recognized them, and, wildly starting from the deck,
shook his uplifted hands with a hideous and terrific frenzy. This
scene was, however, but for an instant; the flank of the wave, as it
bore the vessel along, broke against a projecting rock, and she was
wheeled away by the revulsion to a great distance.

The sailor in the shrouds still stood firm; a second wave, more
appalling than the former, brought the vessel again towards the
cliff. The dog, anticipating what would happen, ran towards the
spot where she was likely to strike. The surge swung her almost to
the top of the precipice,—the sailor leapt from the shrouds, and
caught hold of a projecting rock,—the dog seized him by the jacket
to assist him up, but the ravenous sea was not to lose its prey.—
In the same moment the wave broke, and the vessel was again
tossed away from the rock, and a frightful dash of the breakers tore
down the sailor and the faithful dog. Another tremendous revulsion, almost in the same moment, terminated the fate of the vessel.
As it came roaring along it caught her by the broadside, and dashed
her into ten thousand shivers against an angle of the promontory,
scarcely more than two hundred yards from the spot where the
horror-struck spectators stood. Had she been made of glass, her
destruction and fragments could not have been greater. They
floated like chaff on the waters; and, for the space of four or five
seconds, the foam amidst which they weltered was coloured in
several places with blood.

CHAPTER XXI

THE same gale which proved so fatal on the coast of Caithness, carried the Glasgow party briskly home.[1]

Before their arrival the news of the loss of Mr Walkinshaw had reached the city, and Dirdumwhamle and his son were as busy, as heirs and executors could well be, in taking possession of his fortune, which, besides the estate of Kittlestonheugh, greatly exceeded their most sanguine expectations. They were, however, smitten with no little concern when, on applying to Mr Pitwinnoch, the lawyer, to receive infeftment[2] of the lands, they heard from him, after he had perused the deed of entail, that Robina had no right to the inheritance; but that our friend Walkinshaw[3] was the lawful heir.

It was, however, agreed, as the world, as well as themselves, had uniformly understood and believed that old Grippy had disinherited his eldest son, to say nothing about this important discovery. Walky and Robina accordingly took possession in due form of her father's mansion. Their succession was unquestioned, and they mourned in all the most fashionable pomp of woe for the loss they had sustained, receiving the congratulatory condolence of their friends with the most befitting decorum. To do the lady, however, justice, the tears which she shed were immediate from the heart; for, with all his hereditary propensity to gather and hold, her father had many respectable domestic virtues, and was accounted by the world a fair and honourable man. It is also due to her likewise to mention, that she was not informed, either by her husband or father-in-law, of the mistake they had been all in with regard to the entail; so that, whatever blame did attach to them for the part they played, she was innocent of the fraud.

To Walkinshaw's mother the loss of her brother-in-law was a severe misfortune, for with him perished her annuity of fifty pounds a-year. She entertained, however, a hope that Robina would still continue it; but the feelings arising from the consciousness of an unjust possession of the estate, operated on the mind of Milrookit in such a way, as to make him suddenly become wholly under the influence of avarice. Every necessary expence was grudged; his wife, notwithstanding the wealth she had brought him, was not allowed to enjoy a guinea; in a word, from the day in which Pitwinnoch informed him that she had no right to the property, he was devoured, in the most singular manner, with the most miserly passions and fears.

The old Leddy, for some time after the shock she had met with in the sudden death of her son, mourned with more unaffected sorrow than might have been expected from her character; and having, during that period, invited Mrs Charles to spend a few weeks with her, the loss of the annuity, and conjectures respecting the continuance of it, frequently formed the subject of their conversation.

'It's my notion,' the Leddy would say, 'that Beenie will see to a continuality o' the 'nuity—but Walky's sic a Nabal, that nae doot it maun be a task o' dexterity on her side to get him to agree. Howsever, when they're a' settled, I'll no be mealy-mouthed wi' them. My word! a bien[1] bargain he has gotten wi' her, and I'm wae to think it did nae fa' to your Jamie's luck, who is a laddie o' a winsome temper—just as like his grandfather, my friend that was, as a kittling's like a cat—the only difference being a wee thought mair o' daffing and playrifety.'[2]

Nor was it long after these observations that the Leddy had an opportunity of speaking to her grandchildren on the subject. One day soon after, when they happened to call, she took occasion to remind them how kind she had been at the time of their marriage, and also that, but for her agency, it might never have taken place.

'Noo,' said she, 'there is ae thing I would speak to you anent, though I was in the hope ye would hae spar't me the obligation, by making me a reasonable gratis gift for the cost and outlay I was at, forbye[3] trouble on your account. But the compliment is like the chariot-wheels o' Pharaoh, sae dreigh o' drawing,[4] that I canna afford to be blate[5] wi' you ony langer. Howsever, Walky and Beenie, I hae a projection in my head, the whilk is a thought o' wisdom for you to consider, and it's o' the nature o' a solemn league and covenant. If ye'll consent to alloo Bell Fatherlans her 'nuity of fifty pounds per annus, as it is called, according to law, I'll score you out o' my books for the bed, board, and washing due to me, and a heavy soom it is.'

'Where do you think we are to get fifty pounds a-year?' exclaimed Milrookit. 'Fifty pounds a-year!'

'Just in the same neuk,[6] Walky, where ye found the

Kittlestonheugh estate and the three and twenty thousand pounds o' lying siller, Beenie's braw tocher,' replied the Leddy; 'and I think ye're a very crunkly[1] character, though your name's no Habakkuk, to gi'e me sic a constipation[2] o' an answer.'

'I can assure you, Leddy,' said he, 'if it was a thing within the compass of my power, I would na need to be told to be liberal to Mrs Charles; but the burden o' a family's coming upon us, and it's necessary, nay, it's a duty, to consider that charity begins at hame.'

'And what's to become o' her and her dochter? Gude guide us! would the hard nigger let her gang on the session?[3] for I canna help her.'

'All I can say at present,' was his reply, 'that we are in no circumstances to spare any thing like fifty pounds a-year.'

'Then I can tell thee, Walky, I will this very day mak out my count, and every farthing I can extortionate frae thee, meeserable penure pig that thou art, shall be pay't o'er to her to the last fraction, just to wring thy heart o' niggerality.'

'If you have any lawful claim against me, of course I am obliged to pay you.'

'If I hae ony lawful claim?—ye Goliah o' cheatrie[4]—if I hae ony lawful claim?—But I'll say nothing—I'll mak out an account —and there's nae law in Christendom to stop me for charging what I like—my goose shall lay gouden eggs, if the life bide in my bodie.—Ye unicorn of oppression, to speak to me o' law, that was so kind to you—but law ye shall get, and law ye shall hae—and be made as lawful as it's possible for caption and horning,[5] wi' clerk and signet[6] to implement.'

'If you will make your little favours a debt, nobody can prevent you; but I will pay no more than is justly due.'

The Leddy made no reply, but her eyes looked unutterable things; and after sitting for some time in that energetic posture of displeasure, she turned round to Robina, and said, with an accent of the most touching sympathy,—

'Hegh, Beenie! poor lassie! but thou hast ta'en thy sheep to a silly market. A skelp-the-dub[7] creature to upbraid me wi' his justly dues! But crocodile or croakindeil, as I should ca' him, he'll get his ain justly dues.—Mr Milrookit o' Kittlestonheugh, as it's no the fashion when folk hae recourse to the civil war o' a law-plea, to stand on a ceremony, maybe ye'll find some mair pleasant place

than this room, an ye were to tak the pains to gang to the outside
o' my door; and I'll send, through the instrumentality o' a man o'
business, twa lines anent that bit sma' matter for bed, board, and
washing due to me for and frae that time, when, ye ken, Mr Milrookit, ye had na ae stiver to keep yourself and your wife frae
starvation.—So out o' my house, and daur no longer to pollute
my presence, ye partan-handit, grip-and-haud smedy-vyce Mammon[1] o' unrighteousness.'

After this gentle hint, as the Leddy afterwards called it, Milrookit and Robina hastily obeyed her commands, and returned to
their carriage; but before driving home, he thought it necessary,
under the menace he had received, to take the advice of his lawyer,
Mr Pitwinnoch. Some trifling affairs, however, prevented him
from driving immediately to his office, and the consequence was,
that the Leddy, who never allowed the grass to grow in her path,
was there before him.

CHAPTER XXII

'MR PITWINNOCH,' said the Leddy, on being shown into what
she called 'the bottomless pit o' his consulting-room,' where he
wrote alone,—'ye'll be surprised to see me, and troth ye may think
it's no sma' instancy that has brought me sae far afield the day;
for I hae been sic a lamiter[2] with the rheumateese, that, for a' the
last week, I was little better than a nymph o' anguish;[3] my banes
were as sair as if I had been brayed in a mortar,[4] and shot into
Spain. But ye maun know and understand, that I hae a notion to
try my luck and fortune in the rowley-powley[5] o' a law-plea.'

'Indeed!' said the lawyer. 'What has happened?'

'Aye! Mr Pitwinnoch, ye may weel speer;[6] but my twa ungrateful grandchildren, that I did sae muckle for at their marriage, hae
used me waur than I were a Papistical Jew o' Jericho. I just, in my
civil and discreet manner was gi'en them a delicate memento mori[7]
concerning their unsettled count for bed, board, and washing;
when up got Milrookit, as if he would hae flown out at the broad
side o' the house, and threepit[8] that he didna owe me the tenth
part o' half a farthing; and threatened to tak me afore the Lords
for a Cananitish woman,[9] and an extortioner.—Noo, don't you

think that's a nice point, as my worthy father used to say, and music to the ears of a' the Fifteen at Embrough?'[1]

'Mr Milrookit, surely,' said the lawyer, 'can never resist so just a demand. How much is it?'

'But, first and forwards,' replied the Leddy, 'before we come to the condescendence,[2] I should state the case; and, Mr Pitwinnoch, ye maun understand that I hae some knowledge o' what pertains to law, for my father was most extraordinare at it; and so I need not tell you, that it's weel for me the day[3] to know what I know. For Milrookit, as I was saying, having refused, point-blank, Mr Pitwinnoch, to implement the 'nuity of fifty pounds per annus,[4] that your client—(that's a legal word, Mr Pitwinnoch)—that your client settled on my gude-dochter,[5] I told him he would—then and there refusing—be bound over to pay me for the bed, board, and washing. And what would ye think, Mr Pitwinnoch? he responded, with a justly due,—but I'll due him; and though, had he been calm and well-bred, I might have put up with ten pounds; yet, seeing what a ramping lion he made himsel, I'll no faik[6] a farthing o' a thousand, which, at merchants' interest,[7] will enable me to pay the 'nuity. So, when we get it, ye'll hae to find me somebody willing to borrow on an heritable bond.'[8]

'I think you can hardly expect so much as a thousand pounds. If I recollect rightly, Mr and Mrs Milrookit staid but six weeks with you,' said the lawyer.

'Time,' replied the Leddy, 'ye ken, as I hae often heard my father say, was no item in law; and unless there's a statute of vagrancy in the Decisions,[9] or the Raging Magistratom,[10] there can be no doot that I hae't in my power to put what value I please on my house, servitude, and expence, which is the strong ground of the case. Therefore, you will write a letter forthwith to Mr Milrookit of Kittlestonheugh, charging him with a lawful debt, and a' justly due to me, of one thousand pounds, without condescending on particulars at present, as the damages can be afterwards assessed, when we hae gotten payment of the principal, which every body must allow is a most liberal offer on my part.'

It was with some difficulty that Mr Pitwinnoch could preserve himself in a proper state of solemnity to listen to the instructions of his client; but what lawyer would laugh, even in his own 'bottomless pit?' However, he said,—

'Undoubtedly, Mrs Walkinshaw, you have a good ground of

action; but, perhaps, I may be able to effect an amicable arrangement, if you would submit the business to arbitration.'

'Arbitration, Mr Pitwinnoch!' exclaimed the Leddy; 'never propound such a thing to me; for often hae I heard my father say, that arbitration was the greatest cut-throat of legal proceedings that had been devised since the discovery of justice at Amalphi.[1] Na, na—I hae mair sense than to virdict[2] my case wi' any sic pannelling[3] as arbitration. So, law being my only remede, I hope ye'll leave no stone unturned till you hae brought Mr Milrookit's nose to the grindstone; and to help you to haud it there, I hae brought a five pound note as hansel for good luck,—this being the first traffic in legalities that I hae had on my own bottom;[4] for, in the concos mentos o' Watty, my son, ye ken I was keepit back, in order to be brought forward as a witness; but there is no need o' ony decreet o' Court for such an interlocutor[5] on the present occasion.'

The Leddy having, in this clear and learned manner, delivered her instructions, she left the office, and soon after Milrookit was also shown into 'the bottomless pit,' where he gave an account of the transaction, somewhat different, but, perhaps, no nearer the truth. He was, however, not a little surprised to find the pursuer had been there before him, and that she had instructed proceedings. But what struck him with the greatest consternation was a suggestion from Mr Pitwinnoch to compromise the matter.

'Take my advice, Mr Milrookit,' said he, 'and settle this quietly —there is no saying what a law-suit may lead to; and, considering the circumstances under which you hold the estate, don't stir, lest the sleeping dog awake. Let us pacify the old Leddy with two or three hundred pounds.'

'Two or three hundred pounds, for six weeks of starvation! The thing, Mr Pitwinnoch, is ridiculous.'

'True, Sir,' replied the lawyer; 'but then the state of the Entail —you should consider that. Be thankful if she will take a couple of hundreds.'

'Nay, if you counsel me to do that, I have no alternative, and must submit.'

'You will do wisely in at once agreeing,' said Pitwinnoch; and, after some farther conversation to the same effect, Milrookit gave a cheque for two hundred pounds, and retired grumbling.

The lawyer, rejoicing in so speedy and fortunate a settlement, as soon as he left the office, went to the Leddy, exulting in his address.

'Twa hundred pounds!' said she,—'but the fifth part o' my thousand! I'll ne'er tak ony sic payment. Ye'll carry it back to Mr Milrookit, and tell him I'll no faik a plack[1] o' my just debt; and what's mair, if he does na pay me the whole tot down at once, he shall be put to the horn[2] without a moment's delay.'

'I assure you,' replied the lawyer, 'that this is a result far beyond hope—you ought not for a moment to make a word about it; for you must be quite aware that he owes you no such sum as this. You said yourself that ten pounds would have satisfied you.'

'And so it would—but that was before I gaed to law wi' him,' cried the Leddy; 'but seeing now how I hae the rights o' the plea, I'll hae my thousand pounds if the hide be on his snout. Whatna better proof could ye hae o' the justice o' my demand, than that he should hae come down in terror at once wi' two hundred pounds? I hae known my father law for seven years, and even when he won, he had money to pay out of his own pocket—so, wi' sic erls[3] o' victory as ye hae gotten, I would be waur[4] than mad no to stand out. Just gang till[5] him, and come na back to me without the thousand pound—every farthing, Mr Pitwinnoch—and your own costs besides; or, if ye dinna, may be I'll get another man o' business that will do my turn better—for, in an extremity like a law-suit, folk maunna[6] stand on friendships. Had Mr Keelevin been noo to the fore,[7] I would na needed to be put to my peremptors; but, honest man, he's gone. Howsever, there's one Thomas Whitteret, that was his clerk when my friend that's awa[8] made his deed o' settlement—and I hae heard he has a nerve o' ability; so, if ye bring na me the thousand pounds this very afternoon, I'll apply to him to be my agent.'

Mr Pitwinnoch said not a word to this, but left the house, and, running to the Black Bull Inn, ordered a post-chaise, and was at Kittlestonheugh almost as soon as his client. A short conversation settled the business—the very name of Thomas Whitteret, an old clerk of Keelevin, and probably acquainted with the whole affair, was worth five thousand pounds, and, in consequence, in much less time than the Leddy expected, she did receive full payment of her thousand pounds; but, instead of expressing any pleasure at her success, she regretted that she should have made a charge of such moderation, being persuaded, that, had she stood out, the law would have given her double the money.

CHAPTER XXIII

MR PITWINNOCH was instructed to lay out the money at five per cent. interest to pay Mrs Charles the annuity; and one of his clerks mentioned the circumstance to a companion in Mr Whitteret's office. This led to an application from him for the loan, on account of a country gentleman in the neighbourhood, who, having obtained a considerable increase of his rental, was intending to enlarge his mansion, and extend his style of living,—a very common thing at that period, the effects of which are beginning to show themselves,—but, as the Leddy said on another occasion, that's none of our concern at present.

The security offered being unexceptionable, an arrangement was speedily concluded, and an heritable bond[1] for the amount prepared. As the party borrowing the money lived at some distance from the town, Mr Whitteret sent one of his young men to get it signed, and to deliver it to the Leddy. It happened that the youth employed in this business was a little acquainted with the Leddy, and knowing her whimsical humour, when he carried it home he stopped, and fell into conversation with her about Walkinshaw, whom he knew.

'I maun gar[2] his mother write to him,' said the Leddy, 'to tell him what a victory I hae gotten;—for ye maun ken, Willy Keckle, that I hae overcome principalities and powers in this controversy. —Wha ever heard o' thousands o' pounds gotten for sax weeks' bed, board, and washing, like mine? But it was a rightous judgment on the Nabal Milrookit,—whom I'll never speak to again in this world, and no in the next either, I doot, unless he mends his manners. He made an absolute refuse to gie a continuality o' Jamie's mother's 'nuity, which was the because o' my going to law with him for a thousand pounds, value received in bed, board, and washing, for six weeks.—And the case, Willy,—you that's breeding for a limb o' the law,—ye should ken, was sic an absolute fact, that he was obligated by a judicature to pay me down the money.'

Willy Keckle was so amused with her account of the speedy justice which she had obtained, as she said, by instructing Mr Pitwinnoch herself of the 'nice point,' and 'the strong ground,' that he could not refrain from relating the conversation to his master.

Mr Whitteret was diverted with the story; but it seemed so strange and unaccountable, that the amount of the demand, and the readiness with which it was paid, dwelt on his mind as extraordinary circumstances; and he having occasion next day to go into Edinburgh, where Mr Frazer had returned from Glengael, to attend his professional duties, he happened to be invited to dine with a party where that gentleman was, and the company consisting chiefly of lawyers,—as dinner parties unfortunately are in the modern Athens,—he amused them with the story of the Leddy's legal knowledge.

Glengael, from the interest which he took in his young friend, Walkinshaw, whom he had left at the castle, was led to inquire somewhat particularly into the history of the Kittlestonheugh family, expressing his surprise and suspicion, in common with the rest of the company, as to the motives which could have influenced a person of Milrookit's character to comply so readily with a demand so preposterous.

One thing led on to another, and Mr Whitteret recollected something of the deed which had been prepared when he was in Mr Keelevin's office, and how old Grippy died before it was executed. The object of this deed was then discussed, and the idea presenting itself to the mind of Glengael, that, possibly, it might have some connection with the Entail, inquired more particularly respecting the terms of that very extraordinary settlement, expressing his astonishment that it should not have contained a clause to oblige the person marrying the heiress to take the name of Walkinshaw, to which the old man, by all accounts, had been so much attached. The whole affair, the more it was considered, seemed the more mysterious; and the conclusion in the penetrating mind of Mr Frazer was, that Milrookit had undoubtedly some strong reason for so quietly hushing the old Leddy's claim.

His opinion at the moment was, that Robina's father had left a will, making some liberal provision for his sister-in-law's family; and that Milrookit was anxious to stand on such terms with his connections, as would prevent any of them, now that Walkinshaw had left Glasgow, from inquiring too anxiously into the state of his father-in-law's affairs. But, without expressing what was passing in his mind, he so managed the conversation as to draw out the several opinions of his legal brethren. Some of them coincided with his own. There was, however, one old pawkie[1] and shrewd writer to the signet present, who remained silent, but whom Mr Frazer observed attending with an uncommon degree of earnest and eager watchfulness to what was said, practising, in fact, nearly the same sort of policy which prompted himself to lead the conversation.

Mr Pilledge,—for so this W.S.[1] was called—had acquired a considerable fortune and reputation in the Parliament House, by the address with which he discovered dormant rights and legal heirs; and Mr Frazer had no doubt, from the evident interest which he had taken in the Kittlestonheugh story, that he would soon take some steps to ascertain the real motives which had led Milrookit to act in the Leddy's case so inconsistently with his general character. In so far he was, therefore, not displeased to observe his earnestness; but he had often heard it said, that Mr Pilledge was in the practice of making bargains with those clients whose dormant rights he undertook to establish, by which it was insinuated that he had chiefly built up his fortune—his general practice being very limited; and Mr Frazer resolved to watch his movements, in order to protect his young friend.

This opinion of Pilledge was not unfounded; for the same evening, after the party broke up, he accompanied Whitteret to the hotel where he staid, and, in the course of the walk, renewed the conversation respecting the singular entail of old Grippy. The Glasgow lawyer was shrewd enough to perceive, that such unusual interest in a case where he had no concern could not be dictated by the mere wonder and curiosity which the Writer to the Signet affected to express; but, being unacquainted with the general character of Pilledge, he ascribed his questions and conjectures to the effect of professional feelings perplexed by a remarkable case.

But it happened next morning that he had occasion to attend a consultation with Mr Frazer, who, taking an opportunity to revert to the subject, which had so occupied their attention on the preceding afternoon, gave him a hint to be on his guard with respect to Pilledge, suggesting, on Walkinshaw's account, that Whitteret might find it of advantage to himself, could he really ascertain the secret reasons and motives by which the possessor of the Kittlestonheugh estate was actuated.

'It would not give you much trouble,' said he, 'were you to step into the Register Office,[2] and look at the terms of the original deed of entail; for although the disinheritance of the eldest son, as I have always understood, was final, there may be some flaw in the succession with respect to the daughter.'

This extrajudicial advice was not lost. As soon as the consultation was over, Whitteret went to the Register Office, where, not a little to his surprise, he found Pilledge, as Frazer had suspected, already in the act of reading the registered deed of the entail. A short conversation then ensued, in which Whitteret intimated that he had also come for the same purpose.

'Then,' said Pilledge, 'let us go together, for it appears to me that the heirs-female of the sons do not succeed before the heirs whatsoever of the daughters; and Milrookit's right would be preferable to that of his wife, if the eldest son has not left a son.'

'But the eldest son has left a son,' replied Whitteret.

'In that case,' said Pilledge, 'we may make a good thing of it with him. I'll propose to him to undertake his claim upon an agreement for half the rent, in the event of success, and we can divide the bakes.'

'You may save yourself the trouble,' replied Whitteret coolly; 'for I shall write to him by the first post—in the meantime, Mr Frazer has authorized me to act.'

'Frazer! how can he authorize you?' said Pilledge discontentedly.

'He knows that best himself; but the right of the son of the oldest son is so clear, that there will be no room for any proceedings.'

'You are mistaken there,' replied Pilledge, eagerly. 'I never saw a deed yet that I could not drive a horse and cart through, and I should think that Milrookit is not such a fool, as to part with the estate without a struggle. But since you are agent for the heir of entail, I will offer to conduct the respondent's case. I think you said he is rich, independent of the heritable subject.'

This conscientious conversation was abruptly terminated on the part of Whitteret, who immediately went to Mr Frazer, and communicated the important discovery which had been made, with respect to Walkinshaw being the heir of entail. He also mentioned something of what had passed with Mr Pilledge, expressing his apprehensions, from what he knew of Pitwinnoch, Milrookit's man of business, in Glasgow, that Pilledge, with his assistance, might involve the heir in expensive litigation.

Mr Frazer knew enough of the metaphysical ingenuity of the Parliament House, to be aware that, however clear and evident any right might be, it was never beyond the possibility of dispute there, and he immediately suggested that some steps should be taken, to induce Milrookit at once to resign the possession of the property; but, while they were thus speaking Pilledge was already on the road to Glasgow, to apprise Milrookit of what was impending, and to counsel him to resist.

CHAPTER XXIV

FROM the circumstance of Milrookit and Robina staying with the Leddy at the time of their marriage, the porter at the inn, where Pilledge alighted on his arrival at Glasgow, supposed they lived in her house, and conducted him there. But, on reaching the door, seeing the name of Mrs Walkinshaw on a brass plate, not quite so large as the one that the Lord Provost[1] of the royal city sported on the occasion of his Majesty's most gracious visit to the lawful and intellectual metropolis of his ancient kingdom, he resolved to address himself to her, for what purpose it would not be easy to say, further than he thought, perhaps, from what he had heard of her character, that she might be of use in the projected litigation. Accordingly, he applied his hand to the knocker, and was shown into the room where she was sitting alone, spinning.

'You are the lady,' said he, 'I presume, of the late much respected Mr Claud Walkinshaw, commonly styled of Grippy.'

'So they say, for want o' a better,' replied the Leddy, stopping at the same time her wheel and looking up to him; 'but wha are ye, and what's your will?'

'My name is Pilledge. I am a writer to the signet, and I have come to see Mr Milrookit of Kittlestonheugh, respecting an important piece of business;'—and he seated himself unbidden. As he said this, the Leddy pricked up her ears, for, exulting in her own knowledge of the law, by which she had recently so triumphed, as she thought, she became eager to know what the important piece of business could be, and replied,—

'Nae doot, it's anent the law-plea he has been brought into, on account of his property.'

Milrookit had been engaged in no suit whatever, but this was the way she took to trot[2] the Edinburgh writer, and she added,—

'How do ye think it'll gang wi' him? Is there ony prospect o' the Lord Ordinary coming to a decision on the pursuer's petition?'

This really looked so like the language of the Parliament House, considering it came from an old lady, that Pilledge was taken in, and his thoughts running on the entail, he immediately fancied that she alluded to something connected with it, and said,—

'I should think, Madam, that your evidence would be of the utmost importance to the case, and it was to advise with him chiefly as to the line of defence he ought to take that I came from Edinburgh.'

'Nae doot, Sir, I could gie an evidence, and instruct on the merits of the interdict,'[1] said she learnedly; 'but I ne'er hae yet been able to come to a right understanding anent and concerning the different aforesaids set forth in the respondent's reclaiming petition.[2] Noo, I would be greatly obligated if ye would expone to me the nice point, that I may be able to decern accordingly.'

The Writer to the Signet had never heard a clearer argument, either at the bar or on the bench, and he replied,—

'Indeed, Mem, it lies in a very small compass. It appears that the heir-male of your eldest son is the rightful heir of entail; but there are so many difficulties in the terms of the settlement, that I should not be surprised were the Court to set the deed aside, in which case, Mrs Milrookit would still retain the estate, as heir-at-law of her father.'

We must allow the reader to conceive with what feelings the Leddy heard this; but new and wonderful as it was felt to be, she still preserved her juridical gravity, and said,—

'It's vera true what ye say, Sir, that the heir-male of my eldest son,—is a son,—I can easily understand that point o' law;—but can ye tell me how the heir-at-law of her father, Mrs Milrookit that is, came to be a dochter, when it was ay the intent and purpose o' my friend that's awa, the testator, to make no provision but for heirs-male, which his heart, poor man, was overly[3] set on. Howsever, I suppose that's to be considered in the precognition.'[4]

'Certainly, Mem,' replied the Writer to the Signet; 'nothing is more clear than that your husband intended the estate to go, in the first instance, to the heirs-male of his sons; first to those of Walter, the second son; and failing them, to those of George, the third son; and failing them, then to go back to the heirs-male of Charles, the eldest son; and failing them, to the heirs-general of

Margaret, your daughter. It is, therefore, perfectly clear, that Mrs
Milrookit being, as you justly observe, a daughter, the estate,
according to the terms of the settlement, passes her, and goes to
the heir of entail, who is the son of your eldest son.'

'I understand that weel,' said the Leddy; 'it's as plain as a pike-
staff, that my oe[1] Jamie, the soldier-officer, is by right the heir;
and I dinna see how Walky Milrookit, or his wife Beenie, that is,
according to law, Robina, can, by any decreet o' Court, keep him
out of his ain,—poor laddie.'

'It is very natural for you, Mem, to say so; but the case has other
points, and especially as the heir of entail is in the army, I certainly
would not advise Mr Milrookit to surrender.'

'But he'll be maybe counselled better,' rejoined the Leddy,
inwardly rejoicing at the discovery she had made, and anxious to
get rid of the visitor, in order that she might act at once, 'and if
ye'll tak my advice, ye'll no sca'd[2] your lips in other folks' kail.
Mr Pitwinnoch is just as gude a Belzebub's baby for a law-plea, as
ony Writer to the Signet in that bottomless pit, the House o' Parliament in Edinbrough; and since ye hae told me what ye hae done,
it's but right to let you ken what I'll do. As yet I hae had but ae[3]
law-suit, and I trow it was soon brought, by my own mediation, to
a victory; but it winna be lang till I hae another; for if Milrookit
does na consent, the morn's morning,[4] to gie up the Kittlestonheugh, he'll soon fin' again what it is to plea wi' a woman o' my
experience.'

Pilledge was petrified; he saw that he was in the hands of the
Leddy, and that she had completely overreached him. But still he
was resolved that his journey should not be barren if he could
possibly prevent it. He accordingly wished her good afternoon,
and, returning to the inn, ordered a chaise, and proceeded to
Kittlestonheugh.

The moment that he left the Leddy, her cloak and bonnet were
put in requisition, and attended by her maid, on whose arm she
leaned, being still lame with the rheumatism, she sallied forth to
Pinwinnoch's office, resolved on action.

He had not, however, acted on what she called her great Bed
and Board plea entirely to her satisfaction; for she thought, had
he seen the rights of her case as well as she did herself, and had
counselled her better, she might have got much more than a
thousand pounds. She was, therefore, determined, if he showed

the least hesitation in obeying her 'peremptors,' that she would immediately proceed to Mr Whitteret's office, and appoint him her agent. How she happened to imagine that she had any right to institute proceedings against Milrookit, for the restoration of the estate to Walkinshaw, will be best understood by our narrative of what passed at the Consultation.

CHAPTER XXV

'IT was a happy thing for me, Mr Pitwinnoch,' said the Leddy, after being seated in his inner chamber,—'a happy thing, indeed, that I had a father, and sic a father as he was. Weel kent he the rights o' the law; so that I may say I was brought up at the feet o' Gamaliel. But the bed and board plea, Mr Pitwinnoch, that ye thought sae lightly o', and wanted me to mak a sacrifice o' wi' an arbitration, was bairn's play to the case I hae noo in hand. Ye maun ken,[1] then, that I hae ta'en a suspektion in my head, that Milrookit —the de'il rook[2] him for what he did to me—has nae right because[3] to keep, in a wrongous manner, my gudeman's estate and property o' the Kittlestonheugh. 'Deed, Mr Pitwinnoch, ye may glower; but it's my intent and purpose to gar him surrender at discretion, in due course of law. So he'll see what it is to deal wi' a woman o' my legality. In short, Mr Pitwinnoch, I'll mak him fin' that I'm a statute at large; for, as I said before, the thousand pounds was but erls, and a foretaste, that I hae been oure lang, Mr Pitwinnoch, of going to law.'

'You surprise me, Madam,—I cannot understand what you mean,' replied the astonished lawyer.

'Your surprise, and having no understanding, Mr Pitwinnoch, is a symptom to me that ye're no qualified to conduct my case; but, before going to Thomas Whitteret, who, as I am creditably informed, is a man o' a most great capacity, I thought it was but right to sound the depth o' your judgment and learning o' the law; and if I found you o' a proper sufficiency, to gie you a preferment, 'cause ye were my agent in the last plea.'

'But, Madam,' said the astonished lawyer, 'how can you possibly have fancied that Mr Milrookit has not, in right of his wife, properly succeeded to the estate?'

'Because she's no a male-heir—being in terms of the act—but a woman. What say ye to that? Is na that baith a nice point and a ground of action? Na, ye need na look saw constipated, Mr Pitwinnoch, for the heirs-general o' Margaret, the dochter, hae a better right than the heir-at-law o' George, the third and last son, the same being an heir-female.'

'In the name of goodness, where have you, Madam, collected all this stuff?'

'Stuff! Mr Pitwinnoch, is that the way to speak o' my legality? Howsever, since ye're sae dumfoundert, I'll just be as plain's am pleasant wi' you. Stuff truly! I think Mr Whitteret's the man for me.'

'I beg your pardon, Mrs Walkinshaw; but I wish you would be a little more explicit, and come to the point.'

'Have na I come to ae point already, anent the male-heir?'

'True, Madam,' said the lawyer; 'but even, admitting all you have stated to be perfectly correct, Mr Milrookit then has the right in himself, for you know it is to the heirs-general of his mother, and not to herself, that the property goes.'

'Ye need na tell me that. Do you think I dinna ken that he's an heir-general to his mother, being her only child? Ye mak light, I canna but say, o' my understanding, Mr Pitwinnoch.—Howsever, is't no plain that his wife, not being an heir-male, is debarred frae succeeding; and, he being an heir-general, cannot, according to the law of the case, succeed? Surely, Mr Pitwinnoch, that's no to be contested? Therefore, I maintain that he is lawfully bound to renounce the property, and that he shall do the morn's morning if there's a toun-officer in Glasgow.'

'But, Madam, you have no possible right to it,' exclaimed the lawyer, puzzled.

'Me! am I a male-heir? an aged woman, and a grandmother! Surely, Mr Pitwinnoch, your education maun hae been greatly neglekit, to ken so little o' the laws o' nature and nations. No: the heir-male is a young man, the eldest son's only son.'

The lawyer began to quake for his client as the Leddy proceeded,—

'For ye ken that the deed of entail was first on Walter, the second son; and, failing his heirs-male, then on George and his heirs-male; and, failing them, then it went back to Charles the eldest son, and to his heirs-male; if there's law in the land, his

only son ought to be an heir-male, afore Milrookit's wife that's
but an only dochter.'

'Has Mr Whitteret put this into your head?—he was bred wi'
Keelevin, who drew up the deed,' said the lawyer seriously, struck
with the knowledge which the Leddy seemed to have so miracu-
lously acquired of the provisions of the entail.

'I dinna need Mr Whitteret, nor ony siclike, to instruct me in
terms o' law—for I got an inkling and an instinct o' the whole nine
points[1] frae my worthy father, that was himsel bred an advocate,
and had more law-pleas on his hands when he died than ony ither
three lairds in Carrick, Coil, and Cunningham.[2] But no to be my
own trumpeter—ye'll just, Mr Pitwinnoch, write a mandamus[3]
to Milrookit, in a civil manner—mind that; and tell him in the
same, that I'll be greatly obligated if he'll gie up the house and
property of Kittlestonheugh to the heir-male, James Walkinshaw,
his cousin; or, failing therein, ye'll say that I hae implemented you
to pronounce an interlocutor[4] against him; and ye may gie him a
bit hint frae yoursel—in a noty beny[5] at the bottom—that you
advise him to conform, because you are creditably informed that
I mean to pursue him wi' a' the law o' my displeasure.'

'Does your grandson know any thing of this extraordinary
business?' said Pitwinnoch; but the Leddy parried the question
by saying,—

'That's no our present sederunt;[6] but I would ask you, if ye
do not think I hae the justice o' this plea?'

'Indeed, Madam, to say the truth, I shall not be surprised if you
have; but there is no need to be so peremptory—the business may
be as well settled by an amicable arrangement.'

'What's the use of an amicable arrangement? Is na the law the
law? Surely I did na come to a lawyer for sic dowf and dowie[7]
proceedings as amicable arrangements—no, Mr Pitwinnoch, ye
see yoursel that I hae decern't on the rights o' the case, and therefore (for I maun be short wi' you, for talking to me o' amicable
arrangements) ye may save your breath to cool your porridge; my
will and pleasure is, that Walkinshaw Milrookit shall do to-morrow
morning—in manner of law—then and there—dispone and surrender unto the heir-male of the late Claud Walkinshaw of
Kittlestonheugh, in the shire o' Lanark, and synod of Glasgow
and Ayr[8]—all and sundry the houses and lands aforesaid, according to the provisions of an act made and passed in the reign of

our Sovereign Lord the King. Ye see, Mr Pitwinnoch, that I'm no a daw in barrow't feathers, to be picket and pooket[1] in the way I was by sic trash as the Milrookits.'

The Leddy, having thus instructed her lawyer, bade him adieu, and returned home, leaning on her maid's arm, and on the best possible terms with herself, scarcely for a moment doubting a favourable result to a proceeding that in courtesy we must call her second law-suit.

CHAPTER XXVI

THE shipwreck of the third Laird had left an awful impression on the minds of all the Glengael party, who, immediately after that disaster, returned to the castle. To Mrs Eadie it afforded the strongest confirmation that she had inherited the inspiring mantle of her maternal race; and her dreams and visions, which happily for herself were of the most encouraging augury, became more and more frequent, and her language increased in mystery and metaphor.

'Death,' said she, 'has performed his task—the winds of heaven and the ocean waves have obeyed the mandate, and the moon has verified her influence on the destinies of men. But the volume, with the brazen clasps, has not yet been opened—the chronicled wisdom of ages has not yet been unfolded—Antiquity and Learning are still silent in their niches, and their faces veiled.'

It was of no avail to argue with her, even in her soberest moods, against the fatal consequences of yielding so entirely to the somnambulism[2] of her malady. Her friends listened to her with a solemn compassion, and only hoped that, in the course of the summer, some improvement might take place in her health, and allay that extreme occasional excitement of her nervous system which produced such mournful effects on a mind of rare and splendid endowments. In the hopes of this favourable change, it was agreed, when Mr Frazer was called to Edinburgh on professional business, as we have already mentioned, that the family should, on her account, remain till late in the year at Glengael.

Meanwhile Walkinshaw and French Frazer were proceeding with their recruiting; and it was soon evident to the whole party that the latter had attached himself in a particular manner to Mary. Mrs Eadie, if not the first who observed it, was the first who spoke of it; but, instead of using that sort of strain which ladies of a certain age commonly employ on such affairs, she boded of bridal banquets in the loftiest poetry of her prophetical phraseology. The fortunes of Walkinshaw and Ellen were lost sight of in the mystical presages of this new theme, till the letters arrived from Mr Frazer, announcing the discovery of the provisions in the deed of entail, and requesting his young friend to come immediately to Edinburgh. 'The clasped book of antiquity,' said Mrs Eadie, 'is now open. Who shall dispute the oracles of fate?'

But with all the perspicuity of her second sight,[1] she saw nothing of what was passing at Kittlestonheugh on the same afternoon in which these letters reached the castle.

Mr Pilledge, it will be recollected, immediately after his interview with the Leddy, proceeded in a post-chaise to see Milrookit; and, as he was not embarrassed with much professional diffidence, the purpose of his visit was soon explained. The consternation with which Walky heard of the discovery will be easier imagined than described; but something like a ray of hope and pleasure glimmered in the prospect that Pilledge held out of being able either to break the entail, or to procrastinate the contest to an indefinite period at an expence of less than half the rental of the property.

While they were thus engaged in discussing the subject, and Milrookit was entering as cordially into the views of the Edinburgh writer, as could on so short a notice be reasonably expected, Mr Pitwinnoch was announced. The instinct of birds of a feather, as the proverb says, had often before brought him into contact with Pilledge, and a few words of explanation enabled the triumvirate to understand the feelings of each other thoroughly.

'But,' said Pitwinnoch, 'I am instructed to take immediate steps, to establish the rights of the heir of entail.'

'So much the better,' replied Pilledge; 'the business could not be in abler hands. You can act for your client in the most satisfactory manner, and as Mr Milrookit will authorize me to proceed for him, it will be hard if we cannot make a tough pull.'

Mr Pitwinnoch thought so too, and then amused them with a laughable account of the instructions he had received from the Leddy, to demand the surrender of the estate, and the acknowledgment of the heir, in the course of the following day. Pilledge, in like manner, recounted, in his dry and pawkie style, the interview which he had himself with the same ingenious and redoubtable matron; and that nothing might be wanting to the enjoyment of their jokes and funny recitals, Milrookit ordered in wine, and they were all as jocose as possible, when the servant brought a letter—it was from Mr Whitteret, written at the suggestion of Mr Frazer, to whom he had, immediately after parting from Pilledge in the Register Office, communicated the discovery. It simply announced, that steps were taken to serve Walkinshaw heir[1] to the estate, and suggested on account of the relationship of the parties, that it might be as well to obviate, by an admission of the claim, the necessity of any exposure, or of the institution of unpleasant proceedings, for the fraud that had been practised.

Milrookit trembled as he read,—Pitwinnoch looked aghast, for he perceived that his own conduct in the transaction might be sifted; and Pilledge, foreseeing there would be no use for him, quietly took his hat and slipped away, leaving them to their own meditations.

'This is a dreadful calamity,' were the first words that Milrookit uttered, after a silence of several minutes.

'It is a most unlucky discovery,' said Pitwinnoch.

'And this threat of exposure,' responded his client.

'And my character brought into peril!' exclaimed the lawyer.

'Had you not rashly advised me,' said Milrookit, 'I should never for a moment have thought of retaining the property.'

'Both your father and yourself, Sir,' retorted the lawyer, 'thought if it could be done, it ought; I but did my duty as your lawyer, in recommending what you so evidently wished.'

'That is not the fact, Sir,' replied Milrookit, sharply, and the conversation proceeded to become more abrupt and vehement, till the anger of high words assumed the form of action, and the lawyer and his client rushed like two bull-dogs on each other. At that crisis, the door was suddenly opened, and the old Leddy looking in, said,—

'Shake him weel, Mr Pitwinnoch, and if he'll no conform, I redde ye gar him[2] conform.'

The rage of the combatants was instantly extinguished, and they stood pale, and confounded, trembling in every limb.

It had happened, after the Leddy returned home from Pitwinnoch's, that Robina called, in the carriage, to effect, if possible, a reconciliation with her, which, for reasons we need not mention, her husband had engaged her that afternoon to do, and she had, in consequence, brought her, in the spirit of friendship, as she imagined, out to Kittlestonheugh. The Leddy, however, prided herself on being almost as dexterous a diplomatician as she was learned in the law, and she affected to receive her grand-daughter in the spirit of a total oblivion of all injuries.

'Ye ken, Beenie, my dear,' said she, 'that I'm an aged person, and for a' the few and evil days I hae before me in this howling wilderness, it's vera natural that I should like to make a concilia-tion wi' my grand-childer, who, I hope, will a' live in comfort wi' one another—every one getting his own right, for it's a sore thing to go to law, although I hae some reason to know that there are folks in our family that ken mair o' the nine points than they let wit[1]—so I'm cordial glad to see you, Beenie, and I take it so kind, that if ye'll gie me a hurl[2] in the carriage, and send me hame at night, I'll no object to gang wi' you and speer for your gudeman,[3] for whom I hae a' manner o' respek, even though he was a thought unreasonable anent my charge o' moderation for the bed and board.'

But the truth is, that the Leddy, from the moment Robina entered the room, was seized with the thirst of curiosity to know how Milrookit would receive the claim, and had, in this eccentric manner, contrived to get herself taken to the scene of action.

CHAPTER XXVII

RECALLED to their senses by the interruption, both Milrookit and his lawyer saw that their interests and characters were too intimately linked in the consequences of the discovery to allow them to incur the hazards of a public disclosure. Pitwinnoch was the first who recovered his presence of mind, and, with great cleverness, he suddenly turned round, and addressed himself to the Leddy:—

'Though we have had a few words, Mr Milrookit is quite sensible that he has not a shadow of reason to withhold the estate from the heir of entail. He will give it up the moment that it is demanded.'

'Then, I demand it this moment,' exclaimed the Leddy; 'and

out of this house, that was my ain, I'll no depart till Jamie Walkinshaw, the righteous male-heir, comes to tak possession. It was a
most jewdical habit and repute like[1] action o' you, Walky Milrookit, to reset[2] and keep this fine property on a point of law; and
I canna see how ye'll clear your character o' the coom[3] ye hae
brought on't by sic a diminishment of the grounds of the case
between an heir-male and an heir-female.'

Milrookit, seeing his wife coming into the room, and eager to
get the business closed as happily as possible, requested Pitwinnoch to follow him into another apartment; to which they
immediately retired, leaving the ladies together.

'Beenie,' said the Leddy, with the most ineffable self-satisfied
equanimity, 'I hope ye'll prepare yoursel to hear wi' composity the
sore affliction that I'm ordain't to gie you. Eh, Beenie! honesty's a
braw thing; and I'll no say that your gudeman, my ain oe,[4] hasna
been a deevil that should get his dues—what they are, the laws and
lawyers as weel as me ken are little short o' the halter. But, for a'
that, our ain kith and kin, Beenie—we maun jook and let the jawp
gae bye.[5] So I counsel you to pack up your ends and your awls,
and flit your camp wi' a' the speed ye dow[6]; for there's no saying
what a rampageous soldier-officer, whose trade is to shoot folk,
may say or do, when Jamie Walkinshaw comes to ken the battle
that I hae fought wi' sic triumphing.'

Mrs Milrookit, who was totally uninformed either of the circumstances of her situation, or of what had taken place, scarcely
felt more amazement than terror at this speech, and in perceiving
that her grandmother was acquainted with the business which had
brought her husband and Pitwinnoch to such high words, that
their voices were heard before the carriage reached the door.

'What has happened?' was the anxious exclamation of her
alarm.

'Only a discovery that has been made among the Faculty o'
Advocates,[7] that a dochter's no a male-heir. So you being but the
heir-female of George, the third son, by course o' nature the property goes back to the son of Charles the eldest son—he being, in
the words of the act, an heir-male, and your husband, Walkinshaw
Milrookit, being an heir-general of Margaret, the daughter, is, in
a sense o' law, no heir at all, which is the reason that your cousin
Jamie comes in for the estate, and that you and Milrookit must take
up your bed, and walk to some other dwelling-place; for here, at

Kittlestonheugh, ye hae no continued city, Beenie, my dear, and I'm very sorry for you. It's wi' a very heavy heart, and an e'e o' pity, that I'm obligated not to be beautiful on the mountains, but to tell you thir[1] sore news.'

'Then I'm to understand,' replied Robina, with a degree of composure that surprised the Leddy, 'it has been discovered that my uncle Charles' family were not entirely disinherited, but that James succeeds to the estate? It is only to be regretted that this was not known sooner, before we took up our residence here.'

'It's an auld saying, Beenie, and a true saying, as I know from my own experience, that the law is a tether o' length and durability; so ye need be nane surprised, considering the short time bygane since your father's death, that the pannel[2] was na brought to judgment sooner. Indeed, if it had na been by my instrumentality, and the implementing o' the case that I gied to Pitwinnoch, there's no saying how long it would hae been pending afore the Lords.'[3]

While the Leddy was thus delivering what she called her dark sentence o' legality, Pitwinnoch and Milrookit returned into the room, and the former said to the Leddy,—

'I'm happy to inform you, Madam, that Mr Milrookit acts in the handsomest manner. He is quite satisfied that his cousin, Mr Walkinshaw, is the true heir of entail, and is prepared to resign the estate at once.'

'Did na I prove to you, Mr Pitwinnoch, that wi' baith his feet he had na ae[4] leg in law to stand on; but ye misdootit my judgment,' replied the Leddy, exultingly.

'But,' continued the lawyer, 'in consideration of this most honourable acquiescence at once on his part, I have undertaken that ye'll repay the thousand pounds, which, you must be sensible, was a most ridiculous sum for six weeks' bed and board in your house.'

'Truly, and ye're no far wrang, Mr Pitwinnoch. It was a vera ridiculous soom; for, if I had stood out, I might hae got twa thousand, if no mair. But I canna understand how it is possible you can think I'll part wi' my lawful won money for naething.—What's the gieing up[5] o' the estate to the male heir to me? I'll get neither plack nor bawbee by't, unless it please Jamie to gie me a bit present, by way o' a fee, for counselling you how to set about the precognition[6] that's gotten him his right.—Na, na, no ae farthing will I faik.'[7]

'Then, Madam, I shall feel it my duty to advise Mr Milrookit to revive the question, and take the matter into Court upon a ground of error,' said the lawyer.

'Tak it, tak it, pleasure yoursel in that way; ye can do naething mair cordial to me;—but I think ye ought to know, and Milrookit to understand, baith by bed, board, and washing, and heirs-male, what, it is to try the law wi' me.'

The lawyer and his client exchanged looks: the Leddy, however, continued her address,—

'Howsever, Mr Pitwinnoch, sure am I there was no mistake in the business; for ye'll bear in mind that ye made me an offer of twa hundred, the whilk I refused, and then ye brought me my justly due. That settles the point o' law,—tak my word for't.'

'I am afraid,' said Pitwinnoch to his rueful client, 'that there is no chance'—

''Deed no, Mr Pitwinnoch,' replied the Leddy; 'neither pursuer nor respondent has ony chance wi' me in that plea; so just shake your lugs and lie down again. A' your barking would prove afore the Lords but as water spilt on the ground; for the money is in an heritable bond, and the whilk bond is in my hands; that's the strong ground o' the case,—touch it whan ye may.'

Pitwinnoch could with difficulty keep his gravity, and poor Milrookit, finding he had so overreached himself, said,—

'Well, but when you make your will, I trust and hope you will then consider how simply I gave you the money.'

'Mak my will!—that's a delicate hint to an aged woman. I'll no forget that,—and as to your simplicity in paying the justly due for bed, board, and washing,—was na every pound got as if it had been a tooth out o' your head, howkit[1] out by course and force o' law?'

'In truth, Leddy,' said Pitwinnoch, 'we are all friends here, and it's just as well to speak freely. I advised Mr Milrookit to pay you the money, rather than hazard any question that might possibly attract attention to the provisions of the entail; but now since the whole has been brought to an issue, you must be sensible that he suffers enough in losing the estate, and that you ought to give him back the money.'

The Leddy sat for several minutes silent, evidently cogitating an answer, at the end of which she raised her eyes, and said to Pitwinnoch,—

'I can see as far through a milstane as ye can do through a fir

deal,[1] and maybe I may tak it in my head to raise a plea wi' you in
an action of damages, for plotting and libelling in the way that it's
vera visible ye hae done, jointly and severally, in a plea of the crown;
and aiblins[2] I'll no tak less than a thousand pounds;—so, Mr
Pitwinnoch, keep your neck out o' the woody[3] o' a law-plea wi'
me, if ye can; for, in the way of business, I hae done wi' you; and,
as soon as Mr Whitteret comes hame, I'll see whether I ought not
to instruct in a case against you for the art and part[4] conspiracy of
the thousand pounds.'

Milrookit himself was obliged to laugh at the look of consternation with which this thunderclap broke over the lawyer, who,
unable to withstand the absurdity of the threat, and yet alarmed
for the consequences to his reputation, which such an attempt
would entail, hastily retired.

CHAPTER XXVIII

THE Leddy having so happily brought her second law-suit to a
victorious issue, and already menacing a third, did not feel that
her triumph would be complete, until she had obtained the
plaudits of the world; and the first person on whom she resolved
to levy her exactions of applause was naturally enough the mother
of Walkinshaw.

As soon as Pitwinnoch had left the house, she persuaded Milrookit to send the carriage for Mrs Charles, with injunctions to
the coachman not to say a word of what had passed, as she intended
herself to have the pleasure of communicating the glad tidings.
This he very readily agreed to; for, notwithstanding the grudge
which he felt at having been so simply mulcted of so large a sum,
he really felt his mind relieved by the result of the discovery;
perhaps, in complying, he had some sinister view towards the
Leddy's good will—some distant vista of his thousand pounds.

Mrs Charles was a good deal surprised at the message to come
immediately to Kittlestonheugh; and her timid and gentle spirit,
in consequence of learning from the coachman that the old lady
was there, anticipated some disaster to her son. Her fears fluttered
as she drove on alone. The broad dark shadows that had crossed
the path of her past pilgrimage were remembered with melancholy

forebodings, and the twilight of the evening having almost faded into night, she caught gloomy presentiments from the time, and sighed that there was no end to her sorrows.

The season was now advanced into September; and though the air was clear, the darkness of the road, the silence of the fields, and the occasional glimmers of the fire that the horses' hoofs struck from the stones, awakened associations of doubt, anxiety, and danger; but the serene magnificence of the starry heavens inspired hope, and the all-encompassing sky seemed to her the universal wings of Providence, vigilant and protecting with innumerable millions of eyes.

Still the devotional enthusiasm of that fancy was but a transient glow on the habitual pale cast of her thoughts; and she saw before her, in the remainder of her mortal journey, only a continuance of the same road which she had long travelled—a narrow and a difficult track across a sterile waste, harsh with brambles, and bleak and lonely.

So is it often, under the eclipse of fortune, even with the bravest spirits; forgetting how suddenly before, in the darkest hour the views of life have changed, they yield to the aspect of the moment, and breathe the mean and peevish complaints of faithlessness and despondency. Let it not, therefore, be imputed as an unworthy weakness, that a delicate and lowly widow, whose constant experience had been an unbroken succession of disappointments and humiliations, should, in such an hour, and shrinking with the sensibilities of a mother, wonder almost to sinning why she had been made to suffer such a constancy of griefs. But the midnight of her fate was now past, and the dawn was soon to open upon her with all its festal attributes of a bright and joyous morning—though our friend the Leddy was not so brisk in communicating the change as we could have wished.

She was sitting alone in the parlour when the carriage returned; and as the trembling mother was shown into the room, she received her with the most lugubrious face that her features could assume.

'Come awa, Bell Fatherlans,' said she, 'come away, and sit down. O this is a most uncertain world—nothing in it has stability;—the winds blow—the waters run—the grass grows—the snow falls—the day flieth away unto the uttermost parts of the sea, and the night hideth her head in the morning cloud, and perisheth for evermore. Many a lesson we get—many a warning to set our thoughts on things above; but we're ay sinking, sinking, sinking, as the sparks fly upward.—Bell, Bell, we're a' like thorns crackling under a kail-pot.'

'What has occurred?' exclaimed Mrs Charles; 'I beg you'll tell me at once.'

'So I will, when I hae solaced you into a religious frame o' mind to hear me wi' a Christian composity o' temper; for what I maun tell is, though I say't mysel, a something.'

'For goodness and mercy, I entreat you to proceed.—Where is Mr Milrookit? where is Robina?'

'Ye need na hope to see muckle o' them the night,' replied the Leddy. 'Poor folk, they hae gotten their hands filled wi' cares. O Bell, Bell—when I think o't—it's a judgment—it's a judgment, Bell Fatherlans, aboon the capacity o' man! Really, when I consider how I hae been directit—and a' by my own skill, knowledge, wisdom, and understanding—it's past a' comprehension. What would my worthy father hae said had he lived to see the day that his dochter won sic a braw estate by her ain interlocutors?[1]—and what would your gudefather hae said, when he was ay brag bragging o' the conquest he had made o' the Kittlestonheugh o' his ancestors—the whilk took him a lifetime to do—had he seen me, just wi' a single whisk o' dextcrity, a bit touch of the law, make the vera same conquest for your son Jamie Walkinshaw in less than twa hours?'

'You astonish me! to what do you allude? I am amazed, and beginning to be confounded,' said Mrs Charles.

'Indeed it is no wonder,' replied the Leddy; 'for wha would hae thought it, that I, an aged 'literate grandmother, would hae bamboozlet an Embrough Writer to the Signet on a nice point, and found out the ground of an action for damages against that tod o' a bodie[2] Pitwinnoch, for intromitting wi' ane of the four pleas o' the Crown?[3] Had I kent what I ken now, uncle Watty might still hae been to the fore,[4] and in the full possession of his seven lawful senses—for, woman as I am, I would hae been my own man o' business, counsel, and executioner, in the concos mentos sederunt —whereby I was so 'frauded o' my rightful hope and expectation. But Pitwinnoch will soon fin' the weight o' the lion's paw that his doobilcecity has roused in me.'

Mrs Charles, who was much amused by the exultation with which the Leddy had recounted her exploits in the bed and board plea, perceiving that some new triumph equally improbable had occurred, felt her anxieties subside into curiosity; and being now tolerably mistress of her feelings, she again inquired what had happened.

'I'll tell you,' said the Leddy; 'and surely it's right and proper you his mother should know, that, through my implementing, it has been discovered that your son is an heir-male according to law!'

'No possible!' exclaimed the delighted mother, the whole truth flashing at once on her mind.

'Aye, that's just as I might hae expectit—a prophet ne'er got honour in his own country; and so a' the thank I'm to get for my pains is a no possible!' said the Leddy offended, mistaking the meaning of the interjection. 'But it is a true possible; and Milrookit has consentit to adjudicate[1] the estate—so ye see how ye're raised to pride and affluence by my instrumentality. Firstly, by the bed and board plea, I found a mean to revisidend[2] your 'nuity; and secondly, I hae found the libel[3] proven, that Beenie, being a dochter, is an heir-female, and is, by course of law, obligated to renounce the estate.'

'This is most extraordinary news, indeed,' rejoined Mrs Charles, 'after for so many years believing my poor children so destitute;' and a flood of tears happily came to her relief.

'But, Bell Fatherlans,' resumed the Leddy, 'I'll tak you wi' the tear in your ee, as both you and Jamie maun be sensible, that, but for my discerning, this great thing never could hae been brought to a come-to-pass. I hope ye'll confabble thegither anent the loss I sustained by what happened to uncle Watty, and mak me a reasonable compensation out o' the rents; the whilk are noo, as I am creditably informed, better than fifteen hundred pounds per anno Domini, that's the legality for the year o' our Lord;—a sma' matter will be a great satisfaction.'

'Indeed,' said Mrs Charles, 'James owes you much; and your kindness in giving him the bill so generously, I know, has made a very deep impression on his heart.'

'He was ay a blithe and kindly creature,' exclaimed the Leddy, wiping her eye, as if a tear had actually shot into it—'and may be it winna fare the waur[4] wi' him when I'm dead and gone. For I'll let you into a secret—it's my purpose to make a last will and testament, and cut off Milrookit wi' a shilling, for his horridable niggerality about the bed and board concern. Na, for that matter, as ye'll can fen noo without ony 'nuity,[1] but your ain son's affection, I hae a great mind, and I'll do't too—that's what I will—for fear I should be wheedled into an adversary[2] by my dochter Meg for the Milrookits,—I'll gie the thousand pound heritable bond to your Mary for a tocher; is not that most genteel of me? I doot few families hae had a grandmother for their ancestor like yours.'

Some farther conversation to the same effect was continued, and the injustice which Milrookit had attempted seemed to Mrs Charles considerably extenuated by the readiness with which he had acknowledged the rights of her son. For, notwithstanding all the Leddy's triumphant oratory and legal phraseology, she had no difficulty in perceiving the true circumstances of the case.

CHAPTER XXIX

IN the opinion of all the most judicious critics, the Iliad terminated with the death of Hector; but, as Homer has entertained us with the mourning of the Trojans, and the funeral of the hero, we cannot, in our present circumstances, do better than adopt the rule of that great example. For although it must be evident to all our readers that the success of the Leddy in her second law-suit, by placing the heir, in despite of all the devices and stratagem of parchments and Pitwinnoch, in possession of the patrimony of his ancestors, naturally closes the Entail, a work that will, no doubt, outlive the Iliad, still there were so many things immediately consequent on that event, that our story would be imperfect without some account of them.

In the first place, then, Walkinshaw, immediately after the receipt of Frazer's letter, acquainting him with the discovery of the provisions of the deed, returned to Edinburgh, where he arrived on the third day after his friend had heard from Whitteret, the Glasgow writer, that Milrookit, without objection, agreed to surrender the estate. The result of which communication was an immediate and formal declaration from Walkinshaw of his attachment to Ellen, and a cheerful consent from her father, that their marriage, as soon as the necessary preparations could be made, should be celebrated at Glengael.

Upon French Frazer the good fortune of his brother officer was no less decisive, for any scruple that he might have felt in his attachment to Mary, on account of his own circumstances, was removed by an assurance from Walkinshaw that he would, as soon as possible, make a liberal provision both for her and his mother; and in the same letter which Walkinshaw wrote home on his return to Edinburgh, and in which he spoke of his own marriage, he entreated his mother's consent that Mary should accept the hand of Frazer.

On Mrs Eadie, the fulfilment, as she called it, of her visions and predictions, had the most lamentable effect. Her whole spirit became engrossed with the most vague and mystical conceptions; and it was soon evident that an irreparable ruin had fallen upon one of the noblest of minds. Over her latter days we shall, therefore, draw a veil, and conclude her little part in our eventful history with simply mentioning that she never returned to Camrachle; but sunk into rest in the visionary beatitude of her parental solitudes.

Her husband, now a venerable old man, still resides as contentedly as ever in his parish; and, when we last visited him, in his modest mansion, he informed us that he had acquiesced in the wishes of his elders by consenting to receive a helper and successor in the ministry. So far, therefore, as the best, the most constant, and the kindest friends of the disinherited family are concerned, our task is finished: but we have a world of things to tell of the Leddy and the Milrookits, many of which we must reserve till we shall have leisure to write a certain story of incomparable humour and pathos.

In the meantime, we must proceed to mention, that the Leddy, finding it was quite unnecessary to institute any further proceedings, to eject the Milrookits from Kittlestonheugh, as they of their own accord removed, as soon as they found a suitable house, returned to her residence in the royal city, where she resumed her domestic thrift at the spinning-wheel, having resolved not to go on with her action of damages against Pitwinnoch, till she had seen her grandson, who, prior to his marriage, was daily expected.

'For,' as she said to his mother, after consulting with Mr Whitteret, and stating her grounds of action, 'it is not so clear a case as my great bed and board plea—and Mr Whitteret is in some doubt, whether Pitwinnoch should be sent to trial by my instrumentality, or that of Jamie—very sensibly observing—for he's really a man o' the heighth o' discretion yon—that it would be hard for an aged gentlewoman like me, with a straitened jointure, to take up a cause that would, to a moral certainty, be defendit, especially when her grandson is so much better able to afford the expence. The which opinion of counsel has made me sit down with an arrest of judgment for the present, as the only reason I hae for going to law at all is to mak money by it. Howsever, if ye can persuade Jamie to bequeath and dispone to me his right to the damage, which I mean to assess at a thousand pounds, I'll implement Mr Whitteret to pursue.'

'I dare say,' replied Mrs Charles, 'that James will very readily give up to you all his claim; but Mr Pitwinnoch having rectified the mistake he was in, we should forgive and forget.'

'A' weel I wat, Bell Fatherlans, I needna cast my pearls o' great price before swine, by waring[1] my words o' wisdom wi' the like o' you. In truth, it's an awfu' story when I come to think how ye hae been sitting like an effigy on a tomb, wi' your hands baith alike syde, and mento mori written on your vesture and your thigh, instead o' stirring your stumps, as ye ought to hae done—no to let your bairns be rookit[2] o' their right by yon Cain and Abel, the twa cheatrie Milrookits. For sure am I, had no I ta'en the case in hand, ye might hae continued singing Wally, wally, up yon bank, and wally, wally, down yon brae,[3] a' the days o' your tarrying in the tabernacles o' men.'

Her daughter-in-law admitted, that she was, indeed, with all her family, under the greatest obligations to her,—and that, in all probability, but for her happy discovery of the errand on which the writer to the signet had come to Glasgow, they might still have had their rights withheld.

In conversations of this description the time passed at Glasgow, while the preparations for the marriage of Walkinshaw and Ellen were proceeding with all expedient speed at Glengael. Immediately after the ceremony, the happy pair, accompanied by Mary, returned to Edinburgh, where it was determined the marriage of Mary with French Frazer should be celebrated, Mrs Charles and the old lady being equally desirous of being present.

We should not, however, be doing justice to ourselves, as faithful historians, were we to leave the reader under an impression that the Leddy's visit to the lawful metropolis was entirely dictated by affectionate consideration for her grandchildren. She had higher

and more public objects, worthy, indeed, of the spirit with which
she had so triumphantly conducted her causes. But with that
remarkable prudence, so conspicuous in her character, she made
no one acquainted with the real motives by which she was actuated,
—namely, to acquire some knowledge of the criminal law, her
father not having, as she said, 'paid attention to that Court of
Justice, his geni being, like her own, more addicted to the civilities[1]
of the Court o' Session.'

She was led to think of embarking in this course of study, by the
necessity she was often under of making, as she said, her servants
'walk the carpet;' or, in other words, submit to receive those kind
of benedictions to which servants are, in the opinion of all good
administrators of householdry, so often and so justly entitled. It
had occurred to her that, some time or another, occasion might
require that she should carry a delinquent handmaid before the
Magistrates, or even before the Lords; indeed, she was determined
to do so on the very first occurrence of transgression, and, therefore, she was naturally anxious to obtain a little insight of the best
practice in the Parliament House, that she might, as she said herself, be made capable of implementing her man of business how
to proceed.

Walkinshaw, by promising to take every legal step that she
herself could take against Pitwinnoch, had evinced, as she considered it, such a commendable respect for her judgment, that
he endeared himself to her more than ever. He was, in consequence, employed to conduct her to the Parliament House,
that she might hear the pleadings; but by some mistake
he took her to that sink of sin the Theatre, when Othello was
performing, where, as she declared, she had received all the
knowledge of the criminal law she could require, it having been
manifestly shown, that any woman stealing a napkin ought to
be prosecuted with the utmost rigour. But her legal studies
were soon interrupted by the wedding festivities; and when she
returned to Glasgow, alas! she was not long permitted to indulge
her legal pursuits; for various causes combined to deprive the
world of our incomparable heroine. Her doleful exit from the
tents of Time, Law, and Physic, it is now our melancholy duty
to relate, which we shall endeavour to do with all that good-
humoured pathos for which we are so greatly and so deservedly
celebrated. If nobody says we are so distinguished, we must

modestly do it ourselves, never having been able to understand why a candidate for parliament or popularity should be allowed to boast of his virtues more than any other dealer in tales and fictions.

CHAPTER XXX

MARRIAGE feasts, we are creditably informed, as the Leddy would have said, are of greater antiquity than funerals; and those with which the weddings of Walkinshaw and his sister were celebrated, lacked nothing of the customary festivities. The dinners which took place in Edinburgh were, of course, served with all the refinements of taste and dissertations on character, which render the entertainments in the metropolis of Mind occasionally so racy and peculiar. But the cut-and-come-again banquets of Glasgow, as the Leddy called them, following on the return of the Laird and his bride to his patrimonial seat, were, in her opinion, far superior, and she enjoyed them with equal glee and zest.

'Thanks be, and praise,' said she, after returning home from one of those costly piles of food, 'I hae lived to see, at last, something like wedding doings in my family. Charlie's and Bell Fatherlans's was a cauldrife commodity, boding scant and want, and so cam o't[1] —Watty's was a walloping galravitch o' idiocety,[2] and so cam o't   Geordie's was little better than a burial formality, trying to gie a smirk,[3] and so cam o't—as for Meg's and Dirdumwhamle's, theirs was a third marriage—a cauld-kail-het-again[4] affair—and Beenie and Walky's Gretna Green, play-actoring,— Bed, Board, and Washing, bore witness and testimony to whatna kind o' bridal they had. But thir jocose gavaulings are worthy o' the occasion   Let naebody tell me, noo, that the three P's o' Glasgow mean Packages, Puncheons, and Pigtail,[5] for I have seen and known that they may be read in a marginal note Pomp, Punch, and Plenty. To be sure, the Embroshers[6] are no without a genteelity —that maun be condescended to them But I jealouse[7] they're pinched to get gude wine, poor folk—they try sae mony different bottles: naething hae they like a gausie[8] bowl. Therefore, commend me to our ain countryside,—Fatted calves, and feasting

Belshazers,—and let the Embroshers cerimoneez wi' their
Pharaoh's lean kine and Grants and Frazers.'[1]

But often when the heart exults, when the 'bosom's Lord sits
light upon his throne,' it is an omen of sorrow. On the very night
after this happy revel of the spirits, the Leddy caught a fatal cold,
in consequence of standing in the current of a door while the
provost's wife, putting on her pattens, stopped the way, and she
was next morning so indisposed that it was found necessary to call
in Dr Sinney to attend her; who was of opinion, considering she
was upwards of seventy-six, that it might go hard with her if she
did not recover; and, this being communicated to her friends, they
began to prepare themselves for the worst.

Her daughter, the Lady of Dirdumwhamle, came in from the
country, and paid her every mark of attention. At the suggestion
of her husband, she, once or twice, intimated a little anxiety to
know if her mother had made a will; but the Leddy cut her short,
by saying,—

'What's t'at to thee, Meg? I'm sure I'm no dead yet, that t'ou
should be groping about my bit gathering?'[2]

Dirdumwhamle himself rode daily into Glasgow in the most
dutiful manner; but, receiving no satisfaction from the accounts
of his wife respecting the Leddy's affairs, he was, of course, deeply
concerned at her situation; and, on one occasion, when he was
sitting in the most sympathising manner at her bedside, he said,
with an affectionate and tender voice,—

'That he hoped she would soon be well again; but, if it was
ordain't to be otherwise, he trusted she would give her daughter
some small memorial over and by[3] what she might hae alloo't her
in will.'

''Deed,' replied the Leddy, as she sat supported by pillows, and
breathing heavily, 'I'll no forget that—for ye may be sure, when I
intend to dee, that I'll mak my ain hands my executioners.'[4]

'Aye, aye,' rejoined the pathetic Laird, 'I was ay o' that opinion,
and that ye would act a mother's part in your latter end.'

To this the Leddy made no reply; but by accident coughed rather
a little too moistly in his face, which made him shift his seat, and
soon after retire.

He had not long taken his leave, when Milrookit and Robina
came in, both in the most affectionate manner; and, after the
kindest inquiries, they too hoped that she had made her departure

clear with this world, and that, when she was removed to a better, no disputes would arise among surviving friends.

'I'm sure,' said Robina, 'we shall all greatly miss you; and I would be very glad if you would give me some little keepsake out of your own hands, if it were no more than the silver teapot.'

'I canna do that yet, Beenie, my Leddy, for ye ken I'm obligated to gie the Laird and Nell Frizel a tea banquet, as soon's I'm able. But when I'm dead and gone, for we're a' lifelike and a' deathlike, if ye outlive me, ye'll fin' that I was a grandmother.'

'It's pleasant to hear,' said Milrookit, 'that ye hae sic an inward satisfaction of health; but I hope ye'll no tak it ill at my wishing for a token o' my grandfather. I would like if ye would gie me from yourself the old-fashioned gold watch, just because it was my grandfather's, and sae lang in his aught.'[1]

'Aye, Walky, I won'er thou does na wis for me, for I was longer in his aught. Bairns, bairns, I purpose to outlive my last will and testament, so I redde ye keep a calm sough.'

This they thought implied that she had made some provision for them in her last will and testament; and although disappointed in their immediate object, they retired in as complete peace of mind as any affectionate grandchildren like them could retire from a deathbed.

To them succeeded the mother of Walkinshaw.

'Come away, Bell Fatherlans,' said the Leddy—'sit down beside me;' and she took her kindly by the hand. 'The Milrookits, auld and young, hae been here mair ravenous than the worms and cloks[2] of the tomb, for they but devour the dead body; but yon greedy caterpillars would strip me o' leaf and branch afore my time. There was Dirdumwhamle sympathising for a something over and aboon what Meg's to get by the will. Then came Beenie, another of the same, as the Psalmist[3] says, simpering, like a yird tead,[4] for my silver teapot, and syne naething less would serve her gudeman but a solemneesing wheedlie for the auld gold watch. But I'll sympathise, and I'll simper, and I'll wheedle them.—Hae, tak my keys, and gang into the desk-head,[5] and ye'll fin' a bonny sewt pocketbook in the doocot hole[6] next the window, bring't to me.'

Mrs Charles did as she was desired; and when the pocketbook was brought, the old Leddy opened it, and, taking out one of her Robin Carricks, as she called her bills, she said,—

'Bring me a pen that can spell, and I'll indoss this bit hundred

pound to thee, Bell, as an over and aboon;[1] and when ye hae
gotten't, gang and bid Jamie and Mary come to see me, and I'll gie
him the auld gold watch, and her the silver teapot, just as a reward
to the sympathising, simpering, and wheedling Milrookits. For
between ourselves, Bell, my time is no to be lang noo amang you.
I feel the clay-cold fingers o' Death handling my feet; so when I
hae settled my worldly concernments, ye'll send for Dr De'ilfear,
for I would na like to mount into the chariots o' glory without the
help o' an orthodox.'

All that the Leddy required was duly performed. She lingered
for several days; but, at the end of a week from the commencement
of her illness, she closed her eyes, and her death was, after the
funeral, according to the Scottish practice, announced in that loyal
and well-conducted old paper, the Glasgow Courier, as having
taken place, 'to the great regret of all surviving friends'.

CHAPTER XXXI

WE have often lamented that so many worthy people should be
at the expence and trouble of making last wills and testaments,
and yet never enjoy what passes at the reading of them. On all the
different occasions where we have been present at such affecting
ceremonies, it was quite edifying to see how justly the sorrow was
apportioned to the legacies; those enjoying the greatest being
always the most profoundly distressed; their tears, by some sort
of sympathy, flowing exactly in accordance with the amount of
the sums of money, or the value of the chattels which they were
appointed to receive.

But on no other occasion have we ever been so much struck with
the truth of this discovery as on that when, after attending the
Leddy's remains to the family sepulchre, our acquaintance,
Dirdumwhamle, invited us to return to the Leddy's house, in
order to be present at the solemnity. Considering the tenderness
of our feelings, and how much we respect the professed sincerity
of mankind, we ought, perhaps, in justice to ourselves, knowing
how incapable we are of withstanding the mournful melancholy
of such posthumous rites, to have eschewed the invitation of our
sighing and mourning friend.

We were, however, enticed, by a little curiosity, to walk with him arm in arm from the interment, suggesting to him, on the way, every topic of Christian consolation suitable on such occasions, perceiving how much he stood in need of them all.

When we entered the parlour, which had been so often blithened with the jocose spirit of its defunct mistress, we confess that our emotions were almost too great for our fortitude, and that, as we assured the Laird of Dirdumwhamle, our sensibility was so affected that we could, with the utmost difficulty, repress our hysterical sobbings, which he professed with no less sincerity entirely to believe. Alas! such scenes are too common in this transitory scene of things.

Seeing how much we were all in need of a glass of wine, Dirdumwhamle, with that free thought which forms so prominent a feature of his character, suggested to his lady that she should order in the decanters, and, with a bit of the shortbread, enable us to fortify our hearts for the doleful task and duty we had yet to perform.

The decanters were, accordingly, ordered in; the wine poured into the glasses; and all present to each other sighed, as in silence, the reciprocity of good wishes.

After which a pause ensued—a very syncope of sadness—a dwam[1] of woe, as the Leddy herself would have called it, had she been spared, to witness how much we all felt.—But she was gone—she had paid the debt of nature, and done, as Dirdumwhamle said, what we are all in this life ordained to do. It is, therefore, of no consequence to imagine how she could either have acted or felt had she been present at the reading of her last will and testament. In a word, after that hiatus in the essay of mourning, it was proposed, by young Milrookit, that the Leddy's scrutoire should be opened, and the contents thereof examined.

No objection was made on the part of any of the sorrowful and assembled friends,—quite the contrary. They all evinced the most natural solicitude, that every thing proper and lawful should be done. 'It is but showing our respect to the memory of her that is gone,' said Dirdumwhamle, 'to see in what situation she has left her affairs—not that I have any particular interest in the business, but only, considering the near connection between her and my family, it is due to all the relations that the distribution which she has made of her property should be published among them.—It would have been a happy and a comfortable thing to every one who knew her worth had her days been prolonged; but, alas! that was not in her own power. Her time o' this world was brought, by course of nature, to an end, and no man ought to gainsay the ordinances of Providence.—Gudewife, hae ye the key o' the desk-head?'

Mrs Milrookit, his wife, who, during this highly sympathetic conversation, had kept her handkerchief to her eyes, without removing it, put her hand into her pocket, and, bringing forth a bunch of keys, looked for one aside, which, having found, she presented it to her husband, saying, with a sigh, 'That's it.'

He took it in his hand, and, approaching the scrutoire, found, to his surprise, that it was sealed.

'How is this?' cried Dirdumwhamle, in an accent somewhat discordant with the key in which the performers to the concert of woe were attuned.

'I thought,' replied Walkinshaw the Laird, 'that it was but regular, when my grandmother died, that, until we all met, as we are now met, her desk and drawers should be sealed for fear***'

'For fear of what?' Dirdumwhamle was on the point of saying as we thought; but, suddenly checking himself, and, again striking the note of woe, in perfect harmony, he replied,—

'Perfectly right, Laird,—when all things are done in order, no one can have any reason to complain.'

Dirdumwhamle then took off the seal, and applying the key to the lock, opened the desk head, and therein, among other things, found the embroidered pocketbook, so well known to our readers. At the sight of it, the tears of his lady began to flow, and they flowed the faster when, on examining its contents, it was discovered that the hundred pound Robin Carrick was not forthcoming— She having acquired some previous knowledge of its existence, and had, indeed, with her most dutiful husband, made a dead set at it in their last affectionate conversation with the Leddy, with what success the reader is already informed.

A search was then made for the heritable bond for a thousand pounds, but Mrs Charles Walkinshaw surprised us all into extreme sorrow, when, on understanding the object of the search, she informed us that the said bond had been most unaccountably given, as the Milrookits thought, to her daughter for a dowry.

An inventory of the contents of the desk being duly and properly made,—indeed we ourselves took down the particulars in the most complete manner,—an inquest was instituted with respect to the contents of drawers, papers, boxes, trunks, and even into the last pouches that the Leddy had worn; but neither the silver teapot nor the old gold watch were forthcoming. Mrs Charles Walkinshaw, however, again explained, and the explanation was attended by the happiest effects, in so much as to us it served to lessen in a great degree the profound sorrow in which all the Milrookits had been plunged.

But yet no will was found, and Dirdumwhamle was on the point of declaring that the deceased having died intestate, his wife, her daughter, succeeded, of course, to all she had left. But while he was speaking, young Mrs Milrookit happened to cast her eyes into one of the pigeon-holes in the scrutoire head, where, tied with a red tape in the most business-like manner, a will was found,—we shall not say that Dirdumwhamle had previously seen it, but undoubtedly he appeared surprised that it should have been so near his sight and touch, so long unobserved,—which gave us a hint to suggest, that when people make their wills and testaments, they should always tie them with red tape, that none of their heirs, executors, or assigns, may fall into the mistake of not noticing them at the time of the funeral examination, and afterwards, when by themselves, tear or burn them by mistake.

CHAPTER XXXII

IT appeared by this will that the Leddy had, with the exception of a few inconsiderable legacies to the rest of her family, and a trifling memorial of her affection to our friend Walkinshaw, bequeathed all to her daughter, at which that lady, with the greatest propriety, burst out into the most audible lament for her affectionate mother, and Dirdumwhamle, her husband, became himself so agitated with grief, that he was almost unable to proceed with the reading of the affecting document. Having gradually mastered his feelings, he was soon, however, able to condole with Mrs Charles Walkinshaw upon the disappointment she had, no doubt, suffered; observing, by way of consolation, that it was, after all, only what was to have been expected; for the Leddy, the most kind of parents, naturally enough considered her own daughter as the nearest and dearest of all her kith and kin.

During this part of the scene we happened inadvertently to look towards Walkinshaw, and were not a little shocked to observe a degree of levity sparkling in his eyes, quite unbecoming such a sorrowful occasion; and still more distressed were we at the irreverence with which, almost in actual and evident laughter, he inquired at Dirdumwhamle the date of the paper.

It was found to have been made several years before, soon after the decease of poor Walter.

'Indeed!' said Walkinshaw pawkily;[1] 'that's a very important circumstance, for I happen to have another will in my pocket, made at Edinburgh, while the Leddy was there at my marriage, and the contents run somewhat differently.'

The tears of the Lady of Dirdumwhamle were instantaneously dried up, and the most sensitive of Lairds himself appeared very much surprised; while, with some vibrating accent in his voice, he requested that this new last will and testament might be read.

Sorry are we to say it, that, in doing so, Walkinshaw was so little affected, that he even chuckled while he read. This was, no doubt, owing to the little cause he had to grieve, a legacy of five guineas, to buy a ring, being all that the Leddy had bequeathed to him.

This second will, though clearly and distinctly framed, was evidently dictated by the Leddy herself. For it began by declaring, that, having taken it into her most serious consideration, by and with the advice of her private counsel, Mr Frazer of Glengael, whom she appointed executor, she had resolved to make her last will and testament; and after other formalities, couched somewhat in the same strain, she bequeathed sundry legacies to her different grandchildren,—first, as we have said, five guineas, as a token of her particular love, to Walkinshaw, he standing in no need of any farther legacy, and being, over and moreover, indebted to her sagacity for the recovery of his estate. Then followed the enumeration of certain trinkets and Robin Carricks, which were to be delivered over to, and to be held and enjoyed by, Mary, his sister. To this succeeded a declaration, that her daughter Margaret, the wife of Dirdumwhamle, should enjoy the main part of her gathering, in liferent, but not until the Laird, her husband, had paid his debt of nature, and departed out of this world; and if the said legatee did not survive her husband, then the legacy was to go to

Mrs Charles Walkinshaw, the testatrix's daughter-in-law. 'As for my two grateful grandchildren, Walkinshaw Milrookit, and Robina his wife,' continued the spirit of the Leddy to speak in the will, 'I bequeath to them, and their heirs for ever, all and haill[1] that large sum of money which they still stand indebted to me, for and on account of bed, board, and washing, of which debt only the inconsiderable trifle of one thousand pounds was ever paid.'

The testing clause[2] was all that followed this important provision, but the will was in every respect complete, and so complete also was the effect intended, that young Milrookit and his wife Robina immediately rose and retired, without speaking, and Dirdumwhamle and his lady also prepared to go away, neither of them being seemingly in a condition to make any remark on the subject.

Such is the natural conclusion of our story; but perhaps it is expected that we should say something of the subsequent history of Walkinshaw, especially as his wife has brought him nine sons,— 'all male heirs,' as Dirdumwhamle often says with a sigh, when he thinks of his son and Robina having only added daughters to the increasing population of the kingdom. But Walkinshaw's career as a soldier belongs to a more splendid theme, which, as soon as ever we receive a proper hint to do so, with ten thousand pounds to account, we propose to undertake, for he was present at the most splendid achievements of the late universal war. His early campaigns were not, however, brilliant; but, in common with all his companions in arms during the first years of that mighty contest, he still felt, under the repulses of many disasters, that the indisputable heroism of the British spirit was never impaired, and that they were still destined to vindicate their ancient superiority over France.

These heroic breathings do not, however, belong to our domestic story; and, therefore, all we have to add is, that, as often as he revisited his patrimonial home on leave of absence, he found the dinnering of his friends in the royal city almost as hard work as the dragooning of his foes. Since the peace,[3] now that he is finally settled at Kittlestonheugh with all his blushing honours thick upon him, the Lord Provost and Magistrates have never omitted any opportunity in their power of treating him with all that distinction for which, as a corporation, they are so deservedly celebrated. Indeed, there are few communities where there is less of the spirit of ostracism, or where a man of public merit is more honoured by his fellow-citizens, than in Glasgow. Therefore say we in fine,—

LET GLASGOW FLOURISH![1]

APPENDIX

I. THE 1842 TEXT

THE text of *The Entail* as printed in Blackwood's Standard Novels, 1842 and later reprints, introduced many hundreds of minor spelling variations from the Galt text of 1822/3. The intention was clearly to make the novel more 'readable', partly by making Galt's often phonetic spellings closer to recognizable English spellings, and partly by altering his forms to those already familiar to readers of the Waverley Novels. The general effect can be seen from the following samples:

1. *Older spellings brought up to date*: pye > pie; scite > site; tygress > tigress.

2. *Use of apostrophe to suggest an English spelling*: sin > sin'; tilt > til't ['to it']; mak > mak'; tak > tak'; mysel > mysel'; yoursels > yoursel's; telt > tel't ['told']; awa > awa'; mistak > mistak'; deet > dee't ['died'].

3. *Dialect spellings anglicized*: fasson > fashion; Lunnon > Lon'on ['London']; stedfast > steadfast; clok > clock ['beetle']; cou'dna > couldna; wis > wish; wising > wishing; wiss'd > wished; bodie > body; am > I'm; rue't > rued; jigot > gigot ['leg of mutton']; forton > fortun'.

4. *Dialect forms altered to 'Waverley' conventions*: meikle > muckle; sicker > siccar; callour > caller; doure > dure; ouer > o'er; bot > but ['bot the house']; saully > sally; waur't > wair't ['spend it']; straemash > stramash; is nae > isna; sicna > siccan; waur > war ['were'].

5. *Dialect forms with altered stress*: The *Entail* dialect evidently stressed the negative in combinations like 'was na' ['was not'] and 'need na' ['need not']. The 1842 reviser was more familiar with an unstressed form. Hence, for example, had na > hadna; does na > doesna; was na > wasna; hae na > haena ['have not']; is nae > isna [stress and vowel both altered].

II. THE GALT-BLACKWOOD LETTERS

Galt and William Blackwood were regular correspondents from 1819, when Galt first had a 'communication' accepted for the Magazine, until Blackwood's death in 1834. More than a hundred of their letters survive; excerpts have been cited in the Introduction. The whole series provides valuable information on author-publisher relations in the early nineteenth century. The following exchange in mid-1822, when Galt was planning *The Entail*, demonstrates both Galt's strenuous activity during one month and Blackwood's blend of encouragement and editorial control.

[*Galt to Blackwood*][1]

London 8 June 1822

My dear Sir

I was in hopes to have sent you Lady B's book, but the printers have taken more time than was expected and it cannot be ready for the Review of this month. I therefore write to say that it must be reserved for another month and in the meanwhile I trust the professor's or some other's notice of the Lantern will appear. I have been incidentally speaking of a Review number and whenever the subject has been mentioned an instantaneous great expectation was expressed. It will take depend on't, and be admired even though it should prove inferior to what it ought to be.

I intend as I before mentioned to inscribe the Legatees to Mr Finlay—please to give directions that it be done as follows

Inscribed to
Kirkman Finlay Esq
with the best respects of
The Author

The Steamboat I intend for Lord Gwydir, and he has given me leave to do it if I think fit in the character of Mr Duffle—Should

[1] Nat. Lib. Scot. MS. 4008, ff. 178-9.

you however not like the inclosed in that character let it be done
simply as follows

Inscribed to

The Right Honourable

Lord Gwydir

etc. etc. etc.

as a slight tribute of acknowledgement

for the pleasure enjoyed

by his excellent arrangements

in Westminster Hall

at the Coronation of

King George IV*

* which ever you chose let me see the proof by post—

At the same time I am of opinion that the epistle would be better
than any serious inscription—

I have finished another tale for the Quarantine, which I will
send first opportunity and I have a third on the stocks. Sir Andrew
has not proceeded quite so rapidly as I could wish only three sheets
as yet are thrown off, but the composition is going on pretty well—[1]
My parliamentary business is now almost entirely closed for the
season, indeed I expect it will be quite finished before I leave the
foreign office, where I am now writing this, in waiting for an interview with Lord Londonderry to complete it—During the summer
I intend to devote myself exclusively to 'the Entail' which I foresee
will extend to three volumes, the scene will be altogether in Scotland—Edinburgh will come in, but the chief business lies in
Glasgow, and now that all the other concerns are off I wish you
would do as much for me this year as last and then I shall be free
and clear almost at once—Do think of this and believe me

Sincerely Yours
John Galt

---

[1] The second edition of *Sir Andrew Wylie* was (exceptionally for Blackwood)
being printed in London, under Galt's supervision.

[Blackwood to Galt][1]

Edin. 11 June 1822

John Galt Esqr.

My Dear Sir,

I received yours of the 8th in my coach parcel this morning . . . Your article on Lord Aberdeen is very good indeed. I have got the woodcuts done in excellent style by Lizars and they look very well . . . I like your inscription to Mr. Finlay, and if I had not seen Mr Duffle's letter I would have thought that nothing could be better than the inscription to Lord Gwydir. I shall carefully attend to both. Send me the conclusion of the Steam Boat by the coach parcel at the end of the month, if you have not an opportunity sooner . . .

I am glad to hear that your parliamentary labours are drawing to a close, and that you will now be able to devote yourself to the Entail. I am sure it will be good from the outline you gave me of the story and the scenes in which the characters will figure. I hope you will be able to manage it so as that the hero tells the story himself for you may depend upon it, that it is always the most effective way, and it is particularly your forte. You more than any one almost I know, identify the individual, and the Author never himself appears, it is the very being telling his story himself. This is greatly lost when given in the third person. But of all this you must judge, and regulate yourself entirely by your own plan and conception of the story. Think well as to making three volumes.

I need not tell you how happy I will be if I have it in my power to do even more than I did last year. What I did has given us mutual satisfaction, and I trust this will be the case for many years to come.

I am happy to hear your little folks were doing so well and with every good wish.

I am My Dear Sir
Yours truly
W. Blackwood

[1] L.B. 2, ff. 338–41.

[*Galt to Blackwood*][1]

15 June 1822

. . . You would perhaps observe that I have been at Court—this was partly rendered a necessary etiquette by the nature of the business which brought me so much into personal conference with ministers—I understand from Lord B. that my reception at the Levee is what is considered a particularly gracious one, in consequence of the King speaking to me—at the drawing room it was still more marked, for there the gentlemen are not announced, and His Majesty named me as I made my bow—So much perhaps from Sir Andrew . . .

[*Blackwood to Galt*][2]

Edinburgh
22 June 1822

John Galt Esq.

My Dear Sir

I have the pleasure of receiving yours on Thursday, and I was truly glad to hear that Royalty had been so gracious. I hope that this may be of advantage to you in various ways. . . . .

I had a letter from Mr Cadell yesterday, in which he says the new edition of Sir Andrew was to be ready on Thursday. It will I think be a handsome Book. Though I have some doughts as to the propriety of announcing the Entail so soon after the Provost, because folks are apt to say that you are in too great hurry, yet as you think it right yourself, I have advertised it as you will see in this No of Maga. The title is an excellent one, and I weary sadly to see what you have written which I hope you will send me very soon. . . .

There is one thing however that I may remark to you, which is that some of the best things both in the Annals and Provost are admirable as coming from Micah and Pawkie, but they would have lost all their effect had they been given by the Author in the third person. It is something of this kind which has prevented Sir Andrew from being so popular here as he would have been. It is fortunate that Mr Crowe did not send me the article on your

---

[1] Nat. Lib. Scot. MS. 4008, ff. 180-1.   [2] L.B. 3, ff. 3-5.

Novels, for I have got such an article as I am sure you will like. You will easily see who is the author of the article from the noble fire and manly spirit in which it is done. It is certainly time that the calumnies of these cursed Cockneys should be put down and that you yourself should get the credit you are so well entitled to. . . .

[*Galt to Blackwood*][1]

Arundell 23 June 1822

My dear Sir,

In case of any letter from you being in town I write chiefly to say that I have been in this neighbourhood for a few days and will be back in London early next week—Sir Andr. was to be finished by Thursday last—I hope it is so—I find him in all the libraries along the coast, and most of these have two copies of the Provost on the faith of him—Being unknown as I came along I do assure you that I have not been a little amused and gratified, in some instances, by the *sagacity* of the conjectures and speculations about them—all which has given me renewed heart and confidence, in so much that I have constructed the whole fable of my Entail, determined the characters and most of the incidents—I may be mistaken in my anticipation, but I think it will be out of all comparison the most vigorous and lively work I have yet attempted— It may not perhaps have so much outré humour as Sir Andrew, but it will have the additional and greater merit of being a true narrative in the main,—every character and incident founded on realities. It has taken full possession of my fancy and I always know that when I am myself interested I do not fail in the effort—The story will grasp nearly a century, as it comprehends three generations and in so far will embrace a great deal of matter similar in compass to the annals and the provost, besides being complete as a dramatic plot within itself—when I get to town I will probably send you a part of the *first part*, but I am anxious to make arrangements for spending three months in Scotland, where I may be enabled to add to my vernacular vocabulary. I do therefore wish very earnestly that you would again give me a bill at 12 or 15 months for 3 or £400 and the book will be ready before Christmas

[1] Nat. Lib. Scot. MS. 4008, ff. 182-3.

for the public, indeed I should like to begin printing almost as soon as I reach Edinburgh in order that I might exclusively give myself up to the composition and finish it while with you—It is such an immense thing for me to have ease of mind that I hope you will oblige me in this. I am sure you will find it for our mutual advantage—Believe me Truly

Yours

J. Galt

Let me know as soon as you can.

TEXTUAL NOTES

IN this edition, apart from the silent correction of some obvious misprints and the following alterations, the text of 1822/3 is followed. With one exception (discussed in the Notes) these alterations are intended to secure conformity with Galt's normal practice as attested generally throughout the 1822/3 edition. The 1822/3 reading follows the colon:

Page	Line	
24	6	Leddy: leddy
24	16	Leddy: leddy
24	36	Leddy: leddy
26	9	Leddy: lady
26	27	Leddy: leddy
48	1	'the lady': 'the leddy'
48	20	lady: leddy
53	30	Bodle's: Boddle's
76	15	Lady: leddy
88	16	Roger: Rodger
110	17	Lady: Leddy
152	17	Lady: Leddy
154	36	Lady: Leddy
157	31	Lady: Leddy
163	9	Lady: Leddy
167	11	Lady: Leddy
167	38	Leddy: Lady
182	35	Glassford's: Glasford's
195	22	Watty: Wattie
256	15	Lady: Leddy
258	6	wis: wis'
263	12	wising: wis'ing
275	5	Death and the Leddy's: Death, and the Leddy's (see Explanatory Notes)

EXPLANATORY NOTES

ABBREVIATIONS

Annals   *Annals of the Parish*, ed. James Kinsley, 1967.
Autobiography   John Galt, *Autobiography*, 2 vols., 1833.
Graham   H. G. Graham, *The Social Life of Scotland in the Eighteenth Century*, 1899 (1909).
Hamilton   Henry Hamilton, *An Economic History of Scotland in the Eighteenth Century*, 1963.
Herd   D. Herd (ed.), *Ancient and Modern Scottish Songs, Heroic Ballads etc.*, 1776 (1870).
MacGregor   G. MacGregor, *The History of Glasgow*, 1881.
O.E.D.   *Oxford English Dictionary*, 1933.

VOLUME I

Page 3. (1) *Darien Expedition*: the disastrous Scottish colonial venture of 1698–1700.

    (2) *bairnswoman*: nurse.

Page 4. *Death and the Lady*: apart from the nursery tales, this list is of Scottish songs and ballads which had appeared in Herd's collection, 1769 and 1776. 'Tak your auld cloak', Herd, ii. 102; *Chevy Chace*, Herd, i. 54; *Flowers of the Forest*, Herd, i. 214; *Gil Morrice*, Herd, i. 1; *William's Ghost* (*Death and the Lady*), Herd, i. 76.

Page 5. (1) *Whitehill*: rising ground a mile east of the eighteenth-century centre of Glasgow. At this period, Whitehill was open country with a clear view south of Cathkin Braes, Galt's site for Kittlestonheugh. See p. 44, note 2. The date is *c.* 1705.

    (2) *Provost Gorbals*: the modest village of Gorbals was across the river Clyde from Glasgow. The Provost's progress—Gorbals, a city house in Bridgegate, a country house in Whitehill—will be emulated by Claud. Galt has established his major theme in the first chapter.

    (3) *scite*: site. A common eighteenth-century spelling.

Page 6. (1) *hench-hoops*: hoops under a dress, crinoline; *hench*: haunch.

    (2) *soopit*: swept.

    (3) *drooking*: wetting.

    (4) *gart them jook*: caused them to bend.

    (5) *kyteful*: bellyful.

    (6) *divors*: bankrupt's.

(7) *bodie*: person. Galt distinguished it thus from 'body'.

(8) *rookit*: cheated.

(9) *gudedochter*: daughter-in-law.

(10) *croynt awa*: shrank away.

Page 7. (1) *Ist 'tou aye*: are you still (2nd pers. sing.). Galt usually writes *t'ou*.

(2) *sin' his lan' was roupit*: since his land was auctioned.

(3) *I doubt*: I fear.

(4) *oe*: grandchild.

(5) *lucky*: old lady (term of address).

(6) *I'm wae for't*: I am sorry for it.

(7) *sib*: related.

Page 8. (1) *whar dost t'ou*: where do you (2nd pers. sing.).

(2) *lan'*: 'land', a high block of tenements or flats.

(3) *ettle*: strive.

(4) *rumbling laddie*: boisterous boy.

(5) *mair than I hae to gi'e him*: more than I have to give him.

(6) *aught*: possession.

(7) *the waur*: the worse.

(8) *unco*: unusual.

(9) *belyve*: by and by, in the future.

(10) *with a pack*: and so to become a packman, or pedlar.

(11) *bein*: comfortable.

Page 9. (1) *ane of the fifteen*: one of the fifteen Lords of Session, judges of the Court of Session at Edinburgh.

(2) *muckle*: much.

(3) *turnpike stair-case*: spiral flight of stairs.

(4) *Pictish sculptors . . . Glasgow*: an ironic comment on country ignorance; the High Kirk (Glasgow Cathedral) is Gothic.

(5) *lozens*: lozenge-shaped panes.

Page 10. (1) *the independence . . . of the kingdom*: The Scottish parliament (the States of Scotland) ratified in 1707 the legislative Union of England and Scotland.

(2) *near-be-gawn*: parsimonious.

(3) *gairest*: greediest.

Page 11. (1) *whiles*: sometimes.

(2) *prigging*: haggling, 'beating down'.

(3) *higgling*: haggling.

(4) *piazza*: pillared arcade, for protection against rain. Defoe and other travellers commented on this feature of Glasgow architecture.

(5) *where the Exchange now stands*: in 1822 ('now') the 'Exchange' was the Tontine Hotel opened 1784 with a coffee-house, a gathering place for merchants. Claud opens his shop in the business centre of Glasgow.

Page 12. (1) *infeftment*: (Scots law) 'the act of giving symbolical possession of heritable property' (*O.E.D.*).

(2) *sappy*: 'juicy'.

(3) *the lands are but cauld*: Galt set the Grippy on the cold north-facing slopes of Cathkin Braes. See p. 44, note 2.

(4) *ne'er fash your thumb*: never bother yourself. *fash*: trouble.

(5) *ye hae as many een*: you have as many eyes.

(6) *leddy*: lady, mistress of the house. Girzy will soon acquire a capital letter and become simply 'the Leddy'.

Page 13. (1) *couthy*: agreeable. Claud still has his tradesman's affability.

(2) *Plealands*: even a small laird expected to be addressed by his 'estate' title. Claud will insist on it later; see p. 108, note 10.

(3) *doited*: senile.

(4) *playocks*: toys.

(5) *I hae a lang clue to wind*: I have a large ball (e.g. of twine) to wind.

(6) *ettling*: striving.

(7) *blateness*: bashfulness.

(8) *spier*: ask.

(9) *the Ayr carrier*: Plealands was set by Galt in Ayrshire.

(10) *douce*: pleasant, sedate.

(11) *new kirk on the Green Know*: St. Andrew's Church was built on a 'know' (slight hill) above Glasgow Green between 1739 and 1756. Modelled on St. Martin-in-the-Fields, it was a 'prelatic Babel' to an elder in the long-established Tron Kirk; two Glasgow provosts, Aiton (1738) and Dinwiddie (1742), are 'wytid' (blamed) in the elder's diatribe. Cf. MacGregor, pp. 333, 519.

Page 14. (1) *shouther*: shoulder.

(2) *am nae prophet*: I'm no prophet. 'am' is Galt's phonetic rendering in 1822/3. Later editions read 'I'm'.

(3) *chambering*: wenching.

(4) *kist fu' o' whistles*: 'chest full of whistles'; pipe-organ, regarded as 'prelatical' or episcopalian by presbyterians. Cf. *Annals*, p. 32.

(5) *in our own day*: an organ, built by James Watt, installed in St. Andrews in 1807 led to acrimonious discussion. Cf. MacGregor, pp. 391-2.

(6) *like the tod's whelp, aye the aulder the waur*: like the fox's whelp, ever the older, the worse (it is). Proverb.

(7) *a steek or twa*: a stitch or two.

(8) *kithing*: show.

(9) *erls*: earnests; down-payments. Even the godly elder is affected by 'commercial' imagery which finally affects almost every character in the novel.

Page 15. (1) *even down Nabal*: downright nabob, wealthy from India.

(2) *penure pig*: mean wretch.

(3) *oe*: grandchild.

(4) *bien*: 'comfortable', well off. Galt also uses the spelling 'bein'.

(5) *forty-seven*: such precise details emphasize Galt's insistence on a 'real' chronology. The year is *c.* 1746.

(6) *Land*: tall 'tenement' building.

(7) *the close mouth*: the opening to the 'close', the tunnel-like entry to the flats in a 'land'.

(8) *rig-and-fur gamashins*: woollen leggings, knitted in a ribbed ('ridge and furrow') stitch.

Page 16. *Cathcart*: 'old' Cathcart, a village 4 miles south of Glasgow on the Ayr road.

Page 17. (1) *whare are ye gaun*: where are you going.

(2) *ahint*: behind.

(3) *beetles*: dyers beat their cloth with a flat wooden 'beetle'.

(4) *the synod*: ecclesiastical court intermediate between presbytery and General Assembly (*Annals*, p. 227). Glasgow and Ayr comprised one synod, meeting in Glasgow, in the Tron Kirk.

Page 18. (1) *unco cowp*: terrible upset.

(2) *pawkily*: slyly.

(3) *a' to the fore*: all undamaged; *to the fore*: alive.

(4) *yett*: gate.

(5) *books of sederunt . . . Session*: the records of the courts (sederunt, 'they were sitting') at Glasgow and at the Court of Session, Edinburgh.

(6) *carl*: fellow.

Page 19. (1) *Grippy*: Claud's 'territorial' title acknowledges that he is a laird, even if only of a few acres.

(2) *hirpling*: limping.

(3) *the leddy*: lady, mistress. Galt is preparing for Girzy's rise to the status of 'the Leddy'.

(4) *a Dumbarton youth*: a 'proverbial' phrase, variously explained, meaning someone over thirty-six.

Page 20. (1) *cod*: pillow.

(2) *he'll no can thole*: he'll not be able to endure.

(3) *harigals*: pluck (of an animal).

(4) *sonsy*: 'jolly'. The allusion is to the opening of Burns's 'To a Haggis' ('Fair fa' your honest sonsie face').

(5) *float whey*: boiled curds—supplied in place of the elaborate sweets of the later eighteenth century. Galt emphasizes the self-sufficiency and simple table of a laird of the period. Cf. Graham, pp. 9-10.

(6) *heckle*: comb (for dressing flax).

Page 21. (1) *coothy*: agreeable, kindly.

(2) *live at heck and manger*: live with easy access to everything, like a beast with access to the 'heck' (hayrack).

(3) *I trow . . . birring wheel*: I believe Girzy causes them to keep a neat house and a busily rotating wheel.

(4) *teld*: told.

(5) *the leddy's life's in her lip*: the mistress's life is 'in her breath', i.e. 'uncertain'.

(6) *That's looking far ben*: that's looking a long way off (literally, 'deeply within').

(7) *the gear that'll traike*: the stuff that will waste away.

(8) *the Leddy of Grippy*: Girzy is given her title—with a capital letter—from its first mention.

(9) *Grippy*: Claud's 'estate' name. The farm is usually 'the' Grippy.

(10) *gardevin*: whisky-jar containing two quarts. They drink it neat ('entire').

(11) *doited*: silly, senile.

Page 22. (1) *gouk's errand*: fool's errand.

(2) *any sic wastrie*: any such wastefulness.

(3) *whilk*: which. 'Whilk' by this date was restricted to legal and formal usage, and is natural for the litigious laird.

(4) *kittle again in my oe*: come alive again in my grandchild.

Page 24. (1) *gar*: cause.

(2) *claw*: clause.

(3) *her ail's like*: her ailment is like.

(4) *we need na fash*: we need not trouble.

(5) *the frush green kail-custock-like nature o' bairns*: the nature of children, brittle as green kail-stalks.

(6) *braw*: 'brave', fine.

(7) *tak the law o' him for a haverel*: have him legally declared a half-wit.

(8) *ay mislikening Watty at that gait*: always disparaging Watty in that manner.

(9) *linty at the door-cheek*: linnet at the door-post.

(10) *riving his claes*: tearing his clothes.

Page 25. (1) *mawkins*: hares.

(2) *gar folk trow*: cause people to believe.

(3) *the lave o' the warld*: the rest of the world.

(4) *in mutchkins and chapins*: in pints and quarts. The Scots measures were less than the corresponding English ones.

(5) *stoup*: vessel for liquid, usually wooden.

(6) *say his questions*: recite (from memory) the answers to the questions in *The Shorter Catechism*, a manual of presbyterian doctrine.

(7) *the Mother's Carritches*: *The Mother's Catechism for the Young Child*, 1758. A simplified shorter catechism ('carritch') by the Revd. J. Willison.

(8) *callan*: lad.

(9) *ne'er a prin's worth*: never a pin's worth.

(10) *Gude*: God.

(11) *fey*: mad.

(12) *stirk or a stot*: (terms for bullocks, 'stirk' being the younger).

(13) *wrang my wean*: wrong my child.

(14) *I redde ye, tak tent to*: I advise you, be careful of.

Page 26. (1) *ilk is properly yocket*: each is properly joined together.

(2) *cowpit*: overturned.

(3) *a wheen auld dead patriarchs*: a few old dead patriarchs.

(4) *a thrashing . . . bells*: vain labour; *bells*: bubbles. Cf. *Annals*, p. 221.

(5) *Gae but the house*: go to the outer room ('kitchen'). The opposite of 'ben the house'. Claud, in a fair-sized farm-house, still thinks in terms of a two-roomed cottage.

Page 27. (1) *the Mairns Moor*: about 13 miles south of Glasgow on the Ayr road.

(2) *clanjamphry*: company, 'rabble'.

(3) *the guager's rod*: the exciseman's dipstick—the brandy is smuggled. Cf. *Annals*, ch. ii. 'Guager' is the earlier Scottish spelling.

Page 28. *the services*: (of food and drink). For the lavish funeral feasts of the period see Graham, pp. 52–5.

Page 29. *betherel*: beadle (and grave-digger).

Page 30. (1) *Mr Keelevin . . . of Gudetoun*: a 'cross-reference' to *The Provost*, ch. x. *Gudetoun*: Galt's fictional name for his birth-place, Irvine. *Keelevin*: rhymes with 'vine'.

(2) *writer*: legal practitioner; a 'Writer to the Signet', one of the ancient society of law-agents who conducted cases before the Court of Session at Edinburgh. Galt now discloses that the persona of the narrator is that of a lawyer.

(3) *indemnified by Parliament*: Prince Charles Edward (the Young Pretender) forced the whiggish Glasgow magistrates in 1745 to re-equip his invading army. Glasgow shrewdly obtained £10,000 compensation in 1749. Cf. MacGregor, pp. 319–27. Galt's attitude is (as often) heavily ironical.

Page 31. (1) *a bodie*: a person.

(2) *unco like*: strange. Omit speaks ostensibly English, but the intrusive dialect phrase gives him away.

(3) *Cleland*: James Cleland (1770–1840), author of *Annals of Glasgow*, 1816.

Page 32. (1) *Linwood*: Mary Linwood (1755–1845) was well known for exhibitions of embroidery copies of paintings.

(2) *Craiglands . . . Miss Mysie Cunningham*: another of Galt's 'cross-references' to his other works. Cf. *Sir Andrew Wylie*, ch. lxxxix.

(3) *lippen*: trust.

(4) *erls*: earnests.

Page 33. (1) *a heavy soom of lying siller*: a large sum of money 'lying by' (in a merchant bank). The minister's transition from spiritual comfort to commercial consolation is in keeping with the recurring mercantile imagery of *The Entail*.

(2) *we maun . . . thole wi'*: we must compose ourselves to put up with.

(3) *the gudeman*: 'my husband'; *gudeman*: master of the house.

(4) *hing . . . the laft in the kirk*: hang the front of the gallery in the church.

(5) *first cost*: 'at cost price'; at 'wholesale' rates. The commercial imagery overrides the mourning.

(6) *an express to Kilmarnock*: Kilmarnock, being in Ayrshire, was closer than Glasgow for an emergency purchase.

(7) *at the dear rate*: at the retail price.

(8) *needcessited*: one of the Leddy's many malapropisms.

(9) *gear*: possessions. The key-word in this speech and in the novel.

Page 34. (1) *auld daddy's*: grandfather's.

(2) *farls*: slices (of cake).

(3) *twa whangs as big as peats*: two slabs as big as peats. Watty, on his simpler level, continues the imagery of 'gear'.

(4) *every bodie maun alloo*: every person must allow.

Page 35. (1) *thrawn-natured*: obstinate-natured.

(2) *ye should na let it fash you oure muckle*: you should not let it trouble you over much.

(3) *my auld son . . . callan*: my eldest son Charlie's a fine lad.

(4) *though ye canna hae the lairdship . . . expekit*: though you cannot have the estate in one piece, as you maybe expected.

(5) *hae the twa mailings in ae aught*: have the two farms in one title (literally 'possession').

(6) *excambio*: excambion (Scots law), exchange of property.

Page 36. (1) *creel*: basket.

(2) *fasherie*: trouble.

(3) *haverel*: half-wit.

(4) *cognos't*: cognosced (Scots law), judicially pronounced an idiot.

(5) *kittle*: ticklish, 'tricky'.

(6) *Ye ken Jacob . . . Esau*: the Jacob Esau motif will recur throughout the novel.

(7) *jealousing*: suspicion, act of speculating.

(8) *Jacob's mess of porridge*: for 'pottage'. Galt is being ironical.

Page 37. (1) *ye maun warsle*: you must wrestle.

(2) *we dinna ken whar frae*: we do not know where from.

(3) *that gait*: (in) that manner.

(4) *humlet*: humbled.

Page 38. *lameter*: cripple; *hirple*: to walk with a limp.

Page 39. *the States of Scotland*: see p. 10, note 1.

Page 41. *College*: Glasgow College, the University (then in High Street).

Page 42. *Mississippian . . . Ayr Bank: Mississippi*: a game of chance, see *O.E.D.* The Ayr Bank, founded 1769 under aristocratic patronage, suspended payments 1772, ruining many. Cf. Hamilton, pp. 317–23.

Page 43. (1) *Weel, weel, Charlie*: Galt sharply contrasts the English of the college-educated son with the dialect of his father.

(2) *tocherless*: dowerless.

Page 44. (1) *mantua-maker*: maker of gowns, dress-maker (from *manteau*).

(2) *Cathkin Hills*: Galt 'sets' the Grippy precisely, 6 miles south-east of Glasgow in the parish of Carmunnock. Charles's route is the 'old bridge', open country to Rutherglen, Cathkin Braes. The passage that follows is typical romantic landscape writing, but the scenery is precisely localized.

Page 46. (1) Galt makes a 'cross-reference' to characters from Scott's *Rob Roy*, which had appeared in 1817; cf. chs. xxii–xxiii. The Tolbooth, in the period of both novels, was the prison at Glasgow Cross.

(2) *his eighth provostry*: apocryphal.

(3) *O Chrystal!*: a disguised form of 'O Christ!'

(4) *doited*: silly, senile.

(5) *skelpit*: thrashed.

(6) *nearbegaun*: parsimonious.

(7) *cutty*: wretch (only used of women).

(8) *the elect*: those chosen by God for salvation.

(9) *as 'am*: as I am.

(10) *I'll hae the old craighling . . . afore the Lords*: I'll have the old wheezing wretch before the Lords (of Session).

Page 47. (1) *Sicna beauty*: such a beauty (*1842* siccan beauty—assuming a misprint).

(2) *gushet*: piece in form of narrow triangle.

(3) *make an eke*: make an 'addition', and so increase the size.

(4) *like t'ee*: like to ye, like you.

Page 48. (1) *'the lady*: *1822/3* 'the leddy'. Galt in general uses 'Leddy' for Girzy and 'lady' for other women (including the mistress of Plealands). In this chapter he is inconsistent, using 'leddy' twice and 'lady' three times of Lady Plealands, presumably having proofed this chapter before he established his spelling-pattern (see Textual Notes).

(2) *I hae*: Charles (exceptionally) speaks in dialect in this chapter, a further indication of Galt's inattention to detail at this point.

(3) *dure*: hard.

(4) *genty*: gentle, courteous.

(5) *thole . . . the . . . prins*: endure the pins.

(6) *tawpy*: foolish.

Page 49. (1) *gars*: causes.

(2) *snooled*: bullied.

(3) *the gude forgie me*: God forgive me.

(4) *cess*: tax.

(5) *gude-dochter*: daughter-in-law.

Page 50. (1) *name o' gude*: name of God.

(2) *fashed*: troubled.

(3) *jealouse*: suspect.

(4) *wilt t'ou ne'er devaul' wi' sca'ding thy lips*: will you never cease from scalding your lips.

Page 51. (1) *to hae alloo't*: to have allowed.

(2) *flyte*: argument.

(3) *I'm ony bar till't*: I am any bar to it.

(4) *shouthers*: shoulders.

Page 52. (1) *thole*: endure.

(2) *an unco time*: a too-long time; *unco*: unusual, excessive.

(3) *tawpy*: foolish girl.

(4) *gudeman*: husband.

(5) *fashed*: troubled.

Page 53. (1) *cuif*: fool.

(2) *a' the gude to gang to sic a haverel*: all the property to go to such a half-wit.

(3) *a' she hae*: all she has (*1842* has).

(4) *gar*: compel.

(5) *sic a ram-race*: such a blind rush (like a ram).

(6) *Betty Bodle's tocher*: Betty Bodle's dowry. Galt's labels are often ironical; 'bodle' was a small copper coin: 'Miss Twopence'.

(7) *in this gait*: in this manner.

(8) *the morn*: tomorrow.

Page 54. (1) *gie you a het heart*: give you a hot heart.

(2) *Land . . . Close: Land*: tall block of flats; *Close*: tunnel-like entry to a 'land'. The Gallowgate at this date (*c.* 1773) was still in the business centre of Glasgow.

Page 55. (1) *Come awa ben*: come away to the inner room.

(2) *I redde ye . . . tak tent to*: I advise you . . . pay attention to.

Page 56. (1) *yill*: ale.

(2) *tavert bodie*: senseless person.

(3) *the pith o' a windlestrae*: the strength of a stalk of withered grass.

(4) *mair sicker*: more certain (*1842* siccar).

(5) *scantling*: rough draft.

(6) *teetles*: title-deeds.

(7) *As for the bit . . . no fash wi' it*: as for the little savings of ready cash, we'll not trouble with it.

(8) *gudewife*: wife, mistress of a household.

Page 57. (1) *dispone*: (Scots law from Latin *disponere*) dispose.

(2) *sic*: such.

(3) *tocherless tawpy*: dowerless wretch.

(4) *whilk*: which (legal usage only by this date).

(5) *syne*: next.

Page 58. (1) *a' ae heritage*: all one heritable estate.

(2) *braw*: 'brave', fine.

(3) *the Darien*: see p. 3, note 1.

(4) *almous*: alms, gift solicited by begging.

(5) *hae a bairn's part o' your gear*: have a child's (due) portion of your property.

(6) *breeks*: trousers.

(7) *an unco thing*: a strange thing.

(8) *neest*: next.

(9) *doited*: silly, senile.

(10) *tak tent*: take care.

(11) *wis*: wish. This is Galt's usual form for west–country speakers; *1842* almost invariably changed it to 'wish'.

(12) *concos moncos*: Claud's illiterate rendering of 'compos mentis'.

(13) *conjunct*: (Scots law from Latin *conjunctus*) joined.

Page 59. (1) *wise it awa*: direct it away (OE *wisian*, to guide).

(2) *gang the same gait*: go the same way.

(3) *misliken*: disparage.

(4) *an ettling of pains*: a painstaking effort.

(5) *the fifteen at Edinburgh*: the 15 Lords (judges) of the Court of Session.

(6) *Waes me*: woe is me.

(7) *dinna fash your thumb*: do not bother yourself.

(8) *sicker*: certain.

(9) *it winna be the waur*: it will not be the worse.

(10) *a bit will for the moveables and lying siller*: a 'little' will (to deal with) the furniture and the ready cash.

(11) *clearing the wadset*: paying the debt; *wadset*: (Scots law) a form of mortgage.

(12) *ye had na meikle mair*: you had not much more.

Page 60. (1) *haverel*: half-wit.

(2) *come eight days*: in eight days' time.

(3) *wish*: Keelevin (unlike Claud) uses the English form of the word.

(4) *an ye dinna*: if you do not.

(5) *the deil a plack or bawbee*: the devil a penny. 'Plack' and 'bawbee', like 'bodle', were small copper Scottish coins, replaced by sterling in the

early eighteenth century. The older Scottish money terms remained in popular usage until at least the end of the century, particularly in proverbial formulas. Cf. Hamilton, pp. 291-4.

(6) *ellwand*: stick for measuring (cloth, etc.).

(7) *wis*: wish. (Verb. Noun has same dialect spelling.)

Page 61. (1) *na be canny . . . toom-handed*: not be pleasant to go empty-handed.

(2) *a bit bill*: a 'little' bill — Claud is underplaying his 'generosity'.

(3) *tot*: sum.

(4) *an unco almous frae you*: an unusual gift from you.

(5) *fedam*: unnatural conduct before death (fey-dom).

(6) *am mista'en*: I am mistaken (*1842* I'm).

(7) *Flanders baby*: 'wooden doll produced in Netherlands and popular in England in 18th and 19th century' (Webster).

(8) *darling chevalier*: from the Jacobite song 'Charlie is my darling, The young chevalier'.

(9) *na more for ae thing than anither*: not more for one reason rather than another. Claud is deliberately discreet.

(10) *gouk*: fool.

(11) *sumph*: fool.

(12) *the morn's morning*: tomorrow morning.

(13) *Cry ben*: summon in.

(14) *fashes*: troubles.

(15) *The big ha' Bible*: The use of this phrase (from line 103 of Burns's 'The Cotter's Saturday Night') emphasizes the ironical contrast with the happy family prayers and accepted lovers in that poem.

(16) *action sermon*: preached at the administration of the half-yearly sacrament. Cf. *Annals*, p. 218.

Page 62. (1) *Atweel*: assuredly (I wat weel).

(2) *wheest*: hush!

(3) *vengeance . . . government*: the persecution of the Glasgow covenanters. Cf. MacGregor, chs. xxx xxxi.

(4) *waling*: choosing.

(5) *Genesis*: the recurrent Jacob Esau motif of *The Entail*.

Page 63. (1) *are ye no weel*: are you ill; *weel*: well.

(2) *making exercise*: conducting family worship.

(3) *intil oursels*: to ourselves, silently.

(4) *I'll chapse*: I'll choose. Watty uses a formula from a child's game.

(5) *gae but the house*: go back to the kitchen. Claud still thinks in two-room 'but and ben' terms.

(6) *ilk*: each.

(7) *the morn's night*: tomorrow night.

(8) *t'ou daurs*: you dare (2nd pers. sing.).

Page 64. (1) *daffing*: sport, 'fooling around'.

(2) *braw wissing o' joy*: fine offer of joy; *wiss*: put one in the way of obtaining anything (Jamieson).

(3) *garring it loup*: causing it to leap.

(4) *chucky stanes*: smooth pebbles used for child's game; *chuck*: toss.

(5) *doddy and crabbit*: sulky and ill-tempered.

(6) *Wilt t'ou ne'er devaul'*: will you never cease.

Page 65. (1) *gangs like . . . goose's—*: goes like the clatter-bone of a goose's (arse). 'You talk as freely as a goose breaks wind.'

(2) *wha's yon . . . pin*: who is yonder at the gate rattling the door-latch.

(3) *writer*: lawyer.

(4) *a bit canter oure*: a short ride over. Keelevin has ridden the 6 miles from Glasgow.

(5) *ye maunna*: you must not.

(6) *hansel*: a first gift, implying more to follow.

(7) *I redde ye, an he be*: I counsel you, if he is.

(8) *the lave*: the remainder (of the family).

Page 66. (1) *barming o' his lying money*: interest from his cash deposits; *barming*: growth of yeast.

(2) *wadset*: (Scots law) form of mortgage.

(3) *wis*: wish (*1842* wish).

(4) *in your reverence*: in your power.

(5) *faik*: abate.

(6) *pawkie*: sly.

Page 68. (1) *unco like*: strange, unexpected.

(2) *lang-nebbit*: long-nosed.

(3) *gude-dochter*: daughter-in-law.

(4) *cauldrife*: chilly.

(5) *near frien's*: close relations. 'Friend' in Scots is a relation by blood or marriage.

(6) *wiselike*: prudent.

(7) *cried in the kirk . . . Sabbaths*: had the banns of matrimony announced from the pulpit on three consecutive Sundays.

(8) *gude-father*: father-in-law.

(9) *scog*: shelter.

(10) *fain and fey*: 'madly in love'.

(11) *post should get a hag*: a 'hag' (notch) in the post was proverbial for a stroke of luck.

(12) *deil-be-licket*: 'devil-a-thing', nothing.

(13) *am nane*: I am none, I am not (*1842* I'm).

(14) *gieing ony sic almous*: giving any such alms.

(15) *clishmaclaver*: talk wandering from topic to topic.

(16) *banes*: bones.

(17) *baith sides o' a bawbee*: both sides of a halfpenny.

(18) *cry sic things at the Cross*: make a public announcement of such things. The custom survives in Edinburgh, royal proclamations being made at the Mercat Cross. See p. 75, note 1.

Page 69. (1) *well far't*: well-favoured.

(2) *Charlie's no to mean*: Charlie's not to be pitied; *mean*: bemoan.

(3) *unco scrimpit*: very niggardly.

(4) *the morn*: tomorrow.

(5) *het*: hot.

(6) *forton*: fortune (*1842* fortun').

(7) *siller . . . aff a dyke*: money with him goes like snow off a wall.

(8) *tocher*: dowry.

(9) *ballad . . . .* Cf. Herd, 11. 115.

(10) *gear*: property. The Leddy has become infected by the atmosphere of acquisition.

Page 70. the old dowager: 'Lady' Plealands.

Page 71. (1) *redde*: advise.

(2) *unco crew*: great crowd. The Trongate, in the centre of eighteenth-century Glasgow, was crowded on market-day, Wednesday.

(3) *hansel . . . tocherless matrimony*: initial gift for his dowerless wedding.

(4) *Jacob and Esau*: a further echo of the biblical motif.

Page 72. (1) *clavers*: spoken nonsense.

(2) *taigling at this gait*: tarrying in this manner.

(3) *gumshionless cuif*: senseless fool.

(4) *o't's a' my ain*: of it is all my own.

Page 73. (1) *ye need na fash to ca' ben*: you need not trouble to call in.

(2) *writer*: lawyer.

(3) *doited*: silly, senile.

(4) *an unco like thing*: a strange affair.

(5) *sall*: shall.

Page 74. (1) *T'ou's a born idiot . . . t'ou's bidden*: (2nd pers. sing.) you are a born idiot . . . will you not do as you are bidden.

(2) *drum-head*: i.e. parchment.

(3) *a' the gait*: all the way.

(4) *t'ou sall*: you shall.

Page 75. (1) *the Cross*: Glasgow Cross, the site of the (dismantled) medieval Mercat Cross, was the hub of eighteenth-century Glasgow. Claud's shop was near the Cross.

(2) *t'ou'll let nae daffing nor ploys*: you'll let no fooling or sport.

(3) *t'ou'll no be out o' the need o't*: you'll not be free from the necessity of it.

(4) *atween hands*: 'in the meantime'.

Page 77. (1) *am gaun*: I'm going (*1842* I'm).

(2) *pat*: pot.

(3) *cuff o' the neck . . . bailie's*: piece of the neck (mutton) like that of any Glasgow magistrate.

(4) *pile o' barley*: grain of barley.

(5) *wrang me o' auld daddy's mailing*: cheat me of grandfather's farm. Even the idiot Watty is becoming obsessed by 'gear'.

(6) *haud*: hold.

Page 78. (1) *I daur do nae mair*: I dare do no more.

(2) *aiblins bide wi' Kilmarkeckle*: perhaps remain with (the Laird of) Kilmarkeckle.

(3) *Linnaeus*: Carl Linnaeus (1707-78), founder of botanical classification.

Page 79. (1) *kittled*: produced young.

(2) *Duke of Douglas*: had a considerable wooded estate in Lanarkshire.

Page 80. (1) *gar you look sae as ye were fasht*: cause you to look as if you were troubled.

(2) *Beltane*: the May-Day fair.

(3) *coft*: bought.

(4) *Linty*: linnet.

(5) *smeddum*: liveliness.

(6) *garring ye trow*: causing you to believe.

(7) *knowe*: hill.

(8) *I canna gie't*: I cannot give it.

(9) *atweel*: indeed (I wat weel).

(10) *hae dee't*: have died (laughing).

(11) *Maccaba*: snuff (Maccoboy) from Macouba, Martinique, scented with attar of roses.

Page 81. (1) *tak a pree o't*: take a trial (pinch) of it.

(2) *frae Mr Glassford . . . his last cargo*: Glasgow's annual import of tobacco rose to 40,000 'hoggets' (hogsheads) and made the fortunes of 'tobacco lords' like John Glassford (1715-83). Cf. MacGregor, p. 350.

(3) *speer gin*: ask if.

(4) *lown*: calm.

(5) *muckle glad e'en*: great squint eyes.

(6) *wamling*: rolling.

(7) *callour*: fresh, cool (*1842* caller).

(8) *philosopher . . . his hobby*: the reference is to *Tristram Shandy*.

Page 82. (1) *havering sae*: talking idly in this manner.

(2) *come ben*: come in (literally, 'come to the inner room').

(3) *Dist t'ou*: did you.

(4) *Jenny Langlegs*: crane-fly, daddy-longlegs.

(5) *a spider wabster . . . claught it*: a spider weaver as big as a frog, and clutched it.

(6) *intil*: into.

Page 83. (1) *tochered*: dowered.

(2) *the three shires*: Ayrshire, Renfrewshire, Lanarkshire, Glasgow's agricultural 'hinterland'.

(3) *quean*: lass.

(4) *neive like a beer mell*: 'a fist like a flail'. The 'mell' was used to pound 'bear' (rough barley).

(5) *the whilk . . . ilka dykeside*: the which is a baggage that's not to be found at every roadside; *wullease*: 'valise'; *dyke*: field-wall.

(6) *go halffer*: go halves. Watty thinks in terms of children's games

(7) *an ye flooch her weel*: if you coax her well.

(8) *I hae, though*: on the contrary, I have; 'though' has the sense of German *doch*, which is the same word.

(9) *an t'ou was ance marriet*: once you were married.

(10) *no ae word*: not one word.

(11) *t'ou maun just gang o'er the night*: you must just go over tonight.

Page 84. (1) *unco blate*: too bashful.

(2) *parapharnauls*: ornaments.

(3) *to the nines*: to the utmost.

(4) *jealoused*: suspected.

Page 85. (1) *tak tent . . . wiselike*: take care that the lad goes over prudently.

(2) *green for*: long for.

(3) *girns and gowls*: complaints and lamentations.

(4) *creel*: basket.

(5) *hae fa'en just at ance*: have fallen just at once.

(6) *patren*: pattern.

Page 86. *thole a touzle*: endure being rumpled. Galt is echoing the concluding scene of *Tom Jones*.

Page 87. (1) *scaith*: harm.

(2) *plenishing*: furniture.

(3) *sonsy*: jolly, plump.

(4) *amaist*: almost.

(5) *wud*: mad.

Page 88. (1) *the waur o' . . . kiss*: the worse of a little dab of a kiss.

(2) *dawty*: dear.

(3) *a' Mrs Bailie Nicol Jarvie's aught*: all Mrs. Bailie Nicol Jarvie's possession (*Rob Roy* reference).

(4) *shoo ane another*: push one another. Watty continues in child's imagery even when courting.

(5) *chumley-lug*: chimney corner.

(6) *Patie and Roger*: the first episode of Allan Ramsay's *The Gentle Shepherd* (1725), often used as a title for the whole work.

(7) *bookit on Saturday . . . marriet on the Tuesday following*: a couple were 'booked' (registered in the Kirk Session records), and then 'cryed' (had the banns proclaimed) on three Sundays.

(8) *sic a fasherie o' crying*: such a trouble in having the banns called.

(9) *cryed a' out on ae day*: have the banns announced three times on one Sunday. Legal, but carried the implication of suspicious haste.

Page 89. (1) *ourie*: chilled, melancholy.

(2) *wish*: Charles uses the English form, as opposed to his father's 'wis'.

Page 90. (1) *Glengrowlmaghallochan*: a comic invention in mock Gaelic.

(2) *shod wi' roynes*: (the rockers of the cradle) shod with strips of cloth.

(3) *played whir*: spun around (as in a child's game).

Page 91. (1) *He has na . . . greeten out yet*: he has not completed weeping for the loss.

(2) *thir bonny red cheekit shoon*: these bonny red-sided shoes.

(3) *waur*: worse.

(4) *t'ou sall hae a'*: you shall have all.

Page 92. (1) *eke*: addition.

(2) *ca' canny*: go easy.

(3) *step-bairn*: step-child (with no natural expectation of inheritance).

(4) *gaun to hain but for*: going to save only for.

(5) *gi'e Watty a bairn's part o' gear*: give Watty the proportion of family property that a child can naturally expect.

(6) *jealoused*: suspected.

(7) *I'll see til't*: I'll see to it.

(8) *daur to mak or meddle*: dare to take part in or interfere.

Page 93. (1) *bodie*: person.

(2) *infare*: feast at reception of bride into her new home.

(3) *booking*: see p. 88, note 7.

Page 94. *flichtering*: fluttering.

Page 95. (1) *curdooing*: billing and cooing.

(2) *feet-washing*: for these 'boisterous' rites cf. Graham, pp. 186-7.

Page 96. (1) *rung*: stick.

(2) *in my aught*: in my possession.

(3) *stand in the kirk*: stand on the stool (or pillar) of repentance in the church. The Kirk had considerable powers of discipline. Cf. *Annals*, p. 220; Graham, pp. 321 ff.

(4) *scarting*: scratching.

(5) *gait*: manner.

(6) *cleckit*: hatched.

(7) *doon the water . . . wooddie*: ruined ('swept downstream') or strung in a noose.

(8) *glooms*: scowls.

(9) *randy cutty*: boisterous lass.

Page 97. (1) *if t'ou had na been egget*: if you had not been urged.

(2) *a scud like the clap o' a fir deal*: a blow like the slap of a fir plank.

(3) *the waur o't*: the worse of it.

Page 98. (1) *couthy*: genial.

(2) *canny*: auspicious.

(3) *sicker*: certain.

(4) *I hae nae broo o'*: I have no liking for.

(5) *faik*: abate.

Page 99. *Blantyre*: village 2 miles beyond the Grippy from Glasgow.

Page 100. *our twenty-third year*: Galt by such details carefully dissociates himself from the persona of the narrator, consistently keeping 'out of view every thing that might recall the separate existence of the Author' (*Autobiography*, ii. 220).

Page 101. *pree't*: try it.

Page 102. (1) *fou'*: drunk.

(2) *het kail*: hot colewort, soup.

Page 103. (1) *excambio*: (Scots law) excambion, exchange of property.

(2) *the Virginia trade*: Glasgow's rich tobacco trade. The Leddy will ultimately go to live in Virginia Street.

(3) *Brous*: horse-race to bride's new home.

(4) *Infare*: bride's reception feast at new home.

Page 104. (1) *gart me wise it awa*: compelled me to direct it away.

(2) *washer-woman . . . Green of Glasgow*: The 1783 map of Glasgow by John Mennons shows a washing-house on Glasgow Green. For a reproduction see C. A. Oakley, *The Second City*, 1967, p. 17.

(3) *boynes . . . claes*: tubs . . . clothes.

(4) *streaked*: stretched.

(5) *birthright*: an echo of the persistent Jacob–Esau theme.

(6) *to the fore*: alive.

(7) *kent the kittle points*: knew the subtle points.

(8) *your ellwand . . . Latin taliations*: your ellwand would have been a deficient measure compared with the learning of his books and Latin citations; *taliations*: malapropism.

(9) *gudeman, ye's no get . . . ain way*: husband, you will not get all your own way.

(10) *We'll oure for*: we'll (go) over to.

(11) *interlocutor*: (Scots law) order of the Court.

Page 105. (1) *t'at haverel get*: that half-witted child.

(2) *stoor*: fuss.

(3) *straemash*: disturbance (*1842* stramash).

(4) *gaumeril*: fool.

(5) *weans*: children.

(6) *stap*: stop.

(7) *drammock*: pulp.

Page 108. (1) *gie you meikle in hand*: give you much cash down.

(2) *ettling*: striving.

(3) *the whilk maun aye gang*: the which (legal phrase) must always go.

(4) *ye hae a' to-look in that airt*: you have (your) entire expectation in that direction (*1842* omitted the hyphen in 'to-look', and so altered the meaning to 'You have all to look in that direction').

(5) *an ye could throw a bit fifty tilt*: if you could throw in a little (addition of) fifty to it.

(6) *gausey*: jolly.

(7) *clecking*: 'clutch' (of chickens, etc.).

(8) *he put a' past me*: he diverted everything past me.

(9) *had he no deet amang hands in one o' his scrieds*: had he not died meantime in one of his drinking-bouts.

(10) *pendicle*: appendage. Claud insists on his 'full' territorial title.

(11) *wadset*: mortgage.

(12) *a' gangs noo*: everything goes now.

(13) *na ither tocher . . . cockernony*: no other dowry than her hair-band and hair-knot.

Page 109. (1) *I ne'er rue't*: I never regretted.

(2) *oligarchy*: the date of this incident is the mid seventies, when the growing West Indian trade displaced the Virginia trade in tobacco. For a contemporary description of the Glasgow mercantile aristocracy see MacGregor, p. 352. Galt shows great skill in delineating social change.

Page 110. *Malthusian*: The reference, to the *Essay on Population* of 1798, is (exceptionally for Galt) 'out of period'.

Page 111. (1) *cheesset*: a mould in which cheese is pressed.

(2) *the royal city*: Glasgow became a royal burgh by charter in 1636, confirming earlier privileges. Cf. MacGregor, p. 190.

(3) *freaks*: whims.

Page 112. (1) *t'ou canna prefer ane aboon anither*: you cannot prefer one above another.

(2) *gruntel*: snout.

(3) *I'm gaun ower to the crying*: I'm going over for the confinement.

(4) *blithes-meat*: food prepared for visitors at birth of child.

(5) *sourocks . . . lang-kail*: sorrel . . . colewort.

(6) *Patie and Roger*: i.e. *The Gentle Shepherd*, see p. 88, note 6.

> Then fare ye weel, Meg Dorts, an' e'en's ye like,
> I careless cry'd, an' lap in o'er the dyke.

(Act I, sc. i)

> (Farewell, haughty Meg, just as you please.)

The Leddy is well up in older Scottish poetry.

Page 114. Dost t'ou ken what t'ou's saying: do you know what you are saying.

Page 117. (1) *what for a' this fykerie . . . no faſh me*: why all this bother about a lump of earth. Shovel it into a hole and do not trouble me.

(2) *kist*: chest, coffin.

(3) *cleiding*: clothing.

(4) *I wis . . . gane by itsel*: I hope the poor thing has not gone beside himself.

(5) *threeps*: argues.

(6) *hateral*: heap.

(7) *hussy-fellow*: man who undertakes woman's work.

Page 118. (1) *yirden*: earthen.

(2) *ba' o' my muckle tae*: ball of my big toe.

(3) *gar thee rue sic dourness*: compel you to regret such stubbornness.

(4) *cognost*: legally pronounced an idiot.

(5) *I maun noo*: I must now.

Page 119. will ye ne'er divaul: will you never cease.

Page 120. (1) *genty*: neat.

(2) *throughality*: malapropism 'frugality'.

(3) *a bein house . . . but and ben*: a comfortable home and a trim cottage.

(4) *saullying*: sallying (*1842* sallying).

(5) *speat*: spate, flood.

Page 121. (1) *ettling*: striving.

(2) *wised*: directed (OE *wisian*, to guide).

(3) *thole*: 'endure', bear with me.

VOLUME II

Page 123. (1) *CHAPTER I*: Galt, fulfilling his intention that volume ii should begin 'with the commencement of a new act' (see Introduction, p. xiii), opens with Charles's dramatic—and fatal—discovery that he is not the heir of the entail.

Page 124. (1) *to-look*: expectation.

(2) *warslet*: wrestled, struggled.

(3) *I am wae*: I am sorry.

Page 125. (1) *twa mailings*: two farms.

(2) *turning to the left hand*: Galt contrives a skilful shift, from mid-town commercial Glasgow to a 'Gothic' scene, set in the graveyard, the Cathedral, and the ruins of the medieval castle of the bishops of Glasgow above the flooded stream of the Molindinar.

Page 127. (1) *forenent*: opposite.

(2) *a waff o' cauld . . . a bit towt*: a touch (wave) of cold . . . a slight passing fit.

(3) * * * *: this unusual punctuation is intended to indicate Claud's interruption.

Page 128. (1) *He's by common*: he is out of the ordinary.

(2) *jealouse*: suspect.

(3) *I doubt that*: I am afraid that.

(4) *thraw a key*: turn a key, i.e. he has no practical sense.

(5) *hain and hamper*: economize and take on burdens.

Page 129. (1) *mint*: intend.

(2) *niggar*: niggard.

(3) *rookit*: emptied, stripped.

Page 130. *aliment*: (Scots law) annuity, allowance.

Page 131. (1) *tabinet*: silk-wool fabric.

(2) *blae*: blue.

(3) *sneck-drawer*: 'opener of door-latches', crafty person.

(4) *maun be aye steekit*: must be always closed tight; *steek*: stitch.

(5) *coomy*: dirty.

(6) *straemash*: turmoil

(7) *pourie*: small jug.

Page 132. (1) *over . . . thy father's gathering*: over and above the interest on thy father's savings.

(2) *whilk was a gratus amous*: which was a free gift. The Leddy concocts her own legal jargon.

(3) *ony drumhead*: any parchment.

Page 133. (1) *needcessity*: malapropism.

(2) *meal-pock . . . oaken rung*: meal bag . . . oaken stick.

(3) *fleetch*: coax.

(4) *neives*: fists.

(5) *an te life be*: if the life be.

(6) *hag aff*: hack off.

(7) *in thy reverence*: in your power.

(8) *hoggar*: stocking.

Page 134. (1) *host*: cough.

(2) *income*: illness.

(3) *in the scrutoire neuk; t'ou'll aiblins fin'*: in the corner of the desk; maybe you'll find.

Page 135. (1) *lippent to*: trusted in.

(2) *spyniels*: a measure of flax (four hanks) for weaving.

(3) *Dornick*: 'linen' (originally from *Tournai*). Linen spinning and weaving was a considerable local industry. Cf. Hamilton, ch. v.

(4) *harl*: drag.

(5) *a ta'enawa*: a 'taken-away', changeling.

(6) *benweed . . . windlestrae*: ragwort . . . dried grass.

Page 136. (1) *deep and dreigh*: deep (in mud) and miserable.

(2) *thir*: these ('news' in plural here).

(3) *chiel*: lad.

(4) *or the morn*: before tomorrow.

(5) *flyting and fleetching*: arguing and coaxing.

(6) *puddocks grow chucky-stanes*: till frogs grow into pebbles.

(7) *my leafu' lane*: myself lonely and alone.

(8) *epicacco*: ipecacuanha, emetic and purgative used in home medicine.

(9) *telt to gang . . . no weel*: told to go . . . sick (not well).

Page 139. (1) *I wis you meikle joy*: I wish you much joy (*1842* wish . . . muckle).

(2) *ware*: spend.

(3) *An t'ou's sae . . . peremptors*: if you are so precise and insistent ('peremptor', Scots law).

Page 140. (1) *aiblins the neist*: maybe the next.

(2) *Gae bot the house*: go to the kitchen. Galt's repeated 'bot' (usually 'but') indicated an emphatic pronunciation; *1842* prints 'but'.

Page 144. (1) *eydent*: busy.

(2) *scare*: share.

(3) *trumps*: trifles.

(4) *gude, or but only gowd*: Claud at last recognizes that 'gude' (good) and 'gowd' (gold) are not the same.

(5) *his leaf fadeth never*: Watty sings Ps. i. 3 (Scottish metrical version) echoing Claud's biblical 'tree' imagery.

Page 145. *sma cost and cooking*: 'small cost and trouble'.

Page 146. (1) *speed a' ye dow*: speed all you can.

(2) *big*: build.

Page 147. (1) *gang away the day*: go away today.

(2) *ae*: one.

Page 149. (1) *sough*: wailing sound (e.g. of wind).

(2) *Ethiopian . . . Leopard*: Jeremiah xiii. 23.

Page 150. *poortith*: poverty.

(2) *gar me gie*: cause me to give.

(3) *yird*: earth.

(4) *thole*: endure.

(5) *warsle*: struggle.

(6) *doure*: stubborn.

Page 151. (1) *frae ahint the black yett*: from behind the black door.

(2) *erls*: earnests.

Page 152. *Cameronians*: 'covenanters'; presbyterians commemorating the field-preaching of Richard Cameron (d. 1680). The Grippy was close to Bothwell Brig, scene of the covenanters' defeat in 1679.

Page 153. (1) *What for wilt t'ou no*: why will you not.

(2) *greet for't*: weep for it.

(3) *his vera lug*: his very ear.

Page 154. (1) *anent thir bairns*: concerning these children.

(2) *Bell Fatherlans . . . o' our house*: Bell Fatherlans is of too soft a heart to put up with the bustle and trouble of our house.

Page 155. (1) *I hae never kent . . . or amaist*: I have never known . . . or almost.

(2) *shouther*: shoulder.

(3) *I maun dree*: I must undergo.

Page 156. (1) *wean*: child.

(2) *hae her sent till him*: have her sent to him.

(3) *jealouse*: suspect.

(4) *new kythed*: newly shown.

(5) *gin ye like*: if you please.

Page 157. (1) *gane by himsel*: gone out of his wits.

(2) *we have seen . . . Mount Etna*: Galt is drawing on his experiences. Cf. *Voyages and Travels*, 1812, pp. 90-2, where he describes Etna, though in less romantic terms.

Page 158. (1) *ionic curled tie-wig*: wig with tail tied in ribbon. 'The lesser pigtails, long or curly, prevailed for a long time with elderly men' (A. S. Turberville, *Johnson's England*, 1933, i. 392).

(2) *the morn*: tomorrow.

(3) *Lords*: Lords (judges) from the Court of Session, Edinburgh.

Page 159. (1) *betherils*: beadles.

(2) *Deacon . . . of the Wrights*: President of the Glasgow trade guild of Wrights. Cf. MacGregor, pp. 153-8. Claud's status is emphasized.

(3) *Inner High Church*: Glasgow Cathedral (the High Kirk) contained two churches, the Inner and the Outer, with separate ministers, and congregations from separate 'districts'.

Page 160. *unco drumly*: unusually indistinctly.

Page 161. *trotcosey*: woollen riding-garment covering head and shoulders.

Page 162. (1) *a' this rippet for the cheatrie instruments*: all this uproar for the deceitful instruments.

(2) *cognost . . . sederunt and session*: legally recognized in a court record. Scots law terms plus the Leddy's jargon.

Page 163. *cracks at the Yarn Club*: conversations at the Yarn (i.e. 'Story') Club. For Glasgow's many convivial clubs, see Graham, p. 142.

Page 164. (1) *tenth of Nehemiah*: The Leddy is only putting on a show of Bible-reading. This chapter is largely a catalogue of Hebrew names.

(2) *haud*: hold.

(3) *poortith*: poverty.

(4) *Ringan Gilhaise*: a 'cross-reference' to the name of the hero of Galt's next novel, unwritten, but already in his mind.

Page 165. (1) *plea't*: made a plea of, contested.

(2) *thy concos mentis*: one of the Leddy's several garbled renderings of 'compos mentis'.

(3) *pawky*: sly.

(4) *sae ill waur't on thee*: so uselessly expended on you.

Page 167. *kittle*: subtle, ticklish.

Page 168. (1) *even-down*: downright.

(2) *nae farther gain than Mononday was eight days*: no further (time) gone than Monday eight days ago (OE monandæg).

(3) *Deacon Paul, the Glasgow mason*: he is 'president' of his trade guild.

(4) *count . . . pointed the skews*: account of his slater who pointed the gables.

(5) *the doure Ahasuerus*: the inflexible Ahasuerus. Esther viii. 3.

(6) *nane surprised gin*: not surprised if.

(7) *outstrapolous and constipated*: malapropisms.

Page 169. (1) *draughty*: crafty.

(2) *he kens how he jookit*: he knows how he cheated.

(3) *gang to a revisidendo*: go to a revision. The Leddy invents her legal jargon.

(4) *lave*: remainder.

(5) *mitigation*: malapropism, 'litigation'.

(6) *anxieties of merchants*: This dates the incident in the late 1770s, when the American war ruined the Glasgow tobacco trade. Cf. Mac-Gregor, p. 359.

Page 170. (1) *income*: arrival.

(2) *handling*: (troublesome) affair.

(3) *gratus amous*: the Leddy's 'legal Latin'; 'free gift'.

(4) *neither scaith nor scant*: neither harm nor want.

(5) *settle an aliment*: (Scots law) settle an allowance.

(6) *Embrough*: a sly dig at Edinburgh's cultural pretentions.

Page 171. (1) *conomical*: malapropism, 'economical'.

(2) *belyve*: as time goes on.

(3) *lair*: learning.

(4) *gudebrother*: brother-in-law.

(5) *aiblins*: perhaps.

(6) *terrogation . . . naturality*: malapropisms.

(7) *no to be thol't*: not to be endured.

(8) *decreetit douce enough*: adjudged quiet enough.

(9) *gather the haws afore the snaws*: 'gather the fruit before winter'; *haw*: fruit of hawthorn.

(10) *ploy*: sport.

Page 172. (1) *thrangerie butt and ben*: tumult all over the house.

(2) *baby o' the beetle, and dance til't*: baby of the potato-masher and dance to it.

(3) *doos in a doocot*: doves in a dove-cot.

(4) *lade*: load.

(5) *Jenny Nettles*: daddy-longlegs.

Page 173. (1) *a' the cast*: all the facility.

(2) *thou's no blate*: you are not bashful, i.e. 'you are impudent'.

(3) *the fifteen at Embro*: the fifteen (Lords of Session) at Edinburgh.

(4) *misliken*: disparage.

(5) *auld bachle*: old shoe.

Page 174. (1) *term of Martinmas*: 11 November, one of the Scottish term days which concluded a period of house-renting.

(2) *on receiving his rents, he*: i.e. Watty; 'his wishes' in the earlier part of the sentence refers to George. A carelessly written and obscure sentence, unusual in Galt. Watty, now the Laird, has become as 'grippy' or mean as his dead father.

Page 175. (1) *aye sae couthy*: always so genial.

(2) *I would na kent*: I would not (have) known.

(3) *thir*: these.

(4) *rabiator-like*: like a noisy bully.

(5) *get him cognost*: get him legally pronounced an idiot.

(6) *I'll be herri't . . . ae bawbee*: I'll be harried . . . one halfpenny.

(7) *dour*: hard.

(8) *pour*: 'power', amount.

Page 176. (1) *concos montes*: more of the Leddy's 'legal Latin'.

(2) *straemash*: uproar.

(3) *neither buff nor stye*: neither do one thing or another, i.e. 'nothing at all'.

(4) *would na hae gart him . . . wise-like manner*: would not have compelled him to carry the head of his wife's coffin in a sensible manner.

(5) *He did far waur . . . shouthers*: he did far worse, he almost turned me out of the house by the shoulders.

Page 177. (1) *baith a syde cloak*: both a long cloak.

(2) *egget*: incited.

(3) *tak the dods*: take a fit of ill humour.

(4) *a because*: a reason.

(5) *pooking and rooking*: plucking and stripping.

(6) *skailing*: emptying out.

(7) *Hallowe'en*: the eve of All Saints, 31 October; hence 'autumn'.

Page 178. (1) *dirty turnpike stairs of Glasgow*: spiral stairways leading to separate flats in a building. They were open to the public and passing animals.

(2) *art and part*: (Scots law) by contrivance and by actual execution.

(3) *take gude care and no mint*: take good care not to hint.

(4) *jealouse*: suspect.

Page 179. (1) *a bit slaik o' its paw*: a slight blow (lick) of its paw. Watty, to his mother, has suddenly become 'it', not 'he'.

(2) *writer*: lawyer.

(3) *Parliament House*: in Edinburgh, used after the Union of 1707 by the Faculty of Advocates. Hence 'Parliament House' means 'the Law'.

(4) *learned doctor of the Caledonian Padua*: i.e. of Edinburgh. Shakespeare's Portia dressed as a 'learned doctor' of Padua, the home of civil law.

Page 180. (1) *haudthecat*: 'advocate'.

(2) *Brief of Chancery*: *Chancery*: 'a crown office in Edinburgh. From it are issued, in the sovereign's name, brieves of inquest regarding idiocy' (*O.E.D.*). Galt took great care with the legal details. He wrote to Blackwood, 17 December 1822, asking for a copy of *The Entail* to be sent to 'Dr. Mcfarlane who assisted me with some of my law', *Nat. Lib. Scot.* MS. 4008, f. 194.

Page 182. (1) *the day*: today.

(2) *gleds*: kites.

(3) *gang in the gate . . . gleds*: get in the way of the kites.

(4) *Hae ye . . . ark or amrie*: have you any chest or cupboard.

(5) *den himsel*: conceal himself.

(6) *Stockwell*: for Bailie Glassford see p. 81, note 2. The rural north end of Stockwell Street had become the site for several pretentious mansions. Cf. A. MacGeorge, *Old Glasgow*, 1880, p. 155.

(7) *King William himsel*: equestrian statue of William III, erected at Glasgow Cross in 1735.

Page 183. (1) *virl*: ring.

(2) *silver e'e*: (tassel in the form of a) silver eye.

(3) *yird and stane*: earth and stone.

(4) *wally-wae . . . auld Robin Gray*: lament. The song 'Auld Robin Gray' is in Herd, ii. 196.

(5) *fore hammer*: sledge-hammer.

(6) *belter wi' stanes*: pelting with stones.

Page 184. (1) *gang sae like a divor*: go so like a beggar (bankrupt).

(2) *harl't*: dragged.

(3) *talons*: 'talents'.

Page 185. (1) *art and part*: (Scots law) see p. 178, note 2.

(2) *Gardevine*: whisky-jar. The Leddy uses it only for the jingling rhyme with 'Keelevin'.

Page 186. (1) *Man of Business*: legal representative.

(2) *speer*: inquire.

(3) *even doun*: downright.

(4) *sin syne*: for a long time past.

(5) *crack sand*: 'break stones' (sandstone was pounded down for scouring material).

(6) *mak my leaving*: make my living.

Page 188. (1) *tavert*: senseless.

(2) *swattle . . . like a grumphie*: make a swallowing noise . . . like a pig.

Page 189. (1) *naething but the sic like*: nothing but such.

(2) *atweel I wat*: indeed I know.

(3) *flannen polonies, to mak a hap*: flannel petticoats, to make a covering.

(4) *bien carle . . . bonnet-laird*: well-provided fellow . . . small property-owner.

(5) *preses*: president (Latin form used in Scots).

(6) *sosherie*: (from 'social') 'merriment'.

(7) *stately pile*: an ironic reference to the high 'Land', or building.

Page 190 *preeing*: testing by way of trial.

Page 191. *celebrated Professor of Mathematics*: John Anderson (1826 96) was Professor of Physics at the College at this time (late 1770s).

Page 192. (1) *I canna gie*: I cannot give.

(2) *diet*: died.

(3) *send me . . . a garsing*: discharge me, send me 'to grass'.

Page 194. (1) *headcadab*: 'advocate'.

(2) *wi' a het face . . . the morn*: with a hot face . . . tomorrow.

(3) *I hae nae broo*: I have no liking.

(4) *gumle*: confuse.

(5) *flyte*: abusive speech.

(6) *far left to yoursels*: 'beside yourselves', foolish

Page 195. (1) *an that's the gait . . . calm sough*: if that's the way of it, I'll keep a shut mouth; *sough*: noise.

(2) *Catechism*: two versions of the presbyterian question-and-answer manual of doctrine.

(3) *thraw*: twist.

(4) *straemash*: turmoil.

(5) *roley-poleys*: games of chance with a rolling ball—played at the annual fair at Rutherglen, a village between the Grippy and Glasgow.

Page 196. (1) *trance-door*: door between outer door and kitchen.

(2) *mak a kirk and a mill o't*: (proverb) do what you like with it.

Page 197. *speer at*: ask of.

Page 198. (1) *roos*: boast.

(2) *ream*: cream.

Page 200. (1) *thole*: endure.

(2) *lown*: calm.

(3) *wising*: directing (*1842* (erroneously) wishing).

Page 201. (1) *like a randy . . . ever sin syne*: like a quarrelsome person . . . ever since.

(2) *soughs*: noisy sighs.

Page 202. (1) *an aliment will be alloot*: an annuity will be allowed.

(2) *oure true*: too ('over') true.

(3) *the gethering*: the 'gathering', i.e. saved ready money.

Page 203. (1) *an we waur . . . at ance*: if we were to settle at once.

(2) *saut to his kail*: 'salt for his soup'.

(3) *placks*: small coins.

(4) *faik*: abate.

Page 204. *flit*: remove to a different house.

Page 205. (1) *nieves*: fists.

(2) *flat up a turnpike stair*: see p. 178, note 1.

(3) *spirit of improvement*: for the effect of prosperity in the period (late 1770s) see Graham, pp. 135-45.

Page 206. (1) *the Rebellion*: the 1745 Jacobite uprising.

(2) *General Assembly*: the supreme court of the Kirk, held annually in Edinburgh.

Page 209. *the royal city*: Glasgow. See p. 111, note 2.

Page 210. (1) *your new carriage*: The first private carriage in Glasgow was built in 1752. Cf. MacGregor, p. 330. It was still (in the 1770s) a symbol of considerable wealth.

(2) *back jams*: extensions (for servants' quarters) at the rear of the house—in contrast with Claud's 'but and ben'.

Page 211. (1) *it 'ill a' flee . . . wi' ae wing*: it will all fly fast enough with one wing.

(2) *aye a genty bodie*: ever an elegant person.

(3) *gowany brae*: daisy-covered hill.

(4) *Cluty*: the Devil.

Page 212. *forfeiture*: i.e. of estates of the 1745 rebels.

Page 214. (1) *freats*: superstitious beliefs.

(2) *his warsle . . . for the aliment*: his struggle . . . for the allowance.

Page 216. *leil*: faithful.

Page 217. (1) *out o' the body*: 'transported with delight'.

(2) *even down wastrie . . . set-by thing*: downright wastefulness for such a useless set-aside thing.

(3) *dauds and dings*: thrashes and beats.

Page 219. (1) *a Chaldee excellence*: 'a pre-eminent foreteller of the future'. Cf. Daniel ii. 2.

(2) *wising and wiling*: planning and devising stratagems.

(3) *Gude speed the wark*: God speed the work.

(4) *a booking*: see p. 88, note 7.

(5) *thrashing . . . bells*: vain labour; *bells*: bubbles. Cf. *Annals*, p. 34.

(6) *tower . . . Siloam . . . Lebanon*: The Leddy has her towers confused. Cf. Song of Solomon vii. 4; Luke xiii. 4.

(7) *my friend that's awa*: my dead husband; *friend*: 'relation by kin or marriage'.

Page 220. *the genius of design*: the southern fashion for formal landscape-gardening made its way to Scotland in the late eighteenth century. Cf. Graham, p. 17.

Page 221. (1) *tributary . . . to the Cart*: this river-junction identifies 'Cam-rachle' as the village of Pollokshaws, 4 miles from Glasgow on the Irvine road.

(2) *clachan*: village. Galt probably uses this (Gaelic) form to emphasize Mrs Eadie's 'Highland' character.

Page 222. *The American war was over . . . Europe slumbered*: i.e. between 1782 and 1789.

Page 223. (1) *play-actors*: The Leddy's strictures on the Glasgow Dunlop Street Theatre (opened 1785) had much support. Cf. MacGregor, pp. 331, 367, 375. John Home's tragedy, *Douglas*, first produced 1756, roused similar Kirk opposition in Edinburgh.

(2) *foistering*: malapropism, 'posturing'.

(3) *novelle*: This older pronunciation was still retained in Scots. Cf. 'O leave novels / Ye Mauchline belles' (Burns).

(4) *Clarissy Harlots*: The Leddy's novel-references are no more accurate than her biblical ones: Richardson's *Clarissa Harlowe*.

(5) *Damon and Phillis*: merely generic pastoral names here.

(6) *loup-the-window and hey cockalorum-like*: leap-out-of-the-window and boisterous (like a riotous game).

(7) *wha is't wi'*: who is it with.

Page 224. *cuff . . . breeks*: nape (of the neck) . . . trousers.

Page 225. (1) *an old woman*: The Leddy is now seventy-five (see p. 228). This brings the novel's chronology to the late 1880s.

(2) *opened her trenches*: 'began the siege'. Military metaphor.

Page 226. (1) *sic a bein beild biggit*: such a comfortable shelter built.

(2) *low*: blaze.

(3) *gentle-shepherding*: 'pastoral love-affair'. *The Gentle Shepherd* is a favourite source for the Leddy.

(4) *because*: reason.

(5) *to-look*: expectation.

(6) *Here's a tap o' tow*: here's an affair (top of flax to be spun).

(7) *windlestrae-legget tawpie*: thin-legged lass.

Page 227. (1) *callan*: lad.

(2) *or lang*: before long.

(3) *gar me true*: cause me to believe.

(4) *Jenny Cameron*: Prince Charles Edward's mistress, who is 'free and easy' ('leap-over-the-wall'). Cf. *Tom Jones*, xi. 2.

(5) *blin' as well as fey*: blind as well as mad.

(6) *yird tead to a patrick*: an earth toad to a partridge.

(7) *tangs*: tongs.

(8) *the bress*: 'fireplace' (chimney 'breast'—projection above fireplace).

Page 229. *new-light minister*: from the Leddy, a term of contempt. The 'New Lights', an eighteenth-century group of 'liberal' presbyterians. Cf. Graham, p. 379.

Page 230. (1) *sauly*: sally.

(2) *Little-gude*: the Devil.

(3) *lovely young Lavinia*: heroine of the tale in Thomson's *Seasons*, 'Autumn', ll. 170–310.

(4) *begoted*: self-willed.

(5) *dree*: endure.

Page 231. *angel to Balaam*: cf. Numbers, xxii. 31.

Page 232. (1) *distant Grampians*: the whole passage is a romantic 'period' prospect from the south bank of the Clyde.

(2) *carry*: moving cloud.

(3) *porch . . . mansion*: both firmly indicative of the 'improvements' in the Grippy.

Page 233. *house*: i.e. business 'house' (counting-house).

Page 238. *tare*: weight of receptacle of goods—a suitable 'commercial' image, extended in the subsequent conversation.

Page 245. (1) *eild*: age.

(2) *Muirkirk Iron Works*: Galt has 'transferred' this Ayrshire works to the site of the Clyde Iron Works, in Tollcross across the Clyde from the Grippy. Cf. Hamilton, p. 303.

Page 246. (1) *a most alluring picture*: Galt based this 'picture' on 'improvements' in the district like Pollok House, designed by William Adam.

(2) *pirn*: bobbin of spinning-wheel.

Page 247. (1) *cutt*: measured quantity (of yarn).

(2) *anent an outcast*: concerning a quarrel.

(3) *gude kens . . . scant o' cleeding*: God knows if you would not have been as short of covering.

(4) *wud*: mad.

(5) '*Auld Sir Simon the King*': in Herd, ii. 15.

(6) *gaed louping alang*: went leaping along.

Page 248. (1) *siller*: money, 'silver'.

(2) *pookit*: pulled.

(3) *mint*: intend.

(4) *gradawa*: physician ('graduate').

(5) *your ends and your awls*: 'your bits and pieces' (threads and tools metaphor from shoemaking).

(6) *the tow's to spin and the woo's to card*: the flax is not spun and the wool is not carded.

(7) *Scotsman . . . craw's nest*: children's counting-out rhyme. Cf. R. Chalmers, *Popular Rhymes of Scotland* (1826), 1870, pp. 121-3.

VOLUME III

Page 252. (1) *toll-bar house*: one stood at each exit from Glasgow. The toll-bar on the way to Camrachle (i.e. Pollokshaws) was just south of Gorbals village.

(2) *in despite of the Statute*: the toll-keeper was not licensed to sell spirits.

Page 253. *Auld Robin Gray*: song (by Lady Ann Lindsay), in Herd, ii. 196.

Page 257. (1) *a volunteer*: at her own choice (from French).

(2) *ae*: one.

(3) *baith pawkie and auld farrant*: both sly and sagacious.

(4) *fash your head wı' . . . dodrums*: bother yourself with . . . whims.

(5) *sıc a . . . cutty as to hae beguilt*: such an impudent piece as to have beguiled.

Page 258 (1) *rin to the woody*: run (and put his head in) the noose, behave foolishly.

(2) *to gie't drammock*: to give it gruel.

(3) *a fresh clecking . . . deaved and driven doited wi'*: a new brood . . . that I have been so long pestered and driven silly by.

(4) *words of the Psalmist*: a farrago of biblical reminiscences, mainly Hebrews, iii. 17.

(5) *hurl*: ride.

(6) *stoor in your father's een*: dust in your father's eyes.

(7) *whatna scamp or hempie*: what kind of scamp or rogue.

(8) *cast the glaiks in a' our een*: 'blind all our eyes'; *glaiks*: reflections.

(9) *sparrow-blasted*: malapropism, 'flabbergasted'.

(10) *soople fairy*: subtle creature.

Page 259. (1) *as blin' as . . . frae her minny*: as blind as the silly blind person whose wife had him believe that her sweetheart's horse was a milk-cow sent from her mother.

(2) *wising and wyling*: planning and contriving.

(3) *linking by the dykesides*: jaunting by the hedges.

(4) *whatna novelle gied*: what sort of novel gave.

(5) *the ae oe's as sib to me as the ither*: the one grandchild's as kin to me as the other.

(6) *joe*: sweetheart.

(7) *play the Scotch measure or shantruse*: 'play a lively tune'; *shantruse*: a Highland dance (Gaelic *sean-triubhas*).

(8) *wi' the bellows . . . paternostering ancestors*: with the bellows and the broom-handle to some wizard's rhythm of his far-back ancestors of the papistical and paternostering days.

(9) *a Clarissy Harlot wedding*: i.e. runaway, clandestine.

(10) *diffeequalty*: malapropism.

(11) *ye hae gart . . . for Jamie*: you have caused your father to believe that you were beside yourself for Jamie.

(12) *I am ruined and undone*: Beenie tends to talk in the clichés of the sentimental novelist. The Leddy (without flinching) takes her literally.

(13) *loupen-steek*: dropped stitch.

Page 260. (1) *oure gude for you*: too good for you. The Leddy threatens Beenie with the Kirk's disapproval. See p. 96, note 3.

(2) *an irregular marriage*: legal, but 'irregular' because it did not follow the procedures laid down by the Kirk . . . of which the Leddy is openly contemptuous.

(3) *gumflowers*: artificial flowers. Cf. *O.E.D.*

(4) *speaking in sic high English*: speaking in such precise (and rhetorical) English. Galt faithfully reproduces it in Beenie's conversation.

(5) *Mull and Moydart*: Highland areas (and so Gaelic-speaking).

(6) *your luckless clecking*: your unlucky birth; *clecking*: hatching.

(7) *coup*: upset.

Page 261. (1) *thir*: these.

(2) *it's no waur*: it's not worse.

(3) *without fashing your father . . . till it's by hand*: without troubling your father . . . till it's finished with.

Page 262. (1) *by the common o' cousinship*: in addition to the common feature of cousinship.

(2) *tweesh*: between.

(3) *a bit canny shove*: a little artful push.

(4) *his father's ain gett*: his father's own child; *gett* is pejorative, 'brat'.

(5) *thraw*: twist.

Page 263. (1) *a kind of a because to jealouse*: a kind of a reason to suspect.

(2) *ettle*: strive.

(3) *wising*: contriving (*1822/3* wis'ing).

(4) *Hooly*: slowly.

(5) *mess or mell*: have any part in; *mess*: partake (of food); *mell*: mingle, mix.

(6) *an aff-hand ploy*: an unpremeditated sport.

(7) *fey*: mad.

(8) *haud up thy snout in that gait*: hold up your nose in that manner.

Page 264. (1) *Dr Pringle o' Garnock*: a 'cross-reference' to the main character of *The Ayrshire Legatees*.

(2) *throughgality*: malapropism, 'frugality'.

(3) *her direction-books to mak grozette wine . . . gathering straes*: her direction-books for making gooseberry wine for nothing, and her Katy Fisher's cookery, by which she would have us believe she can make thick soup of pebbles and an old horse shoe—we all know, and you know (Laird) worst of all, that she flings away the peas and makes her broth with the pea-pods, or (as the old proverb says) loses (whole) bundles of hay while she gathers (separate) straws. The cookery book was *The Prudent House-wife; or the Complete English Cook* by Mrs. Fisher, London, *c.* 1750.

(4) *bawkie birds*: bats.

(5) *coom*: dirty (verb).

(6) *misleart tumphy*: ignorant fool.

(7) *unco sweert*: very reluctant.

Page 265. (1) *ill put on blateness*: bashfulness, unbecomingly assumed.

(2) *fidging fain*: restlessly eager.

(3) *I hae nae brow*: I have no liking.

(4) *a sound orthodox*: ironical. A wedding in a private house was 'irregular' and against Kirk law. By the late eighteenth century, it was normal with

the better-off, and the 'orthodox' ministers protested in vain. Cf. Graham, pp. 299–300.

(5) *bide*: stay.

(6) *keep the banes green*: keep the bones young.

(7) *cast out wi'* . . . *a sooking grumphie*: object to . . . a sucking pig.

(8) *Renfrew Doctor* . . . *kitchen*: The 'Renfrew Doctor' is apparently apocryphal; *provice*: provost; *kitchen*: 'relish'.

(9) *geck*: toss.

Page 266. *Siddonian*: Mrs. Siddons, the actress, played at the opening of the Dunlop Street Theatre in Glasgow in 1785. Galt first saw her play when he was a boy. Cf. *Autobiography*, i. 31.

Page 268. *discerning spirit*: clairvoyance, 'second sight'—traditionally attributed to Scottish Highlanders.

Page 271. *cadetcy in India*: *cadet*: 'a volunteer in the army, who serves in the expectation of a commission' (Walker's Dictionary, 1827).

Page 274. (1) *unco like*: strange.

(2) *jigot o' mutton* . . . *florentine pye*: leg of mutton, a fine young turkey and a veal pie (*1842* gigot . . . pie).

(3) *forbye*: in addition to.

(4) *stroopless*: spout-less.

(5) *Robin Carrick*: Robert Carrick (1737–1821), Glasgow merchant, for many years manager of the Ship Bank, founded in 1750, 'arch-exemplar of Scottish thriftiness' (W. H. Marwick, *Scotland in Modern Times*, 1964, p. 17).

Page 275. (1) *lang syne*: long since.

(2) *sic Death and the Leddy's confabbles*: 'such grisly talk'. 'Death-and-the-Leddy's' is adjectival in force—the reference is to the 'Death and the Lady' ballad of William's Ghost (Herd, i. 76). All previous editions (including *1822/3*) punctuate 'Death, and the Leddy's', which is meaningless.

(3) *kittle* . . . *sprose o' jocosity*: liven up your thoughts with a little bit of frolic and show of joy.

(4) *lawfu' toll-road*: lawful turnpike road. The marriage, though 'irregular', is legal.

(5) *gouden goun*: golden gown.

(6) *Mathew Henry's Commentary*: Mathew Henry's *Exposition of the Old and New Testament*, a presbyterian 'commentary', appeared in five volumes in 1710. Unless Galt is being ironic, the Leddy is reading one of the later abridgements.

(7) *gouk's errant*: fool's errand.

(8) *callan*: lad.

(9) *taws*: strap (for punishment).

(10) *skeigh*: proud.

(11) *gie that . . . bodie . . . a shoogle*: give that . . . person . . . a shake.

(12) *bars o' Ayr*: sand-bars at mouth of river Ayr, which 'roared' in certain weathers.

Page 276. (1) *Cupar*: (in Fife) proverbial for obstinacy: 'He that will to Cupar, maun to Cupar.'

(2) *a' sorrow till him*: all sorrow to him.

(3) *ramstam*: impetuous person; *flea-luggit*: crazy, 'with a flea in his ear'.

(4) *bir*: energy.

(5) *sae doure*: so hard.

(6) *no to fash you*: not to trouble you.

(7) *straemash*: turmoil.

(8) *drunken drammatical divor*: drunken beggar-actor. A Joycean blend of 'dram' and 'drama'.

(9) *on ajee*: on askew.

(10) *no uncos*: not strange affairs.

Page 277. (1) *thraw*: 'twist', i.e. prejudice.

(2) *snuffies*: sulks.

(3) *Chevy Chase*: 'confusion', i.e. Robina's children will not be those of an imprudent match.

(4) *be seen on the plane-stanes*: only the centre of Glasgow at the Cross was paved, and 'the plane-stanes' (flagged pavement) was the exclusive parade-ground of the wealthy merchants. For a contemporary engraving see C. A. Oakley, *The Second City*, 1967, p. 15. The phrase in context here implies: 'You cannot hold your head up among your wealthy friends.'

(5) *as we're to hae a bit ploy . . . bide wi' us . . . carve the bubblyjock*: as we're to have a little sport . . . stay with us . . . carve the turkey.

(6) *diject*: malapropism 'dissect'.

Page 278. (1) *mim as a May puddock*: quiet as a May (i.e. young) frog.

(2) *statute*: malapropism, 'statue'—Parliament House contained several.

(3) *Moll-on-the-coals*: the Leddy's pun on 'melancholy'.

(4) *sic a doolie doomster*: such a sad stroke of doom; *doomster*: judge.

(5) *fa' knicketty-knock . . . till our harns are splattered*: fall, knocking ourselves about . . . till our brains are splattered.

(6) *I ne'er think o' minting, and this toast ye maun a' mak a lippy*: I never think of attempting, and this toast you must all fill to the lip of the glass.

Page 279. (1) *propine*: pledge, toast.

(2) *Death, Eternity, and Co. great wholesale merchants*: The Leddy plays ironically on the commercial imagery that runs through *The Entail*.

(3) *glaik*: gleam, reflection.

(4) *hairst*: 'harvest', autumn.

(5) *overly gair anent*: too greedy concerning.

Page 280. (1) *stroop*: spout.

(2) *If that's the gait o't, ye shall hae't as ye will hae't*: if that's the way of it, you shall have it as you insist on having it. This precise 'English' use of 'shall' and 'will' is unusual in Scots.

(3) *the night*: tonight.

(4) *If your worthy father . . . wi' sic unreverence*: if your worthy father had been alive, you would not dared to have spoken with such unreverence.

(5) *lights*: makes light of.

(6) *unco warrandice*: malapropism, 'strange warrant'.

(7) *the day*: today.

Page 281. *The man's gaen by himsel . . . he has scartit and dintit*: the man's gone beside himself . . . he has scratched and dented.

Page 285. (1) *joe*: sweetheart.

(2) *crown-o'-the causey*: 'middle of the street'; *causey*: causeway.

Page 286. (1) *the wyte o' ony sic Gretna Green job*: the blame for any such Gretna Green affair; *Gretna Green*: traditional scene for 'irregular' but legal Scottish marriages.

(2) *hobbleshaw*: hubbub.

(3) *De'il-belickit*: nothing, 'Devil-a-thing'.

(4) *your uncle's Jamaica skippers*: George is in the profitable West India rum and sugar trade, which replaced the tobacco trade ruined by the American war.

(5) *smoor't it wi' ingons*: smothered it with onions.

(6) *hesp o' seven heere yarn*: hank of seven-strand yarn.

(7) *teugh*: tough.

(8) *gar the house dirl*: cause the house to ring.

(9) *wis'd*: wished (as opposed to *wised*: 'directed').

Page 287. (1) *your grandfather . . . no mere man*: I'll never maintain that your grandfather was anything but just a man.

(2) *deacon*: 'master'.

(3) *interlocutor frae the Lord Ordinary*: (Scots law) judgement from the judge assigned to a specific case.

(4) *expiscate*: malapropism, 'explain', explicate.

(5) *scantling*: draft.

(6) *sic graceless getts*: such graceless offsprings.

(7) *belyve*: soon.

Page 288. (1) *Robin Carrick*: i.e. the Ship Bank. See p. 274, note 5.

(2) *the impudent smytcher, wi' my haining*: the impudent brat, with my saving.

(3) *speir for thy aunty*: ask concerning your aunty.

(4) *to be rookit . . . glaikit jocklandys*: to be stripped of small coins by two foolish wastrels.

Page 289. *the King's army*: Appointments to a commission in this period were made by the King at home, and by the commander-in-chief abroad.

Page 290. *recals*: This spelling of 'recalls' was used from the seventeenth to the nineteenth century.

Page 293. *carmagnols*: (nickname) French revolutionary soldiers.

Page 294. (1) *Garb of Old Gaul*: a military march-tune.
(2) *Lochaber no more*: a lament. In Herd, i. 256.
(3) *all hail hereafter*: cf. *Macbeth*, I. iii. 50.

Page 296. *man of business*: lawyer.

Page 297. (1) *Black Bull*: This inn was the starting-point for several coaches and the Greenock 'fly'. Cf. 1790 Glasgow Directory cited in MacGregor, pp. 393-4.
(2) *devauling*: ceasing.
(3) *change-house*: originally inn where horses were changed; by late eighteenth century general term for a small inn.
(4) *nabal*: ironic, 'wealthy man'.
(5) *niggerality*: malapropism, 'niggard' plus 'liberality'.

Page 298. (1) *Toomgarnels*: 'Empty Bins'—a poor village.
(2) *I'll hae them . . . Chambers*: I'll have them up on a charge of injury before the Clerk (of the Court of Session).
(3) *a braw Andrew Ferrara*: a fine sword.
(4) *It's no for a courtesy . . . sic firlots*: it's not for a courtesy of street gossip that he's throwing his mouldy pennies in such quantities; *firlot*: measure of grain.
(5) *discerning spirit*: power of divination, 'second sight'.
(6) *whaup*: curlew, 'alien bird' (in the nest).
(7) *Logan Braes*: The song by Burns (1793) was based on a 1789 poem by John Mayne. Cf. *Oxford Book of Scottish Verse*, 1966, p. 362.
(8) *deevil's buckie . . . a' the lave*: perverse person . . . all the remainder.

Page 299. (1) *hanselling thy knapsack*: making a gift for your equipment.
(2) *pawkie*: sly.
(3) *yird*: earth.

Page 300. *Macpherson's Ossian*: an ironical comment on its exotic 'Celtic' prose style.

Page 301. *Pythian*: 'oracular', from the Pythian oracle at Delphi in Greek mythology.

Page 302. *Her Highland astrology*: Galt by such phrases reveals, even in the text of his novel, his sense of dissatisfaction with much of the third volume. See Introduction, p. xiv. Cf. 'I have just received a queer letter about the Entail . . . from an astrologising friend, who is in *raptures* with

Mrs. Eadie. He thinks her . . . superior to "the Leddy" . . . nothing has occurred for some time that has diverted me so much as this *nonsense*'— Galt to Blackwood, 27 Jan. 1823, *Nat. Lib. Scot.* MS. 4010, f. 178.

Page 303. *A circumstance . . . occurred at this time*: This clumsy introduction brings in a series of contrived incidents whereby all the main characters are coincidentally brought together for the denouement. This is where Blackwood 'interfered' (see Introduction, pp. xiii–xiv). The sea voyage round Scotland is notably sketchy. The whole chapter (like others in volume iii) is padding.

Page 304. *Glottiani*: 'citizens of Glasgow'. 'Glottiana' was (and is) the Glasgow University term for the 'nation' of students from Lanarkshire.

Page 305. *canny twa and twae toun of Aberdeenawa*: Aberdeen was originally two separate towns. Galt, like most southern Scots, professes to find the dialect of Aberdeen incomprehensible. *-awa*: 'the vicinity of', cf. 'hereawa'.

Page 306. *scites*: the older spelling of 'sites' (*1842* sites).

Page 308. *extinguisher-less . . . turrets*: turrets that had lost their conical roofs (shaped like candle-extinguishers). But I suspect Galt wrote 'extinguisher-like', and did not see the misprint.

Page 310. *the son of her early lover*: this implausible coincidence is on a par with much of the 'good and striking story' incidents of volume iii.

Page 312. (1) *storm*: 'The sunny summer storm was introduced to allow of a description of the northern coast of Scotland, which I vividly received from Miss Sinclair, a daughter of the distinguished baronet' (*Autobiography*, ii. 238). This admission confirms his padding-out of the third volume.

(2) *partan*: crab.

Page 313. (1) *hartisans*: battlements.

(2) *related . . . the mournful legends*: Galt is still filling out with extraneous material.

Page 315. *sosherie*: ('social') sociable entertainment.

Page 317. *oure soon*: too ('over') soon.

Page 319. *bernacle*: 'barnacle', sea-bird.

Page 323. (1) *The same gale . . . carried the Glasgow party briskly home*: with this transition, Galt leaves romantic fiction (and Blackwood's conception of a 'lively story') and returns 'home' to the Leddy and his real theme of 'gear'.

(2) *infeftment*: (Scots law) possession.

(3) *our friend Walkinshaw*: not Walkinshaw Milrookit ('Walky'), but James Walkinshaw, son of Charles, grandson of Claud, to whom the entailed estate should now pass by law.

Page 324. (1) *bien*: comfortable.

  (2) *daffing and playrifety*: gaiety and playfulness.

  (3) *forbye*: in addition to.

  (4) *sae dreigh o' drawing*: so slow of motion.

  (5) *blate*: bashful.

  (6) *neuk*: corner.

Page 325. (1) *crunkly*: 'crinkled', shrivelled.

  (2) *constipation*: malapropism.

  (3) *would the hard nigger let her gang on the session*: would the hard niggard let her go on the (charity of the kirk) session.

  (4) *Goliah o' cheatrie*: giant of fraud.

  (5) *caption . . . horning*: (Scots law) arrest . . . legal compulsion to pay a debt.

  (6) *signet*: lawyer (Writer to the Signet).

  (7) *skelp-the-dub*: 'beat-the-dirt', i.e. lowly.

Page 326. (1) *ye partan-handed, grip-and-haud smedy-vice Mammon*: you crab-handed, grip-and-hold, smithy-vice Mammon.

  (2) *sic a lamiter*: such a cripple.

  (3) *nymph o' anguish*: 'child of grief'. Malapropism, 'nymph' for 'imp'.

  (4) *my banes were as sair . . . brayed in a mortar*: my bones were as sore as if I had been squeezed into a mortar—the Leddy is partial to military metaphors.

  (5) *rowley-powley*: game of chance at a fair.

  (6) *ye may weel speer*: you may well ask.

  (7) *momento mori*: malapropism, 'memorandum'.

  (8) *threepit*: argued.

  (9) *a Cananitish woman*: undesirable woman. Cf. Genesis, xxiv. 3.

Page 327. (1) *a' the Fifteen*: all the fifteen (Lords of Session).

  (2) *condescendence*: malapropism, 'conditions'.

  (3) *the day*: today.

  (4) *per annus*: malapropism, 'per annum'. The closeness to 'per anus' is intentional. These innocent 'indecencies' ('constipated', etc.) are part of Galt's conception of the Leddy.

  (5) *gude-dochter*: daughter-in-law.

  (6) *faik*: abate.

  (7) *merchants' interest*: Glasgow banks were all started by merchants, who accepted money on deposit. The Leddy expected 5 per cent. ·

  (8) *borrow on a heritable bond*: *borrow on*: accept as security; *heritable bond*: (Scots law) 'bond for a sum of money, to which is joined a conveyance of land for further security' (*O.E.D.*).

  (9) *the Decisions*: *The Decisions of the Lords of Council and Session*, *1759-61*, a collection made by Sir John Lauder (Lord Fountainhall).

  (10) *the Raging Magistratom*: *Regiam Majestatem* (1609), a collection

of ancient Scottish laws made by Sir John Skene. The Leddy's blend of ignorance and 'erudition' is in character.

Page 328. (1) *Amalphi*: the city of Amalfi established the earliest maritime code of law for the Mediterranean.

(2) *virdict*: 'verdict'—but here a malapropism.

(3) *wi' any sic pannelling*: with any such law-business. In Scots law, 'on the panel' meant 'on one's trial'.

(4) *on my own bottom*: see p. 327, note 4. But the phrase echoes a common shipping term, familiar in an exporting town like Glasgow.

(5) *interlocutor*: (Scots law) judgement.

Page 329. (1) *faik a plack*; abate a halfpenny.

(2) *put to the horn*: (Scots law) declare (someone) an outlaw or a debtor.

(3) *erls*: earnests.

(4) *waur*: worse.

(5) *gang till*: go to.

(6) *maunna*: must not.

(7) *noo to the fore*: now alive.

(8) *my friend that's awa*: my dead husband.

Page 330. (1) *heritable bond*: see p. 327, note 8.

(2) *I maun gar*: I must cause.

Page 331. *pawkie*: sly.

Page 332. (1) *W.S.*: the usual abbreviation for Writer to the Signet.

(2) *Register Office*: This Edinburgh building, designed by Robert Adam, was completed in 1788, only a few years before the scene described. It housed all public documents relating to Scotland.

Page 334. (1) *Lord Provost*: For George IV's visit to Edinburgh in August 1822, the Lord Provost of Glasgow rented a mansion in Edinburgh and had a 'spacious brass plate' fixed to the door. Cf. J. Galt, 'The Gathering of the West', *Blackwood's Magazine*, Sept. 1822, p. 313. Galt (exceptionally) is allowing himself a comment 'out of period'.

(2) *took to trot*: fooled, 'took for a ride'.

Page 335. (1) *interdict*: (Scots law) order of the Court of Session stopping allegedly illegal action.

(2) *reclaiming petition*: (Scots law) an appeal from a judgement of a Lord Ordinary to the Inner House of the Court of Session.

(3) *overly*: too much.

(4) *precognition*: (Scots law) preliminary examination of witnesses.

Page 336. (1) *oe*: grandchild.

(2) *ye'll no sca'd*: you'll not scald.

(3) *ae*: one.

(4) *the morn's morning*: tomorrow morning.

Page 337. (1) *Ye maun ken*: you must know.

   (2) *the de'il rook him*: the Devil strip him.

   (3) *nae right because*: no just reason.

Page 339. (1) *nine points*: 'Possession is nine points of the law' (proverb).

   (2) *Carrick, Coil, Cunningham*: 'the whole of Ayrshire' (which consisted of three districts, Carrick, Kyle, Cunningham). The Leddy's father's estate, Plealands, was in Ayrshire.

   (3) *a mandamus*: a judicial writ (well beyond Pitwinnoch's authority, but there are limits to the Leddy's legal knowledge, if not to her legal vocabulary).

   (4) *pronounce an interlocutor*: (Scots law) issue an Order of Court—equally beyond Pitwinnoch's authority.

   (5) *noty beny*: *nota bene*, footnote.

   (6) *sederunt*: session (Latin 'they were sitting').

   (7) *dowf and dowie*: gloomy and sad.

   (8) *shire o' Lanark . . . Glasgow and Ayr*: Kittlestonheugh was in the county of Lanarkshire, but for church affairs in the Synod of Glasgow and Ayr. This, plus the earlier topographical identification with Cathkin Braes, confirms Carmunnock as the site of the Grippy.

Page 340. (1) *daw in barrow't . . . pooket*: daw in borrowed feathers to be pecked and pulled at.

   (2) *somnambulism*: not 'sleep-walking' but 'indulgence in flights of fancy'. Cf. *O.E.D.*

Page 341. *perspicuity of her second sight*: with this ironical comment (on the intrusive and romantic nature of the Mrs. Eadie episodes) Galt returns the scene to Kittlestonheugh.

Page 342. (1) *to serve Walkinshaw heir*: (Scots law) to declare Walkinshaw heir.

   (2) *I redde you gar him*: I advise you to compel him.

Page 343. (1) *let wit*: 'let on', allow that they know.

   (2) *gie me a hurl*: give me a ride.

   (3) *speer for your gudeman*: ask concerning your husband.

Page 344. (1) *jewdical . . . repute like*: malapropisms, 'injudicious [plus jewish] . . . disreputable'.

   (2) *reset*: (Scots law) receive stolen property.

   (3) *coom*: dirt.

   (4) *your gudeman, my ain oe*: your husband, my own grandchild.

   (5) *we maun jook . . . jawp gae by*: we must stoop down and let the mudsplash go past (us).

   (6) *pack up . . . a' the speed ye dow*: pack up your bits and pieces and break up your camp with all the speed you can.

   (7) *Faculty o' Advocates*: the 'society' of advocates in Edinburgh. The title is still used.

Page 345. (1) *thir*: these ('news' is here plural), 'this sad news'.

(2) *pannel*: (Scots law) 'case'.

(3) *pending afore the Lords*: pending at the Court of Session.

(4) *ae*: one.

(5) *the gieing up*: the giving up.

(6) *precognition*: (Scots law) preliminary examination.

(7) *no ae farthing . . . faik*: not one farthing will I abate.

Page 346. *howkit*: dug.

Page 347. (1) *milstane . . . fir deal*: mill-stone . . . fir plank.

(2) *aiblins*: maybe.

(3) *woody*: halter, noose ('withy').

(4) *art and part*: see p. 178, note 2.

Page 349. (1) *by her ain interlucutors*: (Scots law) by her own judgement.

(2) *tod o' a bodie*: foxy person.

(3) *intromitting . . . four pleas of the Crown*: (Scots law) *intromit*: have dealings. 'Pleas of the Crowne in Scotland be 4, roberie, rape, murder and wilfull fire', 1607 citation in *O.E.D.* As usual, the Leddy exaggerates.

(4) *to the fore*: alive.

Page 350. (1) *adjudicate*: 'to give something controverted to one of the litigants, by a sentence or decision' (Johnson), 'award'.

(2) *revisidend*: malapropism, 'revise'.

(3) *libel*: (Scots law) ground of a charge.

(4) *it winna fare the waur*: it will not fare the worse.

Page 351. (1) *ye'll can fen noo . . . 'nuity*: you'll be able to fend now without any annuity.

(2) *adversary*: malapropism, 'adverse opinion'.

Page 353. (1) *waring*: expending.

(2) *rookit*: plundered.

(3) *Wally, wally . . . brae*: the song is in Herd, i. 81; *wally*: 'alas!'

Page 354. *civilities*: malapropism, 'civil law dealing' (as opposed to criminal law).

Page 355. (1) *a cauldrife commodity . . . and so cam o't*: a chilly affair, presaging scarceness and poverty, and this is what came of it.

(2) *walloping galravitch o' idiocety*: boisterous tumult of idiocy.

(3) *gie a smirk*: give a smile.

(4) *cauld-kail-het-again*: 'reheated dish'.

(5) *Packages, Puncheons, and Pigtail*: the sources of Glasgow's wealth—general cargo, casks of rum, twisted tobacco.

(6) *Embroshers*: 'citizens of Edinburgh'.

(7) *jealouse*: suspect.

(8) *gausie*: jolly.

Page 356. (1) *Grants and Frazers*: Galt is embroidering the traditional rivalries between Glasgow and Edinburgh and their respective 'images'— Glasgow realistic, warm-hearted, and Hanoverian; Edinburgh romantic, genteel, and addicted to tartan ('Grants and Frazers') and literary Jacobitism. There is a concealed sly gibe at the royal visit ('ceremoneez') to Edinburgh, which took place while Galt was writing *The Entail*, when 'writers and writers' clerks' were seen trembling in the breeze, dressed in the Celtic garb' with 'peeled, white, ladylike legs' (Galt in *Blackwood's Magazine*, Sept. 1822, p. 317).

(2) *my bit gathering*: my little saving.

(3) *over and by*: over and in addition.

(4) *executioners*: malapropism, 'executors'.

Page 357. (1) *sae lang in his aught*: so long in his possession.

(2) *cloks*: beetles.

(3) *Psalmist*: The Scottish metrical version of the Psalms uses the phrase 'another of the same' to introduce an alternative rendering of a psalm.

(4) *yird tead*: earth toad.

(5) *gang into the desk head*: go into the (space under the) top of the desk.

(6) *doocot hole*: 'pigeon-hole'; *doocot*: dove-cot.

Page 358. *I'll endoss . . . over and aboon*: I'll endorse this trifling hundred pounds to you, Bell, as an extra ('over and above').

Page 359. *dwam*: sudden fit.

Page 362. *pawkily*: with sly humour.

Page 363. (1) *haill*: 'whole', entire.

(2) *testing clause*: (Scots law) clause 'whereby a formal written deed or instrument is authenticated'. Cf. *O.E.D.*

(3) *since the peace*: This brings the period of the final chapter to 1815.

Page 364. *LET GLASGOW FLOURISH*: the motto on the city's coat of arms.

THE WORLD'S CLASSICS

A complete list of Oxford Paperbacks, including books in The World's Classics, Past Masters, and OPUS Series, can be obtained from the General Publicity Department, Oxford University Press, Walton Street, Oxford OX2 6DP.